Taming the Sooner State

The War Between Lawmen & Outlaws in Oklahoma & Indian Territory 1875-1941

By R.D. Morgan

NEW FORUMS

Stillwater, Okla.
USA

NEW FORUMS PRESS INC.

Published in the United States of America
by New Forums Press, Inc.1018 S. Lewis St.
Stillwater, OK 74074
www.newforums.com

Library of Congress Cataloging-in-Publication Data Pending

This book may be ordered in bulk quantities at discount from New Forums Press, Inc., P.O. Box 876,
Stillwater, OK 74076 [Federal I.D. No. 73 1123239]. Printed in the United States of America.

ISBN 10: 1-58107-139-6
ISBN 13: 978-1-581071-39-9

Cover design by Douglas Dollar.

Contents

Foreword

By Linda Moore

Director, Three Rivers Museum, Muskogee

The very title of this book would seem to be a most ambitious topic. How could the entire Sooner State be tamed? Webster's Dictionary describes the word tame in several ways. When used as a verb, it means to correct by punishment or discipline. Synonyms include such concepts as: chasten, subdue, tone down, and moderate.

Undoubtedly, the men entrusted with keeping the peace and upholding the laws of the land had a monumental task. Over the span of the fifty-plus years detailed in this writing, the methods of doing the job changed dramatically.

In the earlier years, transportation was limited to horses and that demanded hardy souls on both sides of the law. In order to chasten a lawbreaker, one would first have to catch him. This was usually a lengthy process and took sometimes months or years. Once caught, then the acts to subdue, tone down, and moderate could be tried. Only after the outlaw was subdued, could the correction by punishment or discipline be decided, often by the nearest court or judge. If the lawman lost control of the situation and angry victims held sway, sometimes the discipline was decided with a hangman's rope. Other times, when courtroom justice prevailed, perhaps the end result was the same but the punishment was still hanging. For lesser offences, incarceration in a jail cell was in order, and that practice still is the method used to attempt to moderate behavior.

The forward progress into motorized transportation did not really change anything. The outlaws had automobiles, too, and many times, they had better and faster ones than the lawmen. The same thing was true of the weapons used by both. Often, the perpetrator of the crime was better armed than any civil servant who went after him.

Communication was also a consideration because many of the outlaws did not read or write and only had verbal teaching from childhood to instill right from wrong. Some of the lawmen, as well, were illiterate, such as Bass Reeves, and they had to have assistance to read warrants, file reports and document the evidence needed to convict the wrongdoer. As time went by, the number of reports and rules of evidence increased, so that actual pursuit of the offender occasionally was bogged down in paperwork.

To entertain the notion that the Sooner State was actually tame by 1940 is certainly not the point of the book. The efforts made by many brave and dedicated men are what bear the telling of the story. As usual, R.D. Morgan does his usual masterful job of research. With the help of his wife and research partner, he brings out small bits of factual detail that other authors have overlooked.

In each of his books, *Desperadoes: The Rise and Fall of the Poe-Hart Gang*, *The Bad Boys of the Cookson Hills*, *The Bandit Kings of the Cookson Hills*, and *The Tri-State Terror*, he attempts to locate people to interview about their knowledge of events. In addition, he contacts all the known sources of documented facts surrounding the cases, whether they are libraries, museums, courthouses, or even cemeteries. It is not surprising that he was chosen to produce a book on this topic. Its inclusion in a series done to celebrate the Centennial Year of Statehood in Oklahoma is fitting.

Dedication

This book is dedicated to the memory of Glenn Shirley and Ken Butler, pioneers in the preservation of Oklahoma lawmen and outlaw history, and Leona Hopkins Munson, 1937-2006.

Acknowledgments

No book is put together without the help of many. I wish to express my heartfelt gratitude to Rick and Linda Mattix, Richard Jones, Linda Moore, Roger Bell, Herman Kirkwood, Larry Walls, Tony Perrin, Mike Webb, Robert Ernst, Katie Morgan, Dennis Lippe, Henry Jolliff, Bill Guy, Verla Geller, Lester Clark, Henry Peak, Fred Gossett, Jack Hurt, Richard Baine, Ken Butler, Brian Beerman, Marisa Boone, John Strange, Julie Arrowood, and the folks at the Fort Smith National Historic Site, as well as the staffs of several dozen libraries and museums located in six states, which have generously assisted me in my research. I also want to thank my under-appreciated chauffer, photographer, partner, and cherished wife, Naomi, for always being "Game." Lastly, I'd like to convey my gratitude to my publisher, Douglas Dollar, for having faith in my work.

Author's Note

Oklahoma is a state rich in lawmen and outlaw history, truly the last bastion of the "Old West." The state has a tradition of banditry dating back to the time of the Indian Territory. The following account presents a collection of rare photographs, biographical sketches, and true stories offered in chronological order dealing with the epic battle between the forces of law and order and wrongdoers, taking place in a geographic area encompassing the modern state of Oklahoma.

This narrative, which represents nearly ten years of research, is presented in two-part form within a single volume. Part I covers the period of 1875-1919, chronicling events taken from the Indian and Oklahoma Territories to statehood and beyond, while Part II covers the period 1920-1941. This work does not represent an attempt to tell a complete history of lawmen and outlaws in Oklahoma. It is merely offered as a series of prime examples of the genre.

Part I – 1875-1919

The Wild West
& Beyond

In the Beginning – 1875-1906

With the dawn of the nineteenth century, Oklahoma was a vast expanse of untamed wilderness. It was characterized by magnificent near-treeless plains oftentimes blanketed by immense herds of buffalo in the West, a mix of heavily forested bottomlands and gently rolling hills in the center, and a stretch of mountainous hardwood forests slashed by swift flowing rivers to the East. The region was dotted with a widely scattered collection of villages populated by a proud race of nomadic people obsessed with a simple belief in the divinity of Mother Earth. It was a land of unspoiled splendor, devoid of the white man's hand, absent any code of law except ancient tribal customs or the primitive laws of survival and natural selection.

Beginning in 1817 land hungry settlers compelled the federal government to induce certain Native American tribes to voluntarily relocate from their ancestral homelands in the East to the soon to be dubbed Indian Territory granting them large chunks of land they considered worthless. A few isolated military posts were established to oversee the arrangement. In the 1830s, the government upped the ante, instituting a ruthless policy of forced removal of members of the Cherokee, Choctaw, Creek, Chickasaw, and Seminole Nations by way of various overland routes now referred to as the "Trail of Tears." Being violently removed from their established villages and farms and forced to march several hundred miles in oftentimes brutal weather conditions at the point of a bayonet made for poor relations between the tribes and a seemingly heartless government, producing a longstanding atmosphere of mistrust and fear that would over time present a severe cost for both White and Indian in the new land.

The Civil War (1861-65) was a time of bloodthirsty raids throughout the territory by lawless entities representing both northern and southern causes. The Indian Territory marked the geographic beginning of the frontier and the end of established civilization at the time. Law and order was totally absent, except for a minor military presence. Freebooters swept through the region burning and pillaging at will. No one was safe.

As for the native population, while one tribe or part of a tribe associated itself with the north, another would do the opposite, while a third faction attempted to remain neutral. Due to the instability caused by the con-

Jailers and guards standing in front of Fort Smith Federal Courthouse, circa 1890s. Courtesy of Fort Smith National Historical Site.

flict, crops suffered and hunger and disease soon stalked the land. The territory was considered a backwater of the war and neither side cared to spend the time or resources needed to rein in the bushwhackers or the army of criminals, draft dodgers, and aimless drifters who had invaded the land. The best the noncombatants could hope for was to stay one step ahead of the warring factions.

By war's end, the district was dubbed "The Outlaws Roost" and the "Land of the Six-Shooter" by the Eastern press. Due to many of the area's native citizenry swearing their allegiance to the southern cause, the victorious north dealt with the region harshly. The citizens of the Indian Territory would suffer the consequences by being dealt poor and ineffective representation, and consequently were denied adequate roads, policing, public works, medical facilities, and legal refinement.

By the 1870s, the territory was a lawless expanse awash with the dregs of society, some Indian, and others White. While many of the Anglo settlers married into the tribes, others were "Scouting" from various criminal or debtor's courts, and yet a third faction comprised mere illegal land squatters or "Intruders." Many undesirables were attracted to the territory due to its lack of capable law enforcement. At the time, officials estimated, some 15,000 whites populated the area of which only 5,000 were deemed honest citizens gainfully employed in some legal enterprise. The only established law enforcement mechanism concerning Whites was the federal court located initially in Van Buren then Fort Smith, Arkansas. This court, representing the Western District of Arkansas with jurisdiction over the Indian Territory, had a reputation for corruption and inefficiency until the appointment of Isaac Parker in 1875 as the federal judge replacing Judge William Story. Parker was given sweeping powers by the US Government over criminal and civil matters pertaining to the Indian Territory. On taking the bench, the judge instituted far reaching reforms as well as adding to his cadre of deputy marshals. These officers acted as his instrument of justice enabling him to project some semblance of law and order throughout the territory.

Roughly, 200 deputies patrolled the whole of the roadless wilderness that made

Prisoners and guards at Federal Jail, Fort Smith. Courtesy of Fort Smith National Historical Site.

Reunion of retired Marshals and Deputies at Fort Smith. Courtesy of Fort Smith National Historical Site.

up the Indian Nations. Marshals pay averaged $500 per year. They operated on a fee system being paid $2.00 for each arrest and about 8 cents per mile travel pay. Although the deputies were precluded from collecting federal rewards, they were allowed to retrieve bounties offered by state, local, private, and railroad entities. It was a dangerous and thankless job. An estimated seventy marshals were slain in the line of duty within the boundaries of the Indian Territory during the period 1871-1907. While the dime-novel and celluloid-inspired legend – implying these marshals were always of a mind to shoot first and ask questions later – has taken hold in the public consciousness, the truth of the matter is, if a deputy killed a fugitive in the line of duty he lost all his fees and was financially responsible for the man's burial.

Marshals typically made their patrol accompanied by at least one posseman or assistant and a wagon driver who doubled as a cook. They would depart Fort Smith with a single man assigned to the wagon while the others followed on horseback making a broad sweep as far west as Fort Supply rounding up as many as twenty prisoners before heading back east. The journey might take as much as sixty days to complete. The shackled prisoners would march behind the wagon in manacles until nightfall when they were chained together until morning, then their journey would start anew. On arrival at Fort Smith, the prisoners were lodged at the federal jail until they were eventually brought before Judge Parker.

Some of the more well known marshals and deputy marshals serving the various federal courts with jurisdiction in the Indian and Oklahoma Territories were Jacob Yoes, George Crump, Samuel Rutherford, Ben Williams, Heck Thomas, Frank Canton, Bill Tilghman, Chris Madsen, Bass Reeves, E.D. Nix, "Wild" Bill Robbins, Canada H. Thompson, Bill Fossett, Bud Ledbetter, Ransom Payne, Eli "Heck" Bruner, Dave Rusk, Hiram Stephens, and Paden Tolbert.

Shortly after taking office,

Judge Parker sentenced eight persons to die by the hangman's noose. On September 3, 1875, six condemned criminals were publicly hanged simultaneously in a macabre example to lawbreakers. The "Court of the Damned" was now in session.

During his time on the bench, Parker, who was commonly referred to as "The Hanging Judge," sentenced 160 individuals to the gallows of which seventy-nine actually made it to the gibbet that had been nicknamed "The Gates of Hell." He also oversaw 13,490 felony cases garnering 9,454 convictions. Until the arrival of the good judge, the old saying, "No law West of Fort Smith," was quite applicable. Parker's power and prestige was dealt a major blow in 1889 when the Congress gave the US Su-

Deputy US Marshals badges on display at Fort Smith Historic Site. Photo by Naomi Morgan.

Personnel at the federal courthouse and jail, around 1900. Courtesy of Fort Smith National Historical Site.

preme Court power to review his death sentences. Previously, only the president had the right to commute his decisions. The Judge's authority further declined with the land runs starting in the late-1880s when, in a series of complicated moves, other courts were established in Guthrie, Muskogee, Fort Scott and Wichita, Kansas, as well as Paris, Texas, and were given jurisdiction over sections of the Indian Territory previously controlled by Parker's court. Other federal courts were eventually established in McAlester, Ardmore, and Vinita.

In due time, the individual Indian Nations established their own courts and tribal police called The Lighthorse. These tribal entities, which proved to be very efficient in keeping the peace and tracking down outlaws, had no jurisdiction over the large influx of Anglos, many of who were on the run from the authorities back east. Nor did these courts hold sway over Native Americans whose crimes involved white persons. Indian law frequently provided more brutal penalties than Judge Parker's court. When found guilty of a crime the defendant was tied to a tree and whipped for a first offense then whipped more severely for a second. On conviction of a third offense, the defendant was oftentimes executed by either hanging or the firing squad (Choctaw, Seminole, and Creek used the firing squad while Cherokee

and Chickasaw made use of the gibbet). At least thirty-three persons were executed in the Five Civilized Tribes area before statehood. Conditions at the various Native American prisons were abysmal. Inmates worked for their keep, breaking big rocks into little ones with a sledge-hammer, and infractions of the rules were dealt with by liberal doses of solitary confinement and flogging.

Above: Deputy US Marshals at Fort Smith. Courtesy Fort Smith National Historic Site.

Left: Personnel posing in front of new Fort Smith Federal Courthouse on 6th Street. Parker's court was relocated from the old converted army barracks to its new location several blocks East in 1890. Courtesy of Fort Smith National Historical Site.

Railroads, Renegade Cowboys, and Such

When the guns finally fell silent with the ending of the Civil War, capitalists began building railroads reaching as far west as Kansas. With the arrival of the railroads, a host of cash-poor Texas ranchers began driving enormous herds of longhorns north across the Indian Territory on the Western, Chisholm, and Shawnee Trails to railheads in Dodge City, Baxter Springs, Wichita, Hays, and Abilene, Kansas. The nation had developed a taste for beef, and beef they would have. Over time many of the cowboys hailing from the "Lone Star" State who accompanied early cattle drives settled in the territory, some marrying into the various tribes. These bold characters along with some of the more adventurous Texas ranching enterprises began establishing ranches throughout the Western and Central sections of the territory, oftentimes leasing tens of thousands of acres of sweetgrass prairie lands from the various tribes.

The expansion of the railroads across the Indian Territory into Texas, as well as the land rushes beginning in 1889 which carved the country into quarter-section allotments for homesteading purposes, and the liberal use of barbwire and the corresponding reduction of open range, marked the death knell for the big Texas cattle drives. Thus, the landscape of the land began to change, the vast cattle operations began to shrink, and there was less need of the services of an army of cowboys. Instead of homesteading or finding work in town, a host of these independent minded cowpokes turned to riding the "Owl Hoot" Trail, rustling livestock for their daily bread. From there it was just a small step to train and bank robbery.

Some of the more famous cowboys turned outlaw, dating from pre-statehood days, were the notorious Dalton brothers (Grat, Bob, and Emmett) as well as Bill Cook, Henry Starr, Cherokee Bill, Bill Doolin, "Bitter Creek" Newcomb, Charley Pierce, "Little Dick" West, "Blackface" Charley Bryant, Zip Wyatt, Jim French, Bob Rogers, and The Verdigris Kid.

Federal and Territorial Jails

The first federal jail pertaining to the Indian Territory was located in Fort Smith on the grounds of the original military fort situated on a bluff overlooking the mouth of the Poteau River. The prison was built of logs with a thatched roof and dirt floors. Conditions at the jail were so appalling it was locally known as "The Hole in the Wall." In 1872, the prison was relocated to a pair of oversized open rooms located in the basement of the federal court building, which was originally constructed for use as an army barracks in 1846. The condition at the prison, which was known far and wide as "Hell on the Border," was primitive at best and was oftentimes compared to the infamous "Black Hole of Calcutta." Bad food, overcrowding, poor ventilation, widespread infectious diseases, and uncontrolled violence were its mainstay. In 1888, the prison was moved to a newly constructed three-story structure adjoining the old fed-

Hell on the Border Jail located in basement of federal courthouse. Courtesy of Fort Smith Historical Site.

eral courthouse. While it had a capacity to hold some 144 prisoners, the facility sometimes detained as many as 300 within its bleak walls. Most federal inmates sentenced to more than a year in custody were usually transferred to facilities located in Detroit, Michigan, Cleveland, Ohio, and Albany, New York, upon conviction. In 1890 and 1891 respectfully, new jails were opened in Muskogee, I.T. and Guthrie, O.T. Other federal holding facilities servicing the area included those in Fort Scott and Wichita, Kansas, as well as Paris, Texas, along with smaller ones in Vinita, McAlester, and Ardmore. There were two Native American correctional facilities in the Indian Territory. The Cherokee Indian (National) Prison was located in Tahlequah and the Chickasaw National Prison was in Tishomingo. In the Seminole, Creek, and Choctaw Nations, persons convicted of crimes were simply informed when to show up for punishment and amazingly, most did

Left: Prisoners at the Muskogee federal jail complex. Courtesy Okmulgee Public Library.
Below: Federal Courthouse in Muskogee around 1900. Courtesy Three Rivers Museum, Muskogee, OK.

Right: Federal Jail in Muskogee. Courtesy Three Rivers Museum, Muskogee, OK.

Prisoners at the Cherokee National Prison. Courtesy Cherokee Nation.

The Hanging Judge Reigns Over Troubled Lands

Isaac Parker was born in Ohio in 1838. After passing the Ohio bar, he moved to St. Joseph, Missouri, where he practiced law. He was appointed city attorney in 1862 and prosecuting attorney of Buchanan County in 1868. He served two terms in the US Congress 1870-74. After a failed run for the US Senate President Grant appointed him the federal judge for the Western District of Arkansas with full jurisdiction over the wild and wooly outlaw-infested Indian Territory in 1875. Although the good judge's rulings resulted in the hanging of seventy-nine men in a twenty-year period (an average of less than four per year), it should be noted that contrary to popular perception, Parker never personally attended a single execution. The Judge

The Hanging Judge: Isaac C. Parker 1838-1896. Photo courtesy of Fort Smith Historic Site.

was noted as a stern and deeply religious man who literally believed in the biblical concept of an eye for an eye. Between 1883-1896, Parker's jurisdiction was slowly carved away by congress. Shortly after the Western District of Arkansas was completely stripped of its territorial jurisdiction in 1896, Parker took ill and died at his Fort Smith residence. He was buried with honors at the Fort Smith National Cemetery.

Recreation of Judge Parker's court located at the Fort Smith National Historic Site. Photo by Naomi Morgan.

The Gibbet

Standing just south of the old Fort Smith Federal Courthouse, located on its original site, is an exact reproduction of the 1886 gallows. The initial gallows was constructed in the early 1870s with the capacity to hang six men and was replaced in 1886 with a model that had the capability of simultaneously launching twelve souls at a time back to the bosom of their maker. Between 1873-1896, eighty-six men were put to death in thirty-nine separate executions. During a three-year period, 1873-76, twenty-odd executions were open to the public, producing large unruly crowds with an accompanying circus-like atmosphere – peddlers loudly offering roasted peanuts, cotton candy, and lemonade to an impatient crowd of morbid rubberneckers. In 1878, Judge Parker ordered a sixteen-foot-high, whitewashed wooden fence be constructed around the gallows and witnesses allowed inside

The Prince of Hangmen: George Maledon–1830-1911.

German born George Maledon immigrated with his family to America at the age of one. After serving in the Union Army during the Civil War he traveled to Arkansas. There he was employed for a time as a Fort Smith policeman and a Sebastion County Deputy Sheriff, before accepting employment as a Deputy US Marshal working out of the court in Van Buren. When the court moved to Fort Smith, he transferred to the job of jailor and in the mid-1880s was appointed Chief Executioner by Judge Parker. He was paid at the rate of five dollars per head. While employed as hangman he not only sprang the trap on approximately fifty-odd men, but shot and killed two others attempting to escape custody. It was said that the remorseless hangman refused to participate in the execution of any condemned man who wore the blue during the War Between the States. After retiring, he traveled the country displaying his ropes and gallows paraphernalia for several years in carnival shows. Maledon died in 1911 at the Old Soldiers Home in Johnson City, Tennessee. While many historians over the years have credited Maledon as being America's most prolific executioner, this dubious honor may in fact belong to Oklahoma's longtime Chief Executioner Rich Owen, who pulled the switch on fifty-eight condemned men during his career.

Photo courtesy of Ken Butler

Right: Original Fort Smith courthouse and basement jail prior to the second story addition. Courtesy Fort Smith Historic Site.

Old U. S. Jail, Fort Smith, Ark.

by invitation only. The most hanged at one time was six, which occurred twice, while the necks of five individuals were collectively stretched on three separate occasions.

Hangings were generally scheduled for Friday afternoons. Present at each execution were a crowd of invited physicians, ministers, lawyers, lawmen, and relatives of the victims. After a brief religious service, the condemned man, dressed in a new government issued suit, was given the opportunity to spit out his last words before being tied hand and foot. A black hood was draped over the victim's head and the noose fitted before being led to the trapdoor that was promptly sprung with little pause or fanfare. When the body hit the end of the six-foot drop, the crowd typically shuddered and audibly gasped as the unearthly cracking sound made by a breaking neck echoed across the courtyard. At other times the victim slowly strangled to death producing a visually gruesome exhibit of bodily jerking and twisting suggestive of a macabre dance of death, which horrified even the most hardened souls in attendance. After being pronounced dead, the victim's lifeless corpse was left swinging in the wind for approximately thirty minutes before being cut down and loaded into a coffin that was stored nearby and either handed over to his next of kin or quickly buried in a pauper's grave at a local cemetery.

The last execution in Fort Smith took place on July 30, 1896. All eighty-six men were hung for the crime of murder except the five members of the Rufus Buck Gang, who were executed for committing rape. The scaffold was torn down and burned in 1897 by a group of well-meaning citizens who considered the structure a distasteful symbol of the areas wild past. Rumor has it the heavy wooden trapdoor became part of the front porch of an area cabin. For many years neighborhood kids played a game of "Dare." The object of the activity consisted of dashing up to the porch stepping on the "Haunted" trap, then quickly retreating in feigned horror.

Above: The Gallows. Courtesy of Fort Smith Historical Society. Right: Hangman's noose. Courtesy Fort Smith National Historic Site.

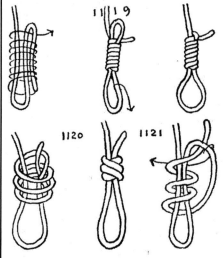

1119. The HANGMAN'S KNOT. This is the knot generally used for the purpose suggested by the name, because it may be counted on to draw up smoothly and not let go. It is conventionally adjusted with the knot immediately in back of and below the left ear.

It is sometimes contended that there should be nine turns to the NOOSE, so that "even if a man has as many lives as a cat, there shall be a full turn for each one of them," and I have heard thirteen turns urged as the proper number on the assumption that there is some connection between bad luck and being hanged.

However, I learned the knot as it is pictured here, with only eight turns, and I have found the preponderance of authority in favor of eight turns only. In Chapter 2 the practical use of the knot is discussed under "Hangman."

1120. A SCAFFOLD KNOT from Diderot's Encyclopedia (1762).

1121. The GALLOWS KNOT. This is the same knot as the last, but differently tied.

Executions by Hanging at Fort Smith –1873-1896

August 15, 1873 - John Childers
October 10, 1873 - Young Wolf
April 3, 1874 - John Billy, Isaac Filmore, and John Pointer
January 15, 1875 - McClish Impson
September 3, 1875 - Edmund Campbell, Daniel Evens, Samuel Fooy, Smoker Mankiller, James Moore, and William Whittington
April 21, 1876 - Gibson Ishtanubbee, William Leach, Orpheus McGee, Isham Seeley, and Aaron Wilson
September 8, 1876 - Samuel Peters, Osey Sanders, John Valley, and Sinker Wilson
December 20, 1878 - John Diggs and John Postoak
August 29, 1879 - William Wiley and Dr. Henri Stewart
September 9, 1881 - William Brown, Abler Manley, Amos Manley, Patrick McGowen, and George Padgett
June 30, 1882 - Edward Fulsom

April 13, 1883 - Robert Massey
June 29, 1883 -William Finch, Martin Joseph, and Te-o-lit-se
July11, 1884 - John Davis, Thomas Thompson, and Jack Weomankiller
April 17, 1885 - William Phillips
June 26, 1885 - James Arcine and William Parchmeal
April 23, 1886 - Joseph Jackson and James Wasson
July 23, 1886 - Calvin James and Lincoln Sprole
August 6, 1886 - Kitt Ross
January 14, 1887 - John T. Echols, James Lamb, Albert O'Dell, and John Stephens
April 8, 1887 - Patrick McCarty
October 7, 1887 - Seaborn Kalijah and Silas Hampton
April 27, 1888 - Jackson Crow, Owen Hill, and George Moss
July 6, 1888 - Gus Bogles
January 25, 1889 - Richard Smith
April 19, 1889 - Malachi Allen and James Mills

August 30, 1889 - Jack Spaniard and William Walker
January 16, 1890 - Harris Austin, John Billy, Jimmon Burris, Sam Goin, Jefferson Jones and Thomas Willis
January 30, 1890 - George Tobler
July 9, 1890 - John Stansberry
June 30, 1891 - Boudinot Crumpton
April 27, 1892 - Sheppard Busby
June 28, 1892 - John Thornton
July 25, 1894 - Lewis Holder
September 20, 1894 - John Pointer
March 17, 1896 - Crawford Goldsby, alias Cherokee Bill
April 30, 1896 - Webber Isaacs, George Pierce, and John Pierce
July 1, 1896 - Rufus Buck, Lewis Davis, Lucky Davis, Maoma July, and Sam Sampson
July 30, 1896 - George Wilson, alias James Casherago

List courtesy Fort Smith National Historic Site

Lawmen

Bass Reeves, 1838-1910

Bass Reeves was one of an estimated fifty black deputy marshals to serve the federal courts in either the Indian or Oklahoma Territories. Born a slave in Texas, Reeves moved to Van Buren, Arkansas, around 1870. Soon after relocating to Arkansas, he was hired as a federal posseman and guard. He served in that capacity until sworn in as a deputy marshal around 1875, remaining in that position until 1907. During his career as a marshal, Reeves was headquartered out of both Fort Smith and Paris, Texas, until transferring to the Muskogee court. Reeves held the distinction of being the first black deputy marshal appointed west of the Mississippi River. While

George J. Crump-1841-1928. Chief US Marshal for the Western District under Judge Parker 1893-1897. Photo courtesy of Muskogee Public Library.

Samuel Rutherford-1859- 1922. Chief US Marshal for the Muskogee court 1895- 1897. Photo courtesy of Muskogee Public Library.

Federal Marshals at Muskogee: Bass Reeves far left middle row, Bud Ledbetter front and center. Courtesy Three Rivers Museum.

ing in Kingfisher, Oklahoma Territory. Fossett served as the Chief Deputy Federal Marshal of the Oklahoma Territory headquartered in Guthrie, 1897-1902, before being appointed US Marshal in 1902. During his service as a deputy, Fossett is credited with slaying several noted outlaws including Doolin-Dalton gang-member "Little Dick" West. In 1908, he occupied the position of city marshal in Waurika before serving as the Chief of Police of Kingfisher 1919-1920. The roaring twenties saw the legendary lawmen working for the Oklahoma City Police Department while simultaneously holding a special commission as a deputy marshal. Bill Fossett died in 1940. He is buried at Kingfisher.

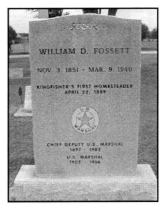

Tombstone of Marshal Fossett in Kingfisher. Photo by Naomi Morgan.

he could neither read nor write, he was noted as a highly respected and extremely courageous peace officer whose real-life adventures easily overshadowed many of the better-known marshals of western lore. Reeves was an expert, steel-nerved, "Shootist" credited with gunning down fourteen men in the line of duty as well as arresting hundreds of desperate lawbreakers during his legendary career in law enforcement. After statehood, he served as a Muskogee city officer for several years until his death in 1910. He was buried at Muskogee's Union Agency Cemetery. Other black lawmen serving the federal courts with distinction prior to statehood were Zeke Miller, William McNat, and Grant Johnson, just to name a few.

William 'Bill' Fossett, 1851-1940.

After spending his youth in Minnesota, Bill Fossett drifted onto the Great Plains where he worked as a cowboy, pushing cattle up the old Chisholm Trail during the 1870s. A plainspoken man noted for his grit and honesty, Fossett served as the assistant city marshal of Caldwell, Kansas, 1881-82 during its heyday as a trailhead for Texas beef on the hoof, before being hired as the city marshal of Kingman. He later acted as a railroad detective before participating in the '89er land run, homestead-

Photo courtesy Richard Jones

Bill Tilghman, 1854-1924

Born in Iowa, Bill Tilghman relocated to Kansas in 1870 seeking adventure and opportunity. He worked as a buffalo hunter and freighter for the railroad before being appointed Deputy Sheriff of Ford County (Dodge City) in 1876, serving under the legendary Bat Masterson. After a few years of rousting Texas cowboys hot off the trail and full of vinegar, Tilghman homesteaded in the Oklahoma Territory in 1889. In 1891, he was appointed deputy federal marshal working out of Guthrie. He served in that position until 1900 when he was elected sheriff of Lincoln County. In 1910, he was elected to the state senate. Soon afterwards, he resigned his senate seat to take on the assignment of Chief of Police of Oklahoma City. He served in that position until his retirement in 1915. During his time as a federal marshal, Tilghman

Photo courtesy of Dennis Lippe.

Grave of Bill Tilghman at Chandler

was most noted for capturing the notorious Bill Doolin at a bathhouse in Eureka Springs, Arkansas, during the mid-1890s.

In 1924, Bill came out of retirement when he was appointed a special officer by Governor Trapp, remanded to clean up the oil-boom community of Cromwell. The small isolated berg had exploded in population in the past year and, as is inevitable in the life of all boomtowns, crime was rampant. Shortly after taking office Bill Tilghman was shot to death when he attempted to arrest a corrupt prohibition officer named Wiley Lynn. Although Lynn was charged with murder, he was acquitted at trial. The celebrated officer was buried at Chandler.

Tilghman's assassin was later involved in a bloody wild-west style shootout with officer Crockett Long in the snack area of a small drug store located in Madill on July 17, 1932. The pair stood flat-footed several feet apart trading shots until both men as well as an innocent bystander lay fatally wounded. At the gunfight's conclusion, Wiley Lynn, sporting four .44 caliber slugs imbedded in his torso, picked himself off the floor and stumbled to a nearby funeral home where he collapsed after informing the undertaker, "I'm afraid I'm going to die. I'm shot to hell."

Chris Madsen, 1851-1944

Chris Madsen was born and raised in Denmark. As a young man he served in the Danish Army before becoming a soldier of fortune fighting in the Franco-Prussian War as well as seeing action with the French Foreign Legion in Algeria. He immigrated to America in 1875 where he promptly joined the 5th US Calvary serving in the Indian Wars. In 1891, he was transferred to Fort Reno, Oklahoma Territory, and decided to settle in the area. That same year he was appointed a deputy US marshal for the Oklahoma Territory where he served with distinction, trading bullets with the likes of "Red Buck" Waightman and other members of the Doolin Gang. Chris Madsen died in 1944. He is buried at the Frisco Cemetery in Yukon.

Photo courtesy Tom Justin.

The Three Guardsmen – Marshals Chris Madsen, Bill Tilghman, and Heck Thomas. Courtesy Ken Butler.

Heck Thomas , left, and posse.

Heck Thomas, 1850-1912

Henry 'Heck' Thomas was probably the most well known and efficient of all the deputy marshals operating in the territories. Born in Georgia, he married and moved to Texas in 1875, where he was employed as a security guard for an express company. He relocated to Fort Smith, Arkansas in 1886, where he accepted an appointment as a Deputy Federal Marshal under Judge Isaac Parker. Thomas was involved in many gunfights and spirited adventures as a marshal, arresting hundreds of lawbreakers. In 1893, he transferred to the Oklahoma Territory working out of the court in Guthrie as a marshal serving with Chris Madsen and Bill Tilghman. The trio was soon dubbed "The Three Guardsmen" by the press. He was

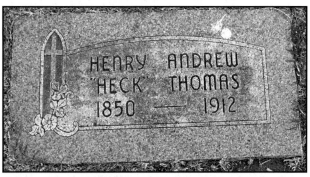

Grave of Heck Thomas. Photo by Naomi Morgan.

credited with killing outlaw Bill Doolin in 1896. The legendary lawman resigned as a marshal in 1902, accepting the position of Chief of Police in Lawton. Heck Thomas died of Brights Disease in 1912, and was buried at Highland Cemetery in Lawton. Some experts believe that his career in law enforcement served as the author's inspiration in the creation of the character of Rooster Cogburn for the book *True Grit,* which was later made into a blockbuster movie starring John Wayne.

Paden Tolbert, 1863-1904

As a Deputy US Marshal, Paden Tolbert was involved in the killing of Ned Christie and the capture of the Jennings Gang, as well as a host of other desperadoes during his sterling career as a territorial lawman. He began working as a marshal for Judge Parker out of the Fort Smith court around 1892. Tolbert died of lung congestion in 1904 in Weleetka. The town of Paden was named for him.

Photo courtesy of Tony Perrin.

Temple Houston: Gunfighting Attorney, 1860-1905

Temple Houston was the eleventh child of Texas hero Sam Houston. An adventurous youth, he worked as a cowpuncher on a trail drive, pushing longhorns into Kansas across the Indian Territory at a tender age. Later he was hired as a clerk on a Mississippi riverboat where he was liberally exposed to the evils of liquor, gambling, and lewd women. Over the next few years, he garnered a reputation for being good with both his fists and a gun. In an attempt to dampen the lad's wild side, his family sent him to law school. After passing his bar examinations at the age of twenty-one, Houston was appointed county attorney for the near lawless Texas panhandle district in 1882, taking up residence in the untamed frontier village of Tascosa. He built a reputation for being a popular but eccentric character, dressing in fringed buckskin clothing and sporting a pair of pearl handled revolvers.

Photo courtesy of Tony Perrin.

Legend has it, Houston once bested the infamous "Billy the Kid" in a bloodless shooting match held on the town's main street.

The enigmatic barrister was elected to the Texas State Senate in 1885. In 1893, he was selected as an observer for the land run into the Cherokee Strip. Attracted to the frontier atmosphere, Houston relocated to Woodward in order to establish a law practice. Over the next few years, the youthful attorney defended a host of criminals and outcasts. He was noted for his wild and unpredictable courtroom behavior, eventually evolving into one of the most charismatic and outlandish figures in the territory. He oftentimes insulted fellow lawyers and witnesses to the extent he was involved in several gun duels, the most famous being the Jennings brothers (Ed, Frank, John, and Al). Evidently, he slighted one of the siblings causing them to attempt to dry gulch him in a saloon where he was lounging with a lawman named Jack Love. When the bullets quit flying Ed Jennings lay dead and his brother John wounded. Although brother Al, who would one day become a semi-famous outlaw connected to several members of the Doolin Gang, swore revenge, nothing ever came of it. Over the years, Houston would be involved in several other gunfights. Temple Houston died of a brain hemorrhage in 1905. He is buried at Woodward.

Indian Lighthorse

Any telling of the history of law enforcement throughout the Indian Territory would be grossly incomplete without mention of the different police entities concerning the various tribes occupying the area. Until statehood, all Five Civilized Tribes (Choctaw, Chickasaw, Cherokee, Creek, and Seminole) possessed independent judicial systems dealing with Native Americans. The enforcement mechanism of those courts was the Tribal Police or Lighthorse. As for the Comanche, Wichita, Kiowa, Arapahoe, and other tribal entities, they too maintained Native Policemen, but usually under white supervision. A separate unique unit of Indian Police with ju-

Lighthorsemen–Indian Territory. Author's private collection.

risdiction throughout the territory operated from Muskogee's Union Agency from 1880 to statehood. Throughout its history, the Indian Lighthorse maintained a reputation for efficiency and bravery.

Outlaws

The Doolin-Dalton Gangs

The infamous Dalton brothers were the sons of James Lewis and Adaline Younger Dalton who originally hailed from Jackson County, Missouri. Adaline was the aunt of the notorious Younger brothers of Jesse James-Younger Gang fame. Over the years, the couple was blessed with fifteen children of which four, Bill, Bob, Grat, and Emmett turned to crime. A fifth son, Frank, was slain in the line of duty in 1887 while employed as a Deputy US Marshal working out of the Fort Smith court.

The family located in the Indian Territory near Vinita in the 1880s where they remained for several years until moving to Kansas. James Dalton died around 1890. Shortly afterwards his widow homesteaded in the Oklahoma Territory near the community of Kingfisher.

Meanwhile, brothers Grat and Bob took jobs acting as Deputy US Marshals working out of the federal courts located in Kansas. Before long, both were accused of stealing horses in the Cherokee Nation as well as peddling moonshine in the Osage country. Soon afterwards, Bob, Grat, and Emmett joined their brother Bill in California where they were suspected of holding up a Southern Pacific train. While Bob and Emmett returned to Oklahoma, Grat and Bill were arrested and charged with the train robbery. In the meantime, Emmett went to work as a cowboy on a ranching concern located near modern-day Cushing where he befriended a charismatic cowpoke named Bill Doolin.

Emmett Dalton mugshot. Kansas State Penitentiary.

Grat Dalton. Courtesy Kansas Historical Society.

Through Doolin, the young man made the acquaintance of a trio of criminal-minded out-of-work-saddle-tramps named Charley Pierce, "Blackface" Charlie Bryant, and "Bitter Creek" Newcomb. Emmett would in turn introduce Doolin and his shady friends to his brother Bob, thus marking the birth of the notorious Doolin-Dalton Gang.

In May 1891, the Dalton brothers, accompanied by Bryant, Pierce, and Newcomb, robbed a Santa Fe train near Wharton, Oklahoma Territory, for $500. A few months later, Deputy Ed Short arrested Charley Bryant. While Short was in the process of transferring his prisoner to the Wichita court by rail, Bryant was somehow able to gain possession of a pistol. The two became involved in a ferocious gun duel that resulted in both men's deaths.

In September, Bob and Emmett, along with Bill

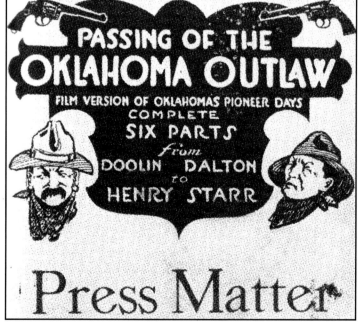

Above: Ad for the silent movie, "The Passing of the Oklahoma Outlaws." Courtesy Rick Mattix.
Left: Bob and Grat Dalton in death. Courtesy Coffeyville, Kansas, Historical Society.

Doolin, Pierce, and Newcomb, looted a KATY railcar near Leliaetta (a long-ago defunct cattle station located a few miles north of Wagoner) for several thousand dollars. A few days after the Leliaetta heist, Grat Dalton, who had recently escaped custody in California, joined his brothers.

The gang's next robbery was a Santa Fe train near Red Rock. On July 14, 1892, they knocked off a train near Adair. An innocent bystander was killed and several others were wounded in the hold-up. After the fiasco in Adair, the boys licked their wounds for several months before the three Daltons, along with Bill Power and Dick Broadwell, attempted to rob two banks at once in Coffeyville, Kansas. The raid was a disaster from start to finish. Bob and Grat were killed by lawmen and vigilantes, as were Power and Broadwell. Emmett was wounded and captured. Also slain in the raid were four Coffeyville citizens. Emmett Dalton would spend the next fifteen years incarcerated in the Kansas State Penitentiary until his parole in 1907. After residing in Bartlesville for several years, he and his newly acquired wife, relocated to California where he died of old age in 1937, his ashes were buried near his mother's final resting place in Kingfisher.

Although the Dalton boys were now out of the picture, the gang reconstituted itself under Bill Doolin's leadership. The group's membership included Charley Pierce, "Little Bill" Raidler, "Bitter Creek" Newcomb, "Dynamite Dick" Clifton, "Arkansas Tom" (Roy Daugherty), "Red" Buck Waightman, "Little" Dick West, "Tulsa Jack" Blake, Ol Yantis, and a score of others who drifted in and out of the group over time. Several weeks after the Coffeyville massacre, Doolin, along with Newcomb, Pierce, and Ol Yantis, saddled up and rode to Kansas where they robbed the Ford County Bank in Spearville for $1,700. Officers caught up with Yantis by month's end, filling him full of lead while the other three bandits hid out at Bee Dunn's ranch, located just south of the community of Ingalls. Bill Dalton, following his brother's example, soon joined the group. Thus, the Doolin-Dalton Gang was reborn.

On June 11, 1893, the group robbed a Santa Fe train near Cimarron, Kansas, for roughly $1,000. In September, a wagonload of federal marshals attempted to ambush the gang on the streets of Ingalls, O.T. The ensuing gunfight resulted in the deaths of three marshals (Dick Speed, Laf Shadley, and Tom Hueston) as well as a pair of innocent bystanders. As for the outlaws, two of their number were wounded

Top: Arkansas Tom and his unmarked grave in Joplin. Photo by Naomi Morgan.
Middle: Contemporary view of Old Condon Bank, on left, Coffeyville, back in the day, on right. Photo by Naomi Morgan.
Above: The Dalton Gang laid out in the aftermath of the Coffeyville raid; (left to right) Bill Power, Bob Dalton, Grat Dalton, and Dick Broadwell. Author's private collection.

and "Arkansas Tom" Daugherty captured. Daugherty was quickly convicted of manslaughter and given a fifty-year prison sentence.

On January 23, 1894, the brigands looted the Citizens Bank of Pawnee for several hundred dollars in cash and coin. In May, they hijacked a bank in Southwest City, Missouri, for $3,500. Shortly after the Missouri bank job, the group split up. Bill Dalton and several others traveled to Texas where they robbed a bank in Longview. Within a month of the heist, Dalton was shot and killed by lawmen near Ardmore. Doolin's bunch continued their deprivations, robbing a train near Dover on April 3, 1895. Soon afterwards, a posse led by Chris Madsen shot and killed Tulsa Jack in a running gunfight. A few weeks after Tulsa Jack's untimely demise, the Dunn brothers lured Charley Pierce and "Bitter Creek" Newcomb to their ranch near Ingalls where the ruthless siblings blasted them into eternity for the reward money. "Little Bill" Raidler was shot and captured by Marshal Bill Tilghman on September 6, 1895. He was convicted of train robbery and sent to prison but paroled in 1903. He died the following year of complications from wounds received during his capture.

In January 1896, Doolin was arrested at a bathhouse in Eureka Springs, Arkansas, by Tilghman. The outlaw was taken to the federal jail in Guthrie where he promptly escaped custody fleeing to the home of his wife's father in Lawson (now Quay). In the early evening hours of August 24, Doolin was shotgunned to death by a party of marshals led by Heck Thomas.

"Red Buck" Weightman was slain by lawmen in 1896 near Cheyenne while "Dynamite Dick" Clifton bit the dust in the fall of 1897 at a location just outside Checotah. His body was transported to Muskogee where he was identified and buried in the old city cemetery at taxpayer's expense. Heck Thomas and his minions of justice killed "Little" Dick West on April 7, 1898.

"Arkansas Tom" was released from prison in 1910. On gaining his parole, he worked on a relative's farm located in Southwest Missouri until ex-Federal Marshal E. D. Nix offered him a job with a movie company that was filming a picture called *The Passing of the Oklahoma Outlaws*. Tom's role consisted of playing himself. After the movie's completion, he drifted to the Joplin area where he was involved in a bank burglary. He was promptly arrested, convicted, and sentenced to an eight-year term at the Missouri pen. When released in 1921 Tom moved

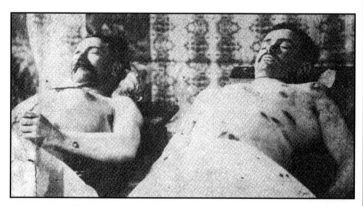

"Bitter Creek" Newcomb (left) and Charley Pierce at the undertakers in Guthrie after being slain at the Dunn Ranch. Author's collection.

Right: Marshal Lafe Shadley, slain in Ingalls battle. Three Rivers Museum.
Right Center: "Little" Dick West at the undertakers in Muskogee. Courtesy Ken Butler.
Far Right: Bill Doolin in death. Author's private collection.

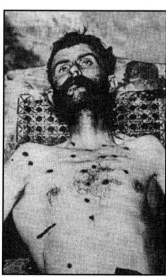

in with his cousin in Galena, Kansas. On November 26, 1923, he and three others robbed a bank in Asbury, Missouri, at gunpoint. The badman was slain in a gunbattle with Joplin detectives on August 16, 1924. "Arkansas Tom," the last surviving member of the Doolin-Dalton Gang, was laid to rest in an unmarked grave at Joplin's Fairview Cemetery with only a handful of witnesses present.

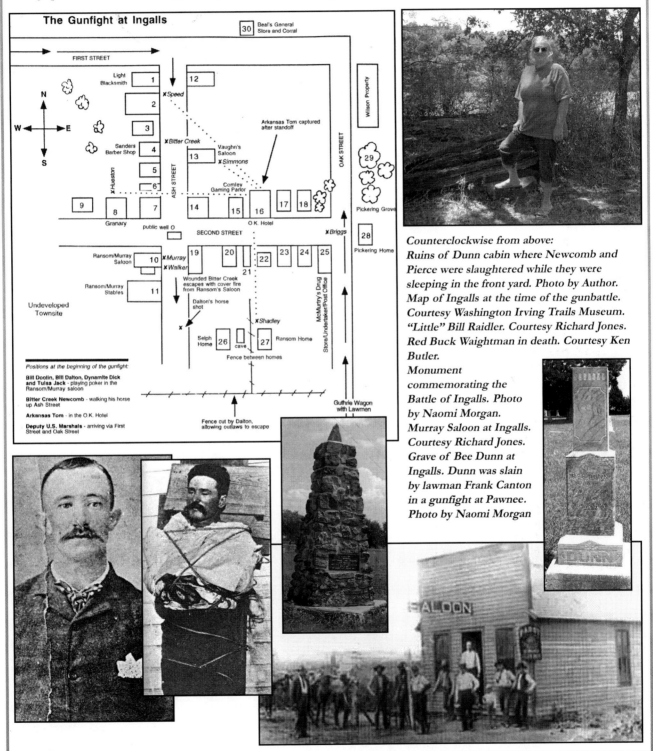

The Gunfight at Ingalls

30 — Beal's General Store and Corral

FIRST STREET

Light Blacksmith — 1

2

3

×Speed

12

N W E S

Sanders Barber Shop — 4 ×Bitter Creek

5

6

×Hueston

9

Granary

8 7

ASH STREET

Vaughn's Saloon — 13 ×Simmons

Comley Gaming Parlor

14 15 16

O.K. Hotel

Arkansas Tom captured after standoff

17 18

public well O

SECOND STREET

Wilson Property

29

Pickering Grove

OAK STREET

×Briggs

28 Pickering Home

Ransom/Murray Saloon — 10 ×Murray ×Walker

Ransom/Murray Stables — 11

Undeveloped Townsite

19 20

Wounded Bitter Creek escapes with cover fire from Ransom's Saloon

Dalton's horse shot

×

Selph Home — 26 cave 27

Fence between homes

22 23 24 25

21

×Shadley

Ransom Home

McMurtry's Drug Store/Undertaker/Post Office

Guthrie Wagon with Lawmen

Fence cut by Dalton, allowing outlaws to escape

Positions at the beginning of the gunfight:

Bill Doolin, Bill Dalton, Dynamite Dick and Tulsa Jack - playing poker in the Ransom/Murray saloon

Bitter Creek Newcomb - walking his horse up Ash Street

Arkansas Tom - in the O.K. Hotel

Deputy U.S. Marshals - arriving via First Street and Oak Street

Counterclockwise from above:
Ruins of Dunn cabin where Newcomb and Pierce were slaughtered while they were sleeping in the front yard. Photo by Author.
Map of Ingalls at the time of the gunbattle. Courtesy Washington Irving Trails Museum.
"Little" Bill Raidler. Courtesy Richard Jones.
Red Buck Waightman in death. Courtesy Ken Butler.
Monument commemorating the Battle of Ingalls. Photo by Naomi Morgan.
Murray Saloon at Ingalls. Courtesy Richard Jones.
Grave of Bee Dunn at Ingalls. Dunn was slain by lawman Frank Canton in a gunfight at Pawnee. Photo by Naomi Morgan

The Bandit Queen: Belle Starr, 1848-1889

The near-mythical "Belle" Starr began her life as Myra Maybelle Shirley, born in 1848 on a farm located near Carthage, Missouri, the daughter of a wealthy innkeeper. When the town was burned by Jayhawkers in 1864, her family drifted to Texas. Legend has it that members of the James-Younger Gang often visited her family in Texas while on the scout. According to tradition, during one of these visits Cole Younger seduced the young lass. Whatever the truth is, Belle became enamored with the outlaw and pledged her love for him throughout her lifetime.

Belle Starr and Blue Duck. Courtesy of Glenn Lemons.

In 1866, Belle married an outlaw named Jim Reed, following him on the "Owl-Hoot" Trail into the Indian Nations where she met and became involved with the Starr clan of brigands led by old Tom Starr. The couple was blessed with two children, Pearl and Ed. In 1874, Reed was slain by lawmen in Paris, Texas.

In 1880, Belle married Sam Starr. The couple made their home on an isolated section of the Canadian River near Porum, which she dubbed Younger's bend. Over time, she turned the place into a bed and breakfast for criminals on the run. In 1882, she and her new husband were charged with horse theft and both were eventually convicted at Fort Smith. Judge Isaac Parker sentenced her to a pair of six-month terms at the Detroit House of Correction. In 1886, Sam Starr was shot and killed at a barn dance by a lawman named Frank West. Widowed for a second time, Belle spent the remainder of her life keeping company with a series of lovers including bandits, Jim July, Jack Spaniard, and Cook Gang member Jim French. Although various writers over the years have attempted to connect her romantically with the notorious Cherokee murderer, Blue Duck, there appears to be little evidence supporting such a claim.

Operating out of her Younger's Bend home, Belle was involved with several others rustling cattle and horses for many years. It is said she would often times visit Fort Smith dressed like a man, armed to the teeth and cussing like a sailor, genuinely delighted with making a spectacle of herself. Although sensationalist writers and reporters would eventually immortalize Belle as the "The Bandit Queen," she was never a bandit in the classic sense, and her reputation was overblown to say the least. Nevertheless, the stories did make good copy.

Right: Contemporary view of Belle Starr's grave located near Porum. Courtesy of Roger Bell. Far Right: Grave of Sam Starr. Photo by Naomi Morgan.

In 1889, Belle was ambushed and shotgunned to death by persons unknown near her home and buried next to her isolated cabin. Within weeks of her death the New York publishers of the popular *Police Gazette* made available a wildly fictitious biography titled "Bella Starr: The Female Jesse James." Although the best selling book was a complete fabrication from beginning to end, the legend soon overtook the facts.

Ironically, Belle's son, Ed Reed, was eventually appointed a Deputy US Marshal and went on to achieve fame for gunning down Zeke and Dick Crittenden on the streets of Wagoner in 1895. The following year he was shot and killed in the line of duty at Claremore when he attempted to arrest a pair of fugitives. Pearl, evolved into a "soiled dove," managing a house of ill repute in Fort Smith and elsewhere for many years.

The case of Belle Starr, "A white woman not Indian" for theft of goods valued at $40. Courtesy of Fort Smith Historic Site.

Ned Christie

Ned Christie was an enigma of sorts. While many thought of him as a Cherokee patriot, others branded him a bloodthirsty outlaw. Born in the Going Snake District on December 14, 1852, Christie was the son of a well-known Cherokee pioneer who had relocated to the Indian Territory via the Trail of Tears. Ned served for a time on the Cherokee National Council. Long an outspoken advocate for the creation of a fully independent Cherokee Nation, he stood in fierce opposition to statehood as well as the expansion of the railroads through Indian lands.

Due to his strong views on Native American separatism and traditional Cherokee values, Christie garnered many enemies among the white power structure. On May 4, 1887, he was falsely accused of

Tombstone of Zeke and Dick Crittenden at IOOF Cemetery located near Hulbert. The brothers were slain by Ed Reed, son of Belle Starr. Photo by Naomi Morgan.

The children of Belle Starr–Ed and Pearl. Courtesy Twin Territories.

Ned Christie in death, surrounded by admiring marshals. Courtesy Glenn Lemons.

In November 1892, a large posse led by Captain G.S. White, accompanied by Federal Marshals Paden Tolbert, Heck Bruner, and Dave Rusk, along with several heavily armed vigilantes surrounded Christie and a pair of youths named Arch Wolf and Charley Hare at the fugitive's rugged, rocky hideout located in modern-day Adair County. After a lengthy but ineffective siege in which possemen expended several thousand rounds of ammunition, the frustrated lawmen resorted to using a small cannon in an effort to force the outlaw-patriot to surrender. When the artillery piece proved useless, the officers placed an over-

killing Deputy Marshal Dan Maples in Tahlequah. Fearing he would not be afforded a fair trial, Ned went on the lam. During the next four years, he was accused of various crimes including the robbery of four isolated stores. In 1889 Deputy Marshals Heck Thomas and L. P. Isbell raided Christie's hideout. A gunfight ensued in which Isbell was wounded and crippled for life. While Ned escaped the scene suffering only a minor wound, Marshal Thomas, in an act of frustration, burned his house to the ground before departing the area with his wounded comrade.

Posse involved in the slaying of Ned Christie. Standing, from left: Wes Bowman, Ab Allen, John Tolbert, Bill Smith, and Tom Johnson. Seated, from left: Dave Rusk, Heck Bruner, Paden Tolbert, Charles Copeland, and Captain G. S. White. Courtesy Glenn Lemons.

Document signed by Chief US Marshal Jacob Yoes concerning the killing of Ned Christie. Courtesy Fort Smith Historic Site. Upper left: Winchester Rifle and Colt .44 cal. revolver once belonging to Ned Christie. Currently on display at Fort Smith Historic Site.

sized charge of dynamite near the structure. When the charge was detonated, it produced a tremendous explosion, which could be heard thirty miles distant. According to reports, the blast erupted with such force it caused the building to rise off its foundation but quickly settled back into position. The only apparent damage to the structure was a gaping hole in the side of the building.

Just moments after the blast, Christie suddenly charged the officers firing a pair of revolvers while issuing a war whoop and gobbling like a turkey. He was cut down in a volley of rifle fire suffering wounds to the head, shoulder, and side. Young Arch Wolf and Mr. Hare were both badly burned in the melee. The body of Ned Christie was transported to Fort Smith where it was tied to a plank and put on public display on the steps of the federal courthouse to serve as an example to so-called "Agitators and Lawbreakers." Over time, Christie has evolved into a heroic and near mystical figure to many of his people.

Rufus Buck

Rufus Buck was possibly the most contemptible brigand the Indian Territory ever produced. During a ten-day period in the summer of 1895, he and several companions committed a half-dozen robberies, two murders, and several atrocious acts of rape in the Creek Nation unleashing a reign of terror that threw the entire territory into a state of mass confusion and fear. He and his gang were finally captured at the conclusion of a lengthy gunbattle with a large posse made up of the Creek Lighthorse, Federal Marshals, and enraged vigilantes. Judge Parker sentenced Buck and four of his crime partners to die for their sins. On July 1, 1896, Buck, Louis and Lucky Davis, Maomi July, and Sam Sampson were simultaneously hung in the courtyard of the Fort Smith Federal Jail. The members of the Buck Gang were the only individuals ever executed at Fort Smith specifically for the crime of rape. While Buck's four pals were secretly buried at Fort Smith's Catholic Cemetery, the outlaw's father arranged for his body to be freighted back to the Creek Nation for burial. Due to the hot weather, the freighters were unable to complete the journey. On reaching Fort Gibson, they hurriedly interred the corpse when it began to grow 'ripe' in the blazing sun.

Rufus Buck Gang. Courtesy Okmulgee Public Library.

The Bill Cook Gang and Cherokee Bill

William Tuttle Cook was for a time the most wanted man in the Indian Territory. Born near Fort Gibson in 1853, Bill lost his father at age five. His mother remarried and the family lived at a series of homesteads in the area. Unable to get along with his stepfather he left home at an early age drifting up to the Osage country where he "Cowboyed" at various ranches.

In 1892, Cook was arrested for introducing liquor and sentenced by Judge Parker to serve a forty-day hitch at the Fort Smith Federal Jail. Two years later, he was charged with horse theft and soon afterwards began his career as a full-fledged outlaw. The same year he and his brother, along with a Texas-born murderer named "Cherokee Bill," (real name Crawford Goldsby) were involved

Bill Cook. Courtesy Ken Butler.

in a shootout, which resulted in the death of Deputy Sequoyah Houston near the tiny settlement of Fourteen Mile Creek in the Cherokee Nation. After the gunbattle, Cook's gang went on a five-month rampage across the territory robbing numerous trains, depots, stores, stages, and lonely travelers as well as committing several murders. Members of the Cook Gang included: Bill's brother, Jim, "Skeeter" Baldwin, "Cherokee Bill," Elmer "Chicken" Lucas, Sam McWilliams (AKA The Verdigris Kid), Henry Munson, and Jim French. The gang's deprivations grew so bold and widespread, area officials demanded the federal government send in a troop of Calvary to help control the situation. On November 8, 1894, "Cherokee Bill" shot and killed a Lenapah merchant named Ernest Melton during a robbery. A few months later, he was captured and transported to Fort Smith in irons where he was charged with Melton's murder.

By early 1895, the gang had been virtually wiped out by federal lawmen and Indian Police. With his crew in tatters, Cook left the territory traveling to New Mexico hoping to stay one step ahead of his pursuers. On January 11, 1895, Bill Cook was captured at an isolated ranch in New Mexico and brought back for trial at Fort Smith where Judge Parker sentenced him to a term of forty years in prison. Cook died in 1900 of natural causes while an inmate at a New York penitentiary. Bill Cook is buried at the IOOF Cemetery located two miles west of Hulbert, as are the notorious Crittenden brothers, who were both slain by Ed Reed, the son of Belle Starr.

After being sentenced to death "Cherokee Bill" managed to have a pistol smuggled into his cell located deep within the bowels of the federal jail. Making a bid to escape Bill shot and killed Jailor Larry Keating. After a fierce gunfight with officers the two sides settled down to a fruitless siege until fellow inmate Henry Starr, who was being held for murdering a federal deputy, was allowed to enter

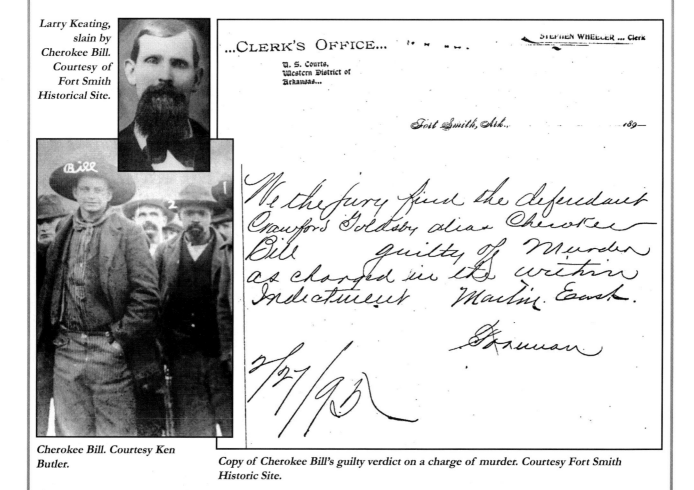

Larry Keating, slain by Cherokee Bill. Courtesy of Fort Smith Historical Site.

...CLERK'S OFFICE...

STEPHEN WHEELER ... Clerk

U. S. Courts,
Western District of
Arkansas...

Fort Smith, Ark., _____ 189—

We the jury find the defendant Crawford Goldsby alias Cherokee Bill guilty of Murder as charged in the within Indictment Martin. Cowsk.

Foreman

2/27/95

Cherokee Bill. Courtesy Ken Butler.

Copy of Cherokee Bill's guilty verdict on a charge of murder. Courtesy Fort Smith Historic Site.

Bill's cell in an attempt to talk the badman into surrendering. Starr's efforts were successful. Bill was promptly tried and convicted of Keating's murder. Judge Parker hammered the twenty-year old rouge with a second death sentence.

"Cherokee Bill" was hanged on March 17, 1896. When asked by the hangman if he had any final words he stated, "I came here to die not make a speech." He was buried at Citizens Cemetery at Fort Gibson.

Grave of Cherokee Bill (Crawford Goldsby) at Fort Gibson Citizens Cemetery. Photo by Naomi Morgan.

United States of America,
Western District of Arkansas.

IN THE CIRCUIT COURT, *Feby* TERM, A. D. 189*5*

UNITED STATES } MURDER.
VERSUS

Crawford Goldsby alias Cherokee Bill

The Grand Jurors of the United States of America, duly selected, empaneled, sworn and charged, to inq in and for the body of the Western District of Arkansas aforesaid, upon their oath present:

THAT *Crawford Goldsby alias Cherokee Bill*

on the *8* day of *Nov* A. D. 189*4* at the *Cherokee* Nation, in the Indian Country, within the Western District of Arkansas aforesaid, with force and arms, in and upon the body of one *Ernest Melton a white man and not an Indian*

then and there being, feloniously, wilfully and of *his* malice aforethought, did make an assault; and that the said *Crawford Goldsby alias Cherokee Bill* with a certain *Gun*

then and there charged with gunpowder and one leaden bullet, which said *Gun* he the said *Crawford Goldsby alias Cherokee Bill* in *his* hand then and there had and held, then and there feloniously, wilfully and of *his* malice aforethought, did discharge and shoot off, to, against and upon the said *Ernest Melton* and that the said *Crawford Goldsby alias Cherokee Bill* with the leaden bullet aforesaid, out of the *Gun* aforesaid, then and there, by force of the gunpowder aforesaid, by the said *Crawford Goldsby alias Cherokee Bill* discharged and shot off as aforesaid, then and there feloniously, wilfully and of *his* malice aforethought, did strike, penetrate and wound *him* the said *Ernest Melton* in and upon the *right side of face and back of the* of *him* the said *Ernest Melton* giving to *him* the said *Ernest Melton Gun* then and there, with the leaden bullet aforesaid, so as aforesaid discharged and shot out of the *Gun* aforesaid

Report of the Federal Grand Jury in the case of Cherokee Bill Courtesy Fort Smith National Historic Site.

Cherokee Bill and his Mother. Courtesy Ken Butler.

Growing Pains – 1907-1919

After statehood, the federal marshals service turned over the bulk of its enforcement duties to newly established county, city, and town police agencies.

By 1906-7, a private organization named the Anti-Horse Theft Association began to take hold in the state, offering large rewards for the capture of thieves in general. In the case of the AHTA, it was never a vigilante organization. The group's effectiveness lay in its ability to band together and offer substantial monetary compensation for information leading to a conviction, and in turn acting as a deterrent to criminal behavior. For example, whereas a single rancher could not offer a $500 reward for the return of a $50 horse, the organization as a whole could. The group's guiding principle was "Many Is One."

Horse-theft was brought back in vogue with the advent of WWI. The great powers placed a high demand on horseflesh for use in hauling wagons, men, and artillery on the killing fields of Europe. By war's end, gangs like the Poe-Hart combination that had previously specialized in stock theft, quickly switched to bank robbery when the demand for livestock dropped to nil.

The mid-teens marked the emergence of the so-called "Auto Bandits." Beginning with the Poe-Hart group, the Lewis-Jones gang, and Henry Starr's bunch, outlaws slowly made the switch from the horse to the car for use in their deprivations. (*The last horseback bank robbery in Oklahoma occurred on June 20, 1929, at the Bank of Caney, Atoka County.)

Noted lawmen of the era include Buck Garrett, Bud Ballew, Hiram Stephens, Bud Ledbetter, John Lung, Joe Wilson, John Johnson, Hi Thompson, "Pussyfoot" Johnson, Sam Tulk, Ed Corbin, Dick Farr, John E. Johnson, Bill Robbins, Sam Ridenhour, Homer Spaulding, Ben F. Smith, and Ralph Stormont. Some of the more famous bandits of the period were Henry Starr, Bert Casey, Joe Davis, Lee Jarrett, "Cottontop" Walker, Jess Littrell, Oscar and "Pony" Poe, Ab Connor, "Kaiser Bill"

Goodman, Ben Cravens, and Tom Slaughter, just to name a few.

The early teens marked the beginning of the oil, gas, and mineral strikes in the state. Oil patch "Boomtowns" began to appear and illegal liquor began to flow like a gusher. The homemade variety making its way into the boom areas was manufactured either locally or in the isolated Cookson or Osage Hills. Although some of the bonded or factory-made stuff originated from Fort Smith, Arkansas, most of it poured into the state directly from the warehouses of William J. "King" Creekmore who owned a huge distillery in the Joplin area. Creekmore was the absolute "King of the Oklahoma Bootleggers," operating in the state from 1908 until his conviction on federal bribery and conspiracy to introduce illegal spirits charges in 1917. "King" Creekmore had a battalion of operatives employed within his complex distribution network, and it was rumored toward the end of his reign he virtually controlled the key elected officials of seven Oklahoma counties.

Lawmen

James Ledbetter

Born and raised in Madison County, Arkansas, Ledbetter was appointed marshal of the rough mining community of Coal around 1879. According to tradition, the town elders hired the young man to police the settlement when they were awed by his beating of several drunken miners half to death with an ax handle in response to their poking fun at his new silk shirt. During the bulk of the 1880s, Ledbetter served as a Johnson County, Arkansas, deputy sheriff.

He then garnered work-guarding payrolls for the KATY Railroad operating in Eastern Arkansas and throughout the Indian Territory. In 1893, Senior Federal Marshal George Crump appointed him to the position of Deputy US Marshal under the auspices of Judge Parker in Fort Smith. Some of the more famous cases he worked

James F. "Uncle Bud" Ledbetter, 1852-1937. Photo courtesy of Three Rivers Museum.

in the Territory included those of Rufus Buck, Bill Cook, and Al Jennings. During the latter 1890s, he operated out of the Muskogee Federal Court working closely with such legal emissaries as Paden Tolbert, H. E. Ridenhour, and Samuel Rutherford. Bud gained a reputation as a fair and fearless officer.

Being a life-long teetotaler, he slaved endlessly to rid the area of the evils of liquor. According to most reports, he was an expert man hunter and a bit of a "Shootist" with an estimated twenty-one notches on his gun. In 1907, he shot and killed several men in a deadly shootout on the streets of Muskogee. His victims in this case were members of a crazed religious cult who had declared war on society.

When interviewed shortly after the gun battle by a reporter from the *Muskogee Phoenix* he stated: "Wasn't much to the affair. I went up there to see what was going on and them fellers started shooting at me so I killed 'em."

Reporter: How come they didn't hit you? There were at least five of them?

Bud: Well, whenever I shoot I always take a step or two sideways then I'm not where I was, you see.

Reporter: Weren't you scared?

Bud: No

Reporter: Were you excited?

Bud: No

Reporter: Nervous?

Bud: I ain't never nervous.

Reporter: Well, you must have felt some unusual sensations standing there being shot at.

Bud: I don't know about sensation or such, but I was a bit fretted.

Reporter: What fretted you?

Bud: Well, when I began firing at that fellow on the porch, I knew I was hitting him with every shot and when he would not fall, it fretted me. Tell you something— Never go after a shooting man with them new fangled .32s. Get ya hurt if ya do. Always take a .45. That knocks 'em down and they don't get up and bother you no more.

Bud left federal service after statehood was declared going to work for the town of Webbers Falls as the town marshal. He was later employed as the marshal in Haskell, and then was appointed Muskogee's Chief of Police in 1908. In 1912, he was elected sheriff of Muskogee County. His term was noted for the destruction of a horde of illegal whiskey stills. Refusing to run for a second term, Bud bought a 160-acre farm and began the life of a gentleman farmer. He was called out of retirement in 1917 when he went to work as a plainclothes officer for the Okmulgee Police Department. The rough-and-tumble oil boomtown had been hampered with a rash of robberies and murders over the past few years and "Uncle Bud," as Ledbetter had recently been dubbed by news reporters and friends, agreed to assist the locals in holding down the criminal element. In

Bud Ledbetter (Center) and posse with confiscated illegal whiskey stills. Courtesy Three Rivers Museum.

mid 1918, he quit his position in Okmulgee in order to spend six months as the town marshal of Haskell where he was paid $150 a month for his services. It was his second assignment in the little railroad settlement. The aging lawman was re-elected to the position of Muskogee County Sheriff in 1925 and again reelected in 1927. Starting to feel his age, he chose not to seek a third term, stating "Those liquor people ran me out of office." He retired to his farm where he died of heart disease with his boots off on July 8, 1937. Over 1,500 people attended his burial at Muskogee's Memorial Cemetery.

Sam Tulk, 1881-1952

Tulk began his career in law enforcement acting as a posse man for Bud Ledbetter. Over the years, he worked as a lawman in Haskell, Muskogee, and Ponca City as well as an investigator for the state crime bureau. He killed at least five men in the line of duty. In 1908, Tulk fatally shot brothers Will and Luther Ligon in separate incidents taking place on the streets of Haskell.

John E. Johnson

John Johnson was the first sheriff of Sequoyah County. His father was slain in the line of duty while working as a territorial lawman. Johnson was the leader of a posse that captured the notorious bank robber Reece Price in 1922. He was later assistant superintendent of the Oklahoma Bureau of Criminal Investigation and Identification.

Hiram Thompson, 1870-1945

Thompson was born in Indiana and relocated to the Oklahoma Territory around 1889 where he was employed as the Undersheriff of Payne County. He was commissioned a Deputy US Marshal in the early 1890s. In 1893, he was one of the officers involved in the "Great Ingalls Raid" in pursuit of the Doolin Gang. Thompson

A brace of pistols once belonging to Bud Ledbetter, on display at Fort Smith Historic Site.

Author holding rifle once belonging to Bud Ledbetter-Gun on display at Three Rivers Museum, Muskogee. Photo by Naomi Morgan.

Grave of Bud Ledbetter, Memorial Park Cemetery Muskogee-Photo by Naomi Morgan

Sam Tulk. Photo courtesy of Tony Perrin.

John E. Johnson. Photo courtesy of Sequoyah County Sheriff's Department.

Hiram "Hi" Thompson. Photo courtesy of Tony Perrin.

later served as a railroad detective before being elected two terms as the Tulsa County Sheriff (1901-2 then 1909-10). Upon completing his second term as sheriff, he was rehired as a deputy marshal. In 1929, he was employed by the Oklahoma City Police Department as the head of their fingerprint bureau. Thompson remained at this position until his death on March 3, 1945. The long-serving lawman was buried at Rose Hill Cemetery Oklahoma City.

Buck Garrett and Bud Ballew

The most famous team of lawmen in the early statehood era was Carter County's Buck Garrett and "Bud" Ballew. In the 1890s, Garrett served as a posseman for various federal marshals in the Ardmore and Paris, Texas, area before traveling to Wyoming where he took part in the bloody Johnson County Range War acting as a "Hired gun." In 1905, he was appointed Chief of Police in Ardmore where he served with distinction until 1910 when he was elected Carter County Sheriff. Upon his election, Garrett picked a double-tough local rancher named David "Bud" Ballew as his deputy. Garrett would go on to serve five terms as sheriff. While he was in office, much of Carter County was made up of a collection of rough and rowdy oilfield boomtowns populated by an army of roughnecks being actively preyed upon by a swarm of pimps, bootleggers, prostitutes, hijackers, and pickpockets. Garrett soon garnered a reputation as a fearless law enforcement officer who efficiently managed to keep the peace in one of the more challenging environments ever faced by a peace officer. His deputy, Bud Ballew, was a talented and willing "Pistelero" who slew at least eight men in various gun-duels during in his time as a lawman. In 1922, both men left office. Later that same year, Ballew came out second best in a gunfight that took place in a domino parlor in Wichita Falls, Texas. Garrett died of natural causes in 1929.

Bud Ballew (left) and Buck Garrett. Author's collection.

Hiram Stephens: Steel-Nerved Lawman

Born in 1869 in Kentucky, Hiram Stephens moved to the Cherokee Nation with his family as a child settling near the village of Braggs. By his early twenties, he had garnered a reputation in the area as a serious hardworking young man of an honorable character. By the mid-1890s, Stephens was talked into joining the local Cherokee Constabulary as a posseman. On February 5, 1895, Judge Isaac Parker appointed him a Deputy US Marshal for the Western District of Arkansas and the Indian Nations.

Several months after Stephens received his commission, the notorious Verdigris Kid, along with George Sanders, and a youth named Sam Butler, hoorayed the town of Braggs. In quick time, Officers Stephens, as well as Johnson Manning, were notified of the disturbance. When the lawmen approached Tom Madden's Store, where the outlaws were holed up, the bandits fired on them killing Manning's horse. Stephens responded by killing the Verdigris Kid where he stood. A general firefight broke out in which several citizens joined in. A clerk named Morris was struck by a fatal round while Butler was wounded, but still game. Suddenly, the two remaining highwaymen bolted for their horses. Sanders fell dead under the withering fire emitting from the officers' Winchesters. Butler safely made his way into the timber, fleeing to his residence located on the Verdigris River, where a deputy marshal named John Davis discovered him in the front yard leaning against an apple tree bleeding profusely. The two fired on one another simultaneously. Both men ultimately died of their wounds.

Over the next few years, Stephens was responsible for the arrest of numerous badmen plying their trade in the Illinois District. The young man married a half-blood Cherokee maiden in 1895. Around 1905 Stephens moved to Alluwe. Shortly after statehood, he was elected the first

Carter County Sheriff Buck Garrett (Front and Center) with deputies.
Courtesy Muskogee Public Library.

Sheriff of Rogers County, holding the position for six years. He later served as the Chief of Police in Chelsea.

In 1917, he was part of a posse that ambushed and killed three members of the notorious Poe-Hart Gang near Okmulgee. In April of 1919, Stephens was appointed Chief of Police of Pawhuska. His first day on the job he shot a man named Roy Tinker when Tinker refused to drop a pistol he was holding. After the shooting, he hired a taxi to transport his still living victim to the front door of the Johnson Funeral Home where he dropped the wounded man off. When the funeral director protested his leaving the gunshot victim at his place instead of the local hospital saying, "This man is not yet dead." Stephens responded, "What's the difference, he soon will be!" Tinker later died of his wounds. Immediately after the incident, Stephens resigned his post, taking a position as a special prohibition agent for the Bureau of Indian Affairs, working out of the Osage District. One week after the Pawhuska shooting, he gunned down a bootlegger named William Borham. It was reported that during his career he slew at least a dozen men in the line of duty. Stephens retired from law enforcement around 1925. The legendary lawman died in 1934.

Joe Wilson: Federal Marshal

Joseph Allen Wilson was born in Carlile, Georgia, on March 10, 1882. He moved to the Indian Territory as a youth before the turn of the century. His family settled near the community of Prices Chapel located in modern-day Sequoyah County. Wilson was married in 1902 and over the years blessed with the birth of three daughters and as many sons. In 1905, he was appointed village constable.

Soon after statehood, he was named to the position of Sequoyah County Deputy Sheriff under the county's first sheriff, John E. Johnson. In 1913, Wilson was appointed Deputy US Marshal for the Eastern District of Oklahoma headquartered out of Muskogee. His duties often focused on eradicating the production and distribution of illegal liquor. His jurisdiction included the heart of "moonshine" country, the wild and woolly Cookson Hills where whiskey making had become a cottage industry taken up by many of the natives owing to the area being a poverty-ridden district, poor for farming due to the rocky soil and totally lacking in industry. Wilson, who often times worked hand in hand with the legendary Federal Revenuer "Pussyfoot" Johnson, once reported there were so many stills operating in the area that on a cold morning one could see the smoke and smell the mash cooking long before arriving in the hills.

In the early 1920s, it was estimated 200 to 300 active stills were operating on the Illinois River alone. In 1918, Wilson and a posse of officers raided a still located in a cave near Marble City, which had the capacity to produce 1,000 gallons of hooch at a time.

Highlights of Wilson's career occurring during his stint as a marshal include the arrest of a notorious anti-government agitator named 'Dock' Copeland, who had been charged with sedition under the Espionage Act. Copeland had been stirring up the hill-folk with his anti-war sentiment during the First World War, encouraging young men to dodge the draft. When the marshal, accompanied by a local officer, attempted to capture the agitator Copeland took a pot shot at the lawmen. Wilson responded by plugging the traitor four times with a .45 pistol.

Later that year, Wilson participated in the arrest of the infamous trio of Levi "Mount" Cookson, "Cottontop" Walker, and "Kaiser Bill" Goodman who had recently robbed the bank of Gore on horseback. In 1921, he apprehended a man named Fleetwood who was operating a massive still near the settlement of Brushy. It appears the still was a community affair, area citizens each owning a share of the operation, shareholders were required to contribute so much corn and ingredients for their share of the product. When the defendant appeared before a magistrate the unrepentant soul implored the judge to "Hurry up and get this over your honor so I can go back and finish running that last batch of mash!"

In early 1922, several area youths broke into the Akins Post Office stealing $300 in pennies. Wilson was sent to investigate. Suspicion quickly fell on eighteen-year-old Charley Floyd (Soon to be known as "Pretty Boy" Floyd). While young Floyd was vigorously questioned in the affair, no charges were filed against him. Several years later, Wilson, along with two Sallisaw officers, arrested Floyd in regards to a Missouri robbery. On hearing of "Pretty Boys" violent demise in 1934, Wilson told newspaper reporters, "I knew him from the time he was eight-years-old. He was a good boy until he and those others broke into that post office. Just a prank, but I figured he would be trouble." Adding, "He was a great baseball player when he was a lad. Played first base. He should of stuck with baseball."

On the afternoon of June 2, 1922, three men rode horseback into the town of Muldrow, robbing the First National Bank of $17,000 in cash and coin. A massive posse that included Wilson and John Johnson set forth after the hijackers. When the posse caught up with the desperadoes near the community of Liberty, there was a quick exchange of fire. One of the bandits, Reece Price, was struck by the lawmen's initial volley falling from his horse. Price, who was plenty "game," remounted and returned fire. The posse responded with a second volley. Hit in the shoulder and buttocks with buckshot the outlaw and horse pitched to the ground violently rolling down a hillside coming to rest against a cedar tree. Meanwhile, the feisty outlaw's two partners desperately fled across a wide field spurning their mounts to action. Wilson dismounted and laying his .44-40 cal. Winchester rifle over his saddle, took aim, squeezed the trigger and brought down one of the riders with a single well-placed shot. The third fugitive, later identified as Charlie Price, escaped into the timber reportedly by forcing his horse to leap a four-rail fence. Later that year, Wilson resigned his

position as federal marshal taking a job as an investigator for the Kansas City Southern Railroad. In 1933, he briefly worked for the state as a stolen car operative before being reappointed to the position of deputy marshal.

On the afternoon of January 20, 1934, Wilson was driving from the Eastern Oklahoma town of Watts bound for Stillwell on Highway #59 when suddenly a car containing two individuals flagged him down on an isolated section of the road. On stopping one of the men exited the rig informing Wilson he was having car trouble and asked for a screwdriver. Wilson was complying with the request when he noticed the man had pulled a pistol. The marshal quickly yanked out his own gun and began exchanging shots with the man. One round fired by the individual struck Wilson in the chest but miraculously deflected off his pocket watch thus saving his life. Wilson fired two rounds, both striking the protagonist in the head killing him. By then, the second man had leaped from the car. Wilson leveled his revolver directly at his stomach and inquired, "You want some too buster?" The man surrendered peacefully. The dead man was identified as thirty-two year-old Oren B. "Red" Edgmon. The second subject was recognized as Earl Williams. Apparently, the pair had been on a robbery spree knocking off a series of filling stations and stores throughout Texas and Arkansas. Williams had recently escaped from the Okmulgee County Jail with several others including the notorious Clarence Eno, who had participated in at least a half-dozen bank robberies in Oklahoma and Kansas as a member of the Wilbur Underhill-Ford Bradshaw Gang. It appears Eno and Williams split up soon after the escape. Williams later connected with Edgmon and began their mini-crime spree.

In the latter 1930s, Wilson joined the effort to stem the tide of illegal hard liquor flowing into Oklahoma via the Fort Smith-Moffett whiskey trail. The area around Moffett had evolved into a wide-open honky-tonk strewn district dubbed "Little Juarez." Although federal and state operatives were able to arrest dozens of whiskey peddlers and confiscate massive quantities of hooch, their efforts seemed to have little effect. When asked by a reporter if it was possible for the authorities to slow down the river of booze coming in from Arkansas, Wilson calmly replied, "Probably not, but we will teach the ones we catch a pretty expensive lesson."

On the afternoon of June 11, 1946, Federal Marshals Wilson and William Thomas were assigned the mission of transporting two prisoners to Leavenworth Federal Prison from the federal holding facility in Muskogee. One of the prisoners, Ronald Jobe of Coalgate had been sentenced to a two-year term for cheating on his taxes while the second man was twenty-year-old red-haired Donald Dube of Massachusetts, who had been convicted of stealing a car in his home state and driving it to Pauls Valley where he was apprehended while trying to cash a phony check. Dube was a born looser having already served two terms in reform school for assault with a deadly weapon. Soon after his release from the reformatory, he stole a car and went on a crime spree robbing a hotel clerk in Owensburg, Kentucky, of $175 before assaulting a filling station operator and stealing a tank full of gas on the way out of town. The following day he was captured in Pauls Valley.

Near the community of Victory Junction, Kansas, Dube made a dive at a pistol the officers had stashed in the car's glove box. After wrestling with the officers for a moment, he broke free, grabbed the gun and shot Joe Wilson five times, once in the head. Deputy Thomas, after he got the car stopped and pulled on to the shoulder, responded by emptying his Colt automatic into Dube. The assailant was pronounced dead on arrival at a Kansas City hospital while Wilson was judged to be in critical condition. Amazingly, the feisty lawman would recover. Shortly afterwards, Joe Wilson retired from law enforcement.

Joe Wilson died on January 16, 1969, at a nursing home in Fort Smith, Arkansas, and he was buried at Sallisaw, Oklahoma. His passing marked the end of an era. He was the last living member of that famed fraternity of federal lawmen, which included Bill Tilghman, "Wild Bill" Robbins, and Bud Ledbetter, whose careers began on horseback and ended with the use of the automobile.

Outlaws

The "Bearcat" Henry Starr, 1873-1921

Cherokee tribesman Henry Starr was undoubtedly the most prolific bank robber in American history, even outdoing Jesse James in that department. Henry, who was the nephew of the notorious "Bandit Queen" Belle Starr, was born at Fort Gibson, Indian Territory, in 1873. After

an uneventful childhood, Henry drifted about the country working as a wrangler on a few of the big ranches until one day in 1891 when he was arrested for introducing liquor into the territory. For the remainder of his life Starr would claim he was innocent of the charge and in turn blame his mistreatment by the arresting officers as his motivation for turning to a life of crime.

Henry Starr "The Bearcat" – the most prolific bank robber in American history. Courtesy Ken Butler.

Days after his release from custody, Henry conducted a crime spree robbing the train depot in Nowata as well as stores in Lenapah and Sequoyah. On December 13, 1892, Deputy US Marshal Floyd Wilson caught up with the young bandit in an open field located near Lenapah and the two began exchanging fire. At the conclusion of a brief firefight, Wilson fell from his saddle gravely wounded. Starr approached the downed officer and mercilessly fired another round into his body. After looting a few more stores and train depots, the youth then hijacked his first bank in Caney, Kansas. He later held-up an MKT train near Pryor Creek before robbing a bank in Bentonville, Arkansas, for $11,000. The budding outlaw was captured with his sidekick, Kid Wilson, in Colorado Springs, Colorado, on July 3, 1893. While Wilson pled guilty to armed robbery and was sentenced to twenty-four years in federal prison, Starr was convicted of the murder of Deputy Floyd Wilson and given a death sentence by "Hanging Judge" Isaac Parker. Henry's lawyer promptly appealed the case and to Parker's extreme annoyance, the badman was granted a new trial by the US Supreme Court. During his stay at the Fort Smith Federal Prison awaiting disposition of his case, Starr assisted lawmen in disarming the notorious Cherokee Bill after the murderer had somehow gotten hold of a pistol and killed a jailor. On Starr's request, the desperate lawmen allowed him to visit Bill in his cell where he talked the killer into surrendering.

Although Henry was eventually convicted of Wilson's murder a second time, the higher courts again reversed the decision. In 1897, Henry's lawyers arranged a plea agreement with the court where the bandit plead guilty to a reduced charge of manslaughter and accepted a sentence of fourteen-years in the federal slammer. President Theodore Roosevelt, an admirer of everything western, including bank robbers, foolishly commuted the badman's sentence in 1901.

Shortly after gaining his freedom Henry married and was blessed with a son, who he named Theodore Roosevelt Starr in honor of his benefactor. After taking a short stab at living the honest life, the temptation of easy money proved too much for the unrepentant desperado. It appears his downfall can be directly connected to his love of gambling. When he went on a loosing streak, he rejoined his recently freed crime partner, Kid Wilson, and the pair hijacked banks in Tyro, Kansas, Hoffman, Oklahoma, and Amity, Colorado. On May 13, 1908, Henry was captured in Arizona and sent to Colorado where he was convicted of the Amity job, being sentenced to a seven to twenty-five year term. Kid Wilson escaped custody and was never heard of again. While

Paul Curry, the lad who shot Henry Starr during the Stroud bank robbery attempt.

in prison Henry kept occupied by writing his autobiography titled: *Thrilling Events: the Life of Henry Starr.*

Upon his parole in 1913, Starr and several acquaintances went on a robbery spree unmatched in the journals of criminal history raiding banks at Keystone, Kiefer, Tupelo, Pontotoc, Byers, Glencoe, Wardville, Carney, Owasso, Garber, Vera, Preston, and Terlton, Oklahoma. On March 27, 1915, Starr, along with Charley Johnson, Bud Maxfield, Joe Davis, and several others attempted to loot two banks at once in Stroud. While the majority of the gang was able to make their getaway out of town on horseback, Henry was shot down by a seventeen-year-old youth named Paul Curry. After pleading guilty to bank robbery, the gravely wounded bandit was sentenced to twenty-five years imprisonment.

Paroled in 1919 Starr entered the motion picture business. Although it appears his "Silent" films made money, the old robber was somehow hustled out of his profits by a group of swindlers. Coming up short of cash due to his ever-present gambling debts, Starr once again turned to what he knew best, bank robbery. The charismatic bandit hurriedly formed a gang that included area brigands Ed Lockhart, Charley Brackett, and Rufus

Kid Wilson, partner of Henry Starr. Author's private collection.

Contemporary view of Stroud National Bank robbed by Starr Gang in 1915. **Photo by Naomi Morgan.**

Rollen. The quartet promptly robbed several small banks in Arkansas and Missouri before attempting to loot the Peoples National Bank in Harrison, Arkansas, on the morning of February 18, 1921. Just moments after Henry entered the building flashing a pistol and announcing it was a holdup, a banker slipped into a walk-in vault where he retrieved a loaded rifle. When Starr bent down to rummage through a small safe the bookkeeper shot him in the back. On observing their leader hit the floor in a bloody heap, Starr's partners fled the bank in a panic roaring out of town in a stolen automobile. While he lie paralyzed on his deathbed the bandit bragged, "I've robbed more banks than any man," Henry Starr died a few days after the attempted bank robbery and was buried at the Dewey, Oklahoma, Cemetery in an unmarked grave.

The Porum Range War

A year before statehood, a bloody range war, which could be favorably compared in intensity with the 1880s Lincoln County War that involved the likes of "Billy the Kid," broke out in southern Muskogee County between two large ranching concerns both located near Porum. One of the factions was led by a well established land baron known as Judge Hester. The ramrod of the second group was "Old Man" Sam Davis, who with his five sons, Cicero, Jack, Bob, Amon, and Sam, ran cattle on about 2000 acres. Apparently, the initial motivation for the feud concerned Hester's suspicion that members of the Davis family along with their ally, Pony Starr, (cousin of Belle and Henry) were rustling his stock. During the

Joe Davis under arrest. Courtesy Ken Butler.

initial stages of the dispute, at least three men were slain in an ambush. When Muskogee County Deputies Jim Work and Bud Robertson attempted to serve a warrant on Bob Davis for cattle rustling in 1911, all hell broke loose leaving Work dead and several others wounded.

As a result of the gun battle, several of the Davis clan were arrested and held in Muskogee. On May 29, 1911, a large posse attempted to arrest Pony Starr and Joe Davis (son of Jack) at Starr's ranch. A gunfight broke out leaving four posseman dead and several wounded. Over the next year, at least three others were slain in connection with the feud. Eventually Starr and Joe Davis left the area defusing the violent atmosphere. Joe Davis turned outlaw, assisting Henry Starr in the failed Stroud robbery before hijacking a train near Eufaula. In 1916, he participated in a train robbery in Arizona. A few months after the Arizona raid Davis and others looted banks in Bromide and Boswell, Oklahoma, before his capture at Purcell. He was eventually convicted of the Arizona train robbery and given 25 years at Leavenworth Federal Penitentiary. The outlaw was paroled in 1931 and died in Sand Springs of natural causes in 1979 at the age of 86.

A Tragedy in Okmulgee

On the afternoon of November 15, 1908, a black man named Newt Deckard (or Decker, spelled both ways in news accounts) was involved in a drunken quarrel with a Creek Indian named Jim Grayson over the price of a duck. When Deckard struck the lad in a fit of intoxication, Grayson hurriedly filed a complaint with the Okmulgee Police. In response to receiving the grievance, Assistant Police Chief Henry Klaber promptly hitched up his buggy and sped to Deckard's small shanty with his twelve-year-old son and the Indian youth in tow. Deckard reacted to the lawman's presence by opening fire on the officer, who in turn emptied his six-shooter at his assailant but missed his target. Deckard, realizing the lawmen was out of bullets, approached to within a few feet of him before cold-bloodedly firing a well-aimed round which entered Klaber's throat killing him instantly. Two African-American neighbors, Felix and Ralph Chapman, hearing the gunshots, picked up the fallen officer's pistol and attempted to return fire not realizing the gun was empty of cartridges. Deckard shot and killed both men before retreating into his house.

Soon afterwards, Police Chief Samuel 'Dick' Farr,

Charred remains of Okmulgee mass murderer. Courtesy of Okmulgee Public Library.

scorched home, they discovered Deckard's body in a state of near total incineration.

In the days following the tragedy the town of Okmulgee was in a state of near panic, many citizens expected a race riot to erupt in response to the death of a black man at the hands of the police. Thankfully, nothing of the sort happened, probably due to the fact the majority of the vigilantes who had exchanged fire with Deckard were African-Americans, as were several of his victims. Sheriff Robinson was buried at Beggs while Assistant Chief Kleber was interred at the Okmulgee Cemetery under the eyes of nearly 1000 mourners.

Elmer McCurdy

The story of Elmer McCurdy is one of the most bizarre tales of the Old West. Born around 1880 in Maine, Elmer quit school at an early age in order to see the world. After a few years of knocking around, he joined the army. After he was discharged from the service on November 7, 1910, Elmer drifted to St. Joseph, Missouri, where he was promptly arrested for suspicion of burglary. While residing in the Buchanan County Jail, the young man made the acquaintance of Walter Jarrett, oldest of the notorious Jarrett brothers of Cedar Creek Gang fame, who was being held on a charge of public intoxication. The two must of hit it off since Walter, who had already done a hitch in the Missouri State Prison for second-degree burglary, informed the youth that once he gained his release, look him up in Oklahoma. Soon after he was sprung, Elmer journeyed south to reconnect with his newfound friend.

On the evening of March 23, 1911, Elmer joined Walter and his brothers, Lee and Glen, along with Ab Connor in an attempt to hijack the express car of an Iron Mountain Railroad train near Lenapah, Oklahoma. Evidently, things started going downhill when Elmer, who bragged of being an explosives expert in the army, set too large of a charge on the safe blowing the iron box into the neighboring county. The profits ended up being slim but it beat working. Shortly after the heist, the gang split up and Walter was quickly captured and jailed. Upon being convicted and sentenced to a twenty-five year sentence for the train heist, Jarrett escaped from the confines of the Muskogee Federal Detention Facility fleeing back to the Osage Country where he single-handedly robbed the Bank of Prue on the morning of October

accompanied by Okmulgee County Sheriff Edger Robinson along with another patrolman arrived on the scene and engaged the assailant in a gun duel. Within minutes, Robinson fell dead, a bullet striking him directly in the forehead. Farr was wounded as was an unidentified deputy sheriff and five other bystanders. With the arrival of reinforcements, the gunfight resumed in which an assembled throng of over 200 lawmen and vigilantes fired over 600 rounds at Deckard's shack. Two hours into the battle the crowd (made up of mostly of colored citizens) set fire to Deckard's home with coal oil forcing the gunman outside where he was peppered with shot before fleeing back into the blazing home. Moments later, witnesses heard a lone shot then silence except the burning of the structure. When the posse finally entered the

12, 1912. The following day he was shot dead by a pair of cowboys when they encountered him crossing the prairie mounted on one of their horses (stolen of course).

Meanwhile, Elmer and a drifter named Amos Hayes attempted to burglarize a bank in Chautauqua, Kansas. The duo broke into the financial institution in the dead of night using a sledgehammer and crowbar. Once more Elmer overestimated the nitro, blowing the safe's exterior door across the room with such force it crashed through the bank's front glass window landing in the street. Unfortunately for them, the safe's interior door remained secured. When lights began to come on throughout the town the two miscreants abandoned their plans departing the area with only a few coins in their pockets. On October 4, 1911, the bungling duo attempted to rob another train near Okesa, but failed miserably, harvesting a mere $40 in cash and coin along with a pint of cheap whiskey for their efforts. In the wake of the train heist, the pair parted ways. Elmer fled to an isolated ranch, finding sanctuary in the hayloft of a barn where he commenced to drink himself insensible. The following morning a posse showed up demanding his surrender. The hung-over outlaw answered their request by taking a couple of ineffective potshots at the lawmen. Minutes later, poor Elmer lay dead from an acute case of lead poisoning.

His remains were transported by wagon to a Pawhuska funeral home where he was embalmed and put in cold storage awaiting his next of kin. As time went on it became apparent no one was going to claim the corpse, so the funeral director pumped his veins full of arsenic and propped him up in a back room standing at permanent attention with an old rifle placed in his hands for effect, eventually becoming a morbid object of local interest. Five years later, a couple of carnival operators outsmarted the undertaker gaining possession of the mummified corpse by claiming they were his grieving relatives. After effortlessly making the career switch from outlaw to showman, Elmer spent the next sixty-odd years making the rounds with a series of carnival sideshows and wax museums.

Elmer McCurdy in death. Courtesy Glenn Lemons.

With the passage of time and the dulling of memories, folks began to assume the mummified corpse was a mannequin of sorts. Hidden under several coats of paint and wax, the shriveled little man became virtually unrecognizable as a human form. Eventually he was sold as a stage prop to a Hollywood production concern and stored in a warehouse located in Long Beach, California. In 1976, a stagehand was moving him to a movie set where they were filming a segment of the "Six Million Dollar Man," when suddenly his arm fell off exposing a bone. The authorities were notified and an autopsy was performed, which uncovered the fact he was indeed human, not wax. A spent bullet, which had been manufactured in 1905, was discovered in his stomach cavity. His organs were reportedly hard as a rock.

After a lengthy investigation, a group of historians and forensic pathologists from both California and Oklahoma confirmed the corpse was that of Elmer McCurdy, Oklahoma badman. The bandit's much traveled body was transported back to Oklahoma where a group of Old West historians made provision for his burial in the Boot Hill section of Guthrie's Summit View Cemetery, the final resting place of Bill Doolin and various other outlaws hailing from the pre-statehood period. Fittingly, Elmer's plain wooden coffin was moved to the cemetery in a horse drawn hearse surrounded by a squad of attendants dressed in cowboy attire, mounted on horseback, and riding in buggies. With great fanfare, the bandit who just wouldn't stay put was finally planted back in the state where his life had officially ended well over a half century ago. A couple of yards of concrete were dumped in the hole to ensure his permanent presence at that local.

Henry Grammer, 1883-1926

The Texas born Grammer was noted as one of the most prolific bootleggers and proficient gunman to ever come out of the Osage Country. Born in 1883, he drifted to Montana at the age of twenty where he worked as a cowboy until killing a man in a barroom gunfight. He

Henry Grammer. Photo courtesy Rick Mattix.

was convicted of manslaughter and promptly sentenced to three years in the Montana State pen. Soon after his release from prison in 1907, he relocated to Ponca City where he joined the Wild West Show from the 101 Ranch, working with such performers as Tom Mix and Bill Pickett. Over time, Grammer came to be known as a world-class rodeo performer. He eventually settled down in the Osage area operating a ranch as well as running one of the largest bootlegging enterprises in the state, oftentimes working hand in hand with legendary whiskey-runner "King" Creekmore providing illegal ardent spirits to an army of oilfield "Roughnecks." During the next few years, he was frequently involved in various gun battles in which he killed and wounded several individuals. Grammer died in a mysterious car wreck in 1926.

The Poe-Hart Gang

In the months before America's involvement in the war to end all wars there came charging out of the west an organized band of cutthroats dubbed the Poe-Hart Gang. This band of desperadoes cut a swath of robbery, murder, and wholesale theft not seen on the frontier since the arrival of the infamous Dalton brothers. The Poe-Hart Gang was noted as Oklahoma's first major group of outlaws to successfully make the switch from the horse to the automobile for use in their deprivations. From their beginnings as an organized crew of horse and cattle rustlers, the gang soon turned to the more lucrative crime of bank robbery.

The original gang was made up of Adolphus L. "Pony or Poem" Poe and his nephew Oscar along with the two Hart brothers, Will and Harry, who hailed from rural Craig County. Others involved in the group were Russell Tucker and Jess Littrell as well as future Cedar Creek Gang members, Lee Jarrett, and his brother-in-law, Albert Connor.

On October 18, 1916, the gang robbed the First National Bank of Centralia for $5,000, making their getaway in an automobile. Oscar Poe and Will Hart were promptly captured in Coffeyville, Kansas, and transported back to Vinita where they were held for trial.

On November 5, the pair escaped from the Craig County Jail with the aide of several confederates and sought refuge in the infamous Blue Canyon. On December 8, the reconstituted gang hijacked the State Bank of Alluwe for $2,500. Three days later, Oscar Poe, aided by the Hart boys and either Russell Tucker or Jess Littrell, held-up the Farmers State Bank in Vinita of $17,000 in cash and coin. On the morning of December 20, the same band of hooligans knocked off the Oklahoma National Bank of Skiatook for $2,800. Two weeks after the Skiatook heist, a posse surrounded the gang in the Blue Canyon. In the ensuing gun battle, Officers Charles Bullock and John Garritson were slain while the fugitives made a clean getaway. On January 12, 1917, the gang looted the First National Bank of Harrah for $4,000.

In response to the gang's latest outrage, the Oklahoma Bankers Association announced a $5,000 reward for the capture of any member of the Poe-Hart combination, "Dead or Alive." Responding to the reward, huge posses of armed vigilantes were organized, setting up

Oscar Poe. Courtesy of Muskogee Phoenix.

roadblocks and swarming over the countryside in search of the fugitives. In the early morning hours of January 18, officers surrounded Jess Littrell and Russell Tucker near the IXL settlement located just north of the town of Boley. When the gunsmoke cleared, Okfuskee County Deputy Sheriff Laf Boulware and outlaw Russell Tucker lay dead, while Jess Littrell was seriously wounded and captured in the melee. Littrell was later convicted of Boulware's murder and given a fifty-year sentence along with a twenty-five year term for the robbery of the Bank of Harrah. The following year the outlaw was convicted of the murder of John Bullock and handed a life sentence, which was later overturned on appeal.

The day after the IXL gun battle, a posse of lawmen, which included Officers Buck George, Hiram Stephens, John Lung, "Wild" Bill Robbins, Mel Bowman, and a private detective named Gustafson, ambushed and killed Oscar Poe and the two Hart brothers near the small community of Nuyaka while they were walking down a footpath moving from one hideout to another. Only part of the loot taken from the gang's recent robberies was recovered leaving future treasure hunters to theorize the badmen had hidden some of their loot in the rugged hills along the Deep Fork River in the vicinity of Nuyaka. As far as is known, no one has yet recovered any of the missing loot.

The morning after the gunbattle, the bodies of Oscar Poe and the Harts were transported to Okmulgee where they were propped up for display behind a large glass window of a local hardware store and viewed by thousands. The following day the trio was buried side by side in unmarked graves at the Okmulgee Park Cemetery.

Jess Littrell was paroled in 1931 and relocated to

Russell Tucker and his final resting place in Nowata. Courtesy Joe Tucker.

Grave of Okfuskee County Deputy Sheriff Laf Boulware, slain by members of the Poe-Hart Gang. Photo by Naomi Morgan.

Arrest warrant out of Nowata County for members of Poe Hart Gang. Courtesy Nowata County Clerk of Court..

Oklahoma City where he worked as a cook in a greasy spoon café as well as being employed as a gas station attendant. In 1933, he was suspected of involvement with the Underhill-Bailey Gang in the robbery of a bank in Black Rock, Arkansas, as well as a burglary in Lawton. He returned to prison in 1939 on a bootlegging charge. Jess Littrell died in 1952. He is buried at Marlow.

As for posseman John Lung, he went on to serve a year as the Chief of Police of Okmulgee before resign-ing to accept a position as Okmulgee County Undersheriff. In 1922, he resigned his post and started his own private detective agency. On September 15, 1922, Lung was shot to death in a gunfight with hoodlums in downtown Sapulpa.

Lawman "Wild" Bill Robbins resigned from the sheriff's department in 1920 and served with the Oklahoma Corporation Commission for many years before taking up farming. The legendary lawman died in 1950.

Grave of Jess Littrell in Marlow. Photo by Naomi Morgan.

Grave of John Garritson, slain by members of the Poe-Hart combination. Photo by Naomi Morgan.

Grave of Charles Bullock killed by members of the Poe-Hart Gang. Photo by Naomi Morgan.

Law Enforcement Advances

In the early days of statehood, the horse was used for patrol and response. By 1918, the automobile had replaced the hay-burner in many departments. Police technology at the time was crude to say the least. For criminal identification, departments and prisons depended on the Bertillon System, which involved taking photographs from several angles of a subject, then taking a series of bodily measurements as well as gathering data such as tattoos, hair, and eye color. Positive identification of a subject usually meant an eyewitness had to physically come forward to visually pick the individual out of a lineup. Education and training for officers was nonexistent. Qualifications for a law enforcement position usually meant size, toughness, and nerve. For equipment, officers relied heavily on the blackjack and six-shooter to enforce the law, especially in the newly created oilfield "Boomtowns." For communications, officers made use of the telephone and telegraph as well as runners.

Left: Bertillon card. Courtesy Rick Mattix.

He is buried at the Okmulgee Park Cemetery. Robbins's obituary stated he first settled in the Indian Territory near Checotah in 1893, hailing from Arkansas. In 1894, he was commissioned a Deputy US Marshal working out of Fort Smith with the likes of Heck Thomas and Paden Tolbert. He later served as a Muskogee County Deputy before accepting a post as Okmulgee County Deputy Sheriff.

"Pony" Poe spent the next forty years knocking about the country working odd jobs and bouncing from jail to jail until his death in a 1963 car accident. He is buried at Ardmore in an unmarked grave. According to old-timers, both he and Jess Littrell were seen at various times over the years lurking about the Deep Fork River bottoms searching for the gang's lost loot.

The Oklahoma State Penitentiary

Before statehood, criminals convicted of offenses committed in the Indian Territory served their time at various federal prisons, while most felons convicted in the Oklahoma Territory were incarcerated at the Kansas State Penitentiary in Lansing.

In 1908, the newly formed state legislature, with the prodding of the recently elected Commissioner of Charities and Corrections, Kate Barnard, voted to construct a state prison and adjacent penal farm in McAlester. Prisoners were returned from Kansas and sent to work building the facility, which was situated on 1,556 acres. The prison's first Warden was R. W. Dick (1909-1916). Over time, numerous industries were created to provide jobs for the inmates. In 1925-6, a separate facility was added for the incarceration of female inmates, while a permanent sub-prison for men was constructed near Stringtown in 1936. Records show some 718 cons were incarcerated at the main prison in 1910, 1,000 in 1915, 1,288 in 1920, 2,788 in 1930 and 3,500 in 1940.

The prison suffered several bloody escapes during its first decades in existence, such as the one in 1914 in which a trio of inmates killed three prison employees and a visiting attorney before they were slain. Ten convicts escaped in 1921 by crawling through a tunnel, while eighteen more tunneled out in 1924. The following year, five cons shorted out the lights and escaped over the wall under the cover of darkness. In 1934, seven inmates tunneled out of the TB ward, while officials discovered a 150-foot tunnel running under the prison yard in 1935. On May 13, 1936, fourteen cons rode out of the prison brickyard in three hijacked cars on a wild bid for freedom. One guard and an inmate were killed in the unsuccessful escape attempt. A few months after the brickyard

Arial view of "Big Mac," early 1940s. Oklahoma Department of Corrections.

Left: Kate Barnard ,1875-1930, America's first woman elected to a statewide office as Oklahoma Commissioner of Charities and Corrections in 1907. Author's collection.

escapade, a pair of inmates took executioner Rich Owens hostage and attempted to trade his life for their freedom. When the pair walked their hostage to the gate and threatened to kill Owens if the guard on duty did not open up, their contrary hostage informed the tower hack to, "Go ahead and shoot. If you hit me it's OK." The guard took him at his word killing both escapees while one of the pair used his last seconds of life to stick a homemade dirk about four inches deep into Owens's back as he fell. Several years later, in 1941, the leader of the '36 bust out, Claude Beavers, along with three others took Warden Jess Dunn and another prison employee hostage, and after forcing their way out of the facility were all gunned down by a sharp-shooting deputy sheriff. Tragically, Dunn and another officer were also slain during the aborted attempt.

In 1909, the Oklahoma State Reformatory was constructed in Granite to house youthful offenders age 14 to 25. Its most famous inmate was pioneer aviator Wiley Post, who served thirteen months of a ten-year sentence at the facility on an armed robbery charge. Post would die in a 1935 Alaska plane crash in the company of world famous humorist Will Rogers. Over the years, several sub-prisons throughout the state were built as well as a host of road or work camps that were often dubbed "Chain Gangs." It should be noted that, to the state's credit, Oklahoma's road camps lacked the reputation for extreme brutality common to those operating in other southern states.

The Granite Reformatory suffered numerous escapes over the years. The more noted incidents occurring at Granite include a group

"Have you got anything with a little pin stripe?"

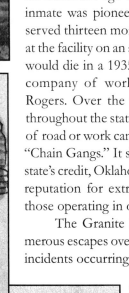

Top: The prison cemetery at Peckerwood Hill, McAlester. Photo courtesy of the Oklahoma Department of Corrections.
Center: Cartoon. Courtesy Rick Mattix.
Left: Oklahoma State Penitentiary, circa 1920s. Oklahoma Department of Corrections.

Guards at McAlester Prison, circa 1915. Courtesy of McAlester News Capitol.

way into the Warden's office, which was occupied by Stenographer Miss Mary Foster, as well as Parole Officer Frank Rice and a visiting lawyer from Muskogee. The lawyer, Judge John R. Thomas, had served as a federal judge for the Northern District of the Indian Territory from 1897 to1901. As they approached the office, Day Sergeant F. C. Godfrey confronted the escapees. A struggle ensued in which Godfrey was fatally shot, as was Bertillon Officer Herman Dover who was working in an adjoining room. Dover was freakishly hit by a stray bullet, which penetrated a door, bounced off a wooden desk, and struck him in the heart.

When the mutineers finally entered the warden's office Miss Foster began to scream hysterically while Thomas stood up and either raised his hands in submission or reached for his cane (reports vary) only to be cold-bloodedly shot down. The escapees then took Foster and Rice hostage, binding their hands with a length of telephone cord intending to use them as human shields

of eight inmates springing loose in 1927, followed by a 1931 mass escape involving ten members of the kitchen detail armed with butcher knives and meat cleavers. On August 15, 1932, twenty-three cons overpowered several guards and a night sergeant making their way to freedom. The nastiest disturbance at the facility occurred in 1935 when thirty-one crudely armed inmates clashed with a cadre of club-wielding guards. Most of the cons backed down when the officers made a show of force, but not until several inmates were seriously injured and a corrections officer slain.

The prison system kept a pack of eighteen bloodhounds on tap for use as trackers. The most famous being Texas-born "Old Boston."

Noted head keepers of the McAlester facility were Warden's R.W. Dick, W.S. Key, Sam Brown, Fred Hunt, and Jess Dunn.

Massacre at McAlester

On the afternoon of January 20, 1914, three inmates, later identified as China Reed, Tom Lane, and Charlie Kuntz, approached the barred gate separating the prison's inner offices from the main cell blocks they presenting Turnkey Jack Martin with a forged pass granting them admittance to the office of the deputy warden. Immediately after the turnkey opened the steel door, Kuntz whipped out a hidden .44 caliber Smith and Wesson revolver shooting the official in the cheek before taking his keys. The desperate inmates then attempted to force their

"Remember, boys, no fair kicking the ball over the fence!"

Over the wall cartoon. Courtesy Rick Mattix.

in their violent rush to freedom. The moment the inmates attempted to exit the main building with their prisoners, Assistant Deputy Warden Pat Oats confronted them with a double-barreled shotgun, but was unable to get a clear shot fearing he would hit the hostages. The inmates, now armed with a second pistol taken off the corpse of one of the slain prison officials, opened fire killing Oats with a round to the heart. Suddenly, a Negro trusty rushed into the hall seizing a small automatic pistol that had fallen from the fatally wounded officer's waistband and fired a single round at the fleeing bandits, the bullet striking Kuntz in the stomach. The inmates reacted by scooping up their wounded pal and charging toward the main gate. By holding a pistol barrel against the hysterical female clerk's head while making loud and threatening gestures, they convinced the tower guards to throw their weapons to the ground and open the gate. The escapees exited the prison and, discovering a single-horse hackney tied up next to the walls, loaded their hostages along with their wounded companion into the rig and rode away from the prison at a fast clip. Apparently, the lady stenographer sat on Lane's lap while Officer Rice was crammed behind the buggy seat. Although confusion reined supreme inside the prison, Chief Telephone Operator L. C. Morton had the good sense to quickly repair the phone line and contact numerous outside locales, informing them of the breakout.

After receiving news of the bust out, Bloodhound Sergeant R. J. Ritchie, who was headquartered at the prison lake, grabbed his Winchester rifle, mounted his horse and began riding toward a small promontory located three-quarters of a mile from the prison walls. On arriving at the hilltop, he took a position behind a large rock ledge that overlooked a dirt lane in hopes of ambushing the escapees.

Back in the crowded buggy, Kuntz, who was bleeding like a

Murder victim, Judge John Thomas. Three Rivers Museum.

stuck hog, begged his companions to stop and tend to his wounds, while Miss Foster, who had taken a stray round to the thigh, continued to scream and wail at the top of her lungs, pleading to be released. Parole Officer Rice, in an act of compassion asked Kuntz if he wanted to make a dying declaration, to which one of the other inmates retorted, "You'll be the one making a dying statement if you don't shut up!"

Once the buggy came abreast of Ritchie's position the officer delivered two well-placed rounds squarely into Lane's forehead with pinpoint accuracy, the bullets missing Miss Foster's face by just inches, close enough for her to feel the breeze made by the round's passage while being showered with the convict's blood and brain matter. When Kuntz raised his head up, curious as to what was happening, the sharp-shooting dog-keeper plugged him as well. Seconds later, Ritchie issued a single bullet to Reed's head, the round taking out his right eye and half his skull. The convict pitched backward in the buggy seat releasing the leather reins causing the little wagon to lurch out of control bumping and crashing into a ditch throwing the dead as well as the living into a bloody pile on the roadside. According to a statement made by Rice, "I fell from the wagon and hit the frozen ground with a jolt rolling to a stop with my hands still bound. Moments later I heard Mr. Ritchie, now joined by another guard, approach me commenting. 'The other three are dead, I guess we'll kill off this other one as well.' My heart froze when I realized he had mistaken me for a convict and intended on putting me under. I stayed still until he approached and thankfully recognized me as a victim not an escaping inmate." Ritchie later told a news reporter "I'd have killed him too if he didn't already look dead." With that said, the Great McAlester Bustout, the most deadly in state prison history, costing the lives of seven men, came to an end.

When interviewed twenty years after the event, R. J. Ritchie, long retired from prison work and operating a chicken ranch located just outside McAlester, told a reporter, "I don't know how it happened, I shot into that heap of folks in that wagon over and over without hitting the hostages. I couldn't repeat those shots in a hundred years."

Capital Punishment

In 1913, the Oklahoma state legislature substituted electrocution for hanging as the means to put condemned inmates to death. Penologists of the day considered electrocution a more humane and efficient method of execution than hanging. Beginning with murderer Henry Bookman, eighty-two male inmates were legally executed by use of the electric chair and one by hanging at the Oklahoma State Penitentiary between December 10, 1915, and August 10, 1966. By race, these figures can be broken down to four Native Americans, twenty-seven African Americans, and fifty-one Caucasian. Previously, between 1907 (statehood) and 1913, seven men were legally put to death by hanging, all taking place in the counties where the crime occurred. During the same time frame, twenty-six others were lynched without the benefit of legalities. On April 19, 1909, four white men were simultaneously hung in a barn located in Ada. A half-dozen or more of these unlawful lynchings were directly connected to violent outbursts of racial bigotry.

The actual electric chair, which was dubbed "Old Sparky" by the prisoners and press, was built of heavy native oak by a guard named Rich Owen with the assistance of a life-term inmate named John Hurst in the prison's woodworking shop. It was provided with duel switches and had a maximum current of 2,400 volts. Prison officials used a calf as a guinea pig when initially testing the devise. The experiment was a success, efficiently dispatching the animal using the devised method. When used on humans, the current was applied via two hard-wire connections – one to a dampened sponge attached to the calf of the leg, the other to a brine-soaked sponge placed beneath a leather skullcap filled with copper wire fitted to the top of the inmate's shaved head. A black leather, later plastic, mask was used to cover the inmate's face, and the victim was bound to the chair by heavy leather straps. The current was initially turned to almost full blast, 2,300 volts, for roughly a half-minute then reduced to 1,700 volts for another fifteen or twenty seconds or so, then back up to nearly full power for a few seconds. The full 2,400 volts was never used since the high current often caused the victim's hide to burn and emit an unpleasant odor, which witnesses found offensive. The trick was to turn the heat up high enough to allow the doomed man's blood to boil in the heart and brain, but not catch the skin on fire. After waiting a moment for the residual current to leave the body, a licensed physician checked the man's vitals and eventually declared him dead.

The actual chair was located in the prison's basement, directly beneath the warden's office. Death row originally comprised six cells located near the death chamber and assessable by a tunnel. Until the 1940s, executions usually took place just minutes after midnight, thus fellow inmates and the press claimed the doomed indi-

Above: The electric chair. Courtesy Ken Butler.
Right: Ada mass lynching of the slayers of Gus Bobbitt - April 19, 1909. Author' collection.

vidual was about to ride the "Midnight Special." Oklahoma law required that the warden, an executioner, a licensed physician, and the prosecuting attorney of the county where the crime occurred, as well as at least twelve reputable citizens, attend an execution. Naturally, an undertaker was always on hand. Up to two ministers and five relatives of both the condemned and the victim or victims were allowed to attend the grim event. Naturally, a host of curiosity seekers inevitably showed up to observe the ghoulish ceremony. Ironically, Warden R. W. Dick, who was the prison's head keeper at the time of the first electrocution, was openly against the death penalty, insisting, "I am only a cog in the machine."

Condemned men were permitted a last meal of their choosing along with cigarettes, cigars, and soda pop. The press was allowed to visit the doomed man right up to execution time. Shortly before showtime, the inmate had the calf of his right leg and head shaved to provide smooth attachment of the electrodes. He was issued a new suit, minus pockets, and with a cut up the side of

one leg. The prison system felt it was its Christian duty to make the victim feel as comfortable as possible in his final hours. At the last moment, the warden asked the inmate if he had any last words. Surprisingly, most thanked the warden and guards for their fair treatment while on death row. It seemed to be very important to the inmates to be seen as dying "like a man." Most expressed grave fears of faltering or loosing their nerve at the last second. Many made jailhouse religious conversions during their final days although there were some who refused spiritual guidance. The most persons executed in one day was four, and the largest turnout for one of these lethal events seems to have been for the execution of a pair of cop-killers, named Leon Siler and Charlie Sands, in the early morning hours of June 11, 1937, with 400 witnesses in attendance. The starkest example of last words was uttered by another cop-killer, named James Hargus on April 24, 1936. He told a large crowd of witness's just moments before his execution, "I'd like to make a long speech but the warden won't let me, so I'll just set here and let you gentlemen watch me die!"

During its years of use, 1915-1966, the electric chair had five operators. The first was a prison engineer named Treadwell. Sometime around 1918 Treadwell left prison employment and a specialist was brought in from Arkansas. Evidently, the Arkie had a habit of spending the

Old Sparky. Author' private collection.

Executioner Rich Owen, on the job. Courtesy Ken Butler.

hours before executions hitting the bottle in order to work up the nerve to perform his bleak duty. On his second visit to the prison, the specialist was deemed too inebriated to pull the switch. Treadwell's long-time assistant, Rich Owen, stepped up to the plate, and did such a good job he was given the assignment permanently.

Owen was a double-tough, unrepentant soul, who had worked for the prison system since 1909, employed as a shop foreman of sorts. Legend has it he never carried a gun or club; instead he preferred to enforce discipline amongst the cons by use of his iron-hard fists. He reportedly had a bloody past, killing his first man at age thirteen. Over time, he would be tried four times for murder and acquitted. He killed one escaping inmate by beating him to death with a shovel and another by cutting his throat with a knife. In his role as chief executioner (1918-1947), Owen pulled the switch on fifty-eight men and hung one. The singular hanging was that of Arthur Gooch (June 19, 1936) who had been convicted of federal kidnapping charges. It was a messy affair, the noose failed to break Gooch's neck causing him to slowly strangle for a tortuous fifteen minutes before expiring.

Owen claimed to have never lost a moment of sleep due to any aftereffects of his job. In fact, he relished his position. Lying on his deathbed dying of liver cancer in 1948, he told reporters his only regret was the fact he was unable to rise off his bed and pull the switch on the next doomed man waiting in line. He was paid $100 per execution per man except in the case of mass executions when he was compensated $100 for the first man and $50 each thereafter. He painstakingly prepared for each event and took great pride in carrying out his duties in a professional manner. He once stated he gave no more thought to killing an inmate or "Peckerwood" as he called them, than jerking the head off a chicken. "We

should execute more of 'em instead of letting them lie around in their cells being fattened up like hogs on the state dole. I don't know how many I've executed. The day after the event I can't even remember their names." Adding, "It's a pleasure to kill some of those sons of bitches. Just think what they have done to people!"

After Owen's death in 1948, a Bryan County farmer and livestock dealer, named M. E. "Big Boy" Elliott, was named chief executioner. Elliott lasted until his own death on August 12, 1956. He pulled the switch on seven men. Next up to bat was B.V. Glover who had been a guard at the prison for the past six years. Glover retired in February 1966 having also served as executioner for seven events. After Glover's retirement, the prison advertised for the position but there were no takers. Then a guard of twenty-three years seniority named Mike Mayfield took the position for the final act in the saga of the electric chair, pulling the switch on a violent psychopath named James French on August 10, 1966. French was the last man to die in "Old Sparky."

Soon after French's execution, the US Supreme Court declared the use of the electric chair unconstitutional (*cruel and unusual punishment). Eventually lethal injection was substituted for electrocution as a means of execution, and the first to die by that method was Charles Troy Coleman out of Muskogee County.

"Old Sparky" sat in the prison basement for years before being exhibited at a local McAlester museum. Years later the chair was brought back to the prison, and is presently on display at the institution's museum.

Right: Arthur Gooch in his death cell in McAlester. Courtesy Ken Butler.

Far Right: The hanging of Arthur Gooch, the last legal hanging performed in Oklahoma. Courtesy Ken Butler.

Part II – 1920-1941
Boom & Bust

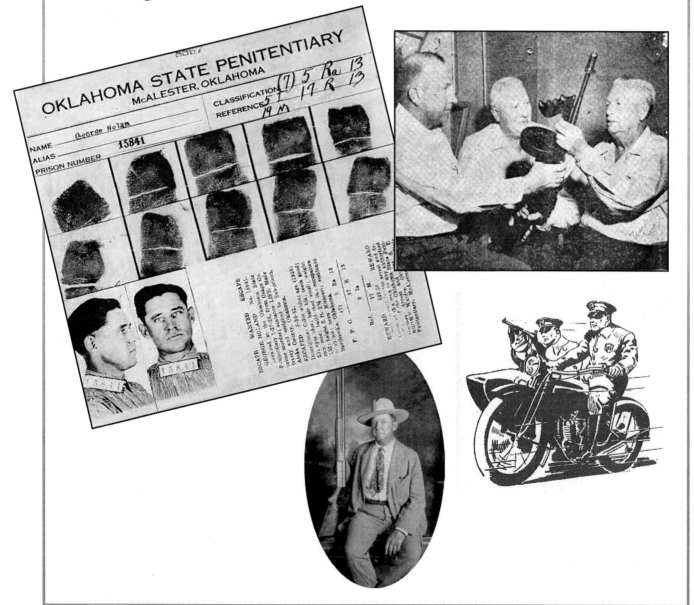

The Roaring Twenties – 1920-1930

The accelerated exploitation of oil, gas, and mining assets throughout the state during the 1920s produced a horde of "Boomtowns" that virtually recreated the infamous rough and tumble cattle-trail settlements of the Wild West Era. Small villages that had previously been characterized as just a fork in the road, such as Whizbang, Ragtown, Wirt, Healdton, Shidler, Picher, Cardin, Cromwell, Burbank, Bighart, Slick, Bowlegs, and Drumright blossomed overnight into clapboard cities populated by not just honest wage earners but an army of card-sharps, common thieves, confidence men, bootleggers, prostitutes, dope peddlers, pickpockets, and hijackers.

The various boomtowns featured fleabag hotels, overpriced greasy spoon cafes, pool halls, so-called "Sporting Houses," and honky-tonk style saloons.

A trio of tough bootleggers, circa 1927. Author's collection.

Crime flourished and the authorities daily discovered murder victims abandoned on the side of a road, in a ditch, floating in oil tanks, and laying in the middle of the street. Muggings and hijackings in dark alleys and on isolated roadways were common. The normal problems associated with vice were further aggravated by the advent of national prohibition. Folks laboring in the boomtowns were not just a hard working lot but hard drinking as well. The demand for "spirits" was met by a horde of whiskey makers and bootleggers. Complicating this problem was the attitude taken by most lawmen of the day that illegal liquor sales and consumption was a victimless crime.

Naturally, when the city fathers of these Sodom and Gomorrahs recruited lawmen to keep the sheep safe from the lions they sought out either oversized goons who possessed no hesitation when it came to the liberal use of a blackjack, or hard men with a reputation for using a deadly six-gun to enforce their edicts.

During the early 1920s, the crime of bank robbery became epidemic in the state, the banner year being 1924 when fifty-seven banks were raided. There was also a notable increase in nighttime bank burglaries perpetrated by steely-nerved "Yeggmen." Noted "Yeggs" of the period were members of the Jeff Duree Gang, the "Gang of Eight," and the Newton brothers, Jess, Joe, Doc, and Willis. Reacting to the rash of hold-ups, the Oklahoma State Bankers Association announced a $250 reward for the capture of bank bandits (Dead or Alive) in 1925. The reward was increased to $300 in 1930 and $500 in 1932. The following year, Association President Eugene Gum announced the organization would continue to pay the standard reward for dead bandits but not, "one thin dime for live ones." Between 1925 and 1929, ten bandits were slain and several dozen others captured by lawmen, armed bankers, or vigilantes with approximately $8,000 in cash rewards distributed by the banker's association.

Responding to the increase of statewide incidents involving serious crime, the authorities created in 1925 an investigative body dubbed the Oklahoma Bureau of Identification and Investigation, which later became known simply as the Oklahoma State Bureau of Investigation. Some of the more noted investigators serving the pioneer investigative agency were Luther Bishop, Jake Sims, Lee Pollack, and Claude Tyler.

Oklahoma ranked second in the nation in bank robberies in both 1924 and 1927, behind Illinois. Prominent daylight bank looters of the decade were Matt and George Kimes, "Dude" Overstreet, "Dutch" Webber, "Goldie" McCollum, Ed Lockhart, Owen Edwards, "Happy" Bohannon. Sam Coker, the Brandon brothers, Henry Cornett, Red Callaway, Whitey Walker, the Cunningham brothers, "Blackie" Thompson, Al Spencer, Dick Gregg, Ab Connor, Earl Jarrett, Chester Purdy, and Walter Philpot.

Lawmen

Alva L. McDonald, 1876-1942

Kentucky born Alva McDonald served in the Spanish-American War with Roosevelt's Rough Riders before relocating to El Reno, Oklahoma Territory, in 1901. He served on the town council for several years prior to being appointed Clerk of the Federal District Court in Fairbanks, Alaska, by President Roosevelt. He returned to El Reno in 1911. McDonald was appointed US Marshal for the Western District of Oklahoma in 1921. During his term in office, he was deeply involved in investigating multiple acts of violence that occurred during the 1922 national railway strike as well as the capture of the "Ghost Bandit" Jeff Duree. On September 15, 1923 he shot and killed outlaw Al Spencer and was instrumental in the apprehension of train robber Frank Nash. McDonald died in 1942.

Luther Bishop, 1885-1926

Bishop was a Town Marshal, County Jailor, Deputy Federal Marshal, and original member of the Oklahoma Bureau of Identification and Investigation. He was widely known as a top-notch investigator. Bishop was mysteriously assassinated at his home in 1926.

Jake Sims, 1890-1966

Texas born Jake Sims was appointed Chief of Police in the boomtown community of Seminole in 1927. Although Sims was small in stature, weighed only 140 pounds, and rarely carried a gun he efficiently maintained law and order in the wild and wooly oil center for over twenty years by means of a combination of sheer physical toughness, overpowering personality, and innate intelligence. Over time, he garnered a reputation as a first-rate investigator, respected by friend and foe alike. A fair-minded and compassionate man, Sims operated his own private soup kitchen for the poor and disenfranchised during the depression years. In 1947, he was appointed the head of Oklahoma's State Bureau of Investigation. He later operated as a private investigator headquartered out of Oklahoma City, 1951 to 1961. Jake Sims died of natural causes in 1966. He is buried at Seminole.

Luther Bishop. Photo courtesy Dennis Lippe and the Oklahoma Law Enforcement Memorial.

Alva L. McDonald. Photo courtesy of Tony Perrin.

Jake Sims. Photo courtesy Tony Perrin.

Billy Shoebox

In chronicling the history of Oklahoma's various boomtowns, circa 1912-30, one frequently encounters lawmen whose characters teetered precariously between good and evil. The characteristics required of an officer serving in such a dangerous atmosphere demanded an individual who was not only fearless and good with a gun, but also able to communicate harshly and sometimes physically manhandle persons representing the most unintelligent, animalistic dregs of society such as drug addicts, violent drunks, gun-crazed hijackers, or straight razor toting ladies of the night. The town elders in these sin-laden communities soon discovered it oftentimes took a professional hired gun to protect the lives and property of honest citizens and merchants from the rough element.

A perfect example of such an arrangement occurred when the town of Picher, in concert with the giant Eagle-Picher Mining Company, procured the services of the infamous William Schmulbach (alias Billy Shoebox) to keep a lid on the criminal element in and around the so-called Tri-State Mining District.

Schmulbach was born in Illinois of German-American parentage around 1876. He drifted to the Joplin, Missouri, area around the turn of the century where he worked as a miner for some years. Over time, he became involved with the town's seedier element, hanging out in saloons and gambling dens drinking, fighting, and carousing from dark until dawn and making a notorious reputation for himself as a rough customer. Eventually the hard-drinking Schmulbach opened his own combination gambling den and brothel located in downtown Joplin.

Around 1907, he married a woman named Jessie and established her as the madam of his prospering house of ill repute. On the night of November 16, 1909, two officers, Tim Graney and George "Will" Smith, were sent to Schmulbach's establishment with orders to shut the place down, ar-resting any suspicious characters on the premises. When the officers arrived, they encountered Jesse and another prostitute named Maude Martin. Both women were arrested and charged with lewd conduct. Since the police station was located nearby, instead of calling for a paddy wagon the lawmen opted to march the women up Main Street toward the jail. At a location a block or two from the cathouse the party encountered Billy Schmulbach who asked, "What's this?" His wife then shrieked, "Bill, they have us under arrest, and one of 'em slapped me around!" The angry gangster responded to this bit of information by whipping out a .32 automatic pistol and shooting Officer Graney in both legs before turning his gun on Patrolman Smith, who pulled his own revolver but failed to fire at the assassin, instead he froze in place with an expression of utter disbelief on his face. The young lawman paid dearly for his hesitation. Schmulbach fired two rounds that tore through the officer's torso fatally wounding him. The moment the bullets quit flying the gunman turned and sprinted to the nearby railyards where he hopped a westbound freight.

Joplin's finest reacted to the shooting by calling out the entire force along with members of the Anti-Horse Theft League. Roadblocks were set up and heavily armed patrols began sweeping through the community with a sense of red-hot anger, raiding every juke joint and bawdyhouse in the district. A $1,200 "Dead or Alive" reward was immediately offered for the brothel owner's capture. Thousands of circulars were sent out across the country to numerous law enforcement agencies. Schmulbach was somehow able to slip the net and ride the rails to Seattle, Washington, where he hid out until he was eventually captured and transported back to Joplin.

Picher in the early days on left, contrasted to a modern day view on the right. Author's collection.

Shortly after his return, the badman was tried and found guilty of Officer Smith's murder. Although a jury sentenced him to a thirty-year hitch at the Missouri State Penitentiary, his sentence was ultimately overturned on appeal and the murderous thug set free.

Upon gaining his release, Schmulbach quietly slipped out of Missouri traveling to the booming zinc mining community of Picher, Oklahoma, where he set up shop in a couple of oversized canvas tents located on the edge of the sprawling makeshift town. It appears he made his livelihood selling illegal rotgut booze as well as operating a gambling parlor and acting as a pimp for several ladies of the night. After making a reputation for himself as a local "Tough," he was hired by the mammoth Eagle-Picher Mining Company to lead a goon squad for the mining concern with orders to keep the peace in their numerous company-run towns located throughout a three county area. With the full backing of the all-powerful company, Schmulbach was able to enforce the law in the manner of a corrupt feudal lord. Although he was investigated on several occasions over the years for extorting money from area businesses for providing "Protection," as well as having his hand in the illicit liquor business, he somehow managed to keep his job. Whether he divested himself of his pimping activities upon gaining employment as a law enforcement officer, is unknown. It is known he remained a degenerate gambler for the rest of his life.

Grave of Police Officer William Smith shot down by Billy Shoebox in a heated exchange over a lewd woman. Photo by Naomi Morgan.

On the night of June 9, 1926, the rouge lawman was called to a Picher Hotel where two drunks accompanied by a woman were making a disturbance. The pair was later identified as Lee Flournoy and Charley Mayes, who had recently robbed a Kansas bank. Both Flournoy and Mayes were incorrigible violent criminals of the worst stripe, being involved in the past in the crimes of murder, armed robbery, kidnapping, and bootlegging. A gangster moll named Vivian Chase was rooming with the duo at the hotel.

Schmulbach, who apparently had no idea of the men's identities at the time, offered a stern warning to the trio to quiet down or face arrest. All was peaceful for an hour until the partiers hopped in their car and began motoring up and down the town's main drag shooting out streetlights and shop windows. Schmulbach, now joined by Ottawa County Deputy Sheriff M. L. Woolsey, arrived at the scene where they promptly became involved in a gunfight with the heavily armed hooligans. After being outgunned, the two officers drove to the police station where they armed themselves with a pair of high-powered rifles. Returning to the scene of the previous gunbattle, the lawmen noticed the badmen kneeling by their car changing a tire, which had previously been punctured by the officer's pistol fire. When the coppers approached the pair, they opened fire. Schmulbach returned fire shooting one of the men in the forehead killing him instantly while Woolsey shot and killed the second individual sending a bullet into his heart. Suddenly, Picher City Officer Grover McCleary unexpectedly arrived on the scene. Startled by the officer's abrupt appearance Schmulbach accidentally shot and seriously wounded the patrolman. Miss Chase, who was unharmed, was arrested and held as a material witness.

In December of 1926, the notorious cop-killer Wilbur Underhill visited the Picher area shooting a youth named Fred Smyth in a robbery attempt. Schmulbach arrived on the scene and on spotting a suspicious acting individual who somewhat matched Underhill's physical characteristics, ordered the fellow to halt. The man reacted by turning toward the officer and began throwing rocks his way. Billy answered the crude assault by shooting the man in the leg. The youth, identified as a drifter named Roy Epperson, was later charged with public drunkenness and resisting arrest.

In November 1927, Officer Schmulbach shot and killed an unarmed Kansas farmer he claimed was attempting to burglarize a business. Although many members of the community questioned the officer's judgment at the time, he was eventually cleared of any wrongdoing in the episode. On the afternoon of October 4, 1930, the itchy-triggered lawman fatally gunned-down a Picher druggist named Frank Carlock. Schmulbach claimed the druggist had attempted to kill him with a .22 cal. squirrel rifle found in the rumble seat of his car. Many suspected the motivation for the killing was the fact Carlock owed the cop a bundle of money in delinquent gambling debts. On this occasion, the errant officer was arrested and charged with murder. On December 16, 1930, Schmulbach was found guilty of first-degree murder and sentenced to a life term. The gray haired, stocky built fifty-six–year-old miscreant arrived at McAlester on December 1930. He was paroled on December 20, 1935, and given a full pardon in 1938.

Joseph W. Anderson, 1884 -1966

One of America's most accomplished officers, Joe Anderson, was involved in the pursuit and capture of many of Oklahoma's noted "Public Enemies" of the 1920s-1930s. Over time, he garnered a reputation within the law enforcement community as being a steady hand, unmatched in bravery and intellect. Anderson began his career in law enforcement around 1915 acting as a Special Investigator for the mammoth Eagle-Picher Mining Company located in Ottawa County. In 1926, he took part in the hunt for Wilbur Underhill who was suspected of committing numerous robberies in the Tri-State Min-

Clockwise from top left: Joe Anderson (Center). Photo courtesy True Crime Magazine. Joe Anderson presenting a Thompson machinegun to Miami Chief of Police A. C. Masterson and Sheriff Ben Stanley. Courtesy Malaka Hayes. Joe Anderson, late in life. Courtesy Malaka Hayes. Grave of Joe Anderson–Zena Cemetery, Delaware County, OK Photo by Naomi Morgan. The notorious Tommy Hill of South Coffeyville – fixer and set-up man for several generations of Oklahoma outlaws. Courtesy Malaka Hayes.

ing District, as well as murdering an Okmulgee drug store clerk. In 1928, he was appointed chief of police of Cardin. Anderson participated in the apprehension and subsequent slaying of bank robber Jake Fleagle in 1930. The following year he was appointed Chief of Police of Oxford, Kansas. In 1933, he was a member of the posse that captured the notorious Eno brothers in Bristow. While employed by the newly created Kansas Highway Patrol, Anderson spent several months effectively working undercover in the wilds of the notorious Cookson Hills posing as a tramp, bird-dogging various members of the Underhill-Bradshaw Gang. His undercover work culminated in the eventual arrests of Jim Clark and Hunter Cotner as well as outlaw kingpin Tommy Hill. He also led the dawn raid on an isolated hideout located near Mannford, which resulted in the capture of bank robbers, Glenn Roy Wright, Frank Peterson, and Charlie Cotner. The celebrated lawman was heavily involved in the massive Cookson Hills raid in March 1934. Anderson served as an operative for the Kansas Bureau of Investigation, 1939-55. On retirement, he took up residence in rural Delaware County. Joe Anderson died on July 31, 1966. He was buried at the Zena Cemetery next to his sister.

Allen "Bloodhound" Stanfield

Allen Stanfield was born at Wild Horse, Indian Territory, on June 25, 1894. The following year his father moved the family to Ada where he operated a general store. In 1915, Stanfield married a Shawnee girl. He attended East Central College before serving throughout the decade of the 1920s as an Ada City policeman and Pontotoc County deputy sheriff. In 1933, Stanfield was appointed Deputy US Marshal for the Eastern District of Oklahoma. While acting as a deputy, he was involved in numerous high-profile cases such as the hunt for the Urschel kidnappers, the capture of Arthur Gooch, and the killing of several members of the notorious O'Malley Gang. He was nicknamed "Bloodhound" by Federal Judge Robert Williams due to his expertise in tracking down

Officer Down – Jim Keirsey

On September 17, 1929, three heavily armed individuals entered the First National Bank of Minco harvesting some $5,000 from the vault and tills before departing. A hastily-formed posse caught up with the badmen at a point just east of the community of Tuttle. While the encounter produced a sharp exchange of fire, the robbers were able to escape unscathed. An hour after the gunbattle officers discovered the getaway car abandoned in a weed-choked ditch near a bridge over the Canadian River. A closer inspection of the rig revealed both rear tires were shredded and bloodstains were found on the seats, indicating that at least one of the hijackers had been wounded in the gunfight. A few weeks after the robbery a youth named Freddy Davis was arrested and charged with not only the Minco heist but also the July 12 robbery of the bank of Kendrick. As the result of some very persuasive interrogation techniques, the lad turned informant naming Owen Edwards, a one-time member of both the Whitey Walker and Matt Kimes Gangs, as an accomplice. On the afternoon of November 7, lawmen received a tip indicating the presence of Edwards at a roadhouse in Harjo. A posse made up of Seminole Chief of Police Jake Sims, his assistant Jim Keirsey, State Crime Bureau Agent Claude Tyler, and Seminole County Deputy George Hall met in Seminole and motored to Harjo. Opon arriving at the speakeasy, Sims entered the front of the business while Keirsey and Tyler entered the rear and Hall covered the outside. On encountering the thug, the three lawmen engaged in a ferocious toe-to-toe gun-duel that resulted in the deaths of both Owen Edwards and Officer Keirsey. Incidentally, Keirsey's brother, William "Con" Keirsey, was later killed in the line of duty while serving as a Carter County Deputy Sheriff on December 10, 1930.

Jim Keirsey. Photo courtesy Oklahoma Law Enforcement Memorial.

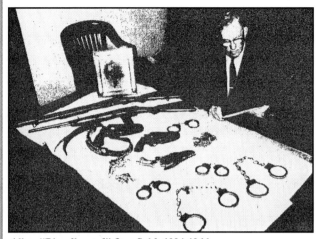

Allen "Bloodhound" Stanfield, 1894-1966.

fugitives from justice. Stanfield retired from the marshals' service in 1961 after twenty-eight years in office. He then served four years, 1961-1965, with the Pontotoc County Sherriff's Department before fully retiring. The legendary lawman died in May 1966.

Outlaws

The Ghost Bandit

One of Oklahoma's more prolific, but lesser known bandits of the 1920s was Jefferson Davis Duree. Dubbed "The Ghost Bandit" by lawmen and the press alike, he was responsible for committing a host of bank and train robberies over a forty-year period (1918-1958). An affable character, Duree, who claimed to be related to Jesse James, was apparently liked and even admired by lawmen to some extent.

The outlaw was born in 1893 on a farm near Bartlesville. His criminal career began with his arrest in 1913 for horse theft. After serving a year at Granite Reformatory, Jeff located to Daughtery where he and his brother operated a poolroom. The billiard

palace soon became the headquarters of an area burglary ring that included Duree, his brother Dan, Ray Terrell, Roland Williams, and Harry Campbell, who would one day be a significant member of the notorious "Ma" Barker Gang.

On the night of September 28, 1921, Jeff and his brother along with two others robbed the Santa Fe # 5 train near Edmond. All four hijackers were eventually arrested and convicted of the heist. Duree was sentenced to a twenty-five-year hitch at Leavenworth Federal Prison but after serving a year was released on appeal bond. On gaining his discharge, Jeff quickly jumped bond and accompanied by his pals Terrell, Williams, and Campbell went on a tear, burglarizing a host of small oilfield banks at Catoosa, Maramec, Lamont, Bristow, Sparks, and Hoffman, Oklahoma, as well as six financial institutions in Kansas.

The gang's MO was to back up to a bank's front door around midnight in a tow-truck and, using a winch and cable, rip the door off its hinges before attaching a cable to the safe. They then winched the strongbox onto the bed of the truck, and motored into the moonlight. The gang was so successful in their ability to motor into a "one-horse" town, burglarize the local bank, and slip away without disturbing a soul, the newspapers began referring to the slippery brigand as "The Ghost Bandit."

In May 1924, Deputy US Marshal Alva McDonald captured Duree hiding out at a small isolated Arizona farm. The outlaw was promptly transported back to

Jeff Duree with grave.

Leavenworth to serve out his sentence. In February of 1939, the bandit was paroled from federal custody and he went to work for the state highway department. A year after his release Duree was convicted of post office robbery and returned to Leavenworth. He was granted his freedom in 1944.

Although one would assume that after spending several decades behind lock and key a fellow would see the error of his ways, but alas, not so with the "Ghost Bandit." In early 1955 he burglarized the State Bank of Helper, Kansas, and in 1958 was shot and wounded by lawmen while sliding out the back window of a closed supermarket in Tulsa. The badman quickly made bond and some months later robbed the State Bank of Peru, Kansas, at gunpoint for $4,000 before disappearing into thin air. A few months after the bank job, the aged outlaw was captured in the company of a "Sporting" woman by a fast moving posse of FBI agents. He was living it up at a ski resort near Denver, Colorado. In mid-1959, Duree was sentenced to a term of "Natural Life" for his involvement in the Peru bank heist.

"The Ghost Bandit" died of a stroke on June 27, 1961, in his prison cell at the Kansas State Penitentiary in Lansing. He was buried in an unmarked grave at Mt. Muncie Cemetery at taxpayer's expense. Incidentally, buried just a few feet away are the two killers who were involved in the infamous Clutter murder case, which was chronicled in the 1967 blockbuster movie, "In Cold Blood."

The Al Spencer Gang

Ethan Allen Spencer was thought to have been the nominal head of a large bandit enterprise operating in the Osage Hills section of Oklahoma in the early 1920s. While he was undoubtedly a bold and resourceful criminal, there has probably been more fiction and hyperbole written concerning his exploits than any other outlaw in Oklahoma history, except perhaps Charley Floyd. Spencer was blamed for robbing between ten and fifty banks in a two-year period. He was pooh-poohed by area newspaper journalists of the day as a modern day Jesse James. Federal Marshal Alva McDonald claimed, "Spencer's crimes were exaggerated. He was a good publicity man." Exactly what crimes he actually committed, and which ones were inventions of creative newsmen, is one for future historians to hash out. Since his death, Spencer has been held up by various historians as being the Dime-Store Godfather of virtually every prominent Oklahoma outlaw operating in the "Sooner" state during the 1920-30s. While it is true that Dick Gregg, Ab Connor, and the Jarretts had some minor association with the bandit chief, others like Henry Starr, Ray Terrill, Wilbur Underhill, Ed Lockhart, and Herman Barker, just to name a few, had little or no connection to Spencer's gang, as was often reported.

What is known of Spencer is that he operated a livery stable in Nowata in his youth before being sentenced to a term in prison for the theft of a calf in 1920. He escaped custody in January 1922 and began scouting.

Frank Nash. Courtesy Rick Mattix.

Earl Thayer. Spencer Lieutenant. Courtesy Master Detective.

Al Spencer. Courtesy Master Detective.

Al Spencer in death. Courtesy Master Detective.

He was definitely involved in the robbery of the Pawhuska Post Office in 1922, as well as the hijacking of banks in Mannford, Oklahoma, Gentry, Arkansas, and Cambridge, Kansas. He also led the band of brigands who committed the last train robbery in Oklahoma near Okesa on August 21, 1923. Although the bandit was accused of committing several murders during his career as a badman, the facts seem to indicate otherwise. Members of Spencer's band of ruffians included Grover Durrill, Riley Dixon, George Curtis, Nick Lemar, Earl Thayer, Henry Wells, Curtis Kelley, Frank Nash, and Whitey Fallon. Others who were associated with the gang at one time or another were area badmen Charley Johnson, Walter Philpot, Bud Maxfield, and Joe Davis.

Toward the end of his illustrious career, a $10,000 reward was posted for his capture, "Dead or Alive." Spencer's luck ran out on September 20, 1923, when he was ambushed and killed by a posse led by US Marshal Alva McDonald at a location just north of Bartlesville. After being viewed in his coffin by an estimated 15,000 morbid curiosity seekers, the bandit was buried at Ball Cemetery in rural Nowata County with much fanfare.

As to the fates of other members of Spencer's gang, Bud Maxfield was killed in the aftermath of the 1923 Mannford bank robbery, while Grover Durrill, George Curtis, Frank Nash, Riley Dixon, Earl Thayer, and Curtis Kelley were all convicted of the Okesa train robbery and sentenced to 25-year terms at Leavenworth Federal Penitentiary. On December 11, 1931, Durrill, Thayer, and George Curtis busted out of Leavenworth in the company of "Ma" Barker Gangster Will Green and several

others. The trio, minus Thayer who was previously captured, was finally cornered in a farmhouse and at the conclusion of a brief firefight with lawmen, Green shot and killed Durrill and Curtis before turning the gun on himself. Earl Thayer died in 1934 from lingering complications caused by exposure suffered during the breakout. Frank "Jelly" Nash escaped from Leavenworth on October 19, 1930, only to be recaptured at Hot Springs, Arkansas, in June 1933. While being escorted back to the "Big Top," Nash, along with four lawmen, were ambushed and killed by multiple gunmen in front of Kansas City's Union Station.

Dave "Ed" Lockhart (1890-1924) Badman From the Hills

David "Ed" Lockhart drifted into the Cookson Hills while still in his teens. Shortly after he was married, he answered the call of duty on America's entrance into the Great War. Upon his return from the trenches in France, where he had been decorated for bravery, he fell into bad company, drinking heavily and gambling. While spending some time in the bootlegging business, he befriended a man named Charlie Brackett who convinced him to join ranks with the notorious Henry Starr in the robbery of a bank in Seligman, Missouri. A few weeks later, Lockhart along with Starr, Brackett, and Rufus Rollins attempted to hijack a bank in Harrison, Arkansas. The robbery failed when a bank clerk fatally shot Starr with a rifle he had previously secreted inside the bank's vault. Starr's pals quickly exited the area, minus their leader.

On December 20, 1921, Lockhart and a companion named Jack Brodie robbed the Illinois Bank of Gore. On January 20, 1922, he and several others including George, Reece, and Charley Price, along with Fred "Cottontop" Walker, looted the First National Bank of Hulbert for $2,300. Lockhart was promptly captured in Huntsville, Arkansas, and confined in the Boone County Jail in Harrison on suspicion of robbing the Harrison bank the previous year. Oklahoma filed extradition papers concerning the Gore heist. Just days after his apprehension, the daring outlaw sawed the bars of his cell and escaped on foot into the rugged Ozark Mountains. In September, he showed back up in Oklahoma, joining the Price boys who were planning to hold up the National Bank of Eureka Springs, Arkansas. Unfortunately for the hijackers, when they exited the financial institution an

Railway flag station at Okesa near where Spencer's band robbed the train. Courtesy Master Detective.

army of armed vigilantes cut them to pieces. Somehow, Lockhart, who was acting as a scout outside the bank at the time of the heist, made his escape, while Charley and George Price along with two others were left dead or dying on the town's main street.

In early 1923, Sequoyah County Deputy Sheriff Perry Chucalate captured Lockhart and Kye Carlile in Sallisaw. Lockhart was quickly convicted of the Gore bank job and sentenced to twenty years at hard labor. After serving only a few months of his sentence, the badman was given a ninety-day leave of absence by Governor Jack Walton. He immediately joined several cronies in Delaware County, operating an auto-theft ring. On October 7, Lockhart was captured by a posse of officers and lodged

The Cedar Creek Gang

The Cedar Creek Gang was an outlaw enterprise hailing from Nowata County, which operated throughout the tri-state area in the years 1918-1926, looting various banks, stores, and other businesses. The group began as a bootlegging ring transporting and selling large amounts of illegal whiskey in various boomtowns located in the Northeast section of the state including the Osage oil district. The Cedar Creek bunch has often been rumored to be an offshoot of the infamous Poe-Hart and Al Spencer Gangs. Members of the gang included the Jarrett brothers, Floyd, Lee, Earl, Glenn, Ralph, and Buster, as well as Albert Connor, Fulton Green, and Tom Slaughter. Their deprivations included the murder of Prohibition Officer Henry Oats in 1925 by Earl Jarrett, as well as the hijacking of banks in Lenapah, Alluwe, Centralia, Shidler, and Burbank. The gang's original leader, Ab Connor, was slain by a Coffeyville, Kansas, storeowner during a 1923 robbery attempt. Tom Slaughter was shot and killed by his running mate after escaping from the Arkansas State Penitentiary where he was being held under a sentence of death. Earl Jarrett was eventually captured and sent to prison for murder and armed robbery, but escaped, fleeing first to Illinois then Ohio, where he died of natural causes posing under an assumed name at a nursing home in 1977. He was buried in a small rural cemetery in West Virginia.

Clockwise from top left: Floyd Jarrett.
Courtesy True Detective.
Fulton Green. Courtesy Master Detective.
Tom Slaughter. Courtesy Master Detective.
Rifle with five notches on stock carried by
Tom Slaughter. Courtesy Master Detective.
Grave of Earl Jarrett alias Howard Martin.
Author's collection.

The old Illinois Bank of Gore. Photo taken near the time it was robbed by Ed Lockhart and Jack Brodie. Author's collection.

and two others looted the Farmers Bank of Burbank. Soon after the bank heist, he was captured near the oilfield community of Lyman, after a brisk gunbattle with lawmen. The outlaw, who was wanted in several locals, was extradited back to Kansas where he was promptly convicted on an armed robbery charge and sentenced to a jolt in the state prison in Lansing. Several years later, he was transported back to Oklahoma due to his promise to testify for the prosecution in the famous Osage murder trials. After giving his testimony, the bandit escaped custody and resumed scouting. Little was heard of Gregg until he looted the much-robbed bank at Centralia in 1928. In the spring of 1929, he and several accomplices knocked off banks in Wynona and Keystone. A few months after the Keystone job the crafty bandit was involved in the robbery of the Peoples State Bank in Wichita, Kansas, for $6,300.

On the morning of August 28, 1929, Gregg and a companion stole a car and motored to the village of Osage where the pair cased the town's small bank, which they planned to rob the following morning. The duo then drove to a Tulsa hideout where they took time to eat, rest, and engage in an all-night drinking binge. The next morning the two brigands flopped into their fliver and began the drive back to Osage with plans of hijacking the bank. Suddenly, at a location in Sand Springs Gregg's car plowed into the rear of another vehicle that was stopped at a stop sign. Gregg reportedly exited his rig and approached the driver of the second car offering to give the man a check

in the Delaware County Jail, but was soon sprung by his friends. Over the next few months, the badman was suspected of involvement in several bank robberies in the Osage country. In March of 1924, Special Officer Mont Grady tracked the outlaw to an isolated farmhouse near Sperry where he shot and killed him in a gunfight. Ed Lockhart was buried at the McCoy Cemetery located near Sallisaw.

Ed's brother, Sam, would later achieve minor fame for perpetrating the 1929 robbery of the bank of Wewoka as well as the hijacking the Vian bank in 1932, and a bank in Logan County Arkansas, the following year. He would eventually be captured and after serving a term at the Arkansas State Penitentiary relocate to Oregon, where he apparently lived out his life as an honest merchant. Sam Lockhart died in 1952. He is buried at the Fort Gibson National Cemetery.

Dick Gregg

Dick Gregg was a well-known hooligan hailing from rural Nowata County, Oklahoma. Gregg was long suspected as being a member of the Al Spencer band of brigands, as well as an active associate of the Cedar Creek Gang. Like most badmen of the era, Gregg began his career as a bootlegger before branching into hijackings and burglaries. In mid-1922, he was suspected of killing Ochelata Night Marshal William Lockett when he and several others were surprised by the lawman while in the act of burglarizing a grocery store. On May 21, 1924, he

Dick Gregg. Photo courtesy of Rick Mattix.

Officer A. L. Bowline. Slain by Dick Gregg near Tulsa. Courtesy Oklahoma Law Enforcement Memorial.

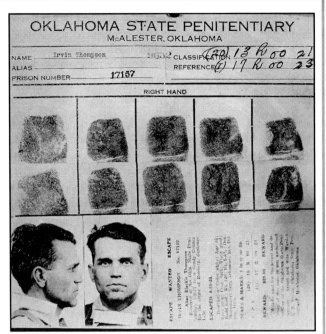

Irvin "Blackie" Thompson OSP Card. Courtesy of Rick Mattix.

"Fighting" Jack Ary, Chief of Police of Drumright, involved in gunbattle with Blackie Thompson. Courtesy of the Tulsa World.

to cover the damages. Moments later two officers, Ross Darrow and Link Bowline, witnessing the crash, approached the scene of the accident to investigate. By this time, Gregg and his companion had departed the area. When questioned, the owner of the second car informed lawmen the driver of the vehicle that had struck his rig appeared intoxicated and was carrying a gun. The officers responded by giving chase. When the cops caught up with the fleeing car, they crowded it to the curb. Officer Bowline cautiously approached the suspicious rig to investigate. Just as he stepped on the automobile's running board Gregg whirled around and shot the lawman in the heart with a .44 caliber slug. Officer Darrow responded by pulling his revolver and ran in the direction of the car firing wildly toward the bandit, who in turn shot him in the chest as well. As he was falling, the dying lawman got off a round at nearly point blank range that exploded into Gregg's temple. Both officers and the badman were pronounced dead at the scene.

Irvin "Blackie" Thompson

Texas born "Blackie" Thompson was one of America's most notorious outlaws of the 1920-1930s. He was first incarcerated at "Big Mac" in 1920 on a five-year sentence for auto theft. On August 3, 1923, he and George Dewey Shipley, along with an unknown individual, robbed the First State Bank of Rush Springs of $3,300. Both Thompson and Shipley were later captured and upon conviction, each given twenty-five year sentences. Thompson promptly escaped custody and on July 2, 1924, he, along with William Weaver (Alias Phoenix Donald), and Joe Clayton shot and killed Drumright Officer U.S. Lenox and wounded Chief of Police Jack Ary at a Creek County roadblock just hours after holding up the nearby Avery bank of $1,500. The outlaw was soon captured and given a life sentence for the murder of Officer Lenox. Thompson would escape from McAlester again in 1933 and go on to participate in numerous bank robberies throughout Texas and Oklahoma as a member of the Whitey Walker Gang. The entire gang was taken into custody in Florida in early 1934. Thompson was extradited to Texas where he was convicted of bank robbery and given a death sentence. He escaped from the Texas State Penitentiary in July 22, 1934. His companions at the time of the breakout were Ray Hamilton, "Whitey" Walker, and several others. The outlaw was fatally cut down by a shotgun blast in a gunbattle with police in Amarillo, Texas, in December 1934.

William Weaver, (Alias Phoenix Donald) 1895-1944

William Weaver was born and raised in Arkansas. After a minor criminal career, he was involved in the 1924 robbery of the First State Bank of Avery as well as the subsequent slaying of Officer U.S. Lenox. Weaver was captured in 1925 and given a life sentence for the lawman's murder. He somehow managed to gain his freedom from the pen in 1931 through a leave of absence and immediately joined up with Alvin Karpis along with Fred and Ma Barker. The newly formed band began vigorously plying their trade, committing a host of burglaries throughout sections of Arkansas and Missouri.

In December 1931, the quartet relocated to St. Paul, Minnesota where they connected with several other underworld types, forming the nucleus of the soon-to-be famous Barker-Karpis Gang. Over the next few years, Weaver was involved in a number of headline grabbing crimes such as kidnapping and bank robbery. He was finally arrested at a Florida hideout in 1935. The outlaw was swiftly convicted of kidnapping and sentenced to life imprisonment. After he was transferred to Alcatraz Prison authorities there noted he was, "A confirmed Public Enemy" and should remain in custody without benefit of parole for the rest of his "Natural Life." William Weaver died of natural causes in 1944 at the Alcatraz prison hospital.

Clockwise from right: Modern day view of location of bloody shootout where Officer U.S. Lenox was slain and Drumright Police Chief Jack Ary was wounded by members of the Blackie Thompson Gang Located near the Drumright cemetery. Photo by Naomi Morgan. William Weaver. NARA. Book-In sheet, Oklahoma State Penitentiary for Phoenix Donald alias William Weaver. Oklahoma Department of Corrections.

George "Ray" Terrill, 1899-1980

Ray Terrill was born in Perkins and left fatherless at an early age. His mother remarried an electrical engineer and the family resided in a series of Creek County oilfield settlements. At the age of eighteen, Terrill committed his first of many crimes, stealing a car on a whim and driving it to Colorado where he was arrested and returned to Oklahoma. The young thug was promptly convicted of auto theft and sentenced to a year and a day at the state pen. While in prison he learned the art of locksmithing from an older more experienced con. Paroled after seven months in the can, he returned to Sapulpa where he fell in with a band of oilfield burglars led by the infamous Jeff Duree. The remainder of the group was identified as Roland Williams, Doc Barker, Alvin Sherwood, and Harry Campbell.

In 1923, he was convicted of an Arkansas burglary, but escaped from Tucker prison after serving a little over a year of his ten-year sentence. He promptly joined the so-called "Gang of Eight," which was originally headquartered out of a pool hall in Miami before relocating to Radium Springs Resort near Salina. Other members of that group were the Barker brothers, Herman and Doc, along with Alvin Sherwood, Elmer Inman, and a rounder named Danny Daniels, along with his hophead sidekick Charles Stalcup (Alias Pale Anderson). This band of expert safecrackers perpetrated at least a dozen bank burglaries as well as scores of other high profile heists in the years 1925-27. They operated throughout six states. Terrill was finally captured in January 1927 in the company of Herman Barker at a residence in Cartersville, Missouri. He was extradited back to Oklahoma but escaped from a

Ray Terrill. Courtesy Rick Mattix.

moving car loaded down with officers just a few miles from the prison gates. The slippery outlaw was nabbed the following month in Hot Springs, Arkansas, and this time officers were able to successfully lodge their prisoner behind the prison walls. He was later convicted of a Pawnee County burglary and sentenced to a twenty-year term. Ray Terrill was paroled back to society in 1936. He lived with his mother in Okmulgee for a time before relocating to Oklahoma City where he operated a nightclub. Terrill moved to California in the 1950s, where he worked as an engineer until retiring to Arizona. The legendary safecracker died in 1980.

As for Terrill's crime partners, Herman Barker committed suicide in Wichita, Kansas, when surrounded by police at the conclusion of a high-speed chase. Charles Stalcup served a lengthy sentence in the Kansas state pen. He died in Arkansas in the mid-1980s at the age of 93. Elmer Inman was involved with the notorious Wilbur Underhill in the mid-1930s. He was sent to "Big Mac" in 1935 where he served a five-year hitch. On his release from the pen, he relocated to Venice, California, where during WW II he hustled sailors selling phony jewelry and such. In 1950, he opened up a jewelry store in Medford, Oregon, which was suspected to have been a fencing operation. The celebrated cat burglar and con man died in a car wreck in 1955 on a twisting highway near Project City, California.

Danny Daniels was convicted of a Colorado burglary and sentenced to a term at the state pen in Canon City where in 1929 he led a bloody riot that resulted in the deaths of eight guards and five convicts. The in-

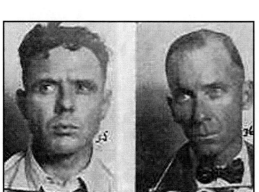

Ray Terrill on left, Elmer Inman on right. Courtesy Rick Mattix.

Danny Daniels. Courtesy Master Detective.

surrection ended when Daniels, realizing his position was hopeless, cold-bloodedly executed several guards and four of his co-conspirators before turning the gun on himself. He was buried in an unmarked paupers grave at the prison cemetery.

Alvin Sherwood would go on to serve several terms in the Kansas pen as well as a jolt in the Oklahoma State Penitentiary for burglary. He died in Lamar, Colorado, in 1958.

Murder in the Osage

The so-called Osage Reign of Terror represents one of the bloodiest chapters in Oklahoma history. In the early 1920s, an Osage County rancher and businessman named William K. "Big Bill" Hale conspired with several others in a deadly scheme to steal the headrights of various Osage tribesmen. He coerced the Indians into willing him their allotted shares of yearly oil fees before killing them one by one. Some of the victims were poisoned while others were shot, knifed, or killed by explosion. Once the victims were disposed of, Hale boldly claimed his bloody inheritance. Nearly two-dozen members of the tribe were murdered before federal officers brought

Hale and his co-conspirators to justice. The massive investigation into the Osage murders by the Bureau of Investigation (the forerunner of the modern FBI) was one of the largest undertaken by the US Department of Justice to date.

The Lawrence Brothers: Evil Incarnate

On the afternoon of June 15, 1924, Muskogee County Sheriff Bud Ledbetter bade "God Speed" to two of his deputies, John Barger and Joe Morgan, as they departed town heading to Texas on a routine assignment concerning the extradition of two miscreants back to Oklahoma to stand trial for auto theft. The fugitives in question were brothers Bill and Babe Lawrence. Both men had lengthy criminal records involving petty theft, vagrancy, and burglary.

Arriving in Texas the following morning, the two officers quickly took charge of the fugitives and began their return trip by car with Deputy Barger at the wheel while Morgan sat next to him in the front seat. The two prisoners were shackled together in the back seat. On an isolated section of road just south of Ft. Worth, Babe Laurence suddenly reached forward yanking Morgan's

Bryan 'Whitey' Walker

A Texas-raised car thief, gambler, burglar, bank robber, and murderer, Walker, and his gang of brigands, looted numerous Texas financial institutions in the mid to latter 1920s. Turning their greedy eyes toward Oklahoma, he and his henchmen hijacked the banks of Allen, Nardin, Purcell, Lomont, and Prague. His chief subordinate was cop-killer Owen Edwards. Other members of his gang of hijackers included Curtis Black, Fred Nave, Freddy Davis, and "Ace" Pendleton. Finally captured in early 1929, he was convicted of armed robbery and sentenced to ninety-nine years as McAlester. On August 30, 1933, Walker along with "Blackie" Thompson and another inmate escaped from "Big Mac" and went on a cross-country crime spree ending with their apprehension in Florida in January 1934. Walker was killed in an escape attempt from the Texas prison in Huntsville on July 22, 1934.

Right: Bryan 'Whitey' Walker, 1897-1934.
Photo courtesy Master Detective.

pistol from his exposed holster. When Morgan attempted to retrieve his firearm, the young thug squeezed the trigger sending a round into Morgan's head. On hearing the deafening blast, Barger lost control of the vehicle causing the rig to fishtail into a steep ditch before crashing into a corner fence post. Turning toward the prisoners Barger found himself staring down the barrel of his companion's handgun. While Babe held the gun on Barger, his brother rifled the deputy's pockets, gaining possession of the keys to the handcuffs and leg shackles. Barger was then ordered to continue driving north. Approaching an open ranch gate, he was instructed to pull into the dirt lane and park under the shade of a small grove of cottonwood trees. After halting the car, Bill Lawrence dragged Morgan's lifeless body to a nearby shallow ditch where it was discarded. The brothers then handcuffed Barger to a fence post before departing the area driving the officer's unmarked patrol car.

Only known photo of the infamous Lawrence brothers. Photo courtesy Michael Webb.

For the next hour the deputy agonizingly shouted for help while in full view of his partner's blood spattered corpse lying just yards from his position. By and by, his screams caught the attention of a ranch hand that was repairing fence nearby. The cowboy took one look at the stark crime scene and refused to assist the officer, instead opting to contact the local sheriff's department. When deputies arrived, Barger, who was severely parched by the hot Texas sun, took one long drink from an offered canteen before telling his tale of woe to the assembled officers. The day after the deadly incident, the Lawrence boys were identified as the perpetrators of a gas station robbery in Jenny Lind, Arkansas. The pair then stole a car in Sedalia, Missouri, before burglarizing several isolated rural general stores in Southwest Missouri and Southeast Kansas.

Although a massive manhunt was undertaken in a five-state area, nothing was seen of the pair of fugitives. On the evening of October 20, Patrolman Charles Wilson spotted a pair of thieves exiting a window of a residence in Livingston, Montana. When the officer and a companion gave chase the suspects fled into a rail yard and were seen climbing into an empty boxcar. When the officers demanded the men's surrender, they answered with a volley of gunshots, one round striking Wilson in the head killing him instantly. While retreating from the scene of the gunbattle, the pair dropped a small leather bag with the name of Joe Morgan etched in gold on its outside flap. A second murder warrant was issued against the pair.

Several weeks later, investigators tracked the brothers to Colorado, but soon lost track of them in the confusion. On the evening of February 4, 1925, Phoenix Police Officer Haze Burch observed two men attempting to siphon gas from a parked car. When the lawman approached the individuals the men shot him down in cold blood. After the shooting scrape, the fugitives fled on foot into the vast, treeless Arizona desert. Throughout the moonless night, several huge posses scoured the area in search of the killers.

The following morning, Constable R. L. McDonald was approached by a Mexican farm worker claiming he had observed a pair of unsavory looking men climbing the side of Tempe Butte, a lofty bald knob located ten miles from the scene of the ambush. McDonald, armed with his trusty Winchester rifle, drove to the base of the butte parked his car and slowly began making his way on foot up the hillside. Near the top of the incline, he spotted the fugitives huddled under a large rock shelf, sound asleep. The officer easily got the drop on the pair, who he described as exhausted, sweat soaked, and disheveled. Bill Lawrence would admit to slaying Officer Burch, but claimed self-defense. Neither man would admit to killing either Deputy Morgan or the Montana officer. Bill was soon convicted of murdering Officer Burch and sentenced to death. He was hanged in the early morning hours of January 8, 1926. His body was brought back to Muskogee by rail for burial. Babe Lawrence was extradited back to Texas where he was convicted of murdering Deputy Morgan and sentenced to life in prison.

Deputy John Barger, who lived the remainder of his life haunted by the memories of that dreadful day in 1924, passed away on April 26, 1938, of natural causes.

"Dude" Overstreet and the Great Shawnee Bank Raid

In the year of our Lord 1924, Oklahoma ranked second in the nation in bank robberies. One of the better known of those robberies was the hijacking of the Federal National Bank of Shawnee. The great Shawnee bank raid was planned in the back room of a small tin shop located in the oilfield community of Bristow. Attending that fateful meeting was the shop owner's nephew, Jimmy "The Dude" Overstreet, his moll Bobbi Livingston, along with an East St. Louis hoodlum named "Little Joe" Marshal, accompanied by his pregnant wife and two of his long-time crime partners, Art Richardson and James Bryce.

Overstreet was an interesting case study. He began his life in crime at age ten when he joined a Shawnee youth gang which specialized in petty thefts and minor burglaries. At the age of eighteen he was arrested for his participation in the bombing of a rail facility at Shawnee during the 1922 nationwide railway strike. After making bond, the youth fled to Tupelo, Mississippi, where he was arrested for burglarizing a jewelry store. Authorities extradited the lad back to Oklahoma where he was convicted of a charge of terrorism and sentenced to a term at Granite Reformatory. In 1923, Overstreet escaped the facility fleeing to East St. Louis, Illinois, where he fell in with a nest of thieves led by a pint-sized degenerate gambler named Joe Marshal. After being arrested in Illinois on suspicion of burglarizing a post office in Salem, "The Dude" (so named for his habit of dressing in fancy attire) escaped custody, fleeing back to Oklahoma accompanied by his new bride and East St. Louis companions.

On December 10, 1924, Overstreet and his gang struck the Federal National Bank of Shawnee, stealing $15,000 in cash and coin. After locking ten employees in the vault, the looters departed in a Cadillac automobile bearing Illinois plates and heading west. The following day the Cadillac was re-

covered, abandoned in an Oklahoma City parking garage. Soon afterwards, detectives arrested Overstreet's wife and another woman at a downtown hotel. The females quickly admitted their identities and ratted out their men folk. Later that same day, two youths hunting squirrels in a wooded area near Bristow discovered the bullet-riddled corpse of "Little Joe" Marshal. The following morning Overstreet was observed boarding a train at Muskogee's Midland Valley depot and traced to Ft. Worth, Texas, where he was promptly captured at a plush downtown hotel, dressed in fashionable golfing tweeds and sporting a bag of golf clubs on his shoulder. He reportedly had $1,000 in cash and a pistol on his person when apprehended. Overstreet was immediately transported back to Shawnee where he admitted his guilt in the bank heist and named his partners. The thug pled guilty to the Shawnee robbery and he was sentenced to a 25-year term at McAlester. Joe Marshal was buried at the Bristow Cemetery in a pauper's grave. In August 1925, Art Richardson was captured in Akron, Ohio. He readily admitted his part in the Shawnee heist, informing his interrogators that Jimmy Overstreet had slain Joe Marshal during a quarrel over the division of spoils. Richardson was in turn handed over to Illinois authorities and convicted of previously robbing a bank in Freeburg. No one was ever officially charged for the murder of Joe Marshal.

On June 2, 1931, Overstreet escaped from the Okla-

Contempary view of the Federal National Bank of Shawnee, robbed by the Overstreet Gang in 1924. Photo by Naomi Morgan.

homa pen by climbing over a wall. In September, he and a companion named James McCoy knocked off the First National Bank of Mt. Clemmons, Michigan, for $14,000. Several months later, the same individuals robbed a bank in Parsons, Kansas, for $3,400. Overstreet was captured in Detroit the following week and confessed to the two bank jobs. He was convicted of the Michigan robbery and sentenced to thirty-five years in prison. A year later, the slippery hoodlum attempted to escape from the Michigan Penitentiary with the use of three sticks of dynamite that had been smuggled into the prison by his long-suffering wife. The attempt was foiled and Overstreet tossed into solitary confinement. The notorious outlaw soon faded into history.

The Kimes Boys

Probably the most famous bank robbers hailing from the 1920s in Oklahoma were the notorious Kimes brothers, Matt and George. Their exploits produced huge attention-grabbing headlines throughout the mid- to latter-part of the decade. The brothers were born in Crawford County, Arkansas, the sons of a sharecropper-turned-bootlegger named Cornelius "Neeley" Kimes. Around 1912 Neeley moved his brood to the Muskogee area where he farmed a bit as well as freighted for the oil companies. In 1918, the Kimes family relocated to the settlement of Shamrock, Creek County, where the father spent his time hauling supplies to the drilling outfits by mule-powered wagon, while moonlighting as a whiskey peddler.

Matt Kimes at the time of his arrest in Arizona. Sheriff John Russell is on his right. Courtesy Okmulgee Public Library.

Meanwhile, the two boys, lacking any supervision from their shiftless father, went native. The pair refused to attend school and began their careers in larceny, stealing anything of value whether it was saddles, horses, tools, or dogs. The boys, now bona fide "Oilfield Trash," also engaged in jack-rolling drunken oilfield workers on the darkened streets of various oil boomtowns located in the Drumright-Cushing Field, when not peddling rotgut liquor for their Pa. Forming friendships with a legion of older, wild-mannered boomtown delinquents, the siblings quickly acquired a taste for liquor, gambling, fighting, and illicit sex. Old-timers relate that Matt was the better natured of the pair. George was surly and closemouthed, whereas his brother possessed an earthy sense of humor along with a charismatic personality.

Before long, the laws began to keep an eye on the lads, rousting them at every turn. Wearing out their welcome, the family drifted to a transient oil camp located between Slick and Beggs where the boys, along with their sister, Nellie, quickly resumed their illicit activities. During the period 1921-24, the lads were suspected of committing a dozen

Mugshot of Matt Kimes. Author's collection.

Roy "Blackie" Wilson-Beggs bank robber. Courtesy Okmulgee Public Library.

Ray Doolin. Courtesy Okmulgee Public Library.

burglaries with several other youths that included Bristow based brothers Clyde and Roy Brandon. In early 1924, the Kimes brothers, one step ahead of the law, fled the area traveling to their uncle's farm located near the small village of Non, where they promptly burglarized the town's general store.

In April 1925, the brothers were convicted of the Non burglary and sentenced to a two-year term in McAlester. Shortly after their release from prison, Matt was arrested in Bristow for auto theft. A week after his capture, the young thug sawed his way out of jail just in time to join his brother and others in the robbery of the Depew Bank for $7,000, followed by the looting of the Farmers National Bank of Beggs for $4,800. On August 25, 1926, the Kimes boys along with the Brandon brothers, Ray Doolin, and an unidentified individual, simultaneously robbed the American State and Covington National Banks in Covington. During the robbery, Matt allegedly refused to take several checks from a elderly woman in the bank, gently comforting her saying, "Its OK Grandma, sit here and be quiet for a spell while we finish up. You'll not be hurt." Two days later, the brothers ran into a roadblock

Detective Mark Lairmore, holding the shotgun taken from Matt Kimes upon his arrest in Arizona. Courtesy Okmulgee Public Library.

manned by officers just west of Sallisaw where they shot and killed Sequoyah County Deputy Sheriff Perry Chuculate and wounded Officer Bert Cotton. Before departing the scene, the boys kidnapped Sallisaw Chief of Police J. C. Woll, releasing him just across the Arkansas border.

Several days later, the Kimes boys were captured near their uncle's farm located near Rudy, Arkansas. A Sequoyah County jury convicted both men for the murder of Deputy Chuculate. George received a twenty-five-year sentence and Matt thirty-five years. Just before Matt's transfer to the state pen, a group led by his sister, Nellie, sprang him from the Sequoyah County Jail.

On January 10, 1927, six bandits looted the Sapulpa bank for $41,000. Kimes was named as suspect, as was outlaw Ray Terrill. In March, Kimes and Terrill along with Elmer Inman, Blackie Wilson, and Owen Edwards were suspected of robbing a bank in Pampa, Texas. In May, Matt, along with the Brandon Boys, Jack Whitehead, and Ray Doolin, hijacked two banks at once in Beggs, killing Chief of Police William J. McAnally in the process. On June 24, 1927, Kimes and Ray Doolin were

Beggs Chief of Police William McAnally, who was slain in Beggs double bank robbery by the Kimes Gang. Okmulgee Public Library.

Sallisaw Chief of Police J.C. Woll. Author's collection.

Sequayah County Deputy Perry Chuculate. Author's collection.

Nellie Kimes. Many suspect she led the raiders in Sallisaw who sprang her brother, Matt. Author's collection.

arrested at a resort near the Grand Canyon in Arizona. Sheriff John Russell along with Deputies Blaine Hill and Mark Lairmore delivered the pair back to Okmulgee, where the badman was convicted of killing Officer McAnally and given the death penalty. His sentence was later commuted to a life sentence.

While incarcerated in Okmulgee, the handsome bandit, who had became a celebrity of sorts, received dozens of "Masher" notes from admiring females. One young flapper wrote, "You are the man of my dreams."

In 1928, lawmen shot and killed Old Neeley Kimes in an altercation at his home in Bowlegs. Later that same year, Nellie Kimes was arrested and tried for the murder of a Sasakwa citizen, but later was acquitted. The authorities arrested Nellie again in 1930, charging her with mail theft. In 1934, she was held for suspicion of twice robbing the Bank of Fairland with Missouri badman Lando Gunter.

In December 1933, prison officials escorting Matt Kimes on a visit to the bedside of his sister Nellie, who had recently been brutally assaulted by an ex-convict named George Noland, shot and killed Noland in an ambush. Although the officers reported Matt was handcuffed in a waiting car while they themselves had slew Noland, many suspected the lawmen had allowed Matt to kill Nolan in return for sharing information concerning the whereabouts of several much wanted criminals. The affair proved to be a major embarrassment to prison officials.

Matt was given a 60-day leave of absence in July 1945. He and a partner named Olif "Chick" Rogers promptly robbed a bank in Morton, Texas, and on December 1, the charismatic outlaw was struck by a poultry truck while crossing a street in North Little Rock, Arkansas, dying on December 14. His body was returned to McAlester where his funeral was overseen by Rev. Alton Parker of the Nazarene Church, before his burial at Van Buren, Arkansas. Nearly 300 persons attended the services.

George Kimes escaped from OSP in 1948. The authorities captured him in Oregon the following year. After his parole in 1958, the ex-badman worked on a cattle ranch located near Warner for a brief time before traveling back west to live out his days. The surly bandit died in California in 1970. Nellie Kimes passed on in 1987. Both Brandon brothers died in prison, Roy in 1928 and Clyde in 1961. They were buried side-by-side at Bristow.

Incidentally, two individuals,

Clockwise, from above: Grave of Perry Chuculate in Sallisaw, slain by the Kimes boys. Photo by Naomi Morgan. Okmulgee Courthouse during trail of Matt Kimes, 1927. Courtesy Okmulgee Public Library. Kimes family at trial of Matt in Okmulgee. Courtesy Okmulgee Public Library.

Roy and Leroy Kimes, who both claimed to be related to George and Matt, would attempt to emulate the exploits of their famous kin.

Leroy, who hailed from Chester, Arkansas, was a professional burglar and escape artist. The first sign of his delinquency occurred in 1930 when he was arrested for breaking into a Van Buren nightclub. After serving a term at the Pine Bluff Reformatory, he spent a hitch at an Arkansas prison farm on a burglary charge. In 1949, Kimes was convicted of robbing a pair of post offices and was given an eight-year stretch to serve at Leavenworth. In 1952, the slippery outlaw escaped cus-tody and upon his capture, he was branded an extreme escape risk and transferred to the maximum-security de-tention facility on Alcatraz Island. He was paroled from federal custody in 1955. In 1957, the incorrigible thief was apprehended in Tulsa for auto theft but eventually released. Kimes was charged with five counts of burglary in 1961 and confined at the MacDonald County Jail in Pineville, Missouri, where he quickly picked the lock on his cell and escaped only to be recaptured several days later. Leroy Kimes died in 1971.

Roy Kimes, a Caddo, Oklahoma, native, was arrested for rape at the age of fourteen and assault with attempt

Clockwise from above: Matt Kimes and Rev. Parker who would later speak at the badman's funeral. Courtesy Tami Babione. Nellie Kimes and husband. Courtesy Tami Babione. George Kimes and friend. Courtesy Tami Babione. Nellie Kimes and others shortly after being arrested on suspicion of murder. Courtesy Seminole Producer. Roy Brandon. Courtesy Okmulgee public Library. Kimes gang member Jack Whitehead. Okmulgee Public Library.

to kill at sixteen. In 1934, he was convicted of highway robbery and sentenced to five years at "Big Mac." The up-and-coming miscreant was paroled in 1937 and the following year he was found guilty of armed robbery and sentenced to a seven-year term. After his release in 1942, he managed to remain free until 1953 when he was con-

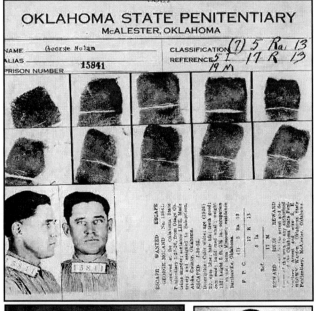

OKLAHOMA STATE PENITENTIARY
McALESTER, OKLAHOMA

NAME   George Nolan   CLASSIFICATION (7) 5 Ra 13
ALIAS   REFERENCE 5 7 17 R 13
PRISON NUMBER   15841   19 M

No. 30598
Name Roy Kimes   Color White Age 21
Rec'd 11-2-34   Term 5-yrs. Max 11-1-39
County Bryan   Min 7-22-37

Crime	High Rob.	COSTS	None	
TRANSFERRED TO O. S. R. 4-28-36.				

No. 38437 OSP
Name Roy Kimes   Color White   Age 25.
Rec'd Oct. 11, 1938   Term (7) Yrs. Max 10/10/45.
County Pittsburg.   NONE   Min 5/27/42.
Crime Robbery with Firearms Cost

2nd. Term		
Discharged by order of warden		
11-16-42.		

Clockwise from above: OSP admission sheet concerning Roy Kimes. Leroy Kimes at Alcatraz. Courtesy NARA. Newlyweds, Matt and wife. Muskogee Democrat. George Noland OSP. Courtesy Michael Webb. Contemporary view of both banks robbed at Beggs by the Kimes Gang. Photos by Naomi Morgan.

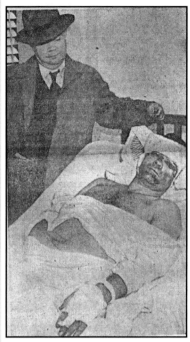

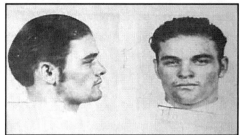

Clockwise from above: Matt Kimes. Okmulgee Public Library. Matt Kimes on his deathbed. Author's collection. Grave of Matt Kimes Van Buren, Arkansas. Photo by Naomi Morgan.

standing on the sidewalk acting as a lookout. In the meantime, the bank guard fired two rounds in the air while shouting at the bandits to "Halt!" The outlaws merely ignored the warning shots and departed the area with a squall of rubber. The amount of the loot stolen by the thieves was estimated to have been $75,000 in mostly bills of large denomination. The bandits take would have been larger had not Mr. Vowell somehow grabbed a packet containing $11,000 from the bag during the scuffle. Police responded with a massive citywide manhunt. A $1,250 reward was offered for each of the robbers (Dead or Alive) by the State Bankers Association. The robbery was noted as the largest to that date in Oklahoma history.

victed of federal bootlegging charges. Just weeks after his release from the Texarkana Federal Detention Facility, he was arrested in Texas and sent to the state pen for two years on a burglary beef. In 1959, he was jailed for shooting a man and brutally assaulting a female in an Oklahoma City barroom incident. The charges were eventually dropped. In 1963, Roy Kimes was shotgunned to death by a Kiowa storeowner when the businessman surprised the outlaw attempting to burglarize his business.

The Bank Messenger Job

On May 24, 1929, twenty-one year-old Bank Messenger Charles Vowell and an armed guard departed the Federal Reserve Bank located in downtown Oklahoma City in a Ford Coupe on their way to deliver $86,000 in cash to the nearby American First National Bank when suddenly a car pulled sharply from the curb into the street cutting them off. An armed man abruptly leaped from the offending automobile, pouncing on to the Ford's running board ordering the two bank employees to hand over the cash. When Vowell refused, the intruder shot him in the arm before wresting the money-laden canvas bag from his grip, then throwing it into the backseat of the accompanying rig driven by an accomplice. After gaining control of the dough, the hijackers pulled back to the curb and picked up another collaborator who had been

A few weeks after the heist, a suspect named Russell "Rusty" Gibson was arrested in a liquor raid in Kansas and extradited back to Oklahoma City for suspicion of participating in the robbery. Approximately $19,000 of the stolen loot was discovered hidden in the rafters of a suburban Kansas City garage rented by Gibson. On August 18, Gibson and another inmate escaped from the Oklahoma County Jail. Sheriff Stanley Rogers immediately assigned one of his best deputies, William Eads, to the case. Eads would spend the next four months fruitlessly scouring various underworld haunts in Kansas City and Chicago on the trail of the slippery bandit. In 1932, an associate of Gibson's named Charles Merritt was arrested in New Orleans and charged with involvement in the robbery. He was quickly convicted and sentenced to twenty-five years at "Big Mac." Two years later James "Cowboy" Hays was apprehended in Seattle, Washington, and promptly extradited back to Oklahoma where he too was tried and convicted of participating in the messenger job. The badman was sentenced to a fifty-year stretch in prison.

In January 1935, Russell Gibson, who had since joined the notorious "Ma" Barker Gang, was slain by FBI agents in a parking lot located next to the apartment where

Right: Wanted poster concerning Russell Gibson. Courtesy Rick Mattix.
Below: Russell Gibson in death. Courtesy Rick Mattix.

he was residing in Chicago. Although the badman was wearing a bulletproof vest at the time, a round fired from a high-powered rifle somehow penetrated the vest. Oklahoma County Sheriff Stanley Rogers, responding to Gibson's violent demise told reporters, "I was hoping to capture him alive so we could put him in Big Mac for a century or two."

The Sheik of Boynton

On August 10, 1929, two out of work oilfield workers named Ben Golden "Goldie" McCollum and Graham "Blackie" Hill knocked off the National Bank of Prague for $3,400. Hill had previously served a stretch in the California penal system for armed robbery before drifting to Oklahoma looking for work, while twenty-one-year-old McCollum was a typical youth of the roaring twenties. Dubbed "The Sheik of Boynton" by his pals, "Goldie," who had quit school at age sixteen, liked to drink homemade hooch from a hip flask, party until

dawn, and participate in all-night area dance-a-thons. His favorite movie star was the original "Sheik," Rudolph Valentino, who the young thug emulated by wearing his hair slicked back using a great quantity of grease and gels. He had a reputation as a real "Jellybean."

McCollum met "Blackie" Hill while laboring as a roughneck in the Seminole oil patch. The pair quickly became pals, pinning their free hours away scheming on how to make some real money, minus the exertion of laboring from sun to sun. They soon began scouting out area banks, hoping to make a quick score and retire to the sunny beaches of California. After quickly going through the loot from the Prague bank job the pair set their greedy eyes on the Peoples National Bank of Checotah. Problem was, in planning the heist the duo failed to take into consideration the local constabulary, which was headed by a bulldog of a county sheriff named Erv Kelley, who had earned the reputation of always getting his man during his career as a lawman.

Shortly before noon on September 12, the wide-eyed pair entered the front lobby of the Checotah bank armed with handguns. After a shout of "Get 'em up!," a crowd of eight customers and two bank employees thrust their hands skyward. While one of the hijackers held sway over the hostages, the other scooped up some

Checotah bank robber and murderer, "Goldie" McCollum. Photo taken at McAlester prison. Courtesy Bob McCollum.

$4,757 in cash and coin before the two maked their get-away in a stolen bright-yellow Pierce-Arrow Sedan equipped with vivid red wire–rim wheels. The car was discovered abandoned in a Bixby garage the day after the heist. A posse, headed by Sheriff Kelley, immediately took to the field, setting up roadblocks and raiding honky-tonks, seedy flop houses, and gambling joints throughout the area. Several days after the robbery, officers received a tip from an informant that put the finger of suspicion on young Goldie, who was quickly picked up by a posse of fast-moving lawmen as he strolled down the streets of Boynton. At the time of his arrest, McCollum was in possession of a pair of pistols and roughly $80 in folding money. Although several witnesses from the Checotah bank robbery positively identified him, Goldie denied all until Sheriff Kelley explained the benefits of cooperating, mainly being allowed to keep his teeth. Lawmen had rough ways back in those days. Upon being educated by Kelley, the youthful "Sheik" began chattering like a treed squirrel, confessing his complicity in the affair, naming his crime-partner, and further informing officers they could find him in Beaumont, Texas, staying with his kinfolk.

That evening, McCollum, accompanied by a half-dozen lawmen, traveled to his mother's farm near Boynton, where the bandit led the cops to a junked out Model T that held $750 of the bank loot in its gas tank. Afterwards, Kelley motored to Hardin County, Texas, where he and several local officers raided a residence discovering Mr. Hill fast asleep on a couch in the living room. After Hill admitted his guilt and turned over $1,600 of the stolen loot, he was escorted back to McIntosh County. He pled guilty to armed robbery and was sentenced to a twenty-five-year stretch at "Big Mac." His pal, "Goldie," also pled guilty and received a twenty-year term. The pair later pled guilty to robbing the Prague bank and were both given an addi-

tional twenty-years to brood about their failed lives. When interviewed just moments after his second sentence was handed down McCollum told reporters, "I don't hold no grudge against the laws but I do believe you will find more principle among bank robbers than murderers."

On the afternoon of April 15, 1934, the "Sheik" was involved in a prison altercation over a card game in which he stabbed a fellow inmate to death with a eight-inch long homemade dirk before rushing across the yard and killing another inmate in the same gruesome manner. Although McCollum was tried, found guilty, and eventually given a ticket to ride "Old Sparky" into the hereafter, the youthful hoodlum had his death sentence commuted to life the following year by Governor Marland. It has been long rumored "Goldie's" mother had literally bought his commutation with the proceeds from the sale of her Boynton farm.

McCollum would escape from the Oklahoma State

Clockwise from above: Goldie McCollum, photo taken a short time before he was murdered. Goldie in repose. McCollum's grave near Marcum, Kentucky. Kentucky residence where Goldie was slain. All photos courtesy Bob McCollum.

Penitentiary in 1954 and remain free until his capture by the FBI in 1958 at an Indianapolis boarding house. During his time on the lam, "Goldie" would be named to the FBI's 'Ten Most Wanted' list. McCollum was given a parole in 1961 with the instruction to "Permanently leave the state." He did just that, relocating to Clay County, Kentucky, where a relative had found him a job working for a coal company. It appears he had finally discovered his notch in life, working a steady job, living in his own house, and attending church. On the evening of August 12, 1963, "Goldie" was robbed and fatally shot in his rural Marcum, Kentucky, home by a pair of local thugs.

Brothers in Crime

On the morning of July 26, 1929, four bandits hijacked the First National Bank of Hooker for $9,822, fleeing in a dark-colored Ford automobile. A large posse was promptly fielded, which soon discovered the abandoned getaway car covered with brush in the nearby Beaver River bottoms. Although officers erected roadblocks and conducted a massive search throughout most of the panhandle region, as well as bordering sections of Kansas and Texas, they discovered no other sign of the hijackers.

Ten months later at a location some two hundred miles southeast of Hooker, the final chapter of the robbery unfolded when Stephens County Sheriff Wal Williams received a report of four thugs holding up a small filling station near Lawton for a measly $1.50, some cigarettes, and a quart of oil. The description of the getaway car matched that of one used in another gas station holdup, which had occurred in nearby Cotton County several weeks earlier. The Sheriff, accompanied by Duncan Chief of Police I. B. Gossett, Undersheriff Ed Sumrill, and a Duncan police officer named McKenzey hopped into the Sheriff's car and sped up the Duncan-Lawton road hoping to cut off the hijackers.

At a point a few miles outside Duncan known as Marlow Junction, the officers pulled alongside a big Buick filled with a quartet of rough-looking men. When informed, "We are officers of the law, pull over!" The bandits reacted by firing a volley of rounds into the officer's car wounding Sheriff Williams and Officer Gossett. Deputy Sumrill answered the attack by squeezing-off a lengthy burst of .45 caliber rounds from a machine gun. That did the trick. The driver of the fleeing car, later identified as Forrest Cunningham, instantly slumped dead at the wheel while his brother, Emanuel, was struck by a round in the stomach, the bullet passing through his body severing his spinal column. A third brother, John, was

Jess Cunningham. Courtesy Oklahoma Department of Corrections.

Sheriff Wal Williams. Courtesy Oklahoma Law Enforcement Memorial.

Chief Gossett. Courtesy Oklahoma Law Enforcement Memorial.

also wounded and immediately surrendered while a fourth Cunningham sibling, nineteen-year-old Jess, fled the car running into a nearby patch of woods. Medical assistance was immediately summoned and the wounded were transported to area hospitals. A massive posse began scouring the countryside for the missing fugitive.

Sheriff Williams expired shortly after his arrival at the hospital while Chief Gossett, who had taken a slug in the abdomen, was listed in critical condition, as was Emanuel Cunningham. Forrest Cunningham was dead at the scene while the third Cunningham brother was listed in fair condition with wounds to the stomach and shoulder. After discovering the men's identities, officers raided the Cunningham home near Comanche, but to no avail. Although, dozens of heavily-armed lawmen and vigilantes beat the bushes for several days, there was no sign of the missing gunman. Officers searching the suspects' vehicle discovered three rifles and four revolvers, along with several hundred rounds of ammunition. The day after the shootout, a farmer living just north of Duncan contacted authorities stating a man matching the description of Jess Cunningham had kidnapped him and his car the previous night. He further declared the fugitive had released him just south of town. The farmer's missing car was discovered later that day abandoned on the side of the road near Marlow with two flat tires.

Monument located at the site of the deadly gunbattle just south of Marlow honoring slain Sheriff Wal Williams. Photo by Naomi Morgan.

Upon interrogation, John Cunningham admitted he and his siblings had robbed the banks in Manitou and Hastings, Oklahoma, in 1928, as well as the banks of Kiowa, Kansas, on March 24, 1929, and the First National Bank in Hooker, Oklahoma, in July. Two weeks after the deadly shootout, Jess Cunningham and his cousin, J. Clifford Moreland, were captured near Crested Butte, Colorado, through information provided by a female snitch. Cunningham was charged with the murder of Sheriff Williams and a host of bank robberies while his cousin was charged with participating in the Manitou bank heist. Both subjects were promptly extradited to the "Sooner" state.

The three surviving Cunningham brothers eventually pled guilty to the murder of Sheriff Williams and were each sentenced to life imprisonment at the state pen in McAlester. On July 29, 1932, John Cunningham finally succumbed to the injuries he had incurred in the 1930 gunfight with officers. Chief Gossett, who was wounded in the same deadly encounter, died in 1939 after suffering nearly a decade of health problems brought on by the injuries he had sustained in the gunbattle. Emanuel Cunningham was permanently crippled and destined to spend the rest of his life in a wheelchair. He was paroled in 1945 and died in a car wreck in 1948. Six years later, Jess Cunningham, along with seven other inmates, escaped from the prison, killing a guard in the process. All eight were charged with murder. Jess was handed a second life sentence. The outlaw was paroled in 1949. His parole was revoked in 1950 when he was apprehended attempting to steal a car. In 1952, he and two others attempted to escape from McAlester via a soap barrel but ultimately were foiled in their efforts. Jess Cunningham was again paroled in 1958.

The citizens of Stephens County eventually placed a granite monument at the intersection of US Highway 81 and State Highway 7, to honor the sacrifice of Sheriff Wal Williams.

Law Enforcement Advances

Advances in police technology during the decade of the 1920s featured the widespread use of the automobile vs. the horse, and one-way radio as well as the reliable telephone and telegraph. Mobile squad car and motorcycle units were now a familiar sight on city streets, and due to the massive increase of automobiles on the road, many of the larger cities established special Auto-Theft Bureaus.

In the late 1920s, a few departments added to their firepower by purchasing machineguns, preferably the .45 caliber Thompson as well as the .30 cal. BAR, for their armories. As for personal identification, the use of fingerprints was beginning to replace the old Bertillon method, and in crime scene investigation, departments still relied on footprint technology and other such crude and usually ineffective methods. Truth serum was introduced and dubbed a grand investigative tool. There existed no reliable crime laboratories in the state, and the State Bureau of Identification and Investigation was in its infancy. Cooperation between city, county, state, and federal departments was in its early stages as well. The beat cop in the major cities was equipped with a sap or nightstick, as well as a pistol and handcuffs. For communication purposes, the telephone call box was used in some of the larger communities. Training for officers was nonexistent, outside of the major cities. On the job training and good old-fashioned horse sense as well as brute force was still the norm.

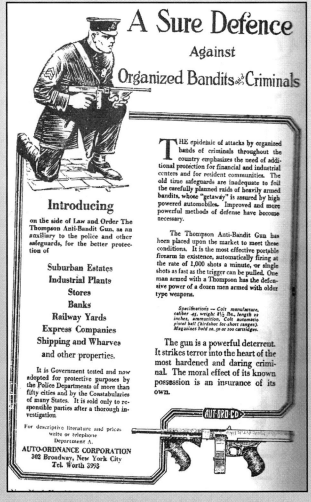

Clockwise from above: Cartoon with caption, "Carry you bag, mister?." Ad for Thompson Machinegun, 1920s. The Tommy gun alias "The Chopper" or "Chicago Typewriter." All courtesy Rick Mattix.

The Dirty '30s and Beyond

The depression-era in Oklahoma can best be characterized as a period of agonizing uncertainty. Oklahoma was especially hard hit by the national economic crisis of 1929-39, suffering an unemployment rate of 35 percent in some parts of the state, along with soaring crime rates. Misery and despair truly stalked the land. Nearly half of Oklahoma's commercial banks failed. Lacking depositor insurance or FDIC at the time, these bank failures left a great many citizens without any savings. The bottom also dropped out of the oil business, throwing tens of thousands out of work. In farm country, crop and livestock prices plummeted and bank foreclosures on farms increased dramatically. A decade-long drought created such dry and parched conditions that much of America's once lush breadbasket turned into a burnt wasteland. Mile-high dust storms dubbed "Black Blizzards" battered the western part of the state. Squalid communities called "Hoovervilles," in honor of the extremely unpopular sitting president, populated by the homeless and disenfranchised sprang up in the major cities, as did bread lines and soup kitchens. Conditions deteriorated to the point that an estimated 70,000 souls fled Oklahoma, emigrating west in a desperate search for jobs and opportunities in what is often disparagingly referred to as the "Great Okie Trek" (1934-1940).

The time and landscape was ripe for the re-emergence of the rural social bandit that had not been seen in the Midwest since the days of the James-Younger Gang in the latter nineteenth century. During the depression-era, a host of high profile bank bandits like "Pretty Boy" Floyd, Wilbur Underhill, Jim Clark, Thomas "Kye" Carlile, Ford Bradshaw, "Big" Bob Brady, and members of the infamous O'Malley Gang, ranged across the land pillaging and plundering the state's financial institutions. Oklahoma led the nation in bank robberies in 1932. The state banker's association estimated some $127,868 in funds was stolen that year, averaging approximately $2,000 per event.

An undercurrent of undeclared class warfare (rich vs. poor) boiled just beneath the surface of society, especially noticeable in the rural sections of the state. Bank bandits were often times viewed by the poor as soldiers in that socio-economic war. Oklahoma was also the very epicenter of the so-called "Midwest Crime Wave." The war between lawmen and outlaws was the news of the day, reported vigorously by newspapers and radio. By the mid 1930s, criminal activity had reached epidemic proportions. The law and order landscape in the 1930s featured not only breathtaking bank robberies but also the newly-fashionable snatch racket. The kidnapping of Oklahoma City oilman Charles Urschel grabbed national headlines, as did the Hamm and Bremer snatches engineered by the one-time Tulsa-based Barker-Karpis Gang. Reports of hundreds of thousands of dollars paid for ransoms caught the attention of a nation gripped in grinding poverty. A horde of federal G-Men soon arrived in the state in order to aide local lawmen.

By the latter 1930s, public opinion began to slowly change in favor of the lawmen, due to the public's weariness of widespread crime along with a slender but noticeable improvement in the economy.

Although the "Public Enemies Era" is best known for producing a host of flashy criminals sporting catchy sounding nicknames such as "Pretty Boy" Floyd, "Machinegun" Kelly, "Baby Face" Nelson, and "Mad Dog" Underhill, the period also produced a healthy group of now nearly forgotten double-tough lawmen like Erv Kelley, Wesley Gage, Mark Lairmore, Grover Bishop, Virgil Cannon, Bill Eads, Frank Smith, Tom Dean, Clay Flowers, Stanley Rogers, Willis Strange, Allen Stanfield, Joe Anderson, Dee Watters, Clarence Hurt, "Jelly" Nash, Ralph Stormont, and John York.

Late in the decade, police and sheriff departments began to modernize under the perseverance of forward-looking lawmen like Oklahoma County Sheriff Stanley Rogers and others. In the early 1930s, many outlaws were typically armed with modern automatic weapons such as the Thompson Machinegun and Browning Automatic

Rifle, while lawmen were often times armed with anti-quated shotguns and single-action six-shooters. What departments did possess modern firearms could rarely spare the funds to buy bullets for target practice. Hijackers typically drove powerful late model cars, while officers depending on the dried–up public dole were forced to patrol with outdated junkers kept together with baling wire and fitted with bald tires. Cash strapped communities and counties simply had no available tax funds and consistently under funded their policing agencies. The two-way radio was virtually nonexistent outside of the big cities, and cooperation between law enforcement agencies was poor. Things began to improve only with the enactment of sweeping federal and state anti-crime measures in the mid-1930s.

The Frame-Up

On the afternoon of November 12, 1930, a well-seasoned but edgy posse made up of nearly a dozen heavily-armed officers lay in wait concealed at various locations around the Marland State Bank. The officers were acting on a tip received from an informant, which implied two men would attempt to rob the bank that very day.

The last time the bank had been robbed was in 1924 when a trio of badmen got away with nearly $5,300. On that occasion, the ensuing manhunt was assisted by the entire film crew of the Trail Dust Moving Picture Company, as well as a plane engaged in shooting aerial shots for the making of a silent "Cowboy" picture at the nearby "101" Ranch. Must have been quite a sight, with two-dozen armed "Hollywood" actors, directors, producers, cameramen, stuntmen, and extras riding hell-bent-for-leather across the prairie, working their horses into a lather while the film crew up in a single prop bi-plane buzzed and sputtered overhead, hot on the trail of genuine real-life outlaws. Unfortunately for the authorities, the brigands make a clean getaway, slipping back to their hideout located in the isolated Osage Hills.

Meanwhile, the team of sharpshooters hidden about the Marland bank on that fateful day in 1930 included Noble County Sheriff H. H. Isham, State Investigators Clint Myers and Claud Tyler, along with several Ponca City officers and a private investigator employed by the Burns Detective Agency named A. B. 'Archibald' Coo-

per. Tagging along with the posse was a nervy newspaper reporter from the *Ponca City News* named Frank Muskrat. Oddly, the officers failed to share the information concerning the impending robbery with either the townspeople or the bankers.

After laying in wait on nearby rooftops, second-story windows, and in alleyways for several hours, the secreted lawmen observed two men, armed with handguns and their faces partially covered by white handkerchiefs, dismount a small "Model A" coupe and enter the financial institution. The officers took a collective breath, checking their weapons in anticipation of the upcoming battle. Meanwhile, inside the bank, one of the individuals confronted Cashier J. E. Roberts, handing him a cotton flour sack demanding the "Dough," while the other man covered a pair of farmers loafing in the lobby. When Roberts appeared to be slow in following instructions, one of the hijackers gave him a swift kick in the backside with the harsh admonition to, "Pick up the pace partner!" After collecting some $3,000 in cash and coin, the bandits locked the hostages in the vault before exiting the building. Standing in the doorway of his corner grocery store and acting as a lookout, storeowner J.W. Elkins, one of the few citizens who had been let in on the situation, gave the "Hi" sign to the posse.

The moment the pair of hijackers hit the pavement all hell broke loose. The posse opened up with a variety of rifle, shotgun, and pistol fire, greeting the robbers with an impenetrable wall of lead without giving them the opportunity to surrender. An ear-shattering crescendo of gunfire punctured the air. Old-timers observing the scene claimed for a few moments they were transported back in time to a previous era when the district was part of the infamous "Cherokee Strip," when the sound of sudden gunfire was a common event. The bandits didn't stand a chance, both men were struck repeatedly while the windows of their getaway car were shattered and the car's steel body punctured so many times it looked like an over-sized minnow bucket. Witnesses stated that, every time one of the outlaws was struck, he jerked like a puppet on a string. Terrified citizens bolted for cover while screaming stray bullets ricocheted off concrete curbs, shattered heavy glass windows and splintered the wooden windowsills of various businesses. The street in front of the bank was quickly littered with concrete chips and dust, shards of glass, pieces of wood, and a host of spent bullet casings. In less than three minutes, the guns fell silent. Wary lawmen approached the bandits with weapons at the ready. Both robbers were discovered lying face down beneath their parked car in an ever-expanding pool of blood. One of the robbers identified as Jimmy Jackson, a twenty-four-year-old Bartlesville native, was stone dead, sporting a half-dozen rounds lodged in his head and torso. A second man, who was later identified as nineteen-year-old Carter Camp, was also found suffering from multiple gunshot wounds.

When officers entered the bank, they located the three victims huddled in the locked vault. When lawmen informed the hostages it was safe for them to come out, adding, "Can you unlock the vault from the inside?," Banker Roberts, who was suffering from a bit of shell shock to say the least, informed them, "Damn right I can unlock it, but I don't know if I'm ready to come out yet or not!" Roberts later informed investigators that as scared as he was during the robbery, the bandits appeared to be even more nervous. "After they shoved us in the vault, the next thing I knew it was boom, boom, boom!"

When questioned at the scene, the surviving bandit told investigators, "We didn't fire a shot. I tried to surrender, but every time I raised a hand to give up they shot me!" The bandit added, "It was a frame-up, another man planned the job and talked us into the deal. When it came time to pull off the heist he crawfished and didn't show!" Camp was quickly transported to the Ponca City Hospital where, despite his many wounds and a serious loss of blood, his condition soon stabilized. Luckily for him, all of his wounds were either superficial or the projectiles had failed to hit any vital organs.

As for Mr. Camp's declaration that a third man had planned the heist then framed him and his dead companion for the job; it appears he was telling the truth. The authorities reluctantly admitted the source of their "Tip" was a scheming Ponca City bootlegger named Chris Weiderkehr, who was currently sitting in a Kay County Jail cell held on liquor charges. Apparently, their informant had been arrested for selling illegal hooch the day before the robbery attempt, and in an effort to cut a deal with the authorities as well as collect a reward, he had squealed on his pals. In a further attempt to garner sympathy from prosecutors, Mr. Weiderkehr was also instrumental in frustrating an attempt to murder a local oilman. He promptly informed his keepers that he was pres-

ently involved in a plot with an area lawyer to commit the murder for hire. It soon became quite apparent to investigators that the bootlegger's character was such that when faced with even minor adversity he would have turned his own Momma into the laws for a reduction in sentence. In the end, the loose-lipped liquor purveyor was given immunity from prosecution as to a charge of conspiracy to rob the Marland bank, as well as issued a check for $62.50 from the banker's association for his part in thwarting the bank heist. Apparently, the association, which had a standing offer of $300 for the capture (Dead or Alive) of any bank robber, had split the $600 reward for the capture of the two bank bandits evenly with all involved. Weiderkehr was later convicted on three counts of illegal distribution of liquor and sentenced to eighteen months in the clink, of which he served less than a year.

Carter Camp was convicted of Robbery with Firearms, and sentenced to eighteen years incarceration. The harsh sentence was vigorously protested as overly severe by area politico E.W. Marland as well as Zack Miller, the owner of the nearby 101 Ranch. Marland spoke out publicly, saying, "The lad was framed by an unscrupulous cohort, then railroaded by a heartless system." Several weeks after Marland was elected Governor of Oklahoma in 1935, one of his first official acts was to parole young Carter Camp, calling his case an injustice. The Governor publicly commented, "It's a shame that even though lawmen knew the whereabouts of Camp and Jackson the night before the bank robbery, they chose not to arrest and hold them for questioning, but instead opted to wait and catch them in the act." Well, there was the reward to consider, and with the ongoing depression, times were hard.

On the morning of June 15, 1936, a bullet-riddled corpse was discovered lying in a roadside ditch at a location eight miles north of Columbus, Kansas, by a tenant farmer. When questioned, the farmer, who lived nearby, stated that although he had heard several shots fired followed by the sound of a car hurriedly leaving the scene the previous night, he had been too scared to investigate until daylight. When the victim's body was searched, investigators discovered several letters addressed to Carter Camp, Bartlesville, Oklahoma. The authorities immediately suspected the victim was one of three men who had recently attempted to rob a clothing store in Pond

Creek, Oklahoma. In that case, Night Marshal William McKay had surprised the burglars in the act and promptly engaged them in a heated gunbattle. McKay was certain at least one of his .44 caliber bullets had found paydirt. The theory was disproved when former Barker-Karpis gangster and escapee from an institution for the criminally insane, Larry "The Chopper" DeVol, was gunned down after killing an officer and wounding another at a bar in Enid on July 8. Moments after DeVol's demise, his crime-partner was arrested and admitted to the Pond Creek job.

Although family members quickly identified the body as that of Carter Camp, the case remained a mystery until August 12, when twenty-five-year-old Richard Hays of El Dorado, Kansas, came forward admitting he had slain Camp when the ex-con attempted to rob him. According to Hays, he picked up Camp, who was hitchhiking near El Dorado, and when he pulled off the dark highway to check a squeaky fan belt, his passenger confronted him with a pistol. A struggle ensued in which Hays somehow gained control of the gun and shot his attacker several times in the torso. Fearing the authorities would not believe his story, he disposed of Camp's body in a nearby ditch and fled the scene. Hays was eventually cleared of all wrongdoing in the young drifters death.

"Ma" Barker and the Boys: Oklahoma's First Family of Brigands

The notorious "Ma" Barker was born Arizona Donnie Clark near Ash Grove, Missouri, in 1873, the daughter of Emeline and John Clark. Her father passed on when she was barely four years of age. The following year her mother married an area farmer named Rueben Reynolds. Arizona or Arrie, as she was called by her family, wed a once divorced pig farmer named George Elias Barker in 1892. The couple set up housekeeping in nearby Aurora where George found employment at an area lead mine. After residing in Aurora for several years, the Barkers sharecropped several different farms in Stone and Christian Counties. Around 1912-1913 the family relocated to Webb City where George was employed as a teamster for a lead mining concern. Over time, the pair was blessed with four sons, Herman (born 1893), fol-

lowed by Lloyd (born 1897), then Arthur, nicknamed "Doc" (born 1899), and finally Fred (born 1903). The boys grew up rough and poor. While all four Barker children were vertically challenged (none attaining a height over 5'6"), what they lacked in height they made up for in meanness. When interviewed in the 1970s, Ben Turner, who attended the Eastern Star School in Riverdale, Missouri, with the Barkers remembered, "They were troublesome kids. When they got into school yard fights they would gang up on ya like yellow jackets."

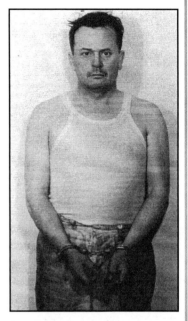

Doc Barker (one tough nut). Courtesy Rick Mattix.

In 1914, the family, minus Herman, who remained in Stone County employed as a farmhand, moved to Tulsa where George worked as a freighter for the Crystal Bottling Company. Ironically, "Ma's stepfather, Rueben Reynolds, who had moved to Tulsa the previous year, found employment as a Tulsa County Deputy Sheriff.

In early 1915, Herman rejoined his family in Tulsa

Early mugshot of Fred Barker, circa 1924, taken at Granite Reformatory. Courtesy Oklahoma Department of Corrections.

where he and another lad were promptly arrested for attempted robbery and sentenced to ninety days at the local prison farm. On his release from incarceration, he traveled to Joplin where he quickly became involved in the city's underworld. In November, Herman and a pair of local toughs named Lee Flournoy and Charley Mayes held up a gambling joint for several thousand dollars. In 1916, the young hooligan was arrested in Springfield and charged with a jewel theft. Although "Ma" tearfully swore in court the wayward youth was at her Tulsa residence on the night of the robbery, Herman was convicted of burglary and given a four-year sentence. Before being transferred to the state pen, the young hooligan escaped from the county jail and spent the next few months drifting across the country engaged as a safecracker and nighttime heist man, He was finally apprehended in Montana and charged with burglarizing a combination clothing store and pool hall in Billings. He was convicted and sentenced to a six-to-twelve-year sentence at the state penitentiary at Deer Lodge, where he remained until his parole in 1920.

Meanwhile, back in Tulsa, Herman's brothers, Lloyd, Freddy, and Arthur (Doc) became entangled with several various local organized groups of juvenile delinquents such as the Bert Prince, the Jacobs, and the Central Park Gangs. During the late teens and early twenties, the Barker boys befriended a host of other criminally minded Tulsa street urchins such as Will Green, Harry Campbell, Volney Davis, Jess Doyle, Larry DeVol, and Glenn Roy Wright, who would remain their crime partners for years to come. Contrary to legend, modern Barker family descendants steadfastly claim none of the boys were involved in criminal activity until the family moved to Tulsa. Actually, there exists little evidence indicating they were mixed up in law

Newspaper report concerning the burglary of the Durnil Store in Muskogee of $6000 in cash and goods. The business was one of dozens looted by the "Gang of Eight." Reader will notice the same issue reporting the escape of Matt Kimes from the Sequoyah County Jail. Muskogee Phoenix.

Right: Doc at Alcatraz. Courtesy Rick Mattix.

Fingerprint card for Arthur "Doc" Barker. Courtesy Oklahoma State Penitentiary.

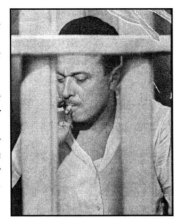

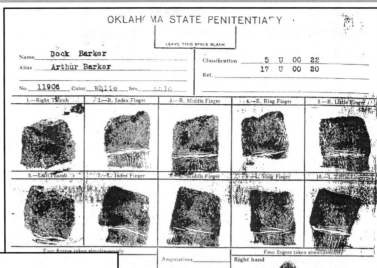

OKLAHOMA STATE PENITENTIARY

LEAVE THIS SPACE BLANK

Name   Dock Barker

Alias   Arthur Barker

Classification   5   U   00   22
                 17   U   00   20

Ref.

No. 11906   Color White   Sex male

1.—Right Thumb | 2.—R. Index Finger | 3.—R. Middle Finger | 4.—R. Ring Finger | 5.—R. Little Finger

6.—Left Thumb | 7.—L. Index Finger | 8.—L. Middle Finger | 9.—L. Ring Finger | 10.—L. Little Finger

Four fingers taken simultaneously

Amputations

Right hand

Left hand

Four fingers taken simultaneously

Prisoner's signature

𝔉𝔢𝔡𝔢𝔯𝔞𝔩 𝔅𝔲𝔯𝔢𝔞𝔲 𝔬𝔣 𝔍𝔫𝔳𝔢𝔰𝔱𝔦𝔤𝔞𝔱𝔦𝔬𝔫

U. S. Department of Justice

San Francisco, California
April 14, 1939

Director
Federal Bureau of Investigation
Washington, D. C.

            Re: ARTHUR E. BARKER, with aliases,
                et al; ESCAPED FEDERAL PRISONERS.

Dear Sir:

        I am transmitting under separate cover a death mask
of ARTHUR E. BARKER, with aliases: DOC BARKER, BOB BARKER,
CLAUD DALE, which was made by PAUL C. GREEN, Technician on the
staff of the Coroner for the City and County of San Francisco.
This death mask was prepared on January 14, 1939, prior to the
autopsy, and was made available through the courtesy of DR.
T. B. W. LELAND, Coroner, City and County of San Francisco. It
is suggested that you may desire to address a communication to
DR. LELAND and MR. GREEN, thanking them for giving this mask to
us.

        It is interesting to note that the attempt to escape
was made on "Friday the Thirteenth", the mortal wounds being inflicted in the early morning hours of that day and BARKER dying
at 5:40 P. M. on Friday the thirteenth. It occurred to me that
you may desire to use this death mask in one of the exhibits at
the Bureau.

                        Very truly yours,

                        N. J. L. PIEPER
                        Special Agent in Charge

LHR/mjd
76-347

                    RECORDED
                        &
                    INDEXED   76- 4175- 37

                            FEDERAL BUREAU OF INVESTIGATION
                                APR 15

Above: Herman Barker, alias Bert Lavender. Courtesy Rick Mattix.
Left: Arthur Osborn, Wyoming officer slain by Herman Barker. Courtesy of Rick Mattix.

Inter-departmental FBI communication concerning the creation of a death mask of Doc Barker, FBI document. Courtesy Rick Mattix.

"CITY AND COUNTY OF SAN FRANCISCO,
STATE OF CALIFORNIA

    INQUISITION taken at Coroner's Court on the 24th day of January,
1939, before THOS. B. W. LELAND, M.D. Coroner of said City and County,
upon the oath of 8 qualified jurors who, being duly summoned and sworn
to inquire into all the circumstances attending the death of ARTHUR
BARKER and by whom the same was produced, and in what manner and when
and where the said deceased came to his death, do say upon their oaths
aforesaid:

    That the said ARTHUR BARKER, male, white, single, about 39 years
old, occupation, laborer, nativity, unknown, residence, Alcatraz Island,
came to his death on January 13, 1939, on Alcatraz Island, from shock
and hemorrhage following gunshot wounds of head and thigh (left),
specimens to toxicologist; negative for alcohol. Specimens to patholo-
gist: Gunshot wound of the head with contusion of the brain and brain
hemorrhage, traumatic.

    And we further find:
    that the said ARTHUR BARKER met his death attempting to escape
from Alcatraz Prison from gunshot wounds inflicted by guards unknown.
From the evidence at hand, we, the jury, believe this escape was made
possible by the failure of the system for guarding prisoners now in use
at Alcatraz Prison and we recommend a drastic improvement by those in
authority. Further, that a more efficient system be adopted for
illumination of shores and waters immediately surrounding the prison; that
the citizens of San Francisco unite in an effort to have a more suitable
location for imprisonment of the type of desperados at present housed at
Alcatraz.

IN WITNESS WHEREOF the said Coroner and the Jurors aforesaid have to this
Inquisition set their hands and seals on the date thereof.

                              s/s   CHAS J. McKEON - Foreman

s/s - R. WILLIAMSON
      J. E. BUTTERFIELD
      J. C. CAIN
      S. SPIELLER
      A. W. LUNDSTROM
      K. D. WEBSTER
      GEO. C. CORY,   Approved - THOS. B. W. LELAND, M.D.
                                              CORONER."

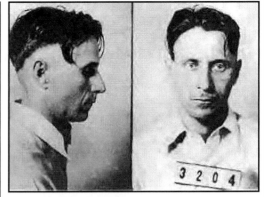

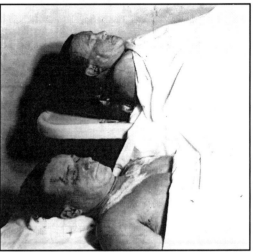

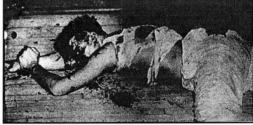

MARRIAGE LICENSE.

#341

STATE OF MISSOURI,   COUNTY OF *Lawrence*

This License Authorizes any Judge, Justice of the Peace, Licensed or Ordained Preacher of the Gospel, or any other person author-
ized under the Laws of this State, to SOLEMNIZE MARRIAGE between *George B. Barker*
of *Aurora* County of *Lawrence* and State of *Missouri*
who is *Over* the age of twenty-one years; and *Arrie Clark*
of *Mt. Vernon* County of *Lawrence* and State of *Missouri* who
Over the age of eighteen years.

WITNESS my hand as Recorder, with the seal of office hereto affixed, at my office in *Mt. Vernon*
the *14* day of *Sept.* 18 *92*

By _____   *W C Trimble*
             Deputy.   RECORDER

STATE OF MISSOURI,
County of *Lawrence* } ss.   THIS IS TO CERTIFY, That the undersigned, *Minister of the Gospel*
did, at *Aurora* in said County, on the *14* day of *September* A. D. 18 *92*, unite in Marriage
above named persons.

                              W B Jackson
                              Minister of the Gospel
Filed for record *Sept 16* 18 *92*
By _____ Deputy.   *W C Trimble* Recorder

MARRIAGE LICENSE.

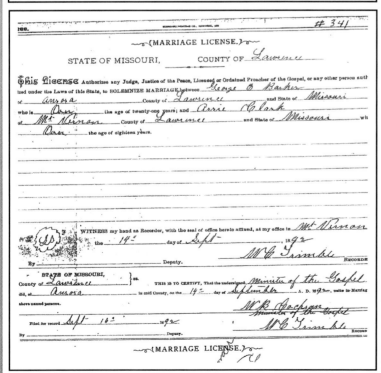

Clockwise from top left: Official Coroners report, County of San Francisco, concerning the death of Doc Barker. Courtesy Rick Mattix. Freddy Barker. Courtesy Rick Mattix. Ma and Fred Barker in death. Courtesy Rick Mattix. Fred Barker, killed by the FBI. Courtesy Rick Mattix. Alvin (Creepy) Karpis. Courtesy Rick Mattix. Marrige License, Arizona and George Barker. Courtesy Verla Geller.

breaking (except for childhood pranks) until that time, except for a few well-worn stories told by old-timers.

In 1922, Lloyd "Red" Barker and Will Green were convicted of a Kansas mail robbery and sentenced to lengthy terms at Leavenworth. The same year, Doc and Volney Davis were convicted of murdering a night watchman named Thomas Sherrill near Tulsa's St. Johns Hospital and were both sent to the Oklahoma state pen for life. The following year, Fred was charged with robbery and eventually sentenced to a five-year hitch at the Granite Reformatory. Upon his release from prison in late 1925 Freddy Barker joined his brother Herman and his faithful traveling companion, Carol Hamilton, becoming a major player in a prolific burglary ring dubbed the "Gang of Eight," which operated out of a pool hall located in Miami as well as Radium Springs Health Resort near Salina. The resort was owned by an ex-judge named Quiliki P. McGhee, who was suspected to have been the brains behind the operation. The group

Ma and a boyfriend, circa 1930; photo taken while the pair was living in South Tulsa. Courtesy Rick Mattix.

robbed dozens of businesses across Oklahoma, Arkansas, and Kansas during the years 1925-27. In early January 1927, Herman and Ray Terrill were both wounded and captured by police in Carterville, Missouri. Herman was transferred to Fayetteville, Arkansas, where he was wanted for participating in the West Fork bank robbery. Soon after his transfer, he escaped custody. On August 1, he murdered Officer Arthur Osborn near Pine Bluffs, Wyoming, while in the company of Carol Hamilton. In the evening hours of August 29, 1927, Herman committed suicide at the conclusion of a gunbattle with police in Wichita, Kansas. Also slain in the gunfight and its aftermath was Officer J. E. Marshal and Oklahoma outlaw Porter Meeks.

In the meantime, Fred was sent to the Kansas pen in 1926 on a burglary charge where he made the acquaintance of an arch criminal named Alvin Karpis (real name Albin Karpowics). Upon his release from prison, Fred reconnected with Karpis, and the pair drifted

Ma Barker (right) with husband and sister. Courtesy Rick Mattix.

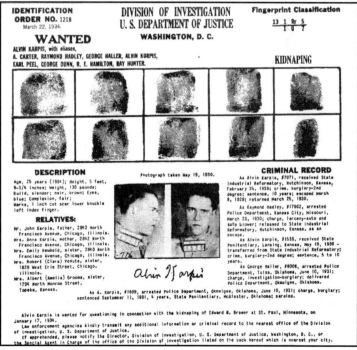

Wanted poster concerning Alvin Karpis. Courtesy Rick Mattix.

to Missouri with Mother Barker and her new boyfriend in tow. By this time, Ma had separated from her husband and taken up with an elderly alcoholic sign painter named Arthur Dunlop. Freddy would later kill Dunlop for having what he referred to as "Loose lips."

On November 8, 1931, Freddy shot and killed Constable Albert Manley in Pocahontas, Arkansas. The following month he and Karpis murdered Sheriff C. Roy Kelly in West Plains, Missouri. Fearing the heat generated from the cop killings, the duo, along with "Ma," sought safety in the then corrupt city of St. Paul, Minnesota, where they joined forces with members of the old Holden-Keating Gang. Over the next few months, the

Barkers, along with Karpis, would organize the largest "Supergang" of the crime-ridden depression-era. Investigators estimated the group numbered thirty to forty hard-core members and close associates. Several of the Barker's boyhood friends would eventually join the group.

In September of 1932, friends of Doc Barker were somehow able to bribe an official to grant him a parole from the Oklahoma State Penitentiary in McAlester, where he was serving a life sentence for murder. He quickly joined his mother and brother in Minnesota. Over the next two years, the group would be responsible for committing a score of cold-blooded murders, as well as a dozen of the nation's largest bank robberies, in which several officers were slain, along with perpetrating the headline generating Hamm and Bremer kidnappings. After the January 17, 1934, Bremer snatch the gang broke apart scattering across the country.

On January 8, 1935, Doc Barker was captured in Chicago by the FBI, and although agents

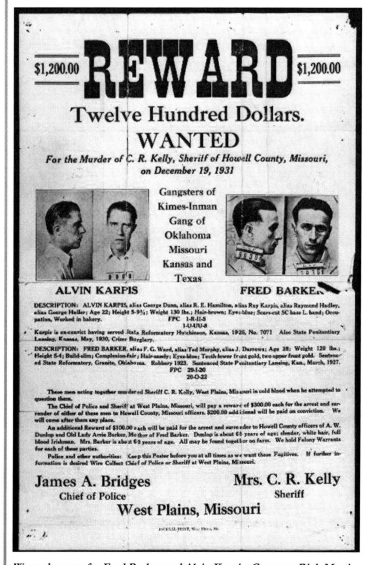

Wanted poster for Fred Barker and Alvin Karpis. Courtesy Rick Mattix.

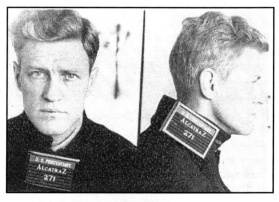

Above: Volney Davis. Courtesy National Archives. Left: Barker-Karpis Gang member Jess Doyle. Courtesy Rick Mattix.

brutalized him during questioning, breaking several thick telephone books over his head, he refused to talk. While searching his apartment, investigators discovered information that suggested his brother and mother were hiding-out in central Florida.

Eight days after Doc's capture, a fast moving contingent of G-Men surrounded a vacation home on Lake Weir, near Oklawaha, Florida, where Ma and Fred were hiding out. When the agents ordered mother and son to surrender, they were answered with machinegun fire. At the conclusion of six-hour gunbattle in which an estimated 700 rounds were exchanged between the antagonists, both Ma and Fred were found dead in an upstairs bedroom. After being stored in a freezer-locker for nearly a year, George Barker had the bodies transported back to Oklahoma and buried next to Herman at a small cemetery near Welch. Soon after the killing of the Barkers, an FBI public relations man put out the improbable story implying "Ma" Barker was the gang's mastermind. His motivation was to cover-up the fact the feds had unintentionally, but probably justifiably, slain an unarmed elderly woman. In reality, there has never been one shred of evidence uncovered over the past seventy-odd years supporting the patently false claim that Ma was any sort of gang leader. By all indications, it appears the old lady merely acted as a front man, chief cook, and bottle-washer for the boys. While her failings as a parent were legion and she obviously benefited materially from her children's illegal activities, "Ma" was certainly not the pistol-packing momma depicted in various movies and books over the decades.

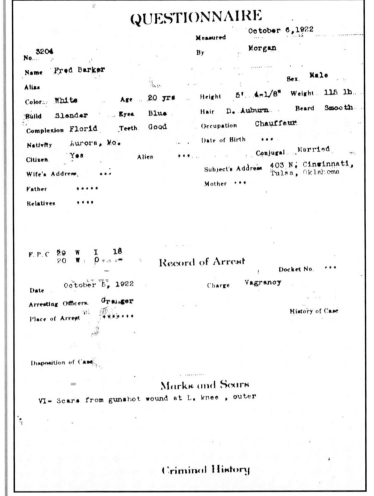

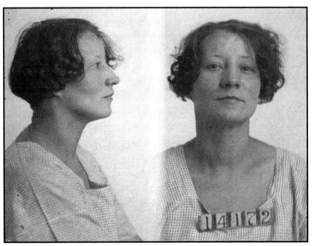

Above: Fred Barker's 1922 arrest record for vagrancy. Courtesy Rick Mattix. Left: Carol Hamilton, Sapulpa gal who became Herman Barker's faithful gunmoll. Courtesy Colorado State Penitentiary. Far left: Lloyd Barker. Courtesy Amazing Detective and Rick Mattix.

Florida residence, Oklawaha, Florida, where Ma and Freddy were slain by agents of the FBI (modern view on left, and picture on right taken at the time of the raid). Author's collection.

Arsenal found in residence on Lake Weir, Florida where Ma and Fred were killed by G-Men. Courtesy Rick Mattix.

Graves of the Barker Clan in Welch, Oklahoma. Photo by Naomi Morgan.

Alvin Karpis and Harry Campbell soon replace Doc and Freddy as America's "most wanted" public enemies. Both are finally captured the following year, but not before committing a host of other robberies. Doc, who

was noted by J. Edger Hoover in a memorandum as, "One of the most dangerous criminals this bureau has ever had to deal with," was sent to Alcatraz Penitentiary for life on a charge of kidnapping. He was killed in an escape attempt in 1939 and was buried in an unmarked grave in California, not next to his kin at Welch, as many have suggested. Alvin Karpis served 33 years in prison before being paroled in 1969. He died in Spain in 1979, a possible suicide. Lloyd Barker was paroled from Leavenworth in 1938, only to be shot-gunned to death by his wife on the steps of their Colorado home in 1949.

The Mysterious Death of Attorney J. Earl Smith

At approximately 9 p.m. on the night of August 17, 1932, a farmer heard what he thought were the sounds of several shots echoing in the darkness coming from an isolated dirt lane near the old Indian Hills Golf Club, located in a remote rural area between Tulsa and Catoosa, Oklahoma. The farmer paid little attention to the explosions figuring it was merely a hunter blasting away at a fleeing rabbit. Sportsmen oftentimes drove the road around dusk with their headlights on bright, attempting to blind or freeze cottontails in place in order to get a clear shot. Although the practice of "Spotlighting" was illegal most people ignored such activities since times were hard and folks were hungry for meat. The farmer didn't give the incident another thought instead simply returned to his chores before strolling back to his house for a late supper.

At five in the morning, two golf course employees on their way to work turned down the rutted lane, which they oftentimes used as a shortcut. After traveling a few hundred feet up the road, the pair noticed an abandoned car with its driver's side door flung open. Pulling their rig over to investigate they spotted a person lying still in the adjacent ditch. To their horror, they observed the suit-clad male figure was covered in blood, especially the head and upper torso. It was soon apparent to the pair the lifeless individual was a victim of some sort of violent trauma. One of the men stayed with the corpse while the other motored back to a nearby filling station phoning the authorities.

Harry Campbell. Courtesy Rick Mattix .

When investigators arrived on the scene, they observed the victim had suffered several gunshot wounds. They searched the body finding a billfold, which contained papers stating it belonged to a Tulsa attorney named J. Earl Smith. Probing through the vehicle detectives noted a bullet had shattered the front windshield. A second round had pierced the car roof smashing the dome light while a third round had damaged the upper portion of the steering wheel. There was blood spatters on the dash and floorboard of the driver's side of the car as well as the presence of blood steaks on the exterior driver's side running board. Blood trails and drag marks were discovered leading from the automobile to the ditch located adjacent to the passenger side of the vehicle, indicating the slayer or slayers had removed the body from the car and drug it into the ditch where it was later found. The body was transported to the morgue and investigators fanned out into the nearby countryside questioning area residents. A pair of detectives drove to the victim's home where they escorted his wife to the morgue in order for her to identify the body.

After making a positive identification, Mrs. Smith informed investigators she had last seen her husband the previous night. Apparently, around 8:15 p.m., their fourteen-year-old daughter answered a ringing phone; the man on the other end of the line was familiar to her. She handed the phone to her dad, who after speaking a few minutes, informed his family he had to meet a man and would return in twenty minutes, "With some money." He never returned alive.

The figure of J. Earl Smith was quite familiar with area police. He was a mobbed-up lawyer, heavily connected to the underworld. Smith moved to Tulsa from Ponca City in 1928 after being charged multiple times there for such crimes as money laundering, hot checks, and participating in a fencing operation as well as conspiring to rob the bank at Kildare. Although he beat the charges on every occasion, he was eventually run out of town by the local authorities. After arriving in Tulsa he partnered up with a prominent legal mouthpiece named Ed Crossland, a one time states assistant attorney general. The two made their offices in the Tulsa World Building downtown. Over the next three or four years the hard drinking Smith, who had a taste for the finer things in life, defended a myriad of area high profile gangsters and underworld notables. In late April 1932, he took on the case of Oklahoma vs. Harry Campbell and Glenn Roy Wright for their suspected participation in the April 15 burglary of the Wilcox Oil Company offices in Tulsa. The Wilcox job was a botched deal from the get go. The burglars broke into the place and evidently cracked the wrong safe getting about $1,000 in cash but missing $175,0000 in negotiable bonds resting in a second steel box located in a back room. Within a week of the heist, Campbell and Wright were arrested and charged with the burglary. Smith

Grave of murdered Tulsa Attorney J. Earl Smith in Rose Hill Cemetery, Tulsa. Photo by Naomi Morgan.

quickly arranged for the suspects to make bond gaining their temporary freedom. By associating himself with the desperate pair, Smith had plunged into some very dangerous waters.

Harry Campbell was a bona fide member of Tulsa's infamous Barker-Karpis Gang. He had been associated with the Barkers since childhood; being raised in the seedy and poverty stricken Central Park area located just east of the downtown district. By 1915, he had joined the notorious Central Park Gang of juvenile delinquents. Around 1918, Campbell joined up with the notorious Jeff Duree and his associates, "Doc" Barker, Roland Williams, Jimmy Lawson, and Ray Terrill burglarizing a dozen or more undersized oilfield community banks as well as numerous other businesses. The following year he married Ica "Billie" Rowell. In 1921, Harry was arrested at a Coweta Hotel on suspicion of bank robbery. Although the police were eventually forced to release him for lack of evidence, it threw a scare in the twenty-one-year-old budding thug causing him to flee to Douglas, Wyoming, where he took a job driving a truck in the oil patch. His wife remained in Tulsa where she filed for divorce informing the court the hoodlum had "abused, choked, and struck her on numerous occasions while engaged in violent fits of jealousy." He remarried in 1923. The union produced a daughter and the couple appeared to live an ordinary life until 1928 when Campbell took to the drink after being forced to quit work due to being seriously injured in a vehicular accident in which he dislocated both knees as well as fracturing his arm and wrist. The pair di-

Grave of Barker-Karpis Gangster Harry Campbell, Rose Hill Cemetery, Tulsa. Photo by Naomi Morgan. Left: Clearwater, Kansas, Constable Robert Hammers, slain by Glenn Wright and Charlie Cotner. Author's private collection.

vorced the following year. In early 1932, Campbell returned to his old haunts and bad acquaintances in Oklahoma where he quickly reconnected with a boyhood pal named Glenn Roy Wright.

The Arkansas born Wright was a vicious habitual criminal and an ever-present menace to polite society. He

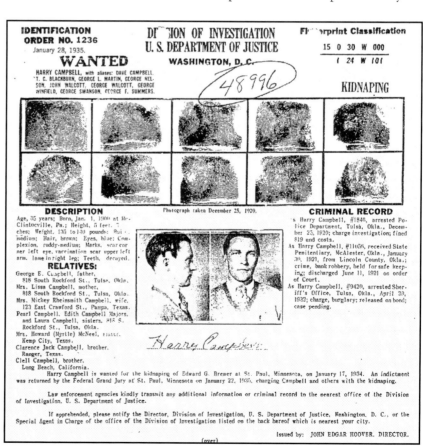

Wanted poster for Harry Campbell. Courtesy Rick Mattix.

first met Campbell as a teen while both men were involved with one of several juvenile gangs in Tulsa. Wright's criminal record began with an arrest for burglary in Tulsa in 1916 for which he was given a suspended sentence. In 1917, he was inducted into the army where he was promptly sentenced to a hitch at the Military Disciplinary Barracks at Leavenworth for striking a superior officer. He was discharged in 1918. In 1920, he pulled a few jobs with Campbell and Terrill in their oilfield bank burglary spree. Within a few months of joining the crew, he was again convicted of burglary in Tulsa and sentenced to a seven-year stretch. In due time he was diagnosed with tuberculosis and was transferred to the Oklahoma TB Hospital in Clinton. Three years later Wright escaped from the facility but was captured the following year and returned to McAlester prison. Just months after gaining

his release from prison in 1926 the young man was convicted of armed robbery and given a ten-year sentence.

Following his latest parole in early 1932, he rejoined his pal Campbell. The pair went on a burglary spree and in early April zeroed in on the Wilcox Oil Company as their next victim. While sitting in the can after his arrest for the Wilcox job, Campbell was informed by a fellow con that he should contact a attorney named Smith who, according to the prison grapevine, not only possessed a good record for acquittals but had a reputation for keeping his mouth shut.

Only hours into the Smith murder investigation, the victim's daughter informed the authorities she recognized the voice of the man who lured her father to his death as belonging to Harry Campbell. According to the daughter and her mother, Campbell had phoned the house numerous times over the past few months, talking to the teenage girl on several of those occasions. Knowing Campbell's reputation, the cops quickly assumed Attorney Smith might have been taken for a "one-way ride" by his new client. The inquiry also uncovered the fact Smith had recently been hired to represent Harvey Bailey, a major bank robber associated with both the Holden-Keating and Barker-Karpis Gangs. Bailey had been arrested in early July at a golf course in Kansas City, Missouri, while in possession of a $500 bond stolen in a June 17, 1932, raid on the Citizens National Bank of Fort Scott, Kansas. When extradited back to Kansas the mobster was identified by several witnesses from the heist naming him as one of the looters. Bailey had previously been suspected by lawmen of being involved in a colossal 1930 $2,000,000 Lincoln, Nebraska, bank robbery.

Within days of his being engaged to represent Bailey, Smith journeyed to Chicago where he picked up a $2,500 money order, which represented a down payment for his le-

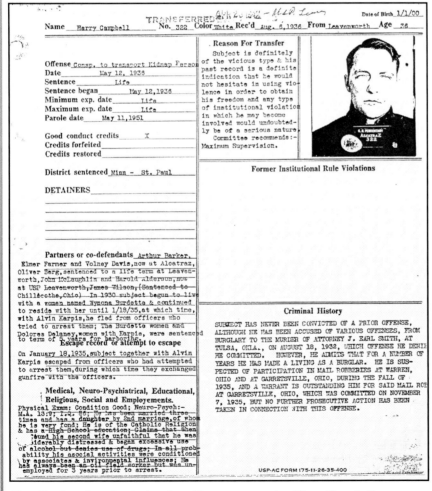

Transfer sheet from Leavenworth to Alcatraz concerning Harry Campbell.
Courtesy NARA.

gal services. On his return to Tulsa the attorney bragged to acquaintances, there was more money to come. In early August, Smith, accompanied by his family, traveled to Fort Scott where he visited with his client and a second lawyer who had been hired as co-council. For some unknown reason when the trial began Smith no-showed Bailey, choosing to stay at home. On August 15, Bailey was found guilty of the Fort Scott job and sentenced to a 10-to 50-year jolt in the Kansas State Penitentiary. When Smith turned up dead two nights later many figured he was "put on the spot" for double-crossing Bailey. When the authorities questioned Bailey over Smith's death the suave bandit sat mum refusing to comment.

Back in Tulsa the investigation dragged on, warrants were issued for Harry Campbell and Glenn Wright for failure to appear for their court date concerning the Wilcox robbery case, neither having been seen for over a week. An autopsy showed Smith had been brutally beaten about the face and shot twice in the head and a third time in the torso, the round entering under the right shoulder and exiting through his mouth knocking out several teeth. Robbery was quickly ruled out as a motive considering the victim's cash filled wallet as well as several gold rings and an expensive gold Hamilton pocket watch were undisturbed by the killers. A transient who had been observed loafing at a filling station located near the murder site was arrested, questioned, and released. Back at Smith's office in the Tulsa World building, his law partner arrived at work the day after the murder only to find the office safe door ajar and its contents missing. Smith's widow would later privately claim her husband had a small fortune in diamonds he had received as a legal fee stashed in the safe. The gems were never recovered and the crime remained unsolved leading some investigators to suspect the burglary was an inside job.

After the coroner released the body, Mrs. Smith had the remains interred at Tulsa's Rose Hill Cemetery.

The following day the widow bundled up her daughters and left town taking up residence in nearby Muskogee where the family spent the rest of the depression living in great poverty under an assumed name. Since it was commonly known she possessed intimate knowledge of her husband's business affairs, the poor woman feared harm from those who suspected she might talk. According to Smith family descendants, the widow was visited by "Ma" Barker just days after her husband's violent demise. The old lady offered a frosted cake as a condolence. After eating a piece of the cake Mrs. Smith became violently ill, prompting her to suspect Ma had attempted to poison her. At another point, the widow was nearly ran over by a speeding car and over the years she received several death threats from unknown parties suggesting she keep silent about what she knew of her husband's untimely death and business in general.

Over time, the authorities settled on two separate theories concerning Smith's murder. One theory sug-

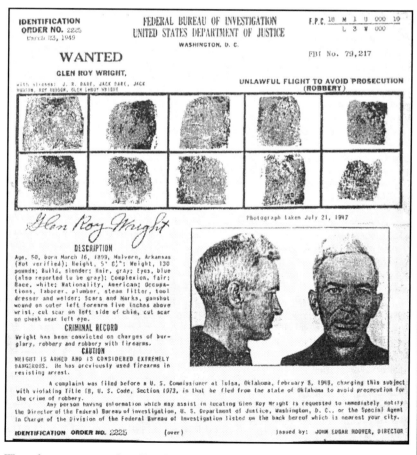

Wanted poster concerning Glen Roy Wright. Courtesy Rick Mattix.

gested Campbell and Wright had killed Smith over a squabble concerning either his fee for defending them in the Wilcox robbery or a disagreement over the laundering of some stolen bonds. Others maintained either Campbell or Fred Barker had executed the attorney over standing up Harvey Bailey at his trial.

Nothing was heard of the either Campbell or Wright until October 17, 1933, when two machine gun wielding individuals matching their descriptions robbed the office of a farm auction house in Stillwater of some $17,000 in cash and coin. After the Stillwater heist Campbell and Wright reportedly split up.

Campbell, now joined by a moll named Wynona Burdette (a Sapulpa native), reconnected with his old pals, the Barkers. On January 16, 1934, he assisted the Barker-Karpis Gang in the kidnapping of wealthy St. Paul, Minnesota, banker Edward Bremer. After collecting a $200,000 ransom Campbell and his girlfriend joined Alvin Karpis and his paramour, Deloris Delaney, (Also a native Oklahoman) at a hideout in Toledo, Ohio. The group laid low for nearly a year until receiving news of the deaths of Ma Barker and her son Fred at the hands of the FBI in Florida. The foursome immediately traveled to Atlantic City where on January 20, 1935, a squad of FBI agents raided the place. After a bloodless gun-duel, the pair managed to escape, but was forced to leave their women behind. On April 24, Karpis, Campbell, and a third individual pulled off a mail heist in Warren, Ohio, and stole $72,000. The following November, the trio, along with a local lad named Fred Hunter, and an ex-con from Oklahoma named Sam Coker held up a train near Garrettsville, Ohio, for $34,000 in cash and $11,000

Glenn Roy Wright. Courtesy Rick Mattix.

in bonds. After the train heist the gang split up, Karpis locating first to Hot Springs, Arkansas, then New Orleans where a posse of federal agents personally led by J. Edger Hoover arrested him and Fred Hunter on May 1, 1936. After Karpis's capture Harry Campbell was named by the FBI as Public Enemy #1 in America. He remained in that dubious position for less than a week.

On May 7, Campbell and Coker were apprehended in an apartment building in Toledo, Ohio. As was the case in the arrest of Karpis, Hoover again accompanied the raiders. His capture made the headlines in every major newspaper in America. Campbell was soon convicted of the Bremer kidnapping (a federal offense) and given a life sentence. After spending a short time at Leavenworth, he was transferred to Alcatraz where he remained until 1942 when he was transferred back to Leavenworth. The outlaw was paroled on December 2, 1959, to his daughter's custody in Amarillo, Texas, where he worked as a motel handyman man until his death in 1974. The infamous badman was buried only a short distance from the eternal resting place of J. Earl Smith at Tulsa's Rose Hill Cemetery.

As for Glenn Wright, after splitting up with Campbell he joined Tommy Hill's South Coffeyville Gang of safecrackers. Other members of this criminal enterprise included one-time Underhill-Bradshaw gang members Charley Cotner and Ira Brackett. Over the next year, the group burglarized a dozen banks in Kansas and Oklahoma. In mid-March

Wright's grave at Memorial Park Cemetery, Tulsa. Photo by Naomi Morgan.

Cotner and Wright shot and killed, a night watchman named Robert Hammers near Wichita, Kansas. The pair, along with a half-dozen others, was captured the following day at Brackett's farmhouse located near Mannford, Oklahoma. Ten empty safes were discovered buried on the property. In May, Wright was convicted of the Stillwater auction heist and given a life sentence. He was never tried for the Kansas murder. The badman escaped custody in 1948 when he was given a leave of absence to visit his ailing mother in Tulsa. Over the next two years, he committed a host of armed robberies and burglaries in the Tulsa area in order to earn his living. The FBI immediately placed him on their "Ten Most Wanted List." Agents of the FBI captured the incorrigible bandit while he was browsing through a drug store magazine rack in Salina, Kansas, on December 14, 1950. He was returned to McAlester where he died of the lingering effects of TB in 1954. Glenn Roy Wright was buried at Memorial Cemetery in Tulsa.

In 1936, a Tulsa raised criminal and Barker Gang associate named Jimmy Lawson, who was currently serving a life sentence at the Kansas State Penitentiary, contacted Tulsa authorities offering to trade information for a reduction in his sentence. Lawson appeared before a Rogers County Grand Jury swearing he was present at the Smith murder, naming the actual killers as Harry Campbell and another Tulsa hood named Edward Snyder, alias "Jew Eddy" Moss. Apparently, nothing came of the affair and the murder of J. Earl Smith remains officially unsolved and open for inquiry to this day.

Larry "The Chopper" DeVol

Lawrence DeVol was born in Ohio in 1903. He and his family moved to Tulsa in 1909 where they operated a small candy store located just off the downtown area. Raised by parents who declined to practice even the smallest semblance of discipline toward their children, the lad refused to attend school, instead spending his days running wild and unsupervised throughout the neighborhood committing numerous petty thefts and acts of vandalism. In 1914, at the age of eleven, he served a four-month sentence at the Oklahoma Reformatory for White Boys in Pauls Valley on a burglary charge. A week after his release the misguided lad was apprehended in the act of stealing articles from a local junk dealer. The following

day he escaped from custody only to be captured several months later while shoplifting from an area grocery store. After his latest arrest a juvenile officer was quoted in the *Tulsa World* saying, "This boy is a real character. He has

Top: Larry "The Chopper" DeVol. Courtesy Rick Mattix.
Above: Jimmy Creighton. Courtesy Joplin Globe.
Left: Enid Officer Cal Palmer, slain by Larry DeVol. Muskogee Phoenix.

been arrested time and again. We don't know what to do with him."

When his father died unexpectedly in 1917, DeVol's mother moved to a small farm on the edge of Tulsa, hoping country life would create a positive change in her son's life. Young Larry reacted to the move by fleeing back to center city joining the notorious Central Park Gang of thieves. After living a year on the streets as a runaway, he was apprehended by juvenile authorities and held for four months at a detention facility until his mother convinced authorities to release him into her custody. In early 1919, he was busted for grand larceny, convicted, and sentenced to a three-year jolt at the Oklahoma State Reformatory in Granite. Two weeks after gaining his freedom from Granite the young man was arrested for bur-

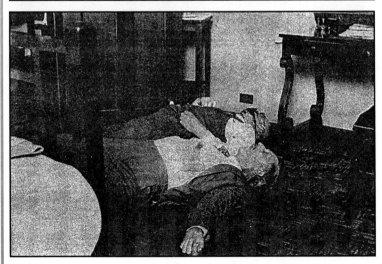

Top: Severs Hotel – scene of the 1930 Muskogee double murders.
Courtesy Sid Burgess.
Above: Severs Hotel death scene, the Smith brothers. **Muskogee Phoenix.**

glary and given a 90-day term at the Tulsa County Jail. Six months later, he was sent back to Granite on another burglary charge.

In early 1926, DeVol was picked up on a grand larceny charge at Pittsburg, Kansas and sentenced to a five-year term at the Kansas Reformatory in Hutchinson. After serving three years of his sentence, DeVol escaped from the facility in the company of another habitual thief named Alvin Karpis on March 9, 1929. Over the next month, the pair drifted across the Midwest pulling B&E jobs until the young man was arrested in Chicago and returned to Hutchinson where the authorities deemed him incorrigible and transferred him to the Kansas State Penitentiary in Lansing to finish out his sentence.

Upon his release from Lansing in early 1930, DeVol quickly hooked up with Karpis and the pair went on another crime spree ending with their arrest in Kansas City for suspicion of burglary on March 23, 1930. While Karpis was returned to Kansas to serve out his sentence, DeVol, using the alias of Leonard Carson at the time, was released on a $1,000 bond. On gaining his discharge the young thug made a beeline back to Tulsa where he connected with his brother Clarence and a hood named Jimmy Creighton, who was on the run from a Nebraska bank robbing charge. The trio spent the next few weeks headquartered out of a hotel in Haskell pulling a few area burglaries.

On May 15, DeVol, using the name of R. L. Benton, and another man were arrested in Muskogee for suspicion of burglarizing the Griffin Food Company. A quick thinking detective noticed DeVol matched the description of one of the suspects in the recent murders of a pair of wealthy Connecticut businessmen at Muskogee's Severs Hotel. The killings, which produced glaring headlines in newspapers nationwide, were thought to have been the work of a pair of professional hitmen. Shortly after his arrest, several witnesses positively identified DeVol as one of the deadly assailants. Not one to hang around very long when the heat was turned up, DeVol jimmied the lock on his cell at the county jail, stole a car, and exited the state in a hurry.

In November, the fugitive shot and killed an officer named John Rose in Kirksville, Missouri, who had attempted to question him. DeVol next turned up in Omaha, Nebraska, where he was hired by the local mob to act as a paid assassin. After taking a series of hapless victims on one-way rides DeVol departed to St. Paul, Minnesota, where he joined up with his old pal Alvin Karpis, who had recently been paroled from the Kansas pen and since become the co-leader along with Freddy Barker of the so-called Barker-Karpis Gang of bank robbers. On March 29, 1932, the group raided a bank in Minneapolis stealing $266,000 in cash and bonds. In June, they looted the Citizens National Bank of Fort Scott, Kansas, of $47,000 before holding up the Cloud National Bank of Concordia, Kansas, for $250,000 in bonds and cash. They then looted the Bank and Trust Co. of Redwood Falls, Minnesota, for $35,000. On October 18, DeVol went solo robbing the bank of Amboy, Minnesota, for $7,000.

In December, the gang raided the Third Northwestern Bank of Minneapolis for $115,000. On this occasion, things got a bit out of hand when a cashier hit the alarm, which was answered by a patrol car containing Officers Ira Evans and Leo Gorski. DeVol, acting as a triggerman, providing cover for the group's getaway cars, reacted to the cop's arrival by literally cutting the pair to ribbons with machinegun fire. Five days after the robbery DeVol was arrested outside a St. Paul apartment house in a state of extreme drunkenness. Police discovered a loaded pistol and $17,000 in cash and bonds stuffed in his pockets. When asked why he failed to resist arrest the pouting hood claimed, "I meant to but I was so liquored up the old arm just wouldn't cooperate with the old bean."

DeVol eventually pled guilty to charges of second-degree murder as well as bank robbery and sentenced to life imprisonment. Three years after his arrival at the Minnesota State Prison in Stillwater, Warden J.J. Sullivan requested his transfer to a mental hospital for treatment saying, "DeVol is one of the most dangerous prisoners ever admitted to this facility. He is a raving maniac and has physically assaulted guards and his fellow inmates on numerous occasions. He refuses to work, and must be kept in solitary confinement most of the time for the safety of the institution." After conducting a mental evaluation, a prison psychiatrist labeled the hoodlum a certified "violent paranoid" and ordered him transferred to the St. Peters Hospital for the Criminally Insane. In 1936, DeVol led a group of thirteen inmates in a mass escape from the hospital. The hoodlum and two other patients, Donald Reeder and a psychotic murderer named Albert Saroko, split from the main group heading south burglarizing their way across the Midwest. Minnesota authorities quickly flooded the country with wanted posters offering a reward for information leading to the capture of the escapees. The poster read, "Larry

BUREAU OF CRIMINAL APPREHENSION
STATE OFFICE BLDG., ST. PAUL. MINN.

Circular No. 255   June 22, 1936

WANTED FOR ESCAPE
Case No. 6504

Age   27 (1932)
Height   5 ft. 8¼ ins.
Weight   157 lbs.
Hair   Medium dark chest-
          nut
Build   Medium
Comp.   Dark
Eyes   Dark hazel

Fingerprint Classification:
    17   29   W   IO
    32   W   I   16

Vaccination scar on upper left arm. Prominent cut scar on elbow Post. of right arm. Faint dimple in chin. Sunken cheeks. Acne rash on face and body. Cut scar over left eye.

LAWRENCE DEVOL
alias
LEONARD BARTON
LAWRENCE DeVOLT
CARSON

On June 8, 1936, this man and fifteen others escaped from the Criminal Ward of the State Insane Hospital, St. Peter, Minn. Twelve of these men have been apprehended and the following are still at large: Lawrence Devol, Frank Gibson, Donald J. Reeder and Albert Soroko.

Lawrence Devol has a long criminal record and was once an associate of Alvin Karpis and the Barker Gang. He was sentenced to the Minnesota State Prison on January 1, 1933, on a life sentence for bank robbery and murder. On December 27, 1935, he was transferred to the St. Peter Hospital. He is a very dangerous criminal and extreme caution should be used in apprehending him.

If located, arrest, hold and notify:

JOHN A. JOHNSON, Sheriff   M. C. PASSOLT, Superintendent
   Nicollet County,   Bureau of Criminal Apprehension
   St. Peter, Minnesota   State Office Building, St. Paul, Minn.

DR. GEORGE H. FREEMAN, Supt.
St. Peter State Hospital, St. Peter, Minnesota

Wanted poster from the Minnesota Hospital for the Criminally Insane for the capture of Larry DeVol. Courtesy Rick Mattix.

DeVol is a very dangerous criminal and extreme caution should be used when attempting to apprehend him. This man is a paranoid maniac who suffers from delusions and is apt to kill anyone suddenly without warning."

After robbing two banks in Kansas and stealing over a dozen automobiles, the trio arrived in Oklahoma where they were involved in two gunfights with the authorities during robberies in both Perry and Pond Creek in which one of the fugitives was wounded, as were three lawmen. Soon afterward, Albert Saroko was shot and killed by police in Oklahoma City attempting to stick up a café.

Larry DeVol, left, and Alvin Karpis, right, under arrest in Kansas City with tools of their trade. Courtesy Rick Mattix.

On July 8, DeVol was drinking beer in a gin-joint in Enid with a prostitute when the tavern owner phoned the cops reporting a suspicious character on the premises. Moments later Officers Cal Palmer and Ralph Knarr arrived at the scene. When the policemen, who were unaware of the badman's identity, approached the thug requesting he, "Come with them," DeVol, his face turning white as a sheet, replied, "OK, but first let me finish my beer." After calmly draining his glass, he placed it on the table then suddenly whipped out a large caliber semi-automatic pistol from his waistband shooting both officers several times at point blank range. The badman ran into the street where he leaped on the running board of a passing car breathlessly informing the driver he was a cop and to, "Drive on!" Just then, two other lawmen arrived and began blasting away at the fleeing fugitive. DeVol responded by shooting one of the cops in the hand as well as wounding a bystander before the officers riddled him with nine rounds. He dropped to the hard pavement, his body withering and jerking convulsively for several moments before becoming stone still. Witnesses said the gunbattle lasted a total of five minutes, resulting in a scene

of unimaginable blood-spattered carnage. When a bevy of ambulances arrived paramedics pronounced Officer Palmer dead at the scene while his partner, who was suffering from four bullet wounds, was rushed to a hospital where he was deemed in critical condition, but somehow managed to survive. A wife and two sons survived the thirty-eight-year-old Palmer. That night hundreds of citizens passed through a local mortuary in order to catch a glimpse of the outlaw's bullet-ridden corpse lying on a cold marble slab. After a coroner's inquest the body of Larry DeVol, who had been positively identified through use of fingerprints, was transported by rail back to Minneapolis, Minnesota, where his body was cremated by his next of kin. In a formal statement to the press, J. Edger Hoover claimed Mr. DeVol was, "Evil incarnate and his death is a relief to all lawmen and honest citizens throughout the Midwest."

"Pretty Boy" Floyd – The Phantom of the Cookson Hills

For better or worse, bank bandit Charley "Pretty Boy" Floyd is now noted as one of Oklahoma's most famous sons. Amongst Oklahomans, he is credited with a higher name recognition factor than any other resident past or present with the exception of Will Rogers or perhaps Mickey Mantle. During his lifetime, the handsome outlaw evolved into an iconic figure attaining folk hero status amongst the state's poor and downtrodden, especially those living in the rural areas. The flamboyant outlaw's attacks upon financial institutions throughout the state during the depression-era were interpreted by a majority of the region's rural poor as an act of retribution against the oppressive ruling class. Tens of thousands of demoralized dirt farmers who had lost everything from farmhouse to outhouse due to widespread bank foreclosures on farms across the state rallied to the desperados cause following his exploits with keen interest via radio and newsprint, some even going as far as directly providing him refuge from the law. Although a reward of over $5,000 was posted for his capture, dead or alive, there were no takers.

During the early 1930s, stories of Floyd's financially assisting the state's oppressed sharecroppers and struggling farmers with cash gifts as well as burning unregistered mortgages during his bank jobs began to appear. How much truth there are to these stories we will never know since over time the legend has overtaken the man. While some, including FBI chief J. Edger Hoover, openly characterized the bandit as a "Dirty yellow rat," others, including songwriter Woody Guthrie, who paid him homage in, "The Balled of Pretty Boy Floyd," thought of him as a modern day Jesse James-like

"Robin Hood" figure, who supposedly robbed the rich in order to give to the poor. Floyd once penned a note to Acting Governor Robert Burns insisting he only robbed, "monied men."

Like Jesse James, the charismatic outlaw seemed to enjoy making a spectacle of his self during robberies, leaping over bank counters in a melodramatic fashion while cracking jokes with his victims. Strangely, he never directly robbed a customer or private citizen during his many hold-ups, instead being satisfied with whatever cash the bank had in its coffers. He also generally showed a good deal of respect to females and the elderly encountered during his heists. Witnesses report his addressing

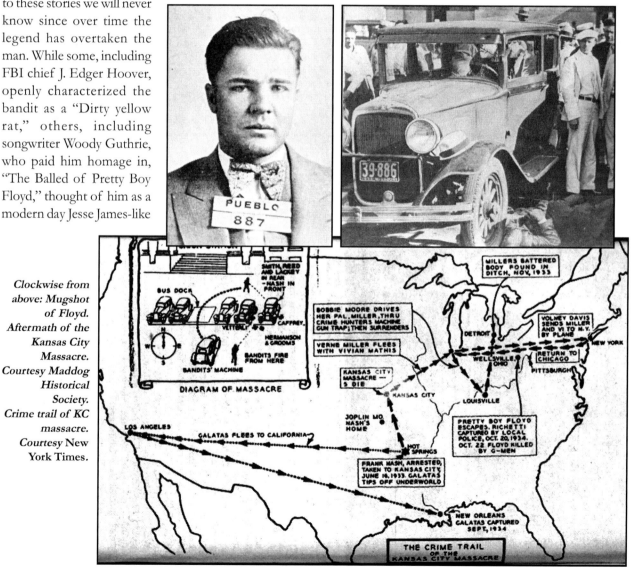

Clockwise from above: Mugshot of Floyd. Aftermath of the Kansas City Massacre. Courtesy Maddog Historical Society. Crime trail of KC massacre. Courtesy New York Times.

female victims as "Ma'am," "Sister," "Grandma," and "Mother" depending on their age. When speaking to older males he good-naturally referred to them as "Dad" or "Grandpa." While departing a robbery, he oftentimes threw quarter and half-dollar coins to assembled crowds of undernourished and poorly clothed children, providing a moment of hope in their otherwise meager lives.

There are several stories as to how the ruggedly handsome and seemingly, fashion conscious outlaw (he oftentimes donned stylish suits along with a silk shirt and tie, topped off with a spiffy fedora and sporting silk underwear, which was the rage of the day) received his nickname. One version implies he was so dubbed by a Kansas City madam while another states he was misidentified by St. Louis authorities as "Pretty Boy" Smith (another bank robber operating around the same time frame).

Charley Arthur Floyd was born in Georgia in 1904 the son of hard-rock Baptist farmers. His family moved to Hanson, Oklahoma, in 1911 where they took up farming. They again relocated a few years later to a farm near the small Sequoyah County community of Akins. The future badman quit school in order to work in the fields at age thirteen. At seventeen, he joined a legion of young men traveling to Kansas to work the seasonal wheat harvest in order to earn some hard money.

Like many other Cookson Hills youths, he learned the art of whiskey

Clockwise from above: Floyd and wife. Courtesy Tulsa World.
McAlester Chief of Police Orin "Ott" Reed, slain in KC massacre. Courtesy Rick Mattix.
Grave of Otto Reed in McAlester. Photo by Naomi Morgan.
Wanted poster issued by FBI concerning "Pretty Boy" Floyd. Author's collection.

making at an early age. Over time, he adapted a taste for a local variety of homemade brew dubbed "Choctaw" beer, a thick, malty, highly fermented substance made of barley, hops, dried fruit, berries, raisons, and sometimes flavored with a pinch of plug tobacco. He enjoyed the brew so much in fact; his pals nicknamed him "Choc."

In 1922, he and another boy burglarized the post office in Akins for a piddling sum. He was questioned about the robbery but the authorities failed to garner enough evidence to charge him with the crime. On June 28, 1924, Floyd married a local girl named Ruby Hardgraves and fathered a son the pair named Charles Dempsey Floyd. The following year he quit the farm and traveled to St. Louis, Missouri, in hopes of finding a good paying job but instead fell into bad company. He and a fellow named Fred Hildebrand went on a crime spree robbing several businesses in the area including a Kroger's Grocery payroll. He was apprehended when he returned to Sallisaw, driving a new car, his pockets flush with cash.

In December 1925, he was convicted of armed robbery and sentenced to a five-year hitch at the Missouri State Penitentiary in Jeff City. On March 7, 1929, Floyd was released from the joint and drifted to Kansas City where he was arrested for vagrancy and suspicion of highway robbery. Upon his release from custody, the unsettled young man traveled to Pueblo, Colorado, where he was again arrested for vagrancy. Soon afterwards, Floyd returned to Kansas City where he was immediately detained when lawmen searching his hotel room discovered two revolvers and a pint of illegal 'Hooch." He was questioned and released.

In November, his father was killed in a backwoods hill feud of sorts. A month later, Floyd was involved in a confrontation with detectives in Kansas City but es-caped unharmed. Fleeing the area, he made his way to Ohio where he joined forces with some local thugs and on February 5, 1930, robbed the Farmers and Merchants Bank of Sylvania for $1,720 but was soon captured in nearby Toledo and charged with the hold-up. Soon after his conviction for bank robbery, the budding outlaw was placed on a passenger train bound for the state prison in Columbus. During the trip, he dramatically escaped custody by leaping from a lavatory window of the moving train, eventually making his way back to Oklahoma.

On March 9, 1931, Floyd, Bill "The Killer" Miller, and a local bootlegger named George Birdwell knocked off the Bank of Earlsboro for $3,000. Days later, Floyd and Miller left the area traveling to Kansas City where they were suspected of involvement in the execution style slaying of two brothers named Wallace and William Ash.

Cartoon. Courtesy Muskogee Times-Democrat.

Police made the assumption the two siblings had been 'rubbed out' as the result of a classic "underworld contract" due to the pair's perceived status as police informants.

In early April, Floyd and Miller robbed the banks of Elliston, Kentucky, and Whitehouse, Ohio. On April 16, the pair was involved in a gunfight with officers in Bowling Green, Ohio, in which Miller was killed along with Officer Ralph Castor. Floyd escaped unharmed making his way back to Kansas City where he was suspected of shooting and killing a federal prohibition agent as well as an innocent bystander during a liquor raid. Returning to Oklahoma, the outlaw, along with his old partner George Birdwell began an extraordinary assault on a series of undersized oilfield banks beginning with the bank in Shamrock on August 4, and then holding up financial institutions in Mor-

WANTED

FOR BANK ROBBERY AND MURDER IN OKLAHOMA.

Charles Arthur (Pretty Boy) Floyd. Age 27 years; 5 feet, 8½ inches tall; weight 170#; muscular build; medium complexion; grey eyes; vaccination scar on left arm; tatoo of Red Cross Nurse on left arm.

George Birdwell, who works with Floyd. 38 years old; 5 feet, 10 or 11 inches tall; weight 160#; sandy or light brown hair; has high cheek bones; wears a small hat on back of his head; walks like a texas cowboy, that is takes short steps.

Charles Floyd

The above men are dangerous characters and officers should be notified that they will shoot on sight.

Any information as to the whereabouts of the above two men should be given to the State Bureau of Criminal Investigation and Identification, State Capital Bldg., Oklahoma City, Okla.

Clockwise from above: Bill "The Killer" Miller. Courtesy Maddog Historical Society. Headline concerning the burial of George Birdwell. Courtesy Seminole Producer. Wanted poster, which appeared in various Midwest newspapers concerning Floyd and Birdwell. Courtesy Michael Webb. George Birdwell (in center) with a pair of acquaintances. Courtesy Michael Webb. Adam Richetti mug shot. Courtesy Missouri State Penitentiary.

ris (twice in three months), Maud, Konawa, and Earlsboro (a repeat performance).

The pair's simple but efficient mode of operations consisted of Birdwell dramatically entering the bank armed with a machinegun, taking up a station in the lobby where he could provide cover for Floyd, who would sud-

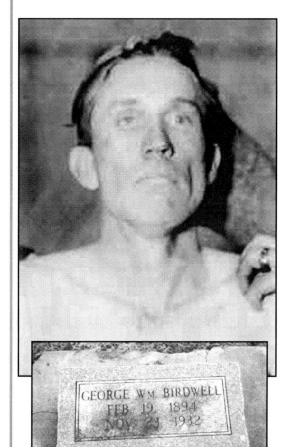

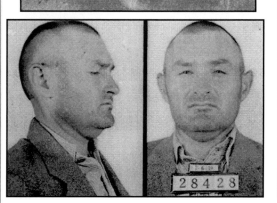

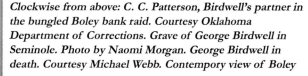

Clockwise from above: C. C. Patterson, Birdwell's partner in the bungled Boley bank raid. Courtesy Oklahoma Department of Corrections. Grave of George Birdwell in Seminole. Photo by Naomi Morgan. George Birdwell in death. Courtesy Michael Webb. Contempory view of Boley bank building where Birdwell was slain. Photo by Naomi Morgan. Contemparary view of Tulsa residence on Young Street where Floyd and Birdwell were nearly captured. Photo by Naomi Morgan. Death certificate of George Birdwell. Courtesy Maggie Birdwell.

denly make his appearance, boldly rushing the teller's counter menacingly waving a pistol about while vigorously demanding the loot. Their "shock and awe" tactics not only proved effective, but painless, the duo never having to pull the trigger during any of their numerous bank raids. Upon completion of the heist the pair would either flee to one of Birdwell's many hideouts in the Central Oklahoma oilfields where the pair were shielded by an army of sympathetic working-class citizens or seek sanctuary in the heavily forested Cookson Hills where Floyd possessed a lifelong familiarity with every hill, holler, cave, and trail. Over time, a legion of lawmen, bounty hunters, and vigilantes entered the hills posing as traveling salesmen, drifters, and sportsmen in hopes of collecting the mounting rewards offered for the badman's capture. None caught even a parting glimpse of the slippery outlaw who moved about the hills like a silent phantom in the night. Clannish hillfolk, living in crude dogtrot cabins located in or near remote backwater mountain settlements, gladly offered him safe haven from his pursuers.

In early 1932, the pair robbed the bank in Castle for $2,600. They were also incorrectly accused of robbing the bank at nearby Paden, an event that had occurred on the same day. There was such an uproar over this particular double bank robbery that incredible pressure was put on Oklahoma's governor to call out the National Guard to join the search for the pair of willow-o-wisp bandits. Soon after the Castle job the bandit was mixed up in a running gunfight on the busy streets of Tulsa but successfully evaded capture. On March 23, the dangerous duo looted the Bank of Meeker for $700.

On the night of April 9, Floyd shot and killed ex-McIntosh County Sheriff turned bounty hunter Erv Kelley near Bixby. Several weeks after the Kelley killing he and Birdwell purportedly robbed the First State Bank of Stonewall for $600. On June 7, the ruthless duo was nearly captured in a shootout near Stonewall but once again miraculously escaped custody. In early November, Floyd

Clockwise from left: Pretty Boy Floyd, a phenomenon of the times, with unidentified woman. Author's collection. Floyd and wife, Ruby, with a friend. Author's collection. Charley Floyd and companion. Courtesy Muskogee Times-Democrat.

returned to his hometown accompanied by the ever-faithful Birdwell and a young gunsel named Aussie Elliott where the trio looted the Sallisaw State Bank of $2,530. When the audacious bandit paused a few moments before entering the bank to greet a hastily assembled mob of rubberneckers, he was cheered and treated like a conquering hero. Shouts of "Give 'em hell, Choc!" were heard emitting from the crowd.

During 1931-32, Floyd was mistakenly suspected of committing dozens of robberies big and small, some as far away as California. On November 23, 1932, Birdwell struck out on his own joining forces with C. C. Patterson and a Negro named Charley Glass in an attempt to loot a bank located in the all-black town of Boley. The raid was a catastrophe. Birdwell and Glass were slain by vigilantes after Birdwell brutally murdered banker D. J. Turner when the gutsy teller set off

an alarm. Patterson was gunned down and captured when he attempted to flee the scene. It was rumored by many that Floyd attended his partner's funeral at Seminole dressed as a woman despite of the presence of host of armed officers. After Birdwell's death, the outlaw went into deep hiding for a period of nearly two years. Various rumors have placed him with the John Dillinger Gang

Clockwise from above: Members of the Ohio posse who killed Floyd. Courtesy Rick Mattix. Newspaper headlines reporting the Great 1934 Cookson Hills Raid. By the time the two-day raid ended, nearly 1,000 officers and National Guardsmen were involved in the search for Floyd as well as members of the Ford Bradshaw Gang. Author's collection. The Conkle farmhouse where Floyd ate his last meal. Courtesy Rick Mattix.

during this period while others imply he either traveled to Cleveland, Ohio, where he worked as muscle for the local mob or bootlegged whiskey in the Kansas City area. Still other stories have him masterminding numerous bank robberies partnering-up with a bevy of lesser-known Oklahoma bandits such as Shine Rush, Coleman Rickerson, and 'Blackie' Smalley.

In June of 1933, Floyd and his new partner, Adam Richetti, were named the chief suspects in the so-called Kansas City Massacre, an event in which a group of assassins mercilessly slew four law officers, including McAlester Chief of Police Otto Reed and the prisoner they were escorting through the parking lot of Kansas City's Union Station Rail Depot. Although Richetti was later convicted and executed for his part in the cop-killings, there is to this day great controversy as to what role Floyd actually played in the gruesome event. What is known of Floyd's movements after the massacre is that in September of 1933, he rented an apartment in Buffalo, New York. In early 1934, police informants reported he was hiding out in a cave near Marble City, Oklahoma. An army of lawmen hailing from Oklahoma, Kansas, and Arkansas, accompanied by several hundred National Guardsmen, launched a massive raid involving some 700 to 1,000 personal into the notorious

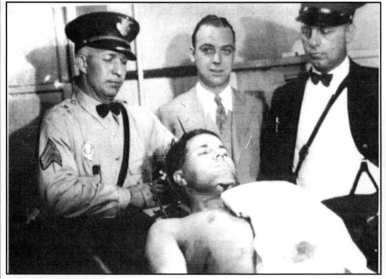

Clockwise from left: Headline concerning Floyd's death. Muskogee Phoenix. Floyd on the slab in Ohio. Courtesy Maddog Historical Society. Grave of Charley Floyd near Akins. Photo by Naomi Morgan.

Clockwise from above: Grave of Ruby Floyd at Bixby. Photo by Naomi Morgan. Grave of E. W. Floyd, the outlaw's brother who took a different trail in life. Photo by Naomi Morgan. Floyd's wife, Ruby, and child, while touring for a "Crime doesn't pay" show. Courtesy Tulsa World.

eating a hearty dinner of pork chops and fruit cobbler he paid the lady of the house a dollar for the vittles before strolling outside where he was spotted by Purvis and company from the road. When the badman attempted to flee on foot across an open field he was shot down. On approaching the bleeding badman, lawmen demanded to know if he had been involved in the Kansas City Massacre. The dying outlaw breathlessly informed them; "I ain't telling you bastards nothing!" The Phantom of the Cookson Hills had met his end. At the time of his death, the badman was wanted for his suspected involvement in a dozen bank robberies and eleven murders.

On searching the outlaw's clothes, agents reported finding a Gruen pocket watch with ten notches scratched on its gold case. Floyd's body was returned to Oklahoma by rail from Ohio where an estimated 30,000 mostly dirt-poor farmers attended his funeral at the small Akins Cemetery. The event was noted as the largest private funeral in Oklahoma history.

Ironically, Floyd's brother, E. W., chose an opposite path in life, serving twenty-two years as the Sheriff of Sequoyah County. The outlaw's longsuffering wife remarried several times and died of cancer at a Broken Arrow nursing home in 1970.

Cookson Hills in an effort to flush out the badman as well as members of the Ford Bradshaw and Barrow Gangs from cover. The oversized raid was largely unsuccessful only yielding arrests of a few nominal bootleggers and petty criminals. The big boys like Floyd and Bradshaw slipped the net.

In October, Floyd and Richetti, accompanied by two female gun molls, departed their New York apartment via automobile heading back to Oklahoma. Around Wellsville, Ohio, their car smashed into a telephone pole in the fog. Sending the girls hitchhiking down the road to fetch a wrecker, the pair made camp on a hillside but were soon spotted by a curious farmer who phoned the law. When several officers attempted to question the pair, Floyd opened fire wounding one of the laws before fleeing the area while Richetti was quickly subdued. Within hours of the shooting, Floyd was identified and an army of lawmen including a group of FBI agents led by the legendary Melvin Purvis arrived on the scene. After several days on the dodge, Floyd, who had recently been named Public Enemy #1 by J. Edger Hoover, sought refuge on a farm owned by a family named Conkle. After

The Unluckiest Bank in Oklahoma: The Morris Robberies

On the morning of September 8, 1931, twenty-two year-old Clara Aggas arrived at Morris State Bank where she worked as a bookkeeper. Her fellow workers Graham Smith and H. L. Mullins greeted the young lady with a nod and a smile. At approximately 8 a.m., a black Model "A" Ford car parked in front of the financial institution. Two men, one described as stout (later identified as Charley Floyd), the other tall and gangly (George Birdwell) entered the bank through the front door. Suddenly, Smith, who was standing on a step-stool resetting the wall clock in the lobby felt a hard jab in the ribs followed by a gruff demand of, "Get off there!" The banker turned to observe a man holding a pistol pointed at his backside. Smith later stated, "I was so scared I don't remember if I fell, slid or jumped off that chair." The three bank employees were ordered to stand against the wall and told, "Do as your told and everyone will be happy but the insurance company," by Birdwell while Floyd rifled the tills for $800 before entering the open vault which contained another $1,000 in cash along with $300 in gold coins. Placing the gold coins on the counter Floyd ordered the employees into the vault and closed the steel door. Before leaving, Floyd requested the bankers to be "sporting" and give him a five-minute head start. In their haste to exit the bank, the pair not only left the gold on the counter but also dropped fifty dollars in change on the floor. In the aftermath of the robbery, witnesses spotted the Model "A" heading south at a leisurely pace. The owner of the "Y" filling station, located just south of town, reported the pair of bandits had bought gas and cigars at his station an hour before the robbery. The little town hadn't seen this much excitement since a pair of "Yeggmen" had attempted to burglarize the First State Bank back in 1914. On that occasion, two individuals broke into the bank under the cover of darkness and attempted to set

off a charge of nitro-glycerin attached to the heavy safe door. Apparently they misjudged the amount of 'juice' needed to blow the door, the ensuing explosion blasted the bank's exterior north wall to bits starting a fire that quickly consumed the entire building as well as a neighboring grocery store.

When interviewed by Okmulgee County Sheriff Jim Stormont, Banker Smith stated, "The short bandit (Floyd) was rather jovial about the whole thing. He never actually threatened anyone but you could tell he meant business. This fellow was obviously no novice at the business of hijacking."

Just two days before Christmas a black late model Ford Sport Coup pulled to the side of the Morris bank. Two individuals dressed in Khaki and donning broad-brimmed fedoras slowly lighted from the rig making their way into the financial institution that was occupied by its three regular full-time employees as well as four customers. Mr. Smith, sitting at his desk going over some figures, glanced up thinking the pair looked familiar. Charley Floyd and his pal had come calling again. Floyd, armed with a Colt automatic pistol, inquired of Smith, "How's business since we were last here?" Smith just shook his head at the gall of the cheery bandit. The outlaw strolled into the lobby surveying the establishment while Birdwell whipped out a submachine gun from under a loose fitting overcoat.

According to Mr. Smith and other witnesses, Birdwell, with a big smile on his face, announced, " Hi boys, we're back for a return engagement." Floyd leaped over the counter quickly scooping up the dough putting it in a large flour sack while informing everyone to "Stand still and shut up." Birdwell commented to the crowd "You're following orders better than the last time and I appreciate that." After gathering up $1,100 in cash and coin, Floyd flippantly stated "We are just taking up a collection for needy orphans and widows for Christmas." While the customers broke into giggles on hearing the remark, the bankers scowled, failing to see the rumor in the remark.

On completion of the heist the collection of witnesses were forced to walk in front of the bandits to their car where Mullins and Smith were ordered to hop on the car's sideboards and told to "Hang on tight." The rob-

Troy Kittrell. Courtesy Oklahoma Department of Corrections.

The late Graham Smith, age ninety, at the time of this photo. Graham was twice robbed by "Pretty Boy" Floyd in his youth. Photo by Naomi Morgan.

bers drove slowly out of town through a crowd of on-lookers who had gathered in front of the bank. Floyd greeted the curious crowd with a tip of his hat and a "Howdy fellers. Stay back now so no one will get hurt." The two hostages were vigorously booted off the running car a mile outside of town.

From all indications, the town marshal followed the bandit's car out of town at a respectful distance. He claimed he "Lost 'em." Although lawmen were notified and roadblocks were set up and area bridges guarded the bandits managed a clean getaway. Floyd was seen a few days later in nearby Haskell getting a haircut with the ever present George Birdwell standing guard just down the street sitting on a bench. According to old-timers, the town law stuck his head out of his office and got into a staring contest with Birdwell who silently shook his head no. The lawman reportedly blinked. There was no trouble in Haskell that day.

The town of Morris once again survived the robbery. However, the events had humiliated the city fathers, local laws, and citizenry. The bank's insurance company was upset to the point of apoplexy. At an emergency meeting of the town council, plans were formulated to defend the bank against further raids. An alarm was installed in the building, local businessmen were requested to bring firearms to work and were assigned shooting positions in the event of another hijacking. The good people of Morris vowed the next time would not be so easy.

The weather report for Morris on May 27, 1932 was described as a high of 72 degrees with little wind and no precipitation. Nevertheless, a storm was about to envelop the little village, which would be remembered for decades.

Around noon three cheap two-bit thieves who had been

Above: Heroine Clara Aggas. Courtesy Okmulgee Public Library. Right: Floyd, wife, and son at Fort Smith, Arkansas hideout. Author's collection.

on a week-long drunken crime spree pulled up to the Morris bank driving a stolen Ford Victoria Coup. The trio was later identified as Troy Kittrell, Roscoe "Red" Ernest and his brother Tom. While Kittrell and Tom Ernest entered the bank that was occupied solely by Clara Aggas, Red Ernest remained at the wheel of the getaway car. Walking behind the counter with guns drawn, the pair ordered Miss Aggas to "Fork over the cash." The plucky lass complied with the demand but not before setting off the burglar alarm, which could be heard on the street. She then commenced to fill the money sacks as slow as possible in order to give the townspeople time to turn their guns on the bank. After the duo rounded up roughly $1,100 in cash and coin, they forced Clara to accompany the bandits to their getaway car to act as a human shield.

Outside in the street Marshal I. Z. Thompson, hearing the alarm, hurried to the neighborhood gas station to retrieve his 32-70 Winchester rifle, which he stashed there in case of just this sort of event before racing to the rear of the station, a position which offered a commanding view of the bank's front door. Meanwhile, Bayron Skinner, the station's owner and Clara's fiancé, armed himself with a shotgun and joined the marshal. Across the street, the owner of the hardware store, Forrest Bradley, ran up

the stairs of his business rifle in hand in order to man a spot at a window overlooking the bank. Several other citizens answered the call to arms quickly taking up stations at their assigned positions.

Suddenly, Red Ernest, noticing Marshal Thompson at the rear of the nearby gas station, raised his shotgun taking a potshot at the officer shattering a plate glass window the lawman was standing under. Thompson, cut by flying glass and shotgun pellets, withdrew from his position to collect his senses. Bradley, observing the action from above the hardware store, reacted by firing two rounds from his 30-30 cal. rifle at the bandit below. The second shot took effect sending the gunman slumping into the front car seat suffering from a gaping head wound.

Meanwhile, the other two hijackers began making their way toward the getaway car, Miss Aggas in tow. All of a sudden, multiple gunshots erupted. Just a few feet from the car door Miss Aggas fell to the ground after being shot in the jaw and shoulder. The two bandits picked her up and pushed her into the rig's back seat before shoving their fallen comrade from the front to the rear seat as well. Just then, a group of bystanders began screaming at the officers and vigilantes to cease fire for fear of further injuring the young teller.

Taking advantage of the lull in the storm the bandits put the pedal to the metal motoring out of town at a rapid clip unmolested. They drove seven miles south to Grayson where they turned west on the Coalton Road. After traveling a few more miles, the bandits turned north on to a dirt lumber road traversing through the heavily forested Deep Fork River bottoms to a point near Flag Lake where the two surviving desperadoes abandoned Miss Aggas and their obviously dead companion making their way on foot into the surrounding thickets. The badly wounded and terrorized bank teller slowly inched her way over the corpse of the dead gunman, exited the car and staggered onto the dirt lane where she agonizingly crawled several hundred yards to the main road before collapsing in a bloody heap. Fortunately, for Clara, Bayron Skinner and a friend, Carl Bay, immediately took up the search for the missing cashier. Skinner later stated, "I just rode in circles until I luckily spotted Clara along the side of the road." Skinner and his partner loaded Miss Clara into his vehicle and sped to the Okmulgee Hospital. Although a massive manhunt was undertaken, nothing was seen of the two missing robbers.

After a brief investigation, lawmen were able to identify the bandits, informing the press, "The Ernest boys are two-bit thugs who may have recently robbed the bank at Shamrock." The robber's car containing the blood-soaked corpse of Red Ernest was towed into Okmulgee. The bullet-ridden car was put on exhibit at the Okmulgee City Hall where the town elders charged a nickel to view the rig. The money was given to the Oklahoma Unemployment Fund. The body was later put on display at the Ward Funeral Home. Throughout the night and the following day, a long line made up of hundreds of curious citizens viewed the dead bandit. At city hospital, surgeons reconstructed Miss Clara's shattered jaw and treated the bullet wound to her shoulder. While she was initially listed in critical condition the gutsy teller would survive and go on to marry her rescuer.

Several weeks after the robbery Troy Kittrell was arrested in Detroit, Michigan, and extradited back to Oklahoma where he was convicted of bank robbery and sentenced to twenty-five years in prison. Tom Ernest was finally captured several years later. The Oklahoma Bankers Association paid a $500 'Dead or Alive' reward to the slayers of Red Ernest.

The Morris State Bank was again held-up in 1978 of $5,000. In that instance, the robbers were quickly rounded up and the stolen cash returned. In 1984, the financial institution was destroyed by a massive tornado. The catastrophic storm killed nine and injured dozens. Oklahoma's unluckiest bank was promptly rebuilt and the financial institution prospers today.

The Death of Erv Kelley

By February 1932, officers tracked the wife of "Pretty Boy" Floyd to a Tulsa address where she and their young son were residing under phony names. The home was immediately put under surveillance. On the night of February 7, lawmen spotted Floyd and his deadly sidekick, George Birdwell, attempting to pay a visit. A gunfight followed by a high-speed chase ensued but the slippery pair again escaped the grip of the law. Investigators Erv Kelley and A. B. Cooper, both working for the Oklahoma Bankers Association, promptly began shadowing Floyd's wife. By this time, a $5,000 cash reward had been offered for the outlaw's capture. On the afternoon of April 8, Ruby Floyd, accompanied by her son, drove to

Erv Kelley, Ex-Checotah Chief of Police and McIntosh County Sheriff turned bounty hunter, slain by "Pretty Boy" Floyd. Author's private collection.

her father's two-room "Shotgun" style home located near Bixby where he worked as a sharecropper for a farmer named Cecil Bennett who lived nearby. On questioning several neighbors, investigators confirmed the phantom bandit had been seen rendezvousing with his wife at the farm in the past. That night a posse made up of Mark Lairmore, Kelley, A.M. Smith, Jim Stormont, Crockett Long, Cooper, and a pal of Kelley's named William Counts met at Lairmore's home in Tulsa to make final preparations for the upcoming raid. Later that night the lawmen drove to the Bennett farm in several cars and set the trap. While Kelley and a pair of recently deputized farmers took stations be-

hind a chicken house located near a gate on the lane that snaked past the Bennett residence on its way to the home of Ruby's father, a second collection of officer's set-up just down the road at a schoolhouse. A third group manned a roadblock a quarter mile south of the Bennett farm at a crossroads. For nearly six hours the lawmen sat transfixed, exposed to the damp foggy night air watching for movement, donning their coats, and stamping their feet to stay warm. A coal oil lamp could be seen shining through a window of the shotgun shack until it was extinguished around midnight.

Around 2 a.m., the laws decided to call it a night and drive into Bixby to an all-night diner for hot coffee and sandwiches. Kelley told the others to go ahead but insisted he would stay at his position for another hour or so. The pair of deputized farmers accompanying Kelley decided to remain with him. Kelley's friend, Bill Counts,

Clockwise from above: Grave of Erv Kelley at Checotah cemetery. Photo by Naomi Morgan. Home of Ruby Floyd's parents located near Bixby. Courtesy Tulsa World. Agent Crockett Long. Courtesy Dennis Lippe and the Oklahoma Law Enforcement Memorial. Modern-day view of spot where Kelley was slain, near Bixby. Photo by Naomi Morgan.

Modern day view of Stonewall bank robbed by Floyd and Birdwell. Photo by Naomi Morgan.

also elected to wait at his position located some 500 yards north of the farm. At a few minutes before 3 a.m., Kelley heard the faint rumbling of an automobile. The car, a green Chevy sedan with the headlights turned off, occupied by a driver and a passenger motored up the lane stopping at a wooden gate located near Kelley's position. When a stocky individual exited the vehicle attempting to open the gate, Kelley, in a suicidal gesture, stepped into the middle of the road with a machinegun cradled in his arms standing a mere eight feet from the vehicle demanding the pair identify themselves. Suddenly, the car's driver popped on the headlights fully illuminating the lawman, turning him into a veritable "Sitting Duck." Both George Birdwell, who was positioned behind the wheel, and Floyd, standing just outside the rig's front passenger door, immediately reacted to Kelley's presence by opening fire with .45 automatic pistols riddling the officer. While falling to the ground, Kelley squeezed the trigger of the chopper releasing nearly a full drum of bullets into the ground. Several rounds ricocheted off the road nicking Floyd in the leg and groin area while the rest harmlessly imbedded into the earth forming a half circle pattern in the ground. The farmers, standing guard nearby, promptly discarded their guns and fled into the darkness in fear for their lives. The two gunmen leaped back into the Chevy and abruptly reversed into a barbwire fence before spinning gravel heading back to the main road.

Meanwhile, William Counts, manning his distant post, sprang into action when he heard two separate loud booms followed by what sounded to him like a string of exploding firecrackers. Counts jumped into his car and headed toward Kelley's station. Suddenly, he noticed the taillights of a car traveling at a high rate of speed heading in a southerly direction. On arriving at Kelley's position, he found his friend prostrate on the ground in a pool of blood. He had been struck five times, mainly in the chest and arms. The clip for his "Tommy gun," which had a capacity of 21 rounds, was nearly empty. Incidentally, it was later discovered that while Kelley was known to have always worn a steel vest on the job, for some unknown reason on that fateful night he had not. Some 3000 persons attended Kelley's funeral. Muskogee County Sheriff V. S. Cannon, who had collaborated with the officer on many manhunts over the years, eulogized him as, " The greatest officer I ever rode with." Bill Counts informed newsmen, "Erv gave those vermin a break and that's what got him killed." Shortly after Kelley's violent demise, his widow was issued a $50 check by the Oklahoma Bankers Association for services rendered.

The day after the shootout, Floyd's wife was interviewed by a reporter from the *Tulsa World*. When informed Kelley had been trailing her husband for three months before the shootout, she laughingly replied: "Well, that son of a bitch won't trail him any longer, will he?"

Decades later Floyd's aged brother-in-law stated in an interview, "A few months before Charley was killed in Ohio he commented to me, 'That Kelley fellow just plain committed suicide stepping out into those headlights and calling us out.'"

Charley Floyd and the Stonewall Raid

Just weeks after the slaying of Erv Kelley, Charley Floyd, and George Birdwell motored to the town of Stonewall, located in south-central Oklahoma, parking their green sedan in front of the First State Bank. As was their habit, the pair preferred to do business at high noon when most folks were home for lunch and skeleton crews usually manned banks. The pair entered the bank ordering the employees and one customer to line up against the wall. Floyd then scooped up roughly $600 from the tills before departing the building with Bankers Furman Gibson and Ed Sallee forced to walk to their front acting as human shields, thus cutting down on the chances of some trigger-happy local hero taking a pot shot at the outlaws.

In the meantime, a crowd of curious citizens gathered in front of the bank rubbernecking to get a view of the two bankers being forced on to the getaway car's running boards before the bandits leisurely motored out of town. At the city limits, the hostages were ordered to jump off the moving car. A stiff boot in the ass by Birdwell backed up the order. A posse was hurriedly formed and sent to the field but failed to catch sight of the fleeing bandits.

An hour after the hold-up a young man named Estel Henson, who had witnessed the robbery from a nearby filling station, was racing down the Ada road on his trusty motorcycle when he suddenly spotted a car parked by the highway manned by two men. A stocky-built individual was sitting behind the wheel while a second man squatted on the running board calmly smoking a cigarette. Assuming they were part of the manhunt, Henson parked his motorbike and approached the pair on foot. He suddenly halted when the stout man leaped out of the car with a pistol in hand saying, "Whoa Hoss, where you think your going?" After explaining his mission, the boy was told, "You better come with us." Leaving his bike racked on the roadside, the lad entered the car sitting in the passenger side of the front seat while the second fellow took a position directly behind him in the backseat. He was quickly informed he was in the company of Charley Floyd and George Birdwell.

A few miles down the road, Floyd, who was driving, noticed they were being followed. He pulled to the side of the highway ordering Henson to lie in the ditch saying, "No sense you getting hurt, boy." "Pretty Boy" quickly withdrew a machine gun from the car and calmly laid its barrel on the fender squeezing off a burst while his companion started popping off rounds from a high-powered rifle at a brisk pace in the direction of the pursing vehicle, which promptly veered off the road crashing into the ditch. The occupants of the car swiftly baled out of the rig running for tall timber. One of the occupants later told reporters he turned back to look at the shooters and noticed they had burst into laughter and

knee-slapping hysterics over their predicament.

With the roadway now clear, the bandits drove into the heavily timbered Canadian River bottoms following a series of dirt roads. At a spot located somewhere between the towns of Allen and Atwood the trio stopped and spent the night, camouflaging their car with tree limbs so as not to be seen from the air. After dining on a meal of potted meat and soda crackers followed up by several shots of moonshine, the trio called it an evening. Early the following morning the bandits departed the area leaving young Henson with a collection of exciting memories and a dollar bill as a souvenir. Henson walked back to civilization informing the posse and the media he would not have turned in the bandits for $10,000 since they had treated him "Square" in his opinion. Later that day the

Top: A.W. Echols and his home near Stonewall where Floyd and Birdwell were involved in shootout with authorities. Courtesy Master Detective. *Above: Barn located on the Echols farm located near Stonewall where Floyd and Birdwell once hid. Courtesy* Master Detective.

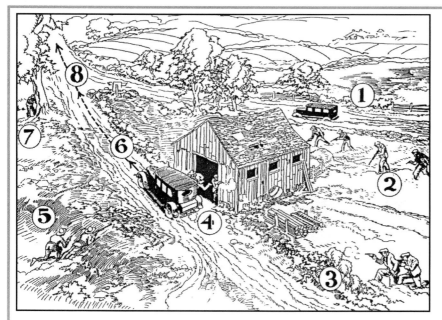

Sketch of Echols farm and raid. Courtesy Master Detective.

lowed the cops at a distance taking stations on a hillside overlooking the Echols farm in order to watch the show. When the sheriff called out to the outlaws to surrender, he was answered with a burst of automatic weapons fire, which sent the lawmen to ground. The bandits then ran to the barn where their car was parked and within moments, the vehicle in question came barreling out of the building heading down the lane gunfire spitting from the rear window. Dozens of .45 rounds sputtered and danced over the officer's heads striking the trees on a nearby hillside, forcing the assembled crowd of curious citizens to flee the area. That's when the best laid plans of the lawmen turned into a comedy of errors.

Obviously grown faint of heart from hearing the angry buzz of a host of lead projectiles snapping past their ears, the officers retreated with their tails between their legs into the woods in order to regroup. Taking advantage of the calm, Ellis Echols herded his family into a storm shelter located in the backyard of his little house. Driving down the farm lane Floyd and Birdwell occasionally noticed a man jump out from cover just long enough to fire a round then flee back into the timber. Birdwell reacted by leaping to of the car's running board and hosing down his tormenters with his machinegun. On reaching a gate, which opened onto the highway, Birdwell got out and opened the gate and, as unbelievable as it sounds, waited for his partner to drive out on to the road before closing and securing the gate. Now that's a true farm boy for you, being courteous enough to properly secure a cattle gate in the middle of a firefight.

Just as the pair was about to exit onto the highway driving on three rims and flattened tires, out of the blue drove up young Estel Henson riding his trusty motorcycle hoping to chew the fat with his new found friends. Birdwell cut loose a solid burst of lead over the youth's head causing him to hit the ditch. Henson later claimed the bandits would not have shot at him if he had been recognized.

The Great Stonewall shootout ended without any-

outlaw's green sedan was sighted by pilot Wiley Post from the air but by the time lawmen arrived in the area they could discover no sign of the rig.

On June 7, a Stonewall farmer named Ellis Echols, who had once befriended George Birdwell while both men were working in the Earlsboro oilfields, heard a knock on the door of his home, which was located less than a mile from town. Echols came to the door and immediately recognized Birdwell, who was accompanied by a stranger. The pair requested a place to stay for a couple of days. They offered to pay and since times were hard, the farmer readily agreed to the proposition. While the arrangement made by Mr. Echols may have been fine and dandy with him, it evidently was not to the liking of his wife, who after observing her husband lay around the barn hours on end with the strangers sipping "Wildcat" whiskey while the cotton needed hoeing, walked to town and informed the laws of the outlaw's presence.

Pontotoc County Sheriff L. E. Franklin promptly began raising a posse to make a raid. Included in the group were Agents Crocket Long, C. M. Reber, and O.P. Ray of the state bureau of investigation. The lawmen got their heads together and came up with a detailed plan of attack. Later that day nine heavily armed officers approached the Echols barn on foot. When news of the raid leaked out, a crowd of town folks gathered and fol-

one receiving so much as a scratch despite the depletion of so many heated rounds being fired. When officers attempted to follow the fugitives, their cars became hopelessly stuck in the mud. Members of the hapless posse later informed newsmen that Floyd and Birdwell must have been wearing bulletproof vests and steel skullcaps since they were certain they had shot the pair repeatedly during the ambush.

The Urschel Kidnapping

On July 22, 1933, millionaire oilman Charles F. Urschel was kidnapped from his Oklahoma City mansion by a gang led by George "Machine Gun" Kelly (real name George Kelly Barnes). The kidnappers transported Urschel, who was married to the widow of oil-magnet Tom Slick, to an isolated ranch owned by Kelly's in-laws located near Paradise, Texas, for safekeeping. The kidnap gang was made up of Kelly, his wife Kathryn, her stepfather "Boss" Shannon, and his son Armon along with a career criminal named Albert Bates. The gang soon contacted Urschel's family demanding a $200,000 ransom. While being held hostage, the oilman astutely took note of his surroundings including the pattern of overhead airplane traffic as well as the weather and the mineral taste of the water he drank. He also purposely left his fingerprints in and around the

cabin and drew his kidnappers into lengthy conversations so he could later recognize their voices.

The ransom was paid just days after the snatch, all in marked $20 bills. On his release, Urschel passed on the information he had collected to the FBI, who after checking airline schedules and weather patterns was able to pinpoint the area where the kidnappers had held their victim. When the feds raided the Shannon Ranch on August 12, they captured Old Man Shannon and his son as well as legendary bank robber Harvey Bailey. Bailey was evidently visiting the ranch after returning a machine gun he had borrowed from Kelly, which he had used in the August 9 robbery of a bank at Kingfisher, Oklahoma, in concert with Wilbur Underhill, Jim Clark, and several

Clockwise, from right: Harvey Bailey – Although convicted of the Urschel snatch, Bailey probably had little or no involvement with the crime. Courtesy Dallas Morning News. *Kathryn Kelly on the left, with her mother and a prison matron at the trial. Courtesy* Daily Oklahoman. *The Shannon cabin where Urschel was held for ransom. Courtesy* Master Detective. *The Urschel mansion in Oklahoma City. Courtesy* True Detective.

other associates. Although Harvey was not involved in the kidnapping, he unfortunately had $1,000 of the ransom money on his person at the time of his arrest, the cash being given him by Kelly for the repayment of an old debt. Kelly and his wife, who were staying at a residence in Fort Worth at the time of the raid, reacted to news of the raid by fleeing to Chicago. Albert Bates was promptly captured in Denver in possession of $660 of the marked ransom bills. He had buried the rest of his share. The Kellys were arrested in Memphis, Tennessee, on September 26. According to FBI Agents, when George Kelly was cornered he declared the famous phrase, "Don't shoot G-Man!" thus making the expression "G-Man" famous for a generation of readers and moviegoers. Whether the outlaw actually uttered the catchy jingle or a FBI publicist made up the slogan is still argued to this day.

After a heated and well-publicized trial, which took place in Oklahoma City, the Kellys as well as Albert Bates and Harvey Bailey were given life sentences for kidnapping. While Kathryn Kelly was sent to a women's prison to serve out her time, the others were eventually shipped to Alcatraz where Bates died of a heart attack in 1948.

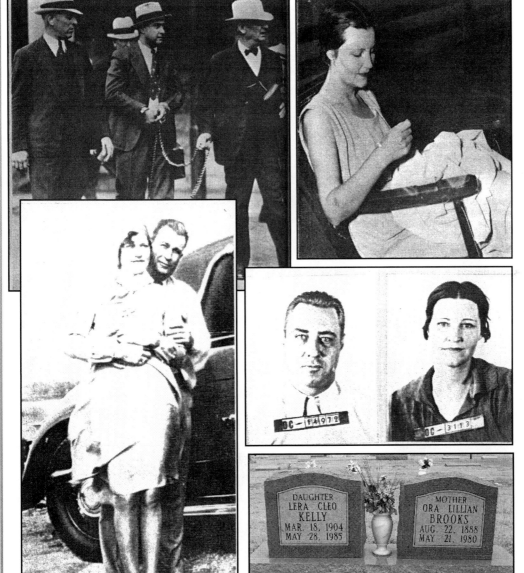

Clockwise from top left: "Machinegun" Kelly in custody. Courtesy True Detective.
Kat Kelly in prison. Courtesy Master Detective.
Kat and George Kelly's mug shots. Courtesy Master Detective.
Grave of Kathryn Kelly and her mother, Tecumseh. Photo by Naomi Morgan.
The Kellys in happier times. Courtesy of Ken Butler.

Clockwise from top left: Kelly leaving court under guard. Courtesy Rick Mattix. George Kelly handcuffed to cell. Courtesy Rick Mattix. Mugshot for George "Machinegun" Kelly. Courtesy Rick Mattix. George Kelly. Courtesy Rick Mattix.

George "Popgun" Kelly, as he was mockingly known to most of his fellow inmates, failed to adapt well to incarceration, once writing his victim (Urschel), "These five words are written in fire on the walls of my cell. 'Nothing can be worth this!'" George Kelly died in prison in 1954. His wife was paroled in 1958. She lived the rest of her life with her mother in Oklahoma City and died in 1985. She is buried at a Tecumseh cemetery.

A Bad Day in Sapulpa

On the afternoon of February 3, 1934, Creek County Sheriff Willis Strange received an anonymous phone tip regarding the presence of several hoodlums hiding out in a small shack on the outskirts of Sapulpa,

Oklahoma. The Sheriff suspected these individuals were part of gang who was responsible for committing several recent filling station robberies in the area. The call marked the beginning of a savage incident, which was long remembered by citizens and lawmen in area.

The residence in question belonged to Lee Davis, an unemployed ex-con, who was listed on the Creek County welfare rolls as receiving $2.00 a week from the area relief fund. The previous year he had been suspected by lawmen of harboring a pair of homegrown burglars in his home. While no charges were brought against him at the time, officers filed his name away for future reference.

Sheriff Strange contacted Sapulpa Chief of Police Tom Brumley asking for his assistance. Brumley informed the Sheriff he'd meet him near the Davis place, which was located just west of Route 66 and the old Liberty Glass plant, northeast of town. Sheriff Strange quickly gathered up a posse that included Deputy Wesley Gage and several others. Brumley, accompanied by Patrolman

Floyd Sellers and several armed volunteers met with Strange at the prearranged spot. The sheriff and Deputy Gage walked up to the front door rapping on it while Brumley and other members of the posse swiftly moved to cover the rear and sides of the house.

Davis emerged from the front door with raised hands while behind him appeared two others, later identified as Aussie (Aulcie) Elliott and Eldon Wilson. When Chief Brumley attempted to enter the back door of the residence, a fourth suspect, identified as Dubert Carolan, suddenly emerged from a nearby root cellar firing a pistol. The lawman took a slug to the right breast dropping to the ground stone dead. The posse, located mainly towards the front of the house, reacted to the sounds of gunfire emitting from the rear of the home by firing at the three suspects standing in the front yard. While Davis hit the ground unwounded and laid still, the other two suspects drew weapons and attempted to flee. In the ensuing melee, both men were shot repeatedly. Elliott died where he fell, his body torn by a shotgun blast fired by Officer Sellers, while Wilson, taking rounds to both the stomach and liver, was still breathing. Sheriff Strange sent a man to a nearby gas station to call for reinforcements and extra ammo.

The gunman who had shot Chief Brumley escaped the scene on foot. Some reports claim Deputy Gage was able to wing the fleeing fugitive in the shoulder in his dash for liberty. Although lawmen lost sight of him, they began combing the hillside near the house. Nearly fifteen minutes after the gunfight a local farmer breathlessly approached the officers claiming the missing gunman had been spotted about 200 yards down the hill from the Davis farm in a weed-choked ravine. The lawmen, led by Sheriff Strange, rushed to the site, where a collection of newly arrived officers and volunteers joined them. The group fanned out and began vigorously searching the small ravine. Suddenly, Sapulpa Policeman C. F. Lloyd spotted the killer crouched behind a rotted tree stump and shouted, "I've got him." The two men fired simultaneously and both were fatally wounded in the quick exchange of bullets. Posse members, not realizing the fugitive was dead, riddled his body with dozens of rounds from pistols, shotguns, and rifles. Back at the Davis house, the severely wounded Eldon Wilson was rushed to the county jail where a doctor was summoned to attend to his injuries. Davis, the character who had harbored the killers, was whisked to the Tulsa County jail for safekeeping. His wife and three screaming children were found unharmed, hiding in the house.

That evening Sheriff Strange phoned Governor William "Alfalfa Bill" Murray requesting the assistance of the National Guard in order to control a quickly forming crowd of angry townspeople who had gathered outside the Creek County Jail where the wounded suspect, Eldon Wilson, was being held. Over 100 guardsmen under the command of Major James Bell were trucked into Sapulpa that evening, quickly

Reward card for Eldon Wilson. Courtesy of Mike Webb.

$50.00 REWARD
Will be paid for the capture and delivery of each of these men to the Sheriff of Osage County, Oklahoma.
All these men are desperate and dangerous.
Escaped from Jail at Pawhuska, Okla., October 28th, 1933

ELDON WILSON
Wanted for Jail Breaking, High-Jacking and Car Theft
Is under 102 year Sentence from Osage Co.
F. P. C.   1 U 1 1 0 12
              1 U 1 1 1 12
Age, 26; Ht., 5'11"; Eyes, Hazel; Wt., 146
Hair, dk. Brown; Comp., medium; Scars,
Thumb, index and middle finger off on left
hand at first joint, bullet wound under left
arm and left breast.

establishing a perimeter around the courthouse. An order was given to the militiamen to "Fix bayonets," Doctors were amazed Wilson was still alive after being riddled with at least a dozen bullets.

An anxious night was passed at the jail where a mob of nearly 1000 citizens had congregated, hurling threats at the prisoner. Nervous guardsmen fingered their rifles as talk of a necktie party was heard coming from agitators in the crowd. The throng of angry citizens, which had thinned considerably as the night wore on, appeared to calm when the sun came up. About 8 a.m. after clinging to life fifteen hours, Wilson died. According to witnesses the outlaw departed this life with a curse on his lips, informing the attending physician, "I'm not going to make it. The dirty bastards got me good!" The anxious crowd dissipated soon after Wilson's death was announced and the National Guardsmen returned to Tulsa.

Grave of Eldon Wilson, Rose Hill Cemetery. Tulsa- Photo by Naomi Morgan.

When reporters inquired as to the personal histories of the pair of outlaws who were shot at the Davis house, they were given an earful. Aussie Elliott, age twenty-two, was a native of Haskell County and a real yahoo. Although the youth had once had been offered an opportunity to play minor league baseball he instead chose a spectacular career in crime. On March 24,1931, he was convicted and sentenced to fifty years at Granite Reformatory for his participation in the 1930 Fort Gibson bank robbery while acting as a member of the Jack Preddy Gang. On August 15, 1932, he and nineteen others escaped from the facility. On November 1, he was identified as the subject who drove the getaway car in the robbery of the Sallisaw State Bank. His companions at the time were identified as "Pretty Boy" Floyd and George Birdwell.

Eldon Wilson, who hailed from Sand Springs, was also a career criminal. In 1924, he was sentenced to a five-year hitch at Granite for auto theft. Wilson was later sent to McAlester on a charge of attempted burglary, escaping the institution on March 25, 1931. Exactly when he joined up with Aussie Elliott is unknown although it was suspected the pair had hijacked the bank at Fairfax along with two others on November 10, 1932. In February 1933, Wilson was engaged in a gunfight with Depew Town Marshal Tom Rigney. Both men were wounded in the gunbattle. Wilson was captured and later transported to Pawhuska where he faced charges of robbing the Fairfax bank. Elliott soon joined him. On April 19, the pair escaped from the jail. On the evening of May 13, 1933, he and Wilson were spotted hiding out in an abandoned shack near Sapulpa. That evening a posse led by Creek County Sheriff Willis Strange raided the place. Although Elliott managed to escape the area on foot, Wilson was cornered and once again shot and captured. Elliott was captured soon afterwards, in the company of another Osage bandit named Joe "Red" Carson. All three were transported to the calaboose in Pawhuska. Elliott was booked along with Red Carson and Paul Evinger of suspicion of slaying a Fairfax filling station operator during a heist committed on May 6, 1933.

On October 28, Wilson and Elliott along with Red Carson once again pulled their Houdini act, escaping the confines of the Osage County Jail. Carson soon split from the group and after committing several outrages was slain by lawmen in Wellington, Kansas, on January 11, 1934. In the months following their second escape from the Pawhuska jail Elliott and Wilson were suspected of killing a Sand Springs cop named J. V. Huskey in early December as well as kidnapping and abusing a pair of Fort Smith patrolmen in late January 1934. The authorities also had the pair pegged for robbing a-half-dozen filling stations during this time frame. Muskogee County Sheriff V. S. Cannon, who dealt with many of the worst criminals to come out of the depression era dubbed Elliott, the "Meanest little rat I ever met."

Elliott's body was claimed by an uncle and transported to Garland, Oklahoma, for burial. Wilson's body was claimed by a sister and interred at Rose Hill Cemetery in Tulsa. When questioned by police, the mortally wounded Eldon Wilson misidentified the third suspect who had killed Chief Brumley and Officer Lloyd as Raymond Moore. On further investigation, the dead man was correctly identified as Dubert Carolan, of Haskell County. He had been sought by lawmen since September 7, 1933, for his participation in a jewelry robbery in Broken Arrow. Carolan and a subject named Clarence Hays had robbed a St. Louis diamond merchant named Charles Weltzmiller of $30,000 worth of rare jewels. Hays was slain by lawmen a few days after the crime near Barnsdall.

Grave of Dubert Carolan in Stigler. Photo by Naomi Morgan.

Carolan's body was claimed by his sister and buried in the City Cemetery in Stigler, Oklahoma, located only a few miles from where Aussie Elliott was interred. The pistol he had used to slay the two officers was tracked to a Tulsa pawnshop. Some of the jewelry he had stolen was discovered hidden in the Davis home when police searched the residence following the shootout while several other pieces, a gold watch, diamond stickpin, and ruby ring were found on the bodies of the suspects.

Chief of Police Brumley was buried at the Kellyville Cemetery. His wife and eleven children survived him.

Attending his funeral were several thousand citizens including two hundred area law officers. Brumley was the third lawman in his family to die at the hands of an outlaw. The chief's brother, Shep, had been shot down in Sapulpa where he was a patrolman in 1922 while attempting to make an arrest. His uncle, Wiley Shelton, who was a Deputy US Marshal, was slain in a gunfight with bandits in 1904. Officer Lloyd was buried with honors at South Heights Cemetery in Sapulpa. His wife and two adopted children survived him.

Lee Davis was promptly charged with Brumley's murder. Creek County Attorney Sebe Christian demanded the death penalty. The trial was reportedly fast-paced and to the point. After deliberating three days, the jury somehow became hopelessly deadlocked. The judge soon declared a mistrial. He was retried in February of 1935. Davis testified at his retrial, he was convinced Officer Floyd Sellers had accidentally shot Chief Brumley in the melee. The other officers at the scene angrily rejected his theory in their testimonies. After fifty-two ballots, the jury came back with a verdict of guilty. Judge J. Harvey Smith sentenced the defendant to life in prison. Davis died in the penitentiary of meningitis several years into his sentence.

With the killer's deaths and Davis's imprisonment, it would seem justice had triumphed in the end. But for the officer's wives, left husbandless, and their thirteen children, left fatherless in the midst of America's worst economic depression, the justice of the courtroom was a fleeting thing, their suffering had only began.

Aussie Elliott and picture of grave. Courtesy Muskogee Phoenix and Naomi Morgan.

Clarence Hurt: G-Man

One of the more widely known urban legends in American history is that of notorious 1930s bandit, John Dillinger. Not nearly as recognizable are the names and stories of the courageous FBI agents who tracked down and slew the celebrated outlaw in front of Chicago's Biograph theatre on a hot summer night in 1934.

One of those agents, Clarence O. Hurt, was born in Illinois in 1897. His family soon relocated to Oklahoma where young Clarence finished school before enlisting in the army during WWI. In 1919, he joined the Oklahoma City Police Department as a patrolman. According to family folklore, Clarence was hired due to his ability to drive both an automobile and a motorcycle, which were quickly becoming important pieces of equipment in law enforcement circles around this time. In 1920, the up and coming young officer was selected to serve as secretary to Chief of Police Calvin T. Linville. The following year he was transferred to traffic duty when a new chief of police was appointed. In 1922, Hurt was involved in a vicious gun duel in which his partner was killed. Several years later, Hurt, and two other officers were placed on detached duty with the US Marshals Service to assist in their investigation of the multiple murders of tribesmen on Oklahoma's Osage Indian Reservation. A gang of cutthroats apparently murdered the Indians in an effort to steal their headrights, which were worth millions of dollars due to the discovery of oil on the reservation.

In 1927, Hurt was assigned as a plainclothes investigator back on the mean streets of Oklahoma City. The following year he was appointed superintendent of the new Auto Theft Bureau. Around this time, Hurt made the acquaintance of a young man named D. A. "Jelly" Bryce. Apparently the pair, who would become lifelong friends, met at a shooting competition, where Hurt, who was a noted marksman, came away so impressed with the lad's shooting abilities he hired him on the spot, assigning him to plainclothes duty.

Clarence Hurt late in life. Courtesy Jack Hurt.

In 1928, Clarence Hurt was appointed Oklahoma City's Assistant Chief of Police. After serving two years in this capacity, he was transferred to the Detective Bureau as a lieutenant. The decade of the '30s would prove to be difficult years for law enforcement. With the ensuing economic depression, crime rates skyrocketed. The early part of the decade also proved to be a time of tragedy and heartfelt misery for Hurt and his extended family. It was during this period his wife's two brothers convinced him to help them attain jobs with the department. Although, the pair made fine officers, it was a decision Hurt regretted. On March 22, 1930, the first of the brothers, John D. "Jack" Gates was slain in the line of duty. Three years later, his sibling, Douglas, was shot and killed by the driver of a stolen car. His killer was convicted of his murder and executed by the state of Oklahoma on January 18, 1934.

In the winter of 1933, Hurt, along with his protégé, "Jelly" Bryce, were recruited into a posse led by US Department of Justice Agent R. H. Colvin, who had received word of the whereabouts of the notorious bank robber Wilbur Underhill. The outlaw, who had been dubbed the "Tri State Terror" by Midwest newspapers, had a long history of violent criminal behavior. As of late, Wilbur had been involved in a prolific crime spree since his May 30, 1933, escape from the Kansas State Prison. He, along with companions, Harvey Bailey, "Big" Bob Brady, Jim Clark, Ed Davis, Ford Bradshaw, "Newt" Clanton, Charlie Cotner, and others had robbed numerous banks and committed several homicides in Oklahoma, Kansas, and Arkansas. The feds had tracked him to a house in Shawnee where he and his newly acquired bride along with a crime partner, Ralph Roe, and his girlfriend, Eva Mae Nichols, were spending the night.

In the early morning hours of December 30, the heavily armed task force, now joined by a group of officers from the Shawnee Police Department and Oklahoma County Sheriff's Department, surrounded the fugitive's lair, each man guarding an exit. Although it was nearly 2 a.m., the lights in the house were still burning. The sounds of a raucous party emitted from the cottage. Hurt and Agent Colvin cautiously approached a rear bedroom window where they spotted Underhill standing near the foot of the bed, the officers called for his surrender. The outlaw responded by grabbing a 9mm Lugar pistol off a nearby table and cutting loose on the lawmen. Hurt, who was armed with a tear gas gun, fired and struck the outlaw hard in the gut with a gas canister while Colvin, carrying a Thompson machine gun, unleashed a full drum of steel-jacketed .45 slugs into the bedroom. A total of more approximately 200 rounds were fired in the ensuing gunfight in which Ralph Roe, along with Wilbur's wife were captured and Eva Nichols severely wounded. She would later die from her injuries. Underhill escaped into the foggy night wearing only his long handle underwear, but was spotted later that morning, passed out on a blood-soaked bed in a downtown furniture store, which authorities suspected was the headquarters of a local fencing operation (stolen goods). He had been wounded numerous times. After receiving treatment at an area hospital, FBI Director J. Edger Hoover, fearing his pals would attempt to liberate him from custody, transferred the badly

wounded desperado to the prison hospital in McAlester where he died within a few days.

The year 1934 was a violent year in America's history. The so-called Midwest Crime Wave was in full bloom. High profile criminals like the infamous "Pretty Boy" Floyd, "Baby Face" Nelson, "Machine Gun" Kelly, "Doc" Barker, Clyde Barrow, and boldest and most well known of them all, John Dillinger, had captured the public's imagination. The nation's newspapers blazed their names on front pages and radio programs touted their deeds. To counteract the sudden appearance and popularity of these catchy named criminals and stem the rising tide of bank robberies throughout the Midwest, a fledgling federal sub-agency of the US Department of Justice, named the Bureau of Investigation was mobilized. An unknown, ex- legal secretary named J. Edger Hoover headed the bureau.

Hoover, who was a bit of a self-promoter, vigorously lobbied Congress for increased powers and funding to enable the bureau to match up with the criminal elements. Strange as it sounds, agents of the bureau at first were not even allowed to carry firearms. Attorney

Agent Gus "Buster" Jones. Author's collection.

Oklahoma City Detective Jelly Bryce. Courtesy Jack Hurt.

General Homer Cummings, with the backing of newly elected President Franklin Roosevelt, threw his full support behind the agency. Apparently, the President was deeply troubled by the fact the public was beginning to look at the big name criminals, especially the bank robbers of the era, as heroic figures. He was also aghast that America's youth might come to see these outlaws as perverse role models. Roosevelt ordered Hoover's agency, which had been renamed the Federal Bureau of Investigation, to use all means available to eradicate these villains.

The director took the President and Attorney General at their word coming up with a bold plan. Recognizing the fact that the majority of the bureau's collage educated "bookworm" agents were mostly just deskbound clerks who didn't stand a chance against the heavily armed desperadoes of the time, he decided to fight fire with fire. The director made the decision to recruit a hand picked squad of hired gunmen or professional "shootists" to go after the big name criminals. Hoover began his search for these new agents in Oklahoma and Texas. He quickly hired Oklahoma City Detectives Clarence Hurt and Jerry Palmer, who joined ranks with Texas Rangers James "Doc" White and Gus "Buster" Jones who were already with the bureau. At Hoover's request, Oklahoma City Chief of Police Watt gave detectives Hurt and Palmer a one-year leave of absence to as he put it, "Go hunting" for the FBI. They were soon joined by Texas born lawman and noted "gunfighter", Charlie Winstead. Within a few months, the bureau, at Hurt's insistence also re-cruited "Jelly" Bryce into their ranks.

After a few weeks of formal training, the men were assigned to Senior Agent Melvin Purvis to work out of the Chicago office. Purvis formed the group into a several so-called "Flying Squads," requiring agents to be packed and ready to board a plane at a moment's notice, speeding to any location whenever one of the well-known gangsters was sighted. Although it was never admitted by the bureau, it later became apparent the orders of the "Flying Squad" was to pursue and kill on sight any of the prominent public enemies on Hoover's list of most wanted.

The first order the Director gave to his special unit was to "Get Dillinger!" who had recently been named "Public Enemy #1" by the US Department of Justice. The outlaw and his gang were wanted for a dozen bank robberies and responsible for numerous murders across the Midwest. On April 3, 1934, members of the "Flying Squad" fatally shot Eddie Green, a Dillinger gang member, in St. Paul, Minnesota.

In mid-July 1934, a pair of

Clockwise from above: Grave of Clarence Hurt-McAlester. Photo by Naomi Morgan. Clarence Hurt's son, Jack, holding pistol his famous father used to shoot John Dillinger. Photo by Naomi Morgan. Sure-Shot Jelly Bryce. Courtesy Jack Hurt.

East Chicago, Indiana, detectives contacted FBI Agent Melvin Purvis informing him they had located a "madam" of a local, "sporting" house named Anna Sage, who wanted to trade information of Dillinger's whereabouts in return for federal assistance with an immigration problem. She apparently met with Purvis the following day, and boldly offered to "finger" the flamboyant outlaw if the feds would promise to "fix" her legal woes. The G-Man leaped at the deal. A call was immediately issued to Clarence Hurt and his fellow members of the "Flying Squad" to get ready for action.

On the hot sweltering afternoon of July 22 Purvis received word from Ms. Sage informing him that she, Dillinger, and one of her "girls" named Polly Hamilton had made plans to take in a movie that very evening. She said, "We will either be at the Marbro or the Biograph theatres in downtown Chicago." Agents were sent to both movie houses in an effort to locate the trio. At 8 p.m., Sage, along with Dillinger and his girlfriend were spotted in the ticket line at the Biograph. A group of seventeen agents of the FBI that included Clarence Hurt immediately surrounded the theatre, which was currently showing the film "Manhattan Melodrama", a gangster movie starring Clark Gable. Purvis wrote in his autobiography, that his plan was to wait until the party in question exited the theatre before having the agents attempt an arrest. Apparently, Purvis had instructed the collection of agents, he would strike a match lighting his cigar as a signal to officers to close in for the kill.

At 10:30 p.m., Sage strolled out of the movie. According to witnesses, the bright orange dress she was wearing appeared blood red when lit up by the marquee lights. A few feet behind her strode Dillinger and his consort hand in hand. According to FBI reports later made public under the Freedom of Information Act, Purvis was shaking so bad from nerves he was unable to light his cigar, so agents reacted on their own intuition. Agent Herman Hollis lock-stepped in behind the outlaw, while Agent Charles Winstead approached to within a few feet of him. Clarence Hurt placed himself directly in front of the outlaw. Suddenly, the bandit, realizing something was up, made a mad dash towards the entrance of a nearby alley while tugging at a revolver stuck in his waistband. Winstead, who was packing a Colt .45 automatic pistol, apparently stopped, took dead aim, and shot him either in the head or back. Agent Hurt, armed with a .38 caliber

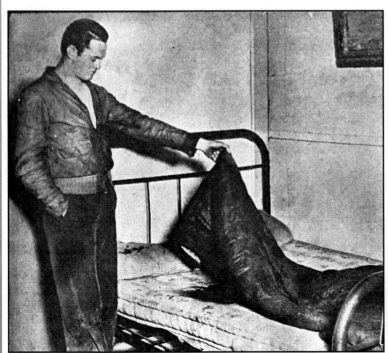

Bloody bed where badman Wilbur Underhill was captured shortly after the Shawnee raid. Courtesy Official Detective.

Bedroom window located at Dewey Street cottage in Shawnee where the assault on Wilbur Underhill began. Photo by Naomi Morgan.

handgun, also fired and hit the fleeing outlaw. In the meantime, Agent Hollis fired his weapon but missed his target wounding two innocent bystanders. Immediately following the volley, Dillinger fell to the concrete, rolled over, and then lay motionless. Agents Hurt and Hollis escorted the bandit's body to a local hospital where he was officially declared dead. According to legend, Hurt then tracked down a priest at the hospital, having him hurriedly say last rites over the departed desperado.

News of the outlaw's demise spread like wildfire. A huge crowd quickly assembled near the scene of the ambush shoving their way towards the alley where Dillinger had recently laid mortally wounded. To enable them to have a souvenir of the event, many in the crowd dipped handkerchiefs in a pool of blood, which had formed where the badman had fallen. The morbidly curious streamed past the site all through the night and the following day. Dillinger's body, which was transported to the Cook County morgue, was put on display for public viewing. For the next thirty-six hours, tens of thousands of citizens stood in line to have a peek at the infamous bad man in death.

Several days later, his father collected Dillinger's remains and buried him at Crown Point Cemetery in Indianapolis, Indiana. Newspapers throughout not only the United States but worldwide reported the bandit's demise with banner headlines. Around this time, several wildly inaccurate rumors surfaced in the media, one widely circulated report wrongly suggested Melvin Purvis had fired the fatal shot which ended the life of the famous fugitive, another implied his betrayer, Anna Sage, had worn a "bright red dress" (actually orange) on that fateful evening as some sort of signal to federal agents. Thus the legend of the "Lady in

Red" was born, a piece of inaccurate folklore, which has persisted for nearly 75 years in the American consciousness.

FBI Director Hoover expressed great satisfaction with the actions of his newly formed "Flying Squad." In the following weeks, the Director, who was full-blown egotist, demonstrated his intent not to share the limelight with others when he refused to reveal the identity of the agents who had slain the famed outlaw. Instead, he insisted the credit for bringing down America's premier public enemy should be given to the FBI in general not any individual agent. The public would have to wait

Above: The Gates brothers. Courtesy Jack Hurt. Right: Oklahoma County plain-clothes deputies, circa 1934. Courtesy Stanley Rogers.

until after Hoover's death in 1972 to find out the identity of the two agents who fired the fatal rounds. Except for Melvin Purvis, none of the agents involved in the Dillinger ambush ever spoke to the press about the event. Even today, there is some controversy whether Hurt or Winstead fired the actual bullet responsible for the bad man's immediate demise. However, since it is an accepted fact both men shot and hit Dillinger on that fateful night, it seems a mute point. Incidentally, shortly after the Dillinger ambush, Agent Hurt put away the gun he used to end the career of the famous outlaw and never carried it again. The pistol, a .38-caliber revolver, was later given to his son, who in turn carried the weapon throughout his own law enforcement career.

In the aftermath of the Dillinger ambush, Anna Sage was given a hefty reward for her part in setting up the outlaw. Although the government had apparently promised her some sort of assistance regarding her immigration status (she was an illegal resident from Romania) she was quickly deported back to her homeland. J. Edger Hoover was given, and graciously received accolades from an appreciative President and Attorney General. Over the next few months the remaining members of Dillinger's gang was hunted down, captured, or killed by Hoover's "Flying Squad." Other "Public Enemies" who were exterminated by the squad during the same period, included the notorious Charles "Pretty Boy" Floyd, and "Baby Face" Nelson.

Hoover and his boys then turned their attention to eradicating the members of the notorious Barker-Karpis Gang. This depraved band of hoodlums, who had originally been based out of Tulsa, Oklahoma, was suspected of a dozen bank jobs along with nearly as many murders. In January 1935, agents surrounded a cottage in Lake Weir, Florida, where "Ma" Barker and her son Freddy were holed up. When ordered to surrender, Freddy Barker fired a full clip of .45 rounds at officers from his submachine gun. Angry lawmen responded in kind, firing tear gas canisters, phosphorous grenades, and 300 rounds of hot ammo into the cottage. The Barkers perished in the crescendo of fire. Following the Florida shootout, gang members Freddie Hunter and Alvin Karpis quickly became the center of attention for Hoover and his crack assault squad.

In May of 1936, federal agents located the pair living in a comfortable flat in New Orleans, Louisiana, near the French Quarter. Members of the "Flying Squad," which included Clarence Hurt and "Jelly" Bryce, immediately set up surveillance of the apartment house in question. Director Hoover was flown to the "Crescent" city without delay, intent on personally taking charge of the operation. On arrival in New Orleans, he was met by Clarence Hurt who drove him to the agent's command post located near the apartment house where the subjects, who were blissfully unaware of the operation going on outside their door, were hiding out.

According to several sources, the plan was for agents to storm the residence as they had the Barker hideaway

Rare action photograph showing the actual capture of bank bandits by Oklahoma County detectives, circa 1935. Courtesy Stanley Rogers.

in Florida. However, even the best of plans can go awry. Apparently, as Agent Hurt was in the act of escorting Director Hoover to a safe spot where he could observe the officer's assault on the residence, Alvin Karpis suddenly and unexpectedly appeared strolling down the steps of the apartment building and nearly collided with Hurt and "Jelly" Bryce. The fugitive, not recognizing the men as lawmen, hopped into his car attempting to start the vehicle. Hurt, paused only a split second before shoving a .351 cal. rifle barrel in the face of America's most wanted outlaw, ordering him to keep his hands on the steering wheel and not move a muscle. A shocked Karpis complied. Hurt, who was quickly joined by a dozen other agents pointing guns at the outlaw, asked the bad man if he was armed. Karpis replied he was not. The lawman retorted "That's good, now I can put the safety back on this rifle before it accidentally goes off."

A few moments after his arrest, Karpis's companion, Freddy Hunter, was spotted trying to mingle with the gathering crowd of rubberneckers in an effort to slip off to parts unknown. Hurt shouted to a fellow agent to "Get that fellow before he gets away." Director Hoover, who was standing in the shadows during the arrest, then approached the man he had named to the top of his most wanted list and loudly proclaimed, "Karpis, you are under arrest." In the confusion, it seems none of the agents had thought to bring a pair of handcuffs, so Hurt pulled off his necktie and bound the desperado's hands and escorted the villain to the federal building for questioning.

When interviewed by the press shortly after Karpis's arrest, Hoover suggested to the assembled crowd of journalist he had personally apprehended the outlaw. The following day, newspapers throughout the nation applauded the Director for his single-handed arrest. This act, which was an obvious deception on Hoover's part, helped to solidify his position as leader of the nation's premier crime-fighting agency. Hoover would remain the unchallenged head of the FBI for the next thirty-four years.

Alvin Karpis was convicted of kidnapping and sentenced to life in prison. He spent the next twenty-five years, longer than any other prisoner, doing time on Alcatraz Island did. He was finally transferred to McNeil Island Federal Penitentiary in 1962 when the government closed "The Rock" permanently. Incidentally, while serving time at McNeil Karpis celled with a minor auto thief named Charles Manson, who would later achieve dubious fame from his involvement in the Sharon Tate-LaBianca murders. Karpis was released from custody in 1969 and deported to Canada where he wrote two books on his experiences. To his dying day, the old outlaw espoused a manacle hatred of J. Edger Hoover, but often expressed a deep respect (or at least fear) for the "Oklahoma boys" who had arrested him. He died in 1979.

"Jelly" Bryce, who once made the cover of Life

John Dillinger "Public Enemy Number One." Courtesy Rick Mattix.

The "Lady in Red." Courtesy True Detective.

magazine due to his fast draw skills and the fact he had shot nearly two dozen bad men in the line of duty during his career, retired from the FBI in 1958. He moved back to Oklahoma where for several years he taught firearms training for the Oklahoma State Highway Patrol. He died in 1974 and buried at Mt. View, Oklahoma. Melvin Purvis was drummed out of the FBI in the latter '30s due to a severe case of professional jealousy existing between him and Director Hoover. Purvis went on to fame and semi-riches when he endorsed a line of wildly successful, "Melvin Purvis, G-man" products (mostly cheap toys, decoder rings and such) sold in boxes of breakfast cereals in the latter 1930s and early '40s. He committed suicide in 1960 with a gun given him by his fellow agents on his retirement from the bureau. Herman Hollis, the agent who had fired and missed the night of the Dillinger ambush, along with Agent Sam Crowley were both killed in a horrific gun battle with "Baby Face" Nelson near Niles, Illinois, on November 27, 1934. Charles Winstead re-

signed from the FBI in 1942 and moved to New Mexico where he ran a ranching operation. He died there in 1973. Clarence Hurt retired from the agency in 1955 moving to a farm near McAlester, Oklahoma. He was elected to the position of Pittsburg County Sheriff in 1958 and re-elected in 1960. He then retired to his ranch. The legendary G-man, whose name would be forever linked to that of John Dillinger's, died on November 5, 1975. He was buried in the Masonic section of Oak Hill Cemetery in McAlester, Oklahoma. Ironically, while Hurt's funeral was being conducted, several thieves burglarized the lawman's ranch house stealing various valuables and vandalizing a large oil painting of J. Edger Hoover.

Irish O'Malley and the Ozark Mountain Boys

The so-called Irish O'Malley Gang was next to the gargantuan Barker-Karpis combination America's largest "Supergang" coming out of the 1930s Midwest Crime Wave. This oversized band of brigands was actually the result of the merging of two organized groups of outlaws, one, the original Irish O'Malley Gang, which was urban in nature, and the other, The Ozark Mountain Boys, who were rural in makeup. The suspected leader of the group was Walter Holland, alias, "Irish" O'Malley. The Missouri born O'Malley became a bootlegger in the St. Louis area shortly after his return from the First World War. Eventually he joined a band of bank robbers in Illinois but was captured and sent to prison in 1922. Upon his release in 1929, he immersed himself back into the St. Louis underworld. In 1933, O'Malley, along with several accom-

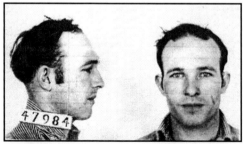

Clockwise from above: Gun-moll Vivian Chase. Courtesy Rick Mattix. Grave of badman Lee Flournoy at Joplin, Missouri. Flournoy and his partner Charley Mayes (husband of Vivian Chase) were slain in a gunbattle with officers in Picher. Photo by Naomi Morgan. Donnie Garrett, white slaver who joined the Muskogee breakout. Courtesy National Archives-NARA. Dewey Gilmore at Leavenworth Prison. US Bureau of Prisons.

plices, kidnapped a wealthy East Alton, Illinois, meatpacker named August Luer, a crime that garnered national headlines. The gang's attempt to collect a $100,000 ransom was unsuccessful.

We next hear of the badman operating in the Kansas City area with a band of prolific burglars, which included Blackie Doyle, John Langan, Dave Sherman, and Clarence Sparger. Also in the group at the time was O'Malley's long-time girlfriend Vivian Chase. Miss Chase was noted by the authorities as one of the most notorious gangster molls of the 1920-1930s. Vivian was born in Nebraska but raised in Southwest Missouri. She married George Chase in 1921 but widowed shortly thereafter when poor George was slain attempting to rob a bank. It appears she worked as a B-Girl or prostitute for the next few years before marrying a Joplin thug named Charlie Mayes. In 1926, she was arrested in

Below: Transfer sheet from Leavenworth to Alcatraz concerning Dewey Gilmore. Courtesy NARA.

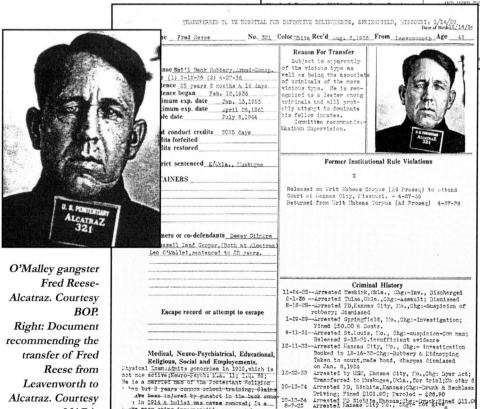

O'Malley gangster Fred Reese- Alcatraz. Courtesy BOP.

Right: Document recommending the transfer of Fred Reese from Leavenworth to Alcatraz. Courtesy NARA.

"Dapper" Dan Heady, a key member of the O'Malley gang, slain by officers following the Muskogee jailbreak. Courtesy of the Heady family.

the aftermath of a bloody gun-battle in the mining community of Picher, Oklahoma, in which her husband and his sidekick Lee Flournoy were both shot down by area lawmen. After her husband's demise, she kept company with a series of small-time Kansas thugs. In 1932, Chase and two men were arrested for suspicion of robbing the First National Bank of North Kansas City for $1,500. A

few weeks after her arrest, Vivian sawed her way out of jail and fled to St. Louis where she hooked-up with O'Malley.

In mid-1933 "Irish" O'Malley was introduced to a nervy, ex-con named "Dapper" Dan Heady. Mr. Heady, who hailed from Springfield, Missouri, in turn connected the gang leader to Leonard Short, a sawed-off, rotund individual of dubious character who led a band of bootleggers whom lawmen had dubbed "The Ozark Mountain Boys." The band operated mostly in and around the Stone-Greene County area, located close to the mountainous Missouri-Arkansas borderlands. Short, the brother of US Congressman Dewey Short had recently led his bloodthirsty group of merrymen away from the illegal liquor trade that was collapsing due to the repeal of prohibition into the bank robbing business. In a two-year time span, the brigands held up financial institutions in Ash Grove, Webb City, Billings, Seneca, and Reeds Springs, Missouri, as well as banks in Galena, Kansas, and Fayetteville, Arkansas. Short's chief henchmen were Dan Heady, Red Melton, Fred Reese, Frank Simmons, Dewey Gilmore, Russell Cooper, Floyd Henderson, Otto Jackson, Buster Cooper, Bob Johnson, and a three hundred pound Cherokee Indian hailing from Claremore, Oklahoma, named "Big Jack" Miller.

On the morning of December 22, 1934, Irish O'Malley joined with Leonard Short, Dan Heady, Jack Miller, Gilmore, Cooper, Reese, and Red Melton in simultaneously hijacking the Okemah National Bank of $12,000 and the First National Bank of Okemah for $5,500. A double daylight bank robbery was a feat rarely attempted in the past and usually with poor results. The Dalton boys tried robbing two banks at once in Coffeyville and they were shot to pieces when the citizens took up arms. In 1915 Henry Starr and company had attempted to pull of a duel bank job in Stroud but failed as well. On the other hand, Matt Kimes successfully held-up a pair of banks on two different occasions, once in Covington and a second time at Beggs.

In the Okemah heists, not a shot was fired and the gang made a clean getaway. Lawmen noted the robbery was one of the most professional in Oklahoma history. While nearly all

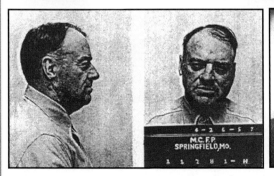

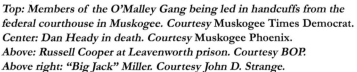

*Top: Members of the O'Malley Gang being led in handcuffs from the federal courthouse in Muskogee. Courtesy **Muskogee Times Democrat.** Center: Dan Heady in death. Courtesy **Muskogee Phoenix.** Above: Russell Cooper at Leavenworth prison. Courtesy **BOP.** Above right: "Big Jack" Miller. Courtesy **John D. Strange.***

of the gang members went to ground, Buster Cooper and Bob Johnson, who were left out of the Okemah raid, robbed the bank in Quapaw for $300 on December 26. A week later, the pair was involved in a gunbattle with Picher lawmen in which Cooper shot and killed Ottawa County Deputy Sheriff Gerald Hodge. Cooper in turn was gunned down by area lawmen while Johnson was captured in Missouri the following day.

On March 2, 1935, the gang, now joined by Clarence Sparger, robbed the First National Bank of Neosho, Missouri, of $17,000. Again, they made a safe departure from the scene. On March 27, the desperadoes knocked off Goldberg's Jewelry Store in Tulsa for $55,000 in rare gems and gold coins. Six weeks later, the outlaw band looted the City National Bank in Fort Smith, Arkansas, for $22,000.

Soon after the Arkansas job, Dewey Gilmore was captured in Texas and turned informant implicating his fellow gang members in various crimes while unveiling their hideouts to the authorities. In short order, the entire gang was apprehended in a series of high profile raids conducted by fast moving squads of heavily armed G-Men. In short order, O'Malley was tried and convicted of the Luer kidnapping and given a life sentence at an Illinois prison. Red Melton, Clarence Sparger, and Fred Reese were given long sentences for the Neosho

bank heist while Dan Heady, Dewey Gilmore, Russill Cooper, and Leonard Short were incarcerated in Muskogee's newly built City-Federal Jail charged with the Okemah bank robberies.

On December 3, 1935, Heady, Gilmore, Cooper, and Short, along with an insignificant thief named John Blackburn and a white-slaver named Donnie Garrett, who were both trustees, escaped from the jail killing Muskogee Chief of Detectives Ben Bolton in the process. During the breakout, a machinegun-wielding Detective Marsh Corgan turned his "chopper" on Blackburn, cutting him to pieces. Over the next few days, hundreds of officers, vigilantes, and National Guardsmen participated in one of the states largest manhunts. On December 6, lawmen led by Deputy US Marshal Allen Stanfield and Muskogee County Sheriff Tom Jordan surrounded the fugitives in a cabin located on the side of Jack Fork Mountain south of McAlester. When ordered to surrender, the fugitives, led by Dan Heady, opened fire. At the gun battle's conclusion, Heady laid dead and his companions wounded

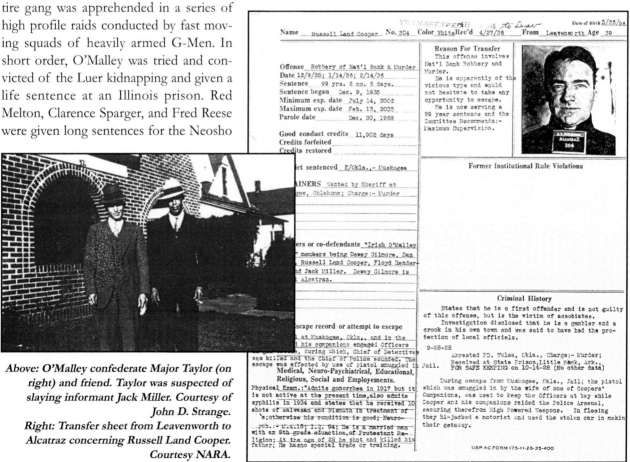

Above: O'Malley confederate Major Taylor (on right) and friend. Taylor was suspected of slaying informant Jack Miller. Courtesy of John D. Strange.
Right: Transfer sheet from Leavenworth to Alcatraz concerning Russell Land Cooper. Courtesy NARA.

and captured. The frozen body of Leonard Short was retrieved from an isolated mountainside hog shed where his companions had abandoned him the previous night when the little bandit had collapsed with pneumonia.

Jack Miller would later turn informant and testify against his fellow gang members, greatly assisting prosecutors in their efforts to convict Gilmore and Cooper of participating in the Okemah robberies. Several years after giving his damming testimony, Miller's bullet-riddled body was discovered lying next to his burning car on an isolated dirt lane located near Chelsea. O'Malley associate and Chelsea native, Robert "Major" Taylor, was the chief suspect in his assassination. While many investigators suspected Miller had been snuffed out for giving testimony against the O'Malley's, others theorized the big man was slain for his participation in the recent robbery of the Route 66 nightclub, which was owned by an un-

derworld figure named Earl "Woodenfoot" Clanton, an uncle of the infamous bank robbing Clanton brothers, Herman and Newt. Incidentally, shortly before his death, Miller and a man named Frank Layton had been arrested for possessing a sawed-off shotgun. The case against the pair for violating the Federal Firearms Act would eventually wind its way to the US Supreme Court. The case (US vs. Miller) was resolved in a controversial landmark ruling regarding the issue of gun control, which is still debated today.

Due to the notoriety of their crimes gang members Dewey Gilmore, Russell Cooper, Red Melton, Fred Reese, Donnie Garrett, and Clarence Sparger would serve the bulk of their lengthy sentences at Alcatraz, America's premiere maximum-security prison located in San Francisco Bay.

In 1939, Walter O'Malley was transferred from the

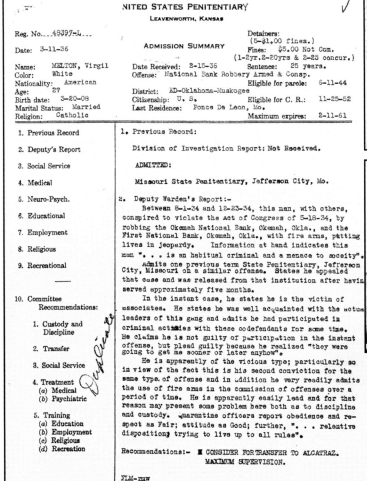

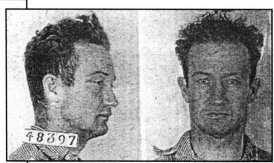

Top: Virgil "Red" Melton in 1936 at Alcatraz. Courtesy NARA.
Above: Virgil Melton in 1959 – a visual example of what twenty-three years behind bars can do to a man's appearance. Courtesy NARA.
Left: Admissions sheet for Red Melton – Leavenworth Penitentiary. Melton participated in at least six bank robberies during his criminal career. Courtesy NARA.

Clockwise from top left: Grave of "Dapper" Dan Heady, Turner Station, Missouri. Photo by Naomi Morgan. Wanted poster for O'Malley gangster Clarence Sparger. Courtesy NARA. Grave of Officer Gerald Hodge, slain by O'Malley outlaws-Miami. Photo by Naomi Morgan.

Illinois State Prison to the state mental hospital for the criminally insane at Menard when doctors diagnosed him as a raving schizophrenic. He died in custody of heart problems in 1944. As for the fate of his gun moll, Vivian Chase, her luck ran out on November 3, 1935, when she was found dead, shot in the head and abandoned in the back seat of a car discarded in a parking lot of a Kansas City hospital.

The Underhill-Bailey-Bradshaw Gangs

On May 30, 1933, eleven hardened convicts escaped from the Kansas State Penitentiary in Lansing. Soon afterwards, the inmates separated into two groups. While the members of the first collection of inmates were quickly captured, the second group, which included master bank robber Harvey "Old Harve" Bailey, along with serial cop-killer "Mad-Dog" Wilbur Underhill, as well as native Oklahomans, Jim Clark, "Big" Bob Brady, and Ed Davis, slipped the dragnet making their way back to Oklahoma. Over the next four months, the escapees robbed banks in Chelsea, Clinton, and Kingfisher, Oklahoma, as well as one in Black Rock, Arkansas. In due time, Bailey was captured in Texas and charged with participating in the Urschel kidnapping, while Davis fled to California. Brady, Clark, and Underhill went on to hijack banks at Geary and Frederick, Oklahoma, before Brady and Clark were captured and returned to prison.

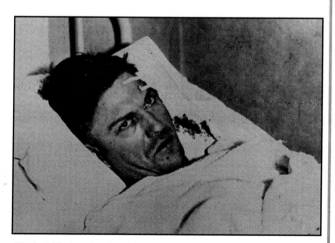

Underhill shortly after his capture in Shawnee. Author's private collection.

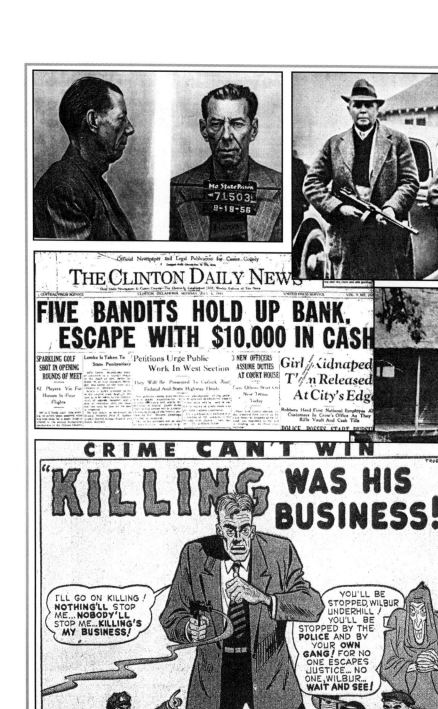

Clockwise from left: "Big" Bob Brady. Courtesy Michael Webb. Deppression-era comic book depiction of Wilbur Underhill. Courtesy Rick Mattix. Newspaper headline concerning the 1933 robbery of the Clinton bank by the Underhill-Bailey Gang. Clarence Eno, a member of the Underhill-Bradshaw Gang. Eno and his four brothers probably set a record when all five were incarcerated in separate prisons at one time in the early 1930s. Courtesy Kansas State Penitentiary. FBI Agents involved in the capture of Wilbur Underhill – R.H. Colvin, left, Paul Hanson, center, K. D. Deaderich, right. Courtesy Jack Hurt. The Bradshaw farm near Vian, a safe haven for the likes of "Pretty Boy" Floyd, Bonnie and Clyde, Wilbur Underhill and members of the Cookson Hills Gang. Courtesy Official detective.

With the rest of the gang now behind bars or out of pocket, Underhill drifted into the thug-infested Cookson Hills of Eastern Oklahoma where he hooked-up with a band of hoodlums led by a vicious gunsel named Ford Bradshaw. The pair, along with Charlie "Cowboy" Cotner, Ed "Newt" Clanton, Charley Dotson, Jim Benge, and the Eno brothers, Clarence and Otis, would make the Bradshaw farm, located near Vian, their headquarters while engaging in an ambitious crime spree. The newly formed gang looted financial institutions in Stuttgart, Arkansas, Baxter Springs and Galena, Kansas, Haskell and Okmulgee, Oklahoma, as well as Nebraska City and York, Nebraska, during the period of October to November 1933. Eventually the gang broke apart, Bradshaw and the Eno boys went on to hijack banks in Wellington, Kansas, as well as Syracuse, Nebraska, while Underhill fled to a series of underworld haunts located in the south-central portion of the state where he formed a new gang,

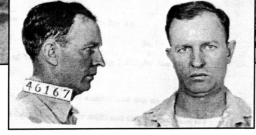

Clockwise from above: Jim Clark. Courtesy NARA. Jim Clark after his release from prison tending rose bushes located behind his residence in Wagoner, Oklahoma. Courtesy Lester Clark. Grave of "Big" Bob Brady, Ada, Oklahoma. Courtesy Larry Walls. Grave of Harvey Bailey-Joplin, MO. Photo by Naomi Morgan. Ford Bradshaw. Courtesy Official Detective. Charlie Cotner. Courtesy Official Detective. Document suggesting the transfer of Jim Clark to Alcatraz. Clark robbed at least a dozen banks in his career. Courtesy NARA.

which promptly robbed banks in Harrah and Coalgate. The noted bandit was finally cornered at a Shawnee residence where he was severely wounded and captured by a heavily armed posse of fast moving G-Men and local officers on a frosty fog-bound December morning. He died the following week at the prison infirmary in McAlester.

Wilbur Underhill would go down in history as the first major criminal to be killed by the FBI. Meanwhile, Underhill's partners in crime soon began dropping like flies. Newt Clanton was slain on the morning of February 4, 1934, in a gunbattle with officers in Chelsea but not before killing Deputy Sheriff Al Powell in the process. Ford Bradshaw was shot and killed by lawmen at a roadhouse near Arkoma on March 3.

Underhill's fellow Kansas prison escapees, Jim Clark and Bob Brady, escaped once again from the Kansas pen on January 19, 1934. Brady was slain by officers near Paola, Kansas, just days after the escape while Clark, along with a third escapee named Frank Delmar, made it back to the 'Sooner' state where they formed a new gang whose membership included notorious badmen Ennis Smiddy and Aubrey "Red" Unsell. Over the next several months, the quartet looted banks in Kingfisher (2nd time), Okeene, Temple, Ryan, and Sentinel, Oklahoma, as well as one in St. Jo, Texas, and two others in Kansas. On the evening of August 1, 1934, Clark was finally captured in the parking lot of a Tulsa apartment complex. The career badman

Modern day view of Kingfisher bank building, robbed twice by members of Underhill-Bailey Gang. Photo by Naomi Morgan.

Author at the grave of Jim Clark. Photo by Naomi Morgan.

Above, left to right: Frank Delmar. Courtesy National Archives. Red Unsell. Courtesy NARA. Ennis Smiddy. Courtesy NARA. Murderer Jack Lloyd, who assisted Underhill in the robbery of the Coalgate Bank. Courtesy NARA. Inset: Grave of outlaw Edward "Newt" Clanton near Chelsea. Clanton was slain in a gunbattle with lawmen. Photo by Naomi Morgan.

was sent to Alcatraz Penitentiary in 1935 and was paroled in 1965. Jim Clark died in 1974, and buried in Wagoner, Oklahoma.

Unsell and Smiddy were soon captured and sent to Alcatraz. Whereas Unsell would eventually be paroled, Smiddy died of liver disease at the prison infirmary in 1941. Harvey Bailey was released from prison in 1965 after serving over thirty years behind bars. He was paroled to Joplin, Missouri, where he married the widow of an ex-crime partner and took up cabinet making along with writing his memoirs. He died in 1979 at the age of 91.

Bonnie and Clyde in Oklahoma with Rick Mattix

Two of the Southwest's most noted desperadoes during the 1930s were Clyde Barrow and Bonnie Parker. Bonnie and Clyde, as they were commonly called, terrorized the country from Texas to Iowa and back over a two-year period, slaughtering at least a dozen men, most of who were peace officers. During their lengthy crime spree, the pair frequently visited Oklahoma.

On the evening of August 5, 1932, Clyde, accompanied by a hoodlum named Ray Hamilton and a third unidentified individual, turned up at a country-dance at Stringtown near Atoka. While the third man entered the dance hall joining the festivities, Clyde and Hamilton remained in their stolen car in the parking lot nipping on a bottle of whiskey. Noticing the men's suspicious behav-

ior, Atoka County Sheriff C.G. Maxwell and Deputy Eugene Moore cautiously approached the car intent on questioning the strangers. The two thugs reacted to the lawmen's appearance by abruptly whipping out a pair of pistols and opening fire, killing Deputy Moore outright while seriously wounding the sheriff. The gunmen then roared off into the night with a host of townspeople in hot pursuit. The killers wrecked their car a short distance away crashing into a railway culvert. The pair, now on foot, flagged down a motorist named Cleve Brady taking his car at gunpoint. Fifteen miles from the scene of the shooting the Brady car lost a wheel. Abandoning the disabled vehicle, Barrow and Hamilton made their way to a farmhouse owned by John Redden. They informed Redden they had been involved in a wreck and had an injured man back at the scene of the accident. When Redden's nephew offered to drive them to a hospital, the pair took

Modern-day view of Bonnie & Clyde death car currently on display at Terribles Casino in Osceola, Iowa.

Barrow gang member Henry Methvin, co-slayer of Cal Campbell near Commerce, Oklahoma. Courtesy Rick Mattix.

Deputy Eugene Moore, slain by Barrow gang near Stringtown, Oklahoma, in 1932. Courtesy Rick Mattix.

Cal Campbell and Percy Boyd. Tulsa World.

Grave of Officer Cal Campbell in Miami. Photo Naomi Morgan.

him hostage and stole his car releasing the poor farmer near the town of Clayton before stealing a another car from a Seminole resident and making their way back to Texas where they abandoned the rig near the community of Grandview.

The Barrow Gang again visited the "Sooner" state in June of 1933 passing through on the way to Ft. Smith, Arkansas, where they hid out in a motor court for several days. On June 23, Clyde's brother Buck killed an officer near Alma, Arkansas, while fleeing a robbery. On July 8, the Barrows raided the National Guard Armory in Enid

where they stole several Browning Automatic Rifles, forty-six Colt .45 pistols, and several thousand rounds of ammunition.

After the Enid heist, the gang stole the car of a Dr. Julian Field containing medical supplies before traveling to Ft. Dodge, Iowa, where they robbed several gas stations. Then it was on to Platte City, Missouri, where the gang was involved in an epic gunbattle with the police. Five days later, the robber band was ambushed at an abandoned amusement park in Iowa by the laws. Although Clyde's brother Buck was slain in the gunfight and his

FAMOUS OUTLAWS
CLYDE BARROW
Terror of the Southwest and his Gun Moll
"BONNIE" PARKER
Modern tigress, fast shooting, cigar smoking, blond Jezebe
MEET DEATH AT GIBSLAND, LA.
ACTUAL AUTHENTIC PICTURES
Taken immediately after the death of these murderous lovers at the hand of the law.

See the Texas Cop Killers - Slayers of 10 men
- Extra Feature -
'BEYOND THE RIO GRANDE'
WITH 5 FAMOUS WESTERN STARS--- Featuring Jack Perrin, Buffalo Bill Jr., Pete Morrison, Franklin Farnum, Edmund Cobb and Starlight, the Wonder Horse.
An All-Talking Western for the Whole Family to See and Hear!

Above: Raymond Hamilton. Author's collection. Left: Clyde Barrow. Courtesy Rick Mattix.

Above: Bonnie and Clyde cohort W.D. Jones. Courtesy Master Detective. Left: Movie Handbill circa 1934 concerning the Barrow Gang. Courtesy Rick Mattix.

wife, Blanche, (born and raised in Garvin County Oklahoma) captured, the rest of the gang again slipped the net traveling back to Texas through Oklahoma.

The Barrow bunch again invaded the state in January of 1934, knocking off the Central National Bank of Poteau for $1,200. In mid-February, the authorities in Oklahoma sent a nearly 1000-man posse made up of lawmen and National Guardsmen into the Cookson Hills, located in the eastern part of the state in an attempt to capture the infamous pair as well as "Pretty Boy" Floyd and Ford Bradshaw. The raid was a dismal failure. On April 1, 1934, Bonnie and Clyde, accompanied by an escaped convict named Henry Methvin, killed a pair of motorcycle policemen near Grapevine, Texas, before traveling back to Oklahoma. A few days later Commerce Constable Cal Campbell received a report concerning some drunks parked on a road southwest of town. Campbell, now accompanied by Police Chief Percy Boyd,

responded to the call. Arriving on the scene the lawmen approached the suspicious car and passengers. The automobile's driver, Clyde Barrow, reacted to the officer's appearance by attempting to drive away but stuck the rig in the mud. Barrow then jumped from the mired car and began firing at the officers with a Browning automatic rifle, as did his cohort, Henry Methvin. Officer Campbell was fatally wounded during the initial volley while Boyd was knocked to the ground by a grazing headshot and captured. The bandits forced Boyd to ride with them on a wild run through Kansas before releasing him near Ft. Scott. Back in Ottawa County Sheriff Dee Watters formed a huge posse but were unable to discover any sign of the desperate pair.

Bonnie and Clyde were slain by a party of officers led by ex-Texas Ranger Frank Hamer in an ambush, which occurred near Gibsland, Louisiana, on May 23, 1934. The father of their associate Henry Methvin had helped set-

Above: Playtime with Bonnie and Clyde. Author's private collection.
Right: Wanted poster concerning the infamous duo. Courtesy Rick Mattix.

up the deadly ambush. Methvin had made a deal with Texas and Louisiana authorities to escape prosecution of crimes committed in those states in return for his informant status but had failed to include Oklahoma in the arrangement. The outlaw was arrested and tried for Cal Campbell's murder. Although a Ottawa County jury found him guilty of murder and sentenced him to die in the electric chair, the Oklahoma Court of Appeals commuted Methvin's sentence to life the following year. While serving time at McAlester, he became renown for his bulldogging abilities displayed at the annual prison rodeo. Methvin was paroled in 1942. He was run over and killed by a freight train near Sulpher, Louisiana in 1948.

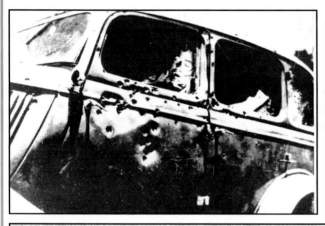

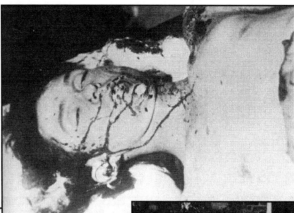

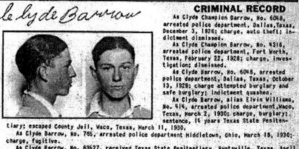

Clockwise from left: Wanted poster concerning Clyde Barrow. Courtesy Rick Mattix. B&C death car, Gibsland, Louisiana, 1934. Courtesy Rick Mattix. Clyde Barrow in death. Courtesy Rick Mattix. Weaponry found in Bonnie and Clyde death car in Louisiana. True Detective.

Law Enforcement Advances

Despite the ongoing economic depression there were many advances made in police work although their implication was limited due to lack of funding. In the art of identification, fingerprinting had fully replaced the crude Bertillon system. Crime scene technology inched ahead using baby steps while in communications the use of the two-way radio installed in patrol cars was pioneered by Oklahoma County Sheriff Stanley Rogers as was the use of the airplane in manhunts. While training for officers in the larger departments improved in the latter 1930s, pay and benefits remained meager. In weaponry, the Thompson machinegun as well as the BAR were finally being distributed en-mass to police departments statewide.

Neither women nor blacks made any appreciable inroads as for employment in the law enforcement community during the 1930s-40s.

In response to the vast number of automobiles on the road and a massive increase in vehicular related fatalities over the past decade, Governor E. W. Marland created the Oklahoma Department of Public Safety, otherwise known as the Highway Patrol in 1937. The initial training period for troopers was three weeks and wages amounted to $150 per month. By 1938, 125 troopers were in uniform patrolling state roadways driving either Ford automobiles or 'Indian' brand motorcycles.

The Thompson Submachine Gun
The Most Effective Portable Fire Arm In Existence

THE ideal weapon for the protection of large estates, ranches, plantations, etc. A combination machine gun and semi-automatic shoulder rifle in the form of a pistol. A compact, tremendously powerful, yet simply operated machine gun weighing only *seven* pounds and having only *thirty* parts. Full automatic, fired from the hip, 1,500 shots per minute. Semi-automatic, fitted with a stock and fired from the shoulder, 50 shots per minute. Magazines hold 50 and 100 cartridges.

THE Thompson Submachine Gun incorporates the simplicity and infallibility of a hand loaded weapon with the effectiveness of a machine gun. It is simple, safe, sturdy, and sure in action. In addition to its increasingly wide use for protection purposes by banks, industrial plants, railroads, mines, ranches, plantations, etc., it has been adopted by leading Police and Constabulary Forces, throughout the world and is unsurpassed for military purposes.

Information and prices promptly supplied on request

AUTO-ORDNANCE CORPORATION
302 Broadway   *Cable address: Autordco*   New York City

Federal Bureau of Investigation
U. S. Department of Justice
J. Edgar Hoover, Director

Firearms Training

PRACTICE WITH VARIOUS TYPES OF ARMS

PISTOL PRACTICE WITH BOBBING TARGETS

SPECIAL AGENTS OF THE BUREAU ARE REQUIRED TO QUALIFY EACH MONTH IN THE USE OF THE REVOLVER, AUTOMATIC PISTOL, SUB-MACHINE GUN, HIGH POWERED RIFLE, SHOTGUN, AND GAS GUNS

PISTOL PRACTICE FROM MOVING AUTOMOBILE

THESE VIEWS SHOW CLASSES OF AGENTS IN TRAINING AT THE U.S. MARINE CORPS BASE AT QUANTICO, VIRGINIA.

WINTER REVOLVER PRACTICE

PRONE RIFLE PRACTICE

"Them mugs look suspicious to me."

Clockwise from left: Cartoon featuring law enforcement humor. Author's collection. Police testing personal body armor the old fashioned way, circa 1925 – crude indeed! Courtesy Rick Mattix. FBI firearms training, 1930s. Courtesy Rick Mattix. Browing Automatic Rifle. Courtesy Rick Mattix.
Opposive page: Sales ad for Thompson Machinegun. Courtesy Rick Mattix. Tulsa city detective division, circa 1935. Courtesy John Lairmore.

Massacre at Big Mac

On the morning of August 10, 1941, Warden Jess Dunn, accompanied by Engineer J. H. Fentress, were strolling about the interior of the Oklahoma State Penitentiary in McAlester, inspecting the prison's public address system in preparation for the upcoming "Behind the Walls" rodeo. Suddenly, inmates Claud Beaver, Hiram Prather, Bill Anderson, and Roy McGee confronted the pair with a selection of straight razors and homemade dirks. While one of the cons grabbed the back of the warden's shirt sliding a razor to his throat, a second man plunged a dirk two full inches into the keeper's back ordering him to "Move toward the gate." The other escapees grabbed Fentress and held knives pressed firmly against his back as well. As the motley assembly of cons and hostages began edging toward the east gate, they unexpectedly ran into a visitor accompanied by his small son. One of the inmates shoved the visitor ordering him to, "Get that kid out of here mister, and I mean now!"

On arriving at the gate, the cons forced Dunn to call up to the tower guards ordering them to throw down their guns. He was further instructed to order them to send a car around for their use. The prisoners then grabbed the weapons and, on the vehicle's arrival, piled in with their hostages, speeding away from the prison proper.

In the meantime, the prison's communications section contacted the area's law enforcement agencies informing them of the escape. Hearing the news of the warden's predicament, Pittsburg County Deputy Sheriff Bill Alexander quickly drove toward the scene slowing down just long enough to pick up County Jailor Tab Ford and a merchant named Bob Pollock, who unknown to him was armed with an unloaded pistol.

On their arrival in the area, Alexander spotted the fleeing vehicle. He responded by blocking the roadway with his cruiser. When the carload of prisoners pulled up the escapees demanded they be given leave or they would be forced to kill their hostages. Alexander responded by informing the cons the warden could pass but the fugitives could not. Suddenly, one of the prisoners fired a pistol round which missed its target. Alexander responded by cutting loose with his .351 cal. rifle killing the driver, Claud Beaver. Another of the escapees quickly took the wheel and put it in reverse speeding the opposite direction motoring several blocks until halting abruptly when he encountered a section of the road where a bridge was out. Sensing the gig was up, one of the cons turned and shot Warden Dunn three time in the head at point-blank range while a second plunged a dirk into his chest repeatedly before bailing out of the rig seeking cover in a nearby ditch. A ferocious gunbattle ensued in which Deputy Ford was fatally wounded while Pollock took a painful round to the shoulder. Alexander returned fire sending a well-placed slug into the skull of McGee, his body sprawling lifelessly into the

Above: Convicts on the job working the "P" Farm. Author's collection.
Top: Jess Dunn, right, and his murderer, inmate Claude Beaver. Courtesy Daily Oklahoman.

Rotunda at Oklahoma State Penitentiary. Photo by Naomi Morgan.

ditch. Seconds later the deputy caught Anderson in the open and pegged him with a pair of rounds to the torso. Observing the fates of his companions, Prather rose out of the ditch, his arms held high begging for mercy. Thus, the battle ended.

Alexander approached the fugitive's car hoping to find the hostages unharmed. Peering into the bullet-riddled car his worst fears were realized, Dunn was slumped in the backseat dead, while the telephone engineer was bound and lying on the floorboard bleeding profusely from a serious knife wound. Strewn about the battlefield, Beavers and McCoy lay dead where they fell, while Anderson, who was gut-shot, appeared to be taking his last gasps of life. He would die in great agony at the prison infirmary. Tab Ford was dead on arrival at the hospital, while Pollock and Fentress would both eventually recover, as would Inmate Prather. Only the sharp-shooting deputy came out unscathed from the battle.

When interviewed shortly after the shootout, Alexander informed reporters, "Some years ago I was a guard here at the prison. One day Jess Dunn informed me 'If there ever should be a break and the convicts take hostages, even if they get me and I tell you not to shoot,

go ahead and shoot." The deputy had clearly taken the warden at his word. A few weeks after the tragic affair, Oklahoma's Governor would officially commend Deputy Alexander for his bravery. Hiram Prather was tried and convicted of Dunn's murder. He was executed on July 14, 1943. According to those present, just prior to pulling the switch on the electric chair, Executioner Rich Owen whispered in the ear of the condemned man he was going to "Fry you like a piece of bacon" for killing his friend, Jess Dunn.

Jess Dunn, a brave and able officer, was buried with honors in his hometown of Ardmore where he had been a law enforcement officer for many years. It stands as an ultimate example of irony that while Jess Dunn was oftentimes criticized for his humane treatment of inmates at "Big Mac" he would suffer such inhumane treatment at their hands. The 'Behind the Walls' prison rodeo, which Dunn had conceived, is now in its sixty-sixth year.

Oklahomans and "The Rock" (Alcatraz)

The US Penitentiary on Alcatraz Island, located in San Francisco Bay, was intimately connected with Oklahoma Lawmen and Outlaw history. It was the repository

Alcatraz – America's Devils Island. Author's collection.

of the most desperate of federal prisoners for three decades until to its closing in 1963. The prison, which had previously served as a military corrections facility, was declared America's principal maximum-security jail in late 1933. During the height of the Midwest Crime Wave, numerous of the facilities inmates either hailed from or had committed headline-grabbing crimes in Oklahoma. Most noted of these prisoners were Alvin Karpis, Arthur "Doc" Barker, "Machine Gun" Kelly, Albert Bates, Harvey Bailey, Jim Clark, Red Melton, Dewey Gilmore, Carl Janaway, Harry Campbell, Frank Delmar, Cecil Snow, Phoenix Donald (William Weaver), Russell Cooper, Donnie Garrett, Malloy Kuykendall, Dale Stamphill, Ted Cole, Ralph Roe, Ennis Smiddy, Aubrey Unsell, Jack Lloyd, Henry Clay Tollett, Roy Kimes, Volney Davis, Dale Stamphill, Clarence Carnes, and Sam Shockley. Several on those on this list were involved in desperate escape attempts from the island bastille…

Dale Stamphill, Oklahoma bank robber and kidnapper involved in a deadly Granite escape in 1935. Courtesy National Archives.

Mugshot of inmate Sam Shockley. Courtesy NARA.

December 16, 1937, Oklahomans Ralph Roe and Ted Cole made their way off the island into the cold waters of San Francisco Bay riding a makeshift raft. The pair was never heard from again. While some have speculated they made their way to freedom, its more likely they drowned in the choppy waters. At the time of his escape, Roe was serving 144 years for the robbery of a Sulpher bank while Cole was serving a fifty-year term for kidnapping a Cushing man.

January 13, 1939, the infamous Doc Barker and several others, including fellow Oklahomans Dale Stamphill and Rufus

McCain, attempted to stage an escape from "The Rock." Rufus McCain had been convicted of the 1935 robbery of the Idabel National Bank while Dale Stamphill was incarcerated for looting the First National Bank of Seiling, Oklahoma, after escaping from Oklahoma's Granite Reformatory with twenty-one others. The escape attempt from the island prison ended in failure, Barker was shot to death by prison guards while his cohorts were quickly captured.

May 21, 1941, Sam Shockley, who was serving time for the 1938 holdup of the Bank of Paoli, was involved in a clumsy and unsuccessful breakout.

May 2, 1946 Sam Shockley and five accomplices were engaged in a bloody escape attempt, which ended with the deaths of two correctional officers and three inmates. The rioters somehow gained possession of some firearms and held several guards hostage until a group

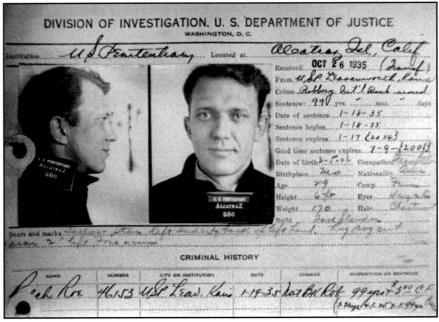

Ralph Roe, one-time member of the Underhill Gang who escaped from Alcatraz in 1937 in the company of Ted Cole. Courtesy NARA.

of heavily armed Marines arrived on the island and began shelling the cellblock with tear gas bombs and bazooka rounds. The Marines eventually fought their way into the bowels of the structure where they lobbed grenades at the rioters. With the killing of three of the conspirators, the riot was quelled and the authorities took back the cellblock. Shockley was executed at San Quinton in 1948 for his part in the affair. Another Oklahoma inmate, Clarence Carnes, a full-blooded Choctaw, also played a part in the disturbance but unlike his fellow conspirators, he was credited with not taking lives, but saving those of several guards who had been taken hostage. Carnes's story was later made into two separate made-for-TV movies.

Carl Lee Janaway, alias "Chick" Janaway, otherwise known as the "Terror of the Ozarks," was born in Arkansas in 1902. He married in 1930 and began working for the Arkansas State Highway Department. The young man seemed to be living a law-abiding existence until 1932 when he robbed a bank located in Hartman, Arkansas. The desperado was soon captured in Tulsa and extradited back to Arkansas where he pleaded guilty to bank robbery charges and promptly sentenced to five years at the state prison in Little Rock. In January 1934, Janaway escaped from the institution going on a

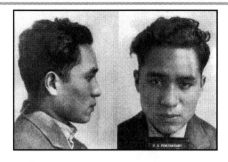

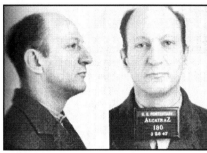

Top: Alcataz mugshot of Clarence Carnes. Courtesy US Bureau of Prisons. Above: Malloy Kuykendall, an incorrigible criminal who led a mass escape from Granite Reformatory before his capture and eventual transfer to "The Rock." Courtesy National Archives.

crime spree burglarizing numerous businesses throughout Western Arkansas and Eastern Oklahoma before being captured in September and sent to the notorious Tucker Prison Farm with two years added to his sentence for escaping custody. He escaped again in mid-1935 and was captured around Christmas, just in time to spend the yuletide season confined in solitary confinement. The incorrigible hoodlum made his way to freedom a third time in April of 1936, fleeing to Oklahoma's Cookson Hills where he hid out for several months night-raiding numerous small stores and farmsteads for his daily bread. In September, he shot and wounded Sequoyah County Deputy Raymond Drake when the officer, along with several others, attempted to ambush him at the

Ford Bradshaw farm located just north of Vian. Soon afterwards, a posse led by Cherokee County Deputy Grover Bishop jumped Janaway and an individual later identified as Estelle Perkins at an isolated hideout located eight miles east of Braggs. When the pair attempted to flee, the posse opened fire-wounding Perkins while Janaway escaped on foot into the heavy timber. Perkins, who was suffering from six buckshot wounds to the abdomen, was transported to a Tahlequah hospital where he admitted the pair was planning to rob a Hulbert bank the following day. He soon succumbed to his wounds. A brief investigation revealed Perkins was a recent escapee from a prison road camp serving a life term for the 1925 slaying of two Ardmore policemen. Reacting to the presence of nearly one hundred possemen arriving in the vicinity, Janaway stole a fisherman's car and drove to Missouri where he hijacked a second vehicle as well as kidnapping the driver. After

Rufus McCain was born in Broken Bow, Oklahoma. He served a one-year sentence for theft beginning in 1931. After his release from prison in 1932, the badman robbed two banks. Captured and sentenced to a twelve-year stretch at "Big Mac," he escaped in early 1935. McCain looted a bank in Broken Bow in May 1935. The outlaw was soon captured and sent to Alcatraz. He was murdered by fellow inmate Henri Young in 1940. Courtesy NARA.

abandoning the rig and driver in East St. Louis, Illinois, the outlaw hired a taxi to transport him to downtown St. Louis where he was confronted by a city cop named Edward Schultz. The two squared off exchanging fire for several minutes until the officer fell struck by rounds in both legs. When the lawman went down the bandit began running across the busy street. Midway through the thoroughfare he was struck by a car and flung onto the pavement suffering a broken leg. Within minutes of the accident, a bevy of angry officers showed up on the scene and took the miscreant into custody.

Janaway was promptly convicted of kidnapping and auto theft for which he was sentenced to fifteen years in the federal prison. Soon after his arrival at Leavenworth the badman was transferred to Alcatraz due to his being branded an extreme escape risk. While serving time on "The Rock" he celled next to gang lord Al Capone. Surviving records from the institu-

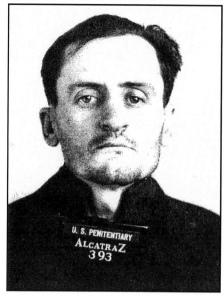
Carl Janaway. Photo courtesy of NARA

tion state he was a "Habitual offender and a menace to society". Records also indicate his mother was presently confined to the Insane Asylum in Vinita while his father was, "The erratic type and likely insane as well."

Janaway was paroled from federal custody in late 1944 and released into the waiting arms of the Sequoyah County authorities that held a warrant for his arrest for the attempted murder of Officer Drake back in 1936. In October of 1945, he was convicted of Assault with Intent to Kill and sentenced to a ten-year term at McAlester. The following year the verdict was overturned and the undersized outlaw (He weighed 96 pounds) was turned loose. Carl Janaway spent the remainder of his life residing in Tahlequah where he operated a paint shop. In his final years, he evolved into a town character spinning his yarns in coffee shops and cafes located near the campus of an area collage. He died at a local nursing home in 1997 at the age of 94.

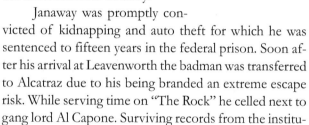

No. 46639   OSP 11-29-03

| Name | Carl Janaway | Color | White | Age | 42 |

Rec'd 10-16-45   Term (10) Years   Max 10-15-55

County Sequoyah   Case No. 3321   Min. 10-13-50

Crime Assault with Intent to Kill

3d Term

C.O. 10-7-46 Above subject released to Sequoyah CountybSheriff by order of Criminal Court of Appeals this date.

Prison document concerning Carl Janaway. Courtesy Oklahoma Department of Corrections.

ADMISSION SUMMARY
U. S. Penitentiary
LEAVENWORTH, KANSAS

1437-ID
Rec'd 7-13-39

Institution Name: J A N A W A Y, Carl   Reg. No.: 50639-L

Reports Received From

F. B. I. **Not Rec'd**   U. S. Attorney **rec'd**   Prosecuting Agency **Not Rec'd**

True Name As above	Offense Kidnapping and Dyer Act Committed	3-3-37
Residence Claimed St. Louis, Mo.	Date Classified	3-31-37
ED:MISSOURI: ST. LOUIS	Sentence 10 yrs. (1-10 yr & 1-5 yr cocur.)	
Date of birth ?-?-02 Age 29	Sentence Begins	2-5-37
Race White	Fine None Eligible for Parole	6-4-40
Country of birth US	Costs None Expires with good time	10-23-43
Citizenship US	Detainers WANTED: COUNTY ATTORNEY Expires full term	2-4-47
Marital Status Separated	SALLISAW, OKLAHOMA. (ASSAULT WITH INTENT TO KILL).	

WANTED: ARKANSAS BOARD OF PENAL INSTITUTIONS, GOULD, ARK.
(ESCAPE)

revious record
2 Deputy's report
3 Social
4 (a) Medical
  (b) Neuro-Psych.
5 (a) Employment
  (b) Educational
  (c) Religious
  (d) Recreational

1. Previous Record : Division of Investigation Report.
   ADMITTED
   #4302 State Pen., Tucker, Ark.

2. DEPUTY WARDEN'S REPORT.
   OFFENSE: Stole from William Hicks, on December 26, 1936, one 1936 Model Ford Coupe bearing Motor No. 2861495, near Doniphan, Missouri, and transported same in interstate commerce to a point near the City of Effingham, in the State of Illinois.
   On December 26, he kidnapped victim William Hicks and transported him in interstate from Doniphan, Missouri to Salem, Illinois. On December 27, 1936, JANAWAY, in his attempt to resist arrest, engaged in a gun battle with a patrolman, inflicting several shotgun wounds in said Patrolman's legs just prior to his arrest at Third St. & Washington Avenue, St. Louis, Missouri.
   INFORMATION INDICATES: No codefendants. He was incarcerated in the Arkansas State Penitentiary, Tucker, Arkansas from 1-3-32 to May 1936, having been convicted of robbery at Harmann, Arkansas, from which institution he ESCAPED. He is WANTED (as above) by the State Courts in St. Louis, Missouri on a charge of assault with intent to kill an officer; and is also wanted (as above) in Salisaw, Oklahoma on 4 charges of grand larceny, as well as two charges of robbery with firearms and 1 charge of assault with intent to kill.
   STATEMENT: This man is at present confined as a patient in the Hospital. No personal interview was held.
   SUMMARY: While this man's present attitude was not determined, it is reasonable to assume in view of the nature of his previous criminal history, that he will always be an habitual violator and always resort to criminal activities in order to live while on the outside. He is definitely of the vicious type and would willingly take part in any disturbance within the institution and as readily take advantage of any opportunity to escape from custody. He will always be a problem.
   QUARANTINE REPORT: None received. Hospital patient.

Recommendations:- CONSIDER FOR TRANSFER TO USP ALCATRAZ, CALIFORNIA WHEN PHYSICAL CONDITION WILL PERMIT. MAXIMUM SUPERVISION.

CJS-mmw

FPI INC—FLK—2-12-36-12000—SETS OF 10—6513

Left: Admissions sheet for Leavenworth Penitentiary concerning Carl Janaway. Courtesy NARA.

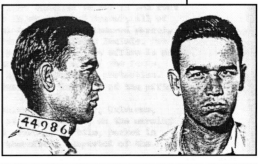

Right: Cecil Snow, a professional burglar who robbed the Dewar post office on February 12, 1934. Captured in the big Cookson Hills Raid on February 17, and sentenced to a ten-year stretch at Alcatraz, Snow had previously done time at Pauls Valley and Granite Reformatories as well as pulling a stretch at McAlester. Courtesy NARA.

Executions by Electricity at the Oklahoma State Penitentiary, 1915-1966

Henry Bookman was executed on the morning of December 10, 1915. He would go down in history as the first to die in Oklahoma's electric chair. Twenty-eight-year-old Bookman, who was African American, had been sentenced to death for the senseless shotgun slaying of a white farmer in rural McIntosh County. According to Bookman, his victim had threatened him a few days before the murder. He was put to death at roughly 1 a.m. and according to news reports had to be physically hauled to the chair by several guards and trustees. Seventy persons attended the event. His last words amounted to admonishing the assembled witnesses to "Be good and love God!" He spent the hours before his death singing gospel songs in his cell. After being placed in the chair, he appeared to fall into a trance. When the warden gave the signal, the executioner, who stood behind a canvas screen, threw the switch and the victim noticeably stiffened then promptly relaxed. The prison physician checked the man for vital signs, found none, and pronounced him dead. Henry Bookman was buried at the prison cemetery, which had been dubbed "Peckerwood Ridge Boneyard."

Cecil Towery-On a hot August day in 1916, Morris, Oklahoma, oilman Charles Vaughn stopped along the highway near the community of Hoffman in order to give a lift to brothers Cecil and Will Towery who apparently had been drinking. The two black men quickly turned on the Good Samaritan, cutting his throat and slicing his body to ribbons with jack knives, ignoring his pleas for mercy. The pair then robbed the body and fled. Cecil Towery was quickly captured near the scene, his hands and shirt covered in blood. His brother was apprehended in the Tulsa rail yards several days later. Both admitted their guilt, blaming the demon rum for their actions. The day after their capture, a mob of citizens attempted to storm the jail in hopes of lynching the pair. Lawmen slipped the two out a side door and hid them in a cornfield until they could be moved to the state penitentiary in McAlester for safekeeping. On November 6, 1916, Cecil Towery was put to death in the electric chair for his crimes.

Willie Williams-At 2:50 a.m. on the day after Christmas 1915, Muskogee Police Officer Sam Neal was on foot patrol when he heard noises in an alley located off Okmulgee Avenue. Neal withdrew his billy club, turned and walked into the dark alley to investigate. Suddenly he bumped into a black man who was running toward the street carrying a burlap sack. When Neal attempted to subdue the man, the interloper turned and shot the officer in the arm. The two grappled and when the wounded officer attempted to pull his own pistol the assassin shot him again in the head. The perpetrator then took the lawman's gun and fled the area on foot into the cold windswept darkness. A few minutes later an off duty streetcar driver discovered the bleeding policeman in the act of crawling into the center of the street. The driver immediately contacted the authorities. On the arrival of a pair of Muskogee detectives, the officer gave them the details of the ambush before passing out. Sam Neal died a few hours later at a local hospital. Neal, a Cherokee Indian, was forty-eight years old, married and the father of four small children. He had been a patrolman for four years.

Investigators quickly discovered a nearby hardware store had been burglarized and a pistol and ammunition stolen. When the assailant was described to the store's owner, he informed lawmen the description fit one of his employees named Willie Williams, alias Will Green. When detectives interviewed his wife, she told officers her husband had left earlier that night intending on getting his hands on a gun in order to shoot a man who had trifled with her on several occasions. She further informed the gumshoes that Williams had showed back up around dawn then left to board a train bound for Porum. At 9 a.m. the morning of the shooting, Deputy Sheriff Shoemake and Porum Police Chief Oscar Poole met the Midland Valley train at the Porum Depot. When the officers sighted the suspect, he and a companion both pulled pistols and attempted to fire on the officers. After exchanging several ineffectual rounds, the officers overpowered the pair and transported them back to Muskogee by car. On their arrival in Muskogee, the duo was incarcerated in the county jail for safekeeping. That night an angry mob of several hundred assembled in front of the jail demanding the prisoners. A rope was soon produced accompanied by shouts of "Hang them." The laws reacted by contacting the governor who immediately dispatched Company F of the local National Guard who quickly surrounded the jail with bayonets at the ready. When the mob, which had been whipped into frenzy by a group of drunken agitators, stormed the jail in force, a company of firemen, backed by the guardsmen, repelled them with blasts from a high-pressure water hose. When the enraged vigilantes assaulted the jail a second time, actually battering down the main door with a pair of steel train rails, Sheriff Barger had the two suspects removed out a side door, dressed as national guardsmen, and taken to nearby Coweta by car. From Coweta the pair was transported via rail to the Tulsa County Jail.

Officer Neal was given a hero's funeral, his casket accompanied by an honor guard to his grave at Muskogee's

Greenhill Cemetery. Williams was eventually tried and found guilty of Neal's murder and sentenced to death by Judge Degraffenreid who commented on sentencing, "I hope the defendant finds the next world better than this one." Williams was executed on the morning of April 13, 1917, in the first triple-header event, where three men were executed in one day. The executions took place just before dawn and were reportedly a chaotic affair. The doomed men spent the hours before their deaths singing gospel hymns and praying with the prison chaplain. Williams sat in the chair first followed by murderers, Charley Young and Chester Taylor. Muskogee County Sheriff John Barger attended the execution saying, "I usually dread going to executions but this time I relish the idea!"

On the evening of December 2, 1916, **Charley Young**, suspecting his live-in girlfriend was passing her favors to several local boys, armed himself and laid in wait until three men arrived at his home under the cover of darkness. Young then waded in amongst them shooting and wounding several. One of his shots went wild and struck and killed a man who was standing on a neighbor's porch fetching his laundry. Although the judge at his trial admitted the murder was probably an accident, he proclaimed, "Young should die since his intentions on that night was to kill someone."

Chester Taylor, a forty-four-year-old black man hailing from Creek County, murdered his wife in a fit of jealousy on the night of August 24, 1916. The deed was committed with the use of the blunt end of an ax. At his trial, Taylor pled self-defense claiming his spouse had attempted to cut him with a knife, so naturally he took an ax to her. Young was buried at "Peckerwood Hill," the prison cemetery.

John Prather and several companions robbed and killed a man on the evening March 9, 1911. After beating their victim senseless and relieving him of his wallet Prather shot and killed the man in a merciless fashion declaring, "I always wanted to kill a white man!" Prather was tried and found guilty of the murder and sentenced to hang in Oklahoma City. While standing on the scaffold just before the rope was draped over his head, the state attorney general appeared in a buggy ordering the executioner to stop the proceedings, stating, "The governor has commuted this man's sentence to life!" Big mistake, on June 27, 1917, Prather murdered his cellmate (Homer Chapman) with a nine-inch long homemade dirk. Prather insisted he killed his bunkie due to his backing out of a scheme to assist him in the planned murder of a prison guard. Shortly afterwards he pled guilty to the crime and was again sentenced to death. When asked by reporters how he felt about his impending execution he stated "I'll stand it like a man." John

Prather rode the 'Midnight Special' on the morning of May 3,1918.

James Brown and a companion robbed and murdered a fisherman named Glenn Jacobs on an isolated road north of Muskogee in 1917. While Brown was soon captured, his pal escaped custody. When Judge Degraffenreid sentenced Brown to death, the defendant retorted, "It's not a fair decision!" He was executed on November 8,1918.

T. R. Braught shot and killed a man in a garage in the small town of Oilton in front of five witnesses while his victim was on his knees pleading for his life. Braught lined up the five witnesses and swore them to back up his story of self-defense. They failed to keep their oaths instead informing and testifying in court against the murderer. Braught was executed on May 23,1919. He was the first white man to take a ride on "Old Sparky."

Monroe Betterton was executed by use of the electric chair on July 11, 1920. His crime was murdering his wife. He was convicted in Craig County.

Next in line for "hot seat" was a pair of Muskogee County murderers named **Robert W. Blakely** and **John Ledbetter**. The two men were executed in a duel event on the morning of February 25, 1921. Blakely had ravaged then brutally murdered his young stepdaughter while Ledbetter had killed a man in a fit of jealousy. Both men found religion shortly before their deaths and a portable copper bathtub was moved into their separate cells for their baptisms. Ledbetter, who was described by the press as a particularly surly individual, maintained his innocence claiming self-defense until the end, protesting his girlfriend had lied on the witness stand. Prior to their executions, the pair ate a last meal of fried liver, hash brown potatoes, cream gravy, applesauce, fried eggs, biscuits, chocolate cake, and milk. They took a nap before a pair of prison employees visited each cell shaving their heads and one leg. Ledbetter was the first to go. He entered the death chamber sporting a red carnation on his lapel provided by the prison chaplain. He was reportedly anxious but kept his nerve to the end. He was declared dead at 12:15 a.m. and his body immediately hauled off on a stretcher to make room for the next man. Blakely was the calmer of the two dying with a smile on his face and a prayer on his lips. He was pronounced dead at 12:25 a.m. Both were buried in Muskogee County cemeteries. Blakely was thirty-nine while Ledbetter thirty-one years of age at the time of their deaths.

Eli Thomas was executed on July 15, 1921, for a murder he committed in LaFlore County. He was twenty-one at the time of his death.

Fifty-some-year-old **Steve Saba** was convicted of stabbing his eighteen-year-old niece Sophia Saba to death at her parent's home in Coalgate on September 18, 1921. Evidently, he had been boarding with his brother's family at the time of the murder. The girl lived long enough to make a dying declaration implicating her uncle who she said attacked her after she refused his advances. Saba was executed on March 17, 1922.

Sam Watkins was executed on May 5,1922, for killing Mrs. Cora Jones. His last words were, "It is that I come here like a man that I can say I will rest forever and am not afraid. This is the first time in my life that I have been in a prison and I am going to be put to death." After he was strapped into the chair he said, "I will meet you all in heaven, and God be with you all."

On a chilly night in April 1923 forty-five year-old **Jack Pope** and twenty-one year-old **Aaron Harvey** of Haworth, McCurtain County got drunked up and slaughtered Pope's wife, two children, and her parents in a blood soaked frenzy motivated by Pope's desire to collect a $2,000 insurance policy in which he was the sole beneficiary. The pair was promptly arrested and both convicted and sentenced to death for their barbarous behavior. The execution date was announced as Sunday, January 13, 1924. Although a group of local clergymen raised a stink protesting the execution of anyone on the Sabbath, the festivities went ahead as scheduled. The event was marred by the fact the prison chaplain, who was against capital punishment, refused to attend forcing the warden to bring in an outside minister. Pope, who was the more nervous of the two, took the chair first with a choir from the Salvation Army singing, "I'm Coming Home With no More Room to Roam" in the background. He offered no last words. When the juice hit him, he reportedly lurched forward straining mightily against the leather straps before suddenly going limp as a rag doll. Moments later, Harvey, who had had a jailhouse religious conversion since his trial, also refused to make a final comment. Forty-one seconds later he met his maker as well. Both Pope and Harvey were buried at Peckerwood Ridge and the $2,000 in insurance money Pope so lusted after was paid to his wife's surviving kin.

On August 9, 1923, **Richard A. Birkes** and Allison Ives robbed the First State Bank of Ketchum at gunpoint. When Cashier Frank Pitts was ordered to hold up his hands in submission, he hesitated. Birkes shot and killed the banker. Rush-

ing out of the bank without even taking a dime, the pair disappeared into the countryside. Both men were eventually captured and while Ives received a life sentence, Birkes, who denied he had pulled the trigger, was given a death sentence. As Birkes' execution date neared, his crime partner signed an affidavit swearing he had been the actual triggerman. When Governor Martin Trapp was presented with this piece of evidence he proclaimed, "Ives's affidavit is worthless since he has already been tried and sentenced. Since he is in no legal jeopardy he can say what he wants." When Birkes' wife and mother showed up at the governor's mansion to plead for his life, Trapp stated, "The grief of these women is a sad thing but there is another woman to be considered, the wife of the victim." A few minutes past midnight on September 5, 1924, Richard Birkes gamely walked to the electric chair dressed in a new blue serge suit, white shirt, and blue tie. He was smoking a cigar stub. Warden Keys told him to, " Go ahead and finish your stogie son." Asked for any last words the condemned man stated in a clear unwavering voice, "I'm not guilty but I am not afraid to die." He was strapped in the seat, the black hood put over his face, and the electrodes attached. Just before the current hit, Birkes shouted, "Goodbye Boys." By all accounts, while Richard Birkes may not have lived well, he died well.

Twenty-one–year-old **Leroy Scott** was sentenced to death for murdering a Pittsburg County taxi-driver. He was executed on May 29,1925.

Johnnie Washington shot and killed an El Dorado, Oklahoma night watchman on November 9, 1924. He was executed on December 4,1925. It took fifty-five seconds and 2300 volts to snuff out his life.

Between midnight and 12:30 a.m. on the morning of June 29, 1928, three men, one white and two black, were executed in McAlester's electric chair. The first to die was **Walter Wigger**, convicted of slaying his girlfriend, Ruth Harris, in Ottawa County. When he entered the death chamber, Wigger demanded the witnesses be removed before five guards crowded him into the chair. A minute later, he was dead. As they were hauling his body off to an adjoining room a Muskogee County murderer named **Theodore Buster** was conducted into the room. He had no last words and it reportedly took two applications of current to extinguish his life. Buster was removed from the room while a third convict named **Willie "Whiskey" O'Neil**, who had slain an Oklahoma City streetcar conductor, was escorted to the chair. He willingly sat down and while being strapped in, smiled and wished the crowd of over 100 witnesses "Good Luck." Both Buster and O'Neil were buried at the prison cemetery. According to press reports Executioner Owen, was quite proud of the fact it took less than thirty minutes to kill all three men. Very businesslike indeed.

On September 2, 1927, **Tom Guest** and two unidentified individuals entered the Canadian Valley State Bank of Asher. Three persons were in the financial institution at the time of the heist. When an employee of the local phone exchange spotted the robbery in progress she rushed across the street to a drug store informing the pharmacist, Bailey Browder, of the event. Young Browder armed himself and took a position in the street directly in front of the bank. When the desperadoes exited the building Browder opened fire. One of the hijackers returned fire, a round striking the druggist. The bullet tore into a lung dropping Browder to the pavement. The bandits piled into the getaway car being driven by a youth named W. J. White, fleeing with $1,800 from the bank's coffers. White, along with Tom Guest were later arrested and charged with the crime. While White copped a plea on the robbery charge and received a ten-year sentence, Guest held out for trial and was convicted and sentenced to death for the druggist's murder. Both men were also suspected of several other recent bank jobs. Guest and a black man named James Edward Forrest, who had been given a death sentence for raping a white woman near Comanche, Oklahoma, were both scheduled for execution on July 17, 1930. At a minute past midnight on the morning of the double execution, Forrest was brought forth into the execution chamber and asked if he had any last words. He calmly said, "I know I am going home," before placing himself in the chair. A crowd of seventy-five persons watched as the young Negro was hit with the heavy current for forty seconds. His body lurched then with the current turned off fell back into the chair. The doctor came forward and after checking his chest with a stethoscope declared, "This man is dead." A witness was overheard saying, "Boy, he was one brave fellow." After the undertakers from Humphries Funeral Home removed the body, Tom Guest was brought in and asked if he had any final statement. Guest loudly stated, "After looking out at this crowd I can tell you I am a better man at heart then some of them." At 12:11 a.m., the Warden nodded to Rich Owen to throw the switch.

A thirty-one year-old Choctaw Indian named **E. S. "Choc" Hembree** was executed on April 17,1931, for the 1930 rape and robbery of a Stephens County schoolteacher. According to several sources, Hembree was electrocuted twice. Apparently, the Warden, who was legally required to physically attend every execution, had departed the death chamber and returned home just moments before the actual execution was carried out. Soon after the physician pronounced the man dead; officials suddenly noticed the Warden's absence. The head-keeper was promptly recalled and the corpse strapped back into the chair in order to repeat the gruesome procedure.

A banker and minor politician named **Paul D. Cole** was executed on July 10, 1931, for the murder of his business partner near Wewoka. Cole was convicted of killing Ernest Irby, a Wewoka druggist in a suspected bootlegging deal gone sour. Irby's bullet-ridden body was discovered by fishermen resting at the bottom of a lake, weighted down with rocks. Cole vigorously denied shooting his pal. On the morning of the execution the condemned man was brought into the death chamber and with sixty spectators looking on and a choir singing "What a friend we have in Jesus" he was placed in the chair and asked if he had any last words. First, he thanked prison personal for their wonderful treatment then he stated, "I did not shoot Ernest Irby. I forgive everyone with no bitterness. God, I confess my sins and repent. Goodbye everyone." A spectator then responded audibly "Goodbye Paul." Cole's death left many unanswered questions concerning Irby's murder. The case against him was not cut and dry. Shortly before his execution, all twelve jurors from his trial signed a document asking Governor Murray to commute Cole's sentence from death to life imprisonment. In the days following the execution a petition was circulated around Wewoka requesting folks donate to the building a small monument, which would be inscribed "Paul Cole—Murdered by the state of Oklahoma." The edifice was never erected.

One hundred and seventeen persons witnessed the August 21, 1931, execution of **Bennie Nichols** who had been convicted of the beating death of an Ada night watchman named Jack Horton. The condemned man's last words were "Warden, I am as innocent as you are…I am to die and I'm an innocent boy. It's a dirty shame."

On the morning of November 26, 1930, thirty-seven-year-old **Henry Lovett** strolled into the lobby of the First National Bank of El Reno sporting a pistol in one hand and a burlap sack in the other. On ordering the eight persons in the financial institution into the vault, a cashier named Burge whipped out a gun and shot the bandit in the chest. Lovett returned fire, his shots going wild. As the gunbattle was in progress a twenty-eight year-old high school wrestling coach Dee Foliart entered the building through a side entrance and was shot in the upper torso, the round entering his right lung. While Lovett and the banker continued to exchange shots Foliart clutched his chest and stumbled into the street where he collapsed in a heap. Meanwhile, back in the bank Lovett was again wounded, taking a slug to the side of the head. The wounded bandit ran from the bank directly into the waiting arms of a group of armed vigilantes. Mr. Foliart would die of his wounds later that night. Lovett survived and was charged with the popular coach's murder as well as robbery with firearms. When informed of the coach's death the outlaw told lawmen, "I'm sorry." The bandit was convicted of both charges in a Canadian County court and sentenced to death. At a few minutes past midnight on September 25, 1931, Henry Lovett was carried to the electric chair by a group of guards. He was reportedly in a trance, had nothing to say, and was unable to respond to questions, looking past the warden and forty witnesses with a blank look on his face and spittle drooling from the side of his mouth. Some suggested the once bold bank bandit had lapsed into a state of insanity since receiving the death penalty. In less than a minute after the black hood had been placed over his face, Lovett would pass from this world and face the supreme judge.

A. M. Harris was executed on June17, 1932, for the murder of a man named Ed Martin in a crowded ward of University Hospital in Oklahoma City on August 17, 1930. It appears the killing occurred in a fit of jealously. A choir made up of a preacher and several guards sang hymns as the condemned man was escorted to the chair. Harris had no last words and died quietly before fifty spectators.

Martin A. Kenney was executed on March 11, 1932, for clubbing an elderly farmer named W. H. Folwell to death near Britton, Oklahoma. His last words were thanking Warden Sam Brown for, "All you done for me." He was pronounced dead at 12:14 a.m.

Charles Fillmore Davis was executed on August 9,1932, for the shooting death of Blaine County Deputy Sheriff Guy Jarvis. Davis killed the officer when he attempted to arrest him for stealing gasoline.

L.J. Adler was executed on August 19, 1932, for the murder of his brother-in-law and his wife near Watonga. He unsuccessfully pled insanity.

Ivory Covington was executed on the morning of January 27, 1933, for the slaying of an elderly Choctaw County farmer named Luther Williams. Just prior to taking his seat in the chair the young black man leaned over to Rich Owens, the executioner, and shouted, "Give me the works!" Owens calmly nodded his head in agreement while pulling the switch. Covington was buried at the prison's cemetery.

Nathan Rightsell was executed on February 24,1933, for the slaying of a railroad detective named J. V. Buchanan near Hugo. When asked for his last words Rightsell said, " All I've got to say is God bless my Mother." He then sat down in the chair without showing any fear. Rightsell had previously told reporters "We all make mistakes and I made mine, I am ready to go and will die like a man." From all indications, he did. Rightsell was interred at Peckerwood Hill.

Charles (Jack) Lattimer was sentenced to death for the 1931 shooting death of his wife at the Lawton home of his mother-in –law. Lattimer, who had previously done time at Leavenworth Federal pen for desertion from the army as well as serving time at both Oklahoma's Granite Reformatory and "Big Mac" for burglary, claimed the shooting was an accident. He was executed on the morning of March 24,1933. He offered no last words. Lattimer was buried at Peckerwood Hill.

On the morning of May 5, 1933, three men, **Procter McDonald**, **Joe L. Martin**, and **Albert Ellis** were put to death in a mass (triple) execution. Martin had beaten a vagrant to death in Noble County when according to Martin the man "Insulted my country." Evidently, Martin and his victim, a Dutch immigrant named Peter Von Nearop, were bumming together (riding the rails) when they got into a physical altercation. After slaying his partner, Martin robbed his victim of $17, then hid the weighted-down corpse in an oil pit. Procter McDonald shot and killed an innocent eight-year-old child named Raymond Butler who got in the way of a 1931 Oilton drug store robbery. McDonald's partner in the raid was killed. Albert Ellis was condemned for aggravated rape. He and another man robbed a Texas family named Weber, who was motoring to the Arbuckle Mountains for a vacation, of three watches before kidnapping the couple's eighteen-year-old daughter. The pair transported the girl to a local cemetery where they tied her to a tombstone before ravaging her. Thankfully, the girl survived the nightmare and was able to testify against the two vicious thugs. Ellis's partner turned snitch and got off with a life sentence.

Martin was the first to enter the death chamber, he faltered when he caught sight of the mesh-enclosed chair but then regained his composure thanking the prison staff for their treatment. He stated, "I bear no ill will and am ready to go." McDonald was next to die. He only smiled and nodded "Goodbye" when asked if he had any final comments. It took two shocks to kill him. Ellis was next in line. He had no last words, but handed the Warden a note in which he attempted to absolve his partner in the rape and robbery of any responsibility in the crime.

Luke Nichols went to the chair for the May 19, 1932, slaying of his sweetheart, Harriet Crawford. His last words were "Warden Brown, I appreciate what you've done for me while I've been here. I love you dearly. I am sorry for what I've done and am sorry I caused the state so much trouble. I am ready to go." He was put to death on May 19,1933, (On the one-year anniversary of the murder). If his last words were any indication, he went to his death the most cooperative and repentant soul to ever pass through those deadly portals.

George and Claude Oliver were both executed on August 25, 1933, for the sadistic murder of a fifteen–year-old girl on November 3, 1932, near Davis, Oklahoma. Claude, who was the older of the two and the uncle of George, married the young female and immediately insured her life for $5,000. Next, he got his nephew to assist him in a plot to murder the girl, which they did. After placing their victim's body in a car, they pushed the rig into a deep ditch and claimed she had met her death in a tragic accident.

Charley Dumas and **Ted Patton** were both executed on the morning of October 20,1933. Patton had slain a boyhood friend at the foot of Wildhorse Mountain near Sallisaw. Even though Patton claimed self-defense, he was eventually convicted and sentenced to death. Just days before his execution Patton's lawyers presented Governor Murray with a petition bearing 1200 names including eight of the twelve jurors from his trial asking for clemency. Murray ignored the document.

Dumas was convicted and sentenced to death out of Coal County for attacking a white girl. When asked if he had any final words Dumas firmly stated, "I feel fine. I got nothing against anybody. Where I'm going, there is no white or black side." He shook hands with the Warden than nonchalantly plopped down in the chair, which was an equal opportunity provider of deadly services. He was pronounced dead at 12:11 a.m. He was buried at the prison cemetery. Patton approached the chair with complete indifference. He stopped in front of the seat and said. " Well, there's the chair and if I had it to do over I'd do just what I did." Over 125 persons attended the event.

William Johnson was executed on November 10,1933, for the clubbing death of a thirty-year-old seamstress named Mary Wofenberger. Johnson, who was a professional burglar, had beaten the woman to death with a claw hammer at her home in Muskogee when she resisted his efforts to rob her. He was buried at the prison cemetery.

Earl Quinn and **Tom Morris** were executed on November 24, 1933. Morris was put to death for the double ax-murder and robbery of Mr. and Mrs. Joe House in McAlester. The thirty-nine-year-old Morris had previously been convicted of committing six other felony crimes. Earl Quinn was executed for the brutal slaying of two innocent young women in Garfield County.

Frank Clark was executed on October 19,1934, for the February 13, 1933, murder of Mrs. Anna Stiles of Idabel. His last words were "Goodbye Captain." One hundred and sixty-five persons witnessed the execution. As with most executions of the day, some spectators turned out to see justice done while others just came for the show.

Ernest Oglesby was executed on January 4, 1935, for the December 3, 1933 murder of Oklahoma City Patrolman Douglas Gates. Ogelsby was a cousin of the notorious Newton Boys Gang of bank burglars.

Twenty-year-old **Robert Cargo** was put to death on May 24, 1935, for the crime of slaying his employer (A. L. Luke) in Bethany with a hatchet on March 7, 1934. Robbery appeared to have been the motive for the murder. His last words were "I want to thank everyone and all my friends for what they have done for me." Over sixty witnesses attended the execution.

Chester Barrett, **Bun Riley**, and **Alfred Rowan** were put to death in a triple event at McAlester on the morning of September 20,1935. Bun Riley was a Pittsburg County bootlegger who lured three of his pals (William Gann, Homer Beasley, and Hobart Watkins) into the woods and after shooting them each once in the head at close range, took an ax and mutilated their copses. The motive for the crime was never established beyond the fact Riley told the authorities he held a grudge against the men. Riley would later "Find religion" in prison.

Chester Barrett of Sapulpa had poisoned three of his children, ages two thru six, for insurance money. At first, he claimed it was an accident then stated he had been unemployed and desperate when he committed the foul deed. He was also "Saved" after he was sentenced to death. His wife would plead with Governor Marland not to commute her husband's sentence to life saying, "We will be much better off without him." In one of his final acts on earth, Barrett gave a bible to a guard requesting he deliver it to his wife. Inside the bible was an obscene, threatening note to his beloved spouse. Barrett would tell reporters "If I get shed of this jam I'm in I will devote my life to doing good works." He spent his final days decorating his cell with pictures of Jesus and handing out religious tracts to other prisoners. Barrett was taken to the prison laundry and baptized before his execution.

Alfred Rowan was sentenced to death for slaying an Altus relief worker named Roy Gentry. All three doomed men ate pork chops for their final meal and Rowan requested an orange that he did not eat. With a 125 witnesses in attendance, the first to die was Chester Barrett, who informed the Warden he was a good man before forgiving his enemies. Riley was next and had nothing to say. Rowan was last to die and told the crowd "If you follow Jesus you will miss all this."

Roy Guyton was executed March 20, 1936, for the shooting-murder of an Oklahoma City night watchman named E.L. Bailey. Guyton was arrested when he tried to pawn a stolen pistol at an Oklahoma City pawnshop. When the gun was tested, it proved to be the weapon used in the night watchman's murder.

On July 22, 1934, an ex-con named **James Hargus**, who was wanted for several armed robberies in Texas and Oklahoma, was exiting a store in Tulsa when a pair of plainclothes officers approached him with drawn guns stating, "Hold on there buddy." Hargus reacted by pulling a pistol and exchanging fire with the officers. When the gunsmoke cleared, Detective Lawrence B. Mitchell laid dead and his partner wounded. Hargus hit the pavement suffering from several .44 caliber wounds to the left arm, which later had to be amputated, and another slug lodged in his temple just under the skin. Miraculously he lived to be convicted of murder and sentenced to death. Hargus would later claim he shot the officers in self-defense not realizing they were cops. At 12:01 on the morning of April 24, 1936, Hargus was escorted into the death chamber with a big smile on his face. His last words were, "I'd like to make a long speech but the warden won't let me, so I'll just sit here and let you gentlemen watch me die."

Twenty-six-year-old **Arthur Gooch** was executed by hanging on June 19, 1936, convicted of the Federal Lindbergh Kidnapping Statute. He was the last man legally hung in Oklahoma. When fitted for his "death suit" just moments before his execution, Gooch joked with guards, saying: "I believe I'll need another "last meal" to fill out these baggy trousers."

On May 31, 1935, **Charlie Sands** and **Leon Siler** robbed the bank of Elgin, Oklahoma, for $600 while their female companions sat outside the financial institution in the getaway car. In response to the hijacking a massive posse was formed. Airplanes were sent aloft. When spotted by a plane the bandits abandoned their car at a point some sixteen miles northeast of Lawton and after wading a creek, invaded a farmhouse occupied by Adrian Medrano, his wife, and baby. When the laws caught up with the quartet, a gunfight ensued in which Medrano as well as Grady County Deputy Sheriff Pete Wilson were killed. The two bandits as well as another officer and a banker were wounded in the fray. Turns out the pair were also suspected of previously murdering a Pauls Valley constable. The twosome was promptly tried and convicted of Deputy Wilson's death and given death sentences. On the morning of June 11, 1937, the duo was executed in the electric chair in front of 400 spectators, the largest crowd to ever observe an execution in Oklahoma. While Siler took his medicine with a smile Sands collapsed at the foot of the chair and had to be carried to his death. According to witnesses when the executioner pulled the switch, smoke curled out from under the skullcap Sands was wearing as well as from the electrode attached to his leg. Neither man offered any final remarks.

The first to go to the chair during the decade of the 1940s was murderer **Ray Mannon** who had shot a man named Skelley to death then dumped his body in an abandoned well located in Wagoner County. He was executed before 200 witnesses at dawn on March 1, 1940. Mannon ate his last meal in his cell (fried chicken) with his mother. As he approached the chair he thanked the Warden and executioner Rich Owen for their kind treatment then said, " I want you all to know I'm going down for another man."

On the morning of March 6, 1939, **Roger Cunningham** strangled his wife, Eudora, to death and disposed of her body in a newly dug sewer ditch in Oklahoma City. He later disposed of her possessions enclosed in three suitcases off a bridge before motoring back to the sewer ditch to watch his wife's corpse be covered with dirt by a bulldozer. Cunningham later confessed to the crime and led authorities to his wife's body. He was charged with murder and convicted. He pled insanity. The judge did not buy his legal ploy and sentenced him to death. Cunningham was executed on November 15, 1940.

Warren Abby was executed on August 29, 1941, for beating his mail-order bride to death near Clinton on October 6, 1939. Abby initially claimed his wife had been killed by a hit and run driver. The two had met through a matrimonial agency. Abby later claimed self-defense saying "She was insanely jealous and wanted to kill me because she thought I was having affairs with other women." Adding, "She constantly carried a gun and threatened my life." Prosecutors did not buy his defense insisting he had killed his wife to get his hands on her money. While on death row Abby told reporters, " I don't think its right for them to execute me." His last words to Warden Fred Hunt were, "I am being killed for an act that was forced on me. There was no premeditation." Abby was buried at the prison cemetery.

J. D. Tuggle was executed on February 9, 1942, for murdering his Aunt and Uncle at their farm near Stratford on May 10, 1940. As he entered the death chamber the smiling convict took a puff on a cigarette, tossed it aside and plopped down in the chair. When asked if he had any last words he calmly stated, "No Warden Hunt. Take care of your self."

Long-term convict **Finley Porter** was executed on the morning of April 16, 1943, for killing his cellmate. Porter claimed to have slain his bunkie in self-defense. He had no last words as he calmly met his death.

On August 10, 1941, four convicts, Claud Beaver, Bill Anderson, Roy McGee and a lifer named **Hiram Prather** kidnapped Warden Jess Dunn and a prison electrician forcing their way out of the prison gates. When passing through the gates they ordered Dunn to tell the guards to throw down their weapons, which they did. The convicts then commandeered a car and attempted to escape the area. Not far from the prison proper, a posse led by Pittsburg County Deputy Sheriff Bill Alexander ambushed the fleeing cons shooting and killing all three but Prather, who was wounded and surrendered. Tragically, Warden Dunn and an ex-guard named Tab Ford were caught in the crossfire and killed as well. The wounded Prather was tried and convicted for the murder of Warden Dunn and sentenced to death. On the morning of July 14, 1943, Hiram Prather was led to the death chamber where sixty-nine witnesses stood in attendance. When asked his final words, Prather told Warden Fred Hunt, "You're holding the best hand now."

A repeat offender named **Amon Johnson** was put to death on March 23, 1945, for the senseless brutal murders of three persons in Lincoln County. After stabbing and beating a farmer named Roy Schat to death, he stole his truck. He then attacked a Mrs. Jorski and her three-year-old daughter at their farm near McLoud. After slashing the pair with a long, jackknife; nearly decapitating them, he went on his merry way. He arrived at his home dressed in bloody clothes, beat his young wife with a belt for backsassing him, then threatened her life with a knife saying, "I already killed three people and if I could breathe life back into them I'd kill 'em again." He then fled the residence on foot. Johnson was later captured by a group of vigilantes. He freely confessed to all three murders. Since no one came forward to claim his body, Johnson was buried at Peckerwood Ridge.

Ciff T. Norman was executed on November 9, 1945, for the rape and attempted murder of a young female whose husband was serving in the military overseas. Although she was unable to talk due to being shot in the mouth, the victim described her attacker through handwritten notes. The doomed man offered no last words.

Alfred C. Bingham was put to death on May 31, 1946, for the August 8, 1943 stabbing death of his estranged wife in Tulsa. According to witnesses, he plunged the knife into his spouse while his young son pleaded with him to spare her. Bingham, who was an unemployed house painter at the time

of the murder, ate a last meal of baked ham and beans. While on death row, he told reporters, "I was drunk and deserve to die." He entered the chamber informing the guards he was not afraid. His last words were "God bless you all, I will see you in heaven."

Also scheduled to die on May 31 was thirty-one-year-old Stanley Steen who with a fellow inmate named Mose Johnson had killed a prison guard named Pat Riley and a fellow convict named L. C. "Blackie" Smalley on December 13, 1943. Steen had been convicted of murdering the guard and was sentenced to death but cheated the executioner by slashing an artery in his right arm the night before his scheduled execution while in his death row cell. How he managed to pull off his suicide while he was being watched 24-7 by two guards is a mystery.

On the afternoon of December 13, 1943, inmates **Mose Johnson** and **Stanley Steen** were sitting around the penitentiary light plant drinking homemade booze and gulping down illegal narcotic pills called "Yellow Jackets" when they decided to rob a fellow inmate named L.C. "Blackie" Smalley who was incarcerated on a forty-year hitch for robbing the Bank of Mill Creek. Blackie, a one-time associate of the notorious bank robber "Pretty Boy" Floyd, in turn sought the protection of Sergeant of the Guard W. H. Riley. When Riley arrived at the light plant to investigate one of the pair of miscreants stabbed him to death with a 14-inch dirk. After killing Riley the two ran to the canteen, where Smalley worked and killed him as well. Johnson was serving a seven-year sentence for manslaughter out of Pittsburg County due to his killing an inmate in the past while Steen was serving a 50-year stretch. Johnson had recently been foiled in an escape attempt from the prison. After it was all sorted out Johnson was convicted of killing Smalley and sentenced to death while Steen was convicted of Riley's death and sentenced to death as well. While the authorities were successful in carrying out the supreme penalty against Johnson on November 1, 1946, Steen was somehow able to have a razor smuggled into his death row cell and commit suicide on the night before his scheduled execution, which was to take place on May 31,1946.

Hardin Broyles was executed on January 30, 1947, for the January 1, 1945 murder of a Seminole County Deputy Sheriff Eric Nicholson. He maintained his innocence to the end saying, "Father I forgive them for what they do. I hope I'll not die in vain." The doomed man lost his nerve at the end and had to be carried to the chair screaming and weeping. This was the final execution where Rich Owens pulled the switch.

A black man named **Lewis Grayson** was executed at 10 p.m. on May 25, 1948, for raping a white girl at a location just north of Muskogee. His execution was the first to be held at night as well as the first for the newly installed executioner "Big Boy" Elliott.

Ben Gould was put to death on September 27, 1948, for the brutal murder of fifty-seven-year-old Mary Lynn of Atoka. Miss Lynn had been beaten then stabbed forty-odd times with an ice pick in the throat and chest. The motive for the killing was robbery. Gould ordered fried chicken for his last meal but left it uneaten. He spent his final hours drinking orange soda pop, smoking cigarettes, and reading comic books. His last words were, "I've nothing against no one. Not even the judge who sentenced me. I'm going to die in peace." Just as he sat in the chair he said, "I'm glad I lived to see this day."

Max E. Klettke was put to death on the evening of January 4, 1951, for shooting and killing a New York man who had given him a ride as he was hitchhiking across the country. Klettke was evidently a drifter and a born looser. According to most reports, he totally lost his nerve when faced with his own death.

An ex-con named **Jearell Hathcox** was executed on July 27, 1951, for the 1950 murder of an Oklahoma City sewage plant guard. Only twenty-five spectators attended the execution of the pint-sized killer. His last words were, "I am innocent. I was framed."

Melburn J. Mott was executed on September 21,1951, for the heinous murder of his six-year-old daughter. Mott slashed his daughter's throat with a butcher knife while under the influence of alcohol and barbiturates. He claimed at trial he had blacked out and did not remember the event. Evidently, the tragic slaying was somehow the result of a domestic quarrel with his estranged wife.

Carl Austin DeWolf was executed for the 1946 shooting death of Tulsa Detective Gerald M. St Clair. His case was very controversial in nature. Conflicting statements were given by many of the eyewitnesses to the crime, some changing their initial testimony when the case came to trial. DeWolf maintained his innocence to the end, claiming he was at a café in Drumright at the time of the killing. He further avowed, the murder weapon, which was found on his person at the time of his arrest, had been given to him several days after the deadly event by a homicidal drifter named Victor Everhart, who was wanted by the authorities for the recent killings of a pair of Tulsa lawmen as well as a Seneca, Missouri, night watchman. Everhart was eventually captured and charged with a bevy of murders including that of Detective St Claire, but promptly escaped from the Tulsa County Jail and was slain by officers at a roadblock near Choteau.

Soon after Everhart's death, DeWolf, who had been convicted of three felonies in the past, was charged with Officer St Clair's murder. Even though he passed a lie-detector test and placed in Drumright at the time of the murder by several reliable witnesses, DeWolf was found guilty and sentenced to death at the conclusion of a stormy two-day trial. Over the next few year's scores of prominent citizens, including a well-known state senator named Kirksey Nix Sr., came to DeWolf's aide convinced he was the victim of injustice and had not received a fair trial. Many of his supporters suspected Victor Everhart as the guilty party in St Clair's murder, loudly asserting DeWolf had been the victim of a police frame-up. Although the defendant's guilt and death sentence was confirmed by the Oklahoma State Court of Appeals and adjudged not worthy of review by the US Supreme Court, Governor Johnson Murray granted DeWolf a record fourteen stays of execution. The Governor even made a rare personal visit to death row in order to question the condemned man. DeWolf steadfastly informed the chief executive, "As God is my judge, I am innocent of the death of St Clair. I never killed anyone in my life." Johnson publicly stated that while he personally believed DeWolf deserved a new trial, he would leave the final resolution of the case in the hands of the State Pardon and Parole Board who ultimately refused to intercede in the case. On the evening of November 16, 1953, the Assistant Warden asked DeWolf if he had any final request, he sheepishly murmured, "A two-mile head start." After being baptized at the prison chapel he was taken to the death chamber where he informed a crowd of witnesses, "I am innocent. You are killing an innocent man!" At 12:08 a.m., the switch was pulled and DeWolf pronounced dead three minutes later.

Hubie F. Fairris was sent to the electric chair at 12:05 a.m. on January 18, 1956, for the July 16, 1954, murder of Oklahoma City Detective Bennie Cravatt. Fairris was the nephew of depression-era badman Raymond Hamilton of Bonnie and Clyde fame. He ate a sandwich for his final meal and his last words, spoken just moments before he died were "If this is the way you want it, this is the way you'll get it!" Fairris donated his eyes to an eye bank before his execution.

Author's note: Executioner M.E. Elliott died on August 12, 1956. B. V. Glover took his place.

On January 11, 1957, **Otto A. Loel** was put to death for the January 10, 1954, stabbing death of thirty-one-year-old Elizabeth Henderson. Apparently, Loel and Miss Henderson were sharing expenses on a cross-country motor trip from California to Ohio when they stopped for the night at an Oklahoma City motel. The following morning the motel's owner discovered Henderson's bloody corpse lying on the floor of her room. She had suffered fourteen stabbing wounds. Loel was later captured in California but declared he had killed the woman in self-defense. According to him, the deceased had assaulted him in the motel room grabbing hold of and hanging on to a sensitive part of his anatomy while demanding he have unnatural relations with her. When that explanation didn't work, he pled insanity. The jury found him guilty of murder and sentenced him to death. On his final day he chain-smoked cigarettes and drank Dr. Pepper. When approaching the chair he took one last drag off his cigarette, threw it to the ground, and mounted the instrument of his destruction. According to numerous witnesses, Loel immediately passed out probably suffering from a heart attack, which most certainly proved to be fatal in nature the moment the executioner pulled the switch.

Former rodeo performer and suspected bootlegger **Robert Hendricks** was put to death on February 5, 1957, for the August 24, 1954, beating death of a Vinita cattle buyer named Rheam Payton. At the time of the killing, Hendricks was on parole from a life sentence pertaining to a 1930 murder conviction out of Seminole County. While incarcerated in the Craig County Jail he attempted suicide with a razor blade. On entering the death chamber, he cursed the officers saying, "I don't accept Christ and by G-d I don't want to be baptized. I won't forgive the prosecutors who framed me." Since no one claimed his body, Hendricks was buried at the prison cemetery.

On the evening of June 17, 1956, a twenty-seven-year-old career criminal named **Edward Leon "Pete" Williams**, who had in the past served terms in various federal correctional facilities for auto theft and armed robbery, stuck-up a Tulsa filling station at gunpoint for the sum of thirty dollars. The following morning, Williams's carjacked a young ministerial student named Tommie Cooke when the lad had stopped his 1949 Oldsmobile at a traffic light in front of the Tulsa Library. After forcing the youth to drive him to a secluded dead-end dirt lane near the small Muskogee County settlement of Taft, Williams instructed his victim to park the car on the edge of the road. He then marched the youth some two hundred yards into the high-weeds located on the banks of the Arkansas River where he placed a gun-barrel (38 cal. revolver) behind his right ear and pulled the trigger. The killer then exited the scene driving the stolen car to Muskogee where he gassed up before continuing his flight south on highway #64 toward Porum. Somewhere along the way, he discarded Cooke's billfold and other personal effects. When he arrived in the small community of Talihina he robbed a store where he once worked as a clerk of $1,000 at gunpoint.

Williams abandoned the car at a point some eighteen miles east of Talihina and continued his journey to nowhere on foot. After wandering through the mountains for a time, he finally made his way back to the highway where he hitchhiked back to town and burglarized a store for food and other supplies. In the meantime, hearing news of the Talihina store robbery, a massive manhunt was organized in the area. After looting the second store, the killer caught another ride forcing a man and woman at gunpoint to drive him to Wilburton where he released the couple before boarding a Greyhound bus. Somewhere between Wilburton and Poteau, he tossed the offending pistol out the window. On his arrival in Poteau, lawmen arrested the youth as he exited the bus.

Williams immediately confessed to all his crimes and led officers to the location of the young would-be minister's body. The defendant was held at the Muskogee jail where he soon escaped custody. He was recaptured the following day. Williams pled guilty to killing Cooke and received a life sentence. The murderer was then transferred to the Tulsa County where he was tried for kidnapping and armed robbery. The prosecutor in the case was James Edmondson, who would later become Oklahoma's Governor. Williams would eventually be convicted of the aggravated kidnapping charge and sentenced to death. Ironically, when seeking a commutation of his sentence, the defendant's lawyers were forced to appear before newly elected Governor Edmondson, who had been the prosecutor in the doomed man's kidnapping case. When interviewed by newsmen on the eve of his execution Williams told the journalists, "When I die tonight, that is as it should be. I killed and they are going to kill me. An eye for an eye...I've been through hell down here and I'm glad it's almost over...but I deserve consideration for clemency since I am a changed man both mentally and spiritually." The condemned man ate a last meal consisting of chocolate pudding and chocolate milk. Pete Williams, his hair now streaked with gray, was put to death on the evening of July 28, 1960, in front to 25 witnesses. He had no final comments. Incidentally, his own father refused to attend the execution saying, "He will just have to take his medicine." Williams was the first person executed by the state for the crime of kidnapping.

On March 31, 1958, **James Spence** and his brother-in-law robbed a surplus store in Lawton. During the heist the duo shot and killed nineteen-year-old Ruth Zimmerman and wounded her husband. While both men were convicted of the slaying and sentenced to death. Governor James Edmondson commuted the brother-in-law's sentence to life when Spence informed the parole board that "Eddie was just along for the ride. He didn't shoot anyone." On the eve of his execution, Spence told reporters, "I'm guilty of the crime, and we have to live by man-made laws." He then asked the warden if he could watch a boxing match on television. The warden responded to the request by having a portable TV installed outside the condemned man's cell so he could view the "Fights." On the evening of August 31, 1960, the condemned man was escorted to the execution chamber where he declined the opportunity to make a final statement. According to all reports, his execution went smoothly.

An Altus taxi-driver named **Ray Allen Young** was executed on December 15, 1960, for the 1959 murder of Highway Patrolman John Barter on a lonely road near Altus. Young and a female friend had been parked on the side of a country road where they planned to ambush his estranged wife. When a car showed up containing his ex-wife's lover, Young took a pot shot at him but missed. Meanwhile, Officer Barter arrived on the scene and attempted to disarm Young, who in turn shot the lawman after informing him, "I bought this gun to kill my wife and no ones going to stop me." Shortly after his capture, Young escaped from jail but he was quickly recaptured. At his trial the defendant stated, "I'm sorry John (Officer Barter) died, he had been a friend of mine for years. We served in the marines together." With twenty persons in attendance Young slowly and deliberately walked to within a few feet of the electric chair where he stopped and told the warden "I wish everyone a Merry Christmas and I hold no hatred for anyone." He was the 80th person to die in the electric chair.

On the morning of August 19, 1960, **Shelby Doggett** and a companion were hitchhiking through downtown Lawton when a man named James Lanman gave them a lift. The pair responded to this act of kindness by robbing then brutally murdering their host. The two were soon captured and both convicted of the murder. Doggett, who admitted he pulled the trigger, was given the death sentence while his pal received a life sentence. While on death row Doggett told reporters, "I am sorry for what I did and sorry for that guy's folks," He added, "I'm better off than my buddy who may have to spend fifty more years locked up in this place." On the day before his scheduled execution, Doggett requested a breakfast of eggs, bacon, and biscuits and a supper consisting of steak, French fries, and salad. Just hours before the end, he told reporters, "I'm ready to go. I think I'm getting what I deserve. I'm going to the chair tonight and it's not as bad as spending the rest of my life cooped up here." At 9:50 p.m. on the evening of October 1, 1962, Doggett was led to the foot of the chair where he made no final statement and after 2300 volts were surged into

his body for 56 seconds, he was declared dead. His remains were released to his family for cremation.

On the morning of August 6, 1960, **Richard Dare** beat his wife to death in the couple's Oklahoma City residence before traveling to his in-law's home intent on killing them as well. When he discovered they were not at home he hid in a back room. On the arrival of his mother-in-law, he strangled her to death and arming himself with a .22 caliber rifle, shot and killed both his father-in-law and nephew when they arrived home. Dare then robbed the bodies of his in-laws for $36 and went on a drunk. After spending a night of debauchery in the company of a lewd woman, the killer was captured near Blanchard. When questioned, he stated, "After the killings, I never slept better in my life." The unrepentant thug was put to death on June 1, 1963.

Author's note: Executioner B. V. Glover retired after this execution, and Mike Mayfield was appointed to the position.

On October 21, 1961, a heavily tattooed career criminal named **James French** strangled his bunkmate with a shoestring in their shared cell at the Oklahoma State Penitentiary. French was presently serving a life-sentence for the brutal 1958 murder of Franklin Boone, which occurred near Stroud. The muscle-bound hoodlum had spent a lifetime drifting from town to town committing various crimes. He had been incarcerated on many occasions. When sentenced to death for killing his cellmate he stated, "Good!" The husky inmate would later beg the judge for his immediate execution. In the days leading up to his death, French admitted to a half-dozen other murders. His motive for killing his bunkie was, "He refused to shape up." The doomed men informed the newly installed executioner, Mike Mayfield, that he intended to come back from the dead and kill his family just for the fun of it. French would claim to be agnostic and forbade any ministers at his execution. On the evening of August 10, 1966, French, flanked by a guard and the warden, strolled to the chair where he sat down with a wide smile on his face. When asked for a final statement he stated, "Everything has been said." The executioner pulled the switch. Smoke curled out from French's collar for a few seconds before the switch was shut down and the inmate declared dead. James French was the last man executed in Oklahoma's electric chair.

A Decade of Oklahoma Bank Robberies, 1924-1934

*Most, but not all, banks robbed during this decade are listed.

-1924-

**Fifty-two banks robbed-Thirty-eight listed-Six bandits killed-Fifty-six arrested-Oklahoma ranked second in the nation behind Illinois for bank robberies in 1924.

*January 2-The **First National Bank of Shidler** is robbed by two unmasked men of $2,000 in cash and coin. Buster Jarrett and Sam Coker are eventually convicted of the raid.

*January 23-The **First National Bank of Pocasset** is robbed by three men of $3,000. The bandits fled in a Hudson automobile. Just west of town, the rig ran low on oil and had to be abandoned. The trio promptly flagged down a Ford driven by George Ingraham. When the driver balked at the idea of giving up his car, the frustrated outlaws fired several rounds into the front windshield, one of the bullets barely missing the poor man's head. Mr. Ingraham swiftly decided to reconsider his position and live another day. The robbers sped off believing they had it made until the Ford blew a tire sending the hapless trio afoot for a second time. Luckily for the robbers the only thing more inept that day then them was the pursuing posse.

*January 31-The **First National Bank of DeNoya** is looted by two unmasked men shortly before noon. The pair forced two employees, Herman Huffine and Lyle Overman, who were the only ones present in the building at the time, to lie on the floor while they rifled the tills and safe of $2,500. The pair escaped in a Ford Touring car heading east. A few hours after the heist, officers cut the bandits trail just south of Pawhuska forcing them into a ditch. In the ensuing firefight a deputy named Dempsey Smith is wounded. One of the bandits is captured while the other escaped on foot. The loot is recovered.

*February 5-The **First National Bank of Shidler** is hijacked of $3,000 by Posey Mitchell and Hinard Fain.

*February 11-The **First National Bank of Gracemont** is robbed of an undetermined amount. Jack Newman, "Happy" Bohannon, and Paul Evanger are convicted of the robbery. Other suspects include Walter O'Quinn and Henry Cornett.

*February 21-The **Farmers State Bank of Burbank** is looted of an undetermined amount. Badman Dick Gregg is suspected as being one of the two looters.

*March 1-The **First National Bank of Kaw City** is robbed of $1500.

*March 3-The **Capitol State Bank of Oklahoma City** is held-up for $1,927 by two men. Jack Mitchell is convicted of heist.

*March 7-Several bandits hold up the **Capitol Hill State Bank** of $1,927.

*May 14-The **Bank of Mustang** is raided. Robbery turns out to be a simple case of embezzlement. Clerk who reported theft along with his brother are arrested.

*May 1-Roy Buxton, age 25, and Robert Brown, age 27, robbed the **Farmers and Merchants Bank of Catoosa** of $2000.

*May 7-The **First National Bank of Addington** is looted of $2,991. The O'Quinn Gang is suspected.

*May 6- Attorney George Crump robs the **Ochalata State Bank**. The bank was robbed in 1923 by Cookson Hills' bad boy Kye Carlile.

*May 21-Two unmasked men loot the **Farmers State Bank of Burbank** for $2,000. During the heist, four employees and a customer are forced to lie on the floor. Before departing, the bandits lock the witnesses into the vault.

*May 28-A lone unmasked bandit robs the **Citizens Bank of Lamont** of $1,111. The bandit entered the deserted bank at the noon hour. Cashier George Cowen was eating his lunch in a back room when he observed a man depart the building with a bag in his hand. Evidently, when the intruder noticed the bank was empty he merely helped himself to the funds and calmly departed the scene so much the wiser and richer.

*June 4-The **Community State Bank of Bristow** is divested of $2,000 at gunpoint. Two robbers entered the institution, which contained four customers and five employees at the time. The bandits harvested the loot and forced all the witnesses into the vault before fleeing. The hostages quickly gained their freedom and gave the alarm. A large posse was organized but was unsuccessful in their efforts to track down the brigands. An eyewitness to the robbery identified one of the hijackers as the notorious Jeff Duree, the so-called "Ghost Bandit." A month after the raid Osage badman Kelsie Morrison is arrested and charged with the heist.

*June 11-**First State Bank of Washington** is looted of $2,475 in cash along with $550 in Liberty Bonds. The bank is robbed by four men and a woman who escape in two cars. The town's Mayor, responding to the bank's alarm, shot and wounded one of the fleeing bandits. The lady involved in the hijacking, Mrs. J. W. O'Quinn, is arrested driving about town a half hour after the heist. Later that day, a large posse of officers arrested the woman's husband (J. Walter O'Quinn) and a companion named Argns Williams near Blanchard. That evening, Deputy Sheriff's Oscar Morgan and James Williams ambushed the other two members of the raiding party at a spot seven miles south of Blanchard. The officer's shoot and kill an ex-con named Claude Bishop and wound his companion, later identified as Guy Wilkerson. A search of Bishop's body uncovers $1,728 of the bank loot.

*June 12-Two masked men rob the **First State Bank of Meridian** of $3,000. According to Cashier Fred McCroskey, two armed men, one about forty years of age, the other crossed-eyed, took all the money in the building except for pennies.

*June 17-Soon after opening for morning's business, two armed men entered the **State Bank of Marland** through the front door while a companion stood guard outside. The robbers gathered up $5,300 before locking a cashier and a book-keeper, along with two customers into the vault. The bandits then fled the bank in two cars, a blue Buick and a Cadillac, traveling East toward the Arkansas River at a high rate of speed. Officers from Osage, Noble, and Kay Counties organized a posse and began pursuit. A plane belonging to the Trail-Dust Moving Picture Company filming overhead shots for a silent Western film being made at the nearby 101 Ranch is sent aloft in an effort to track the desperadoes by air. Due to a $500 reward being posted for the robbers capture, every out of work saddle-tramp in the area as well as a few of the Hollywood types from the film company load their Winchesters, mount "Old Dobbin," and join the hunt. Evidently, the fleeing hijackers successfully make it back to their haunts in the Osage Hills without getting their tail feathers burnt by the guys in the white hats.

*June 20-A single man entered the **Slick National Bank** armed with a heavy revolver. The individual quickly sought out Cashier W.P. Johnson demanding "some money." Johnson complied, handing over $2,500 in cash and gold. The bandit then forced the cashier outside at gunpoint to a waiting car

being driven by an accomplice. The frightened banker was released about five miles outside the town limits.

*June 27- A pair of youthful bandits rob the **Security National Bank of Dewey** of $1,709, taking two bank employee's, G. H. Clewer and Harry Brent, hostage. The pair motored to a spot two miles west of town where they took off on foot abandoning their car and captives. A hurriedly formed posse made up of lawmen and vigilantes followed the pair's trail into the Osage hill country where it was lost.

*July 2-The **Avery State Bank** is robbed of $1,500. Robbers William Weaver (Phoenix Donald), Joe Clayton, and Blackie Thompson kill Drumright Officer U. S. Lennox and severely wound lawman Jack Airy in a gunfight, which occurs at a roadblock located near Drumright shortly after the robbery.

*July 21-The **Uncas State Bank** is looted of $1,500 by Floyd Jarrett, Henry Cornett, Jack Newman, and William "Max" Garden.

*August 10-A pair of well-dressed young men parked in front of the **First National Bank of Prague** driving a large sedan. Upon entering the bank with drawn pistols, they issue the well-worn phrase, "This is a hold-up" to an audience made up of Assistant Cashier K. H. Sutton and Bookkeeper Edna Gaylor. After gathering up the available funds ($2,500), the pair shut the witnesses into the vault, which was fitted with a safety devise that kept the steel door from locking. The duo then escaped in their sedan. Banker Sutton reportedly grabbed an old army rifle he had stashed in the vault and ran outside just in time to take a poorly aimed potshot at the fleeing hijackers. When interviewed by the press, Miss Gaylor was quoted as saying, "They were very nice about the whole thing and never threatened anyone."

*August 21-Four unmasked individuals knock off the **Citizens State Bank of Skedee** for an undetermined amount. On exiting the bank the robbers lock Cashier J. E. Newell and his brother Frank in the vault. The bankers quickly escape and pursue the bandits for several miles before they lost 'em. The hijackers getaway car is discovered abandoned the following day in Osage County.

*September 2- Two unmasked youths raid the **Farmers National Bank of Yale** of $2,500 while a third boy remained with the getaway car parked in a nearby alley. Two bank employees and several customers are locked in the vault. The budding badmen made haste back to the Osage country where they soon found refuge. Since it took some twenty minutes for the hostages to gain their freedom and give the alarm, a pursuit wasn't even bothered with on this occasion.

*September 15-Two unemployed youths, Dan Morris and Earl Robards, enter the **Vera State Bank** armed with revolvers where they are greeted by two female employees. When ordered to "Reach for the sky," one of the clerks, Mrs. Mary Garlinhouse, told the bandit to "Shove it." The lads, not being experienced in the business of bank robbery, commenced to argue and plead with the woman to cooperate. Some minutes into the debate, the irate lady finally grudgingly held up her hands in submission. Meanwhile, a citizen on the street, noticing the goings on at the bank, quickly rounded up a posse of armed citizens who stormed the bank shooting and killing young Mr. Morris, wounded and capturing his crime partner. Following the robbery, her fellow townsmen roundly applauded the obstinate Mrs. Garlinhouse for her stubbornness, which had bought enough time for the citizenry to organize and react to the hijacking in a successful manner.

*October 11-Three men attempt to rob the **Bank of Shidler**. Henry Wells and John Gregg are arrested in connection to the near hijacking.

*October 15-Three men loot the **Canute Bank** of $1,000. A few months after the heist, Ben Parks, a guard at the Darlington Home for Drug Addicts, along with a father and son duo named Patterson are arrested and charged with both the Canute and Sharon bank robberies. The following year "Big" Jim McGraw is also charged with the heist.

*October 25-Two bandits, one described as tall the other short, enter the **Avard State Bank** just before noon. The pair got the drop on Cashier Ed Roberts, who was alone in the bank at the time, demanding he "Give it up!" After plundering the institution of some $1,700 in cash along with another $1,850 in jewelry and bonds, the pair locked Roberts in the vault then leisurely strolled out the front door attracting little or no attention. The robbers made their getaway in a Ford Touring car, which had been stolen several days earlier off the streets of Alva. Mr. Roberts was able to free his self after a half-hour and give the alarm. It was reported nearly every male citizen of the town joined the swiftly formed posse and took to the trail in hot pursuit. The loss was fully covered by insurance.

*October 26-Two men hijack the **Davenport State Bank of Lincoln County** for $1,000. Five witnesses are in the bank at the time. The bandits flee in the direction of Drumright, driving a Ford automobile, quickly melting into the oilfield country. A posse is fielded but the pursuit proves fruitless

*October 30-Four men rob the **First National Bank of Jennings** at high noon before absconding in a small touring car carrying $2,000 of the bank's money stuffed in a feed sack. A carload of officers promptly gave chase. At a point four miles from town, the outlaws decamped from their automobile and concealed themselves in the brush on the roadside intent on ambushing their pursuers. As the big touring car carrying the trio of lawmen came abreast to the hidden bandits, they opened up with shotguns. The officers reacted by departing the kill zone as promptly as the big motorcar could carry them. Two of the officers, who were identified Deputy Sheriff E. R. Wise and City Marshal Frank Mahan, were slightly wounded in the ambush. The driver of the chase car was reportedly unscathed.

*November 6-Yeggmen break into the **Bank of Arcadia** in the early morning hours gaining access through a window, hauling the heavy safe containing $3,000 out the front door to a waiting truck. Guy Falk of Norman is charged in connection to the heist.

*November 7-Two men rob the **First State Bank of Shamrock** of $1,500. On departing the bank, the bandits lock Cashier J. A. Smith and his assistant, Vernon Crouch, in the vault. Smith immediately contacted the authorities from a phone, which had recently been installed in the vault.

*December 10-The **Shawnee Federal National Bank** is robbed of $18,000 by the Dude Overstreet gang.
*See previous article-*Dude Overstreet and the Great Shawnee Raid*.

*December 11- Three men loot the **Bank of Copan** of $500. The bandits force Cashier H. C. Courtney to stand against a wall with his hands raised while they rifle the tills. On completion of the hurried heist, the trio rushed out to the street and mounted a small roadster in which they escaped. Reacting to the commotion, several business owners hurried from their shops firing at the getaway car. It was suspected one of the robbers was wounded in the melee.

*December 15-**First National Bank of Carney** is looted of $3,200 by Ed Bailey, Owen Edwards, Ace Pendleton, and Blackie Thompson. A cashier and a deputy sheriff are wounded in a brief gunfight following the robbery.

*December 26-Three bandits rob the **First National Bank of Jennings** of $2,000. At the conclusion of the robbery, an assistant cashier and customer are locked in the vault. The bandits are last seen motoring toward the Osage country. This event marks the second time the financial institution is robbed in two months.

*December 30-The **Farmers National Bank of Chan-**

dler is robbed by four subjects of $5,900. On the morning of the heist, a false tip was phoned in informing officers someone was planning to rob the Stroud bank that afternoon. While every officer in the county made a mad dash toward Stroud, three bandits entered the front door of the Chandler bank while a fourth individual remained in a running getaway car parked on a side street, located a block from the financial institution. On departing the bank, the robbers locked five employees and a customer in the vault. They were released moments later by Cashier Homer Curry, who had been eating breakfast in a nearby restaurant during the hijacking. Investigators suspect Owen Edwards led the raid while Ed Bailey was the driver of the getaway car.

-1925-

**Seventeen bank robberies occurred, all are noted. Due to the aggressive activities of various vigilante groups created by the Oklahoma State Bankers Association, there was a considerable drop-off in the number of bank jobs pulled in 1924 vs. 1925.

*January 21-A party of yeggs broke into the **Farmers and Merchants Bank of Inola** under the light of the moon. Around 2 a.m. a citizen named A. J. Creighton overheard the thieves drilling into the vault and engaged them in a gunfight. The robbers fled the building running to their truck, which was parked a block away, abandoning a full compliment of burglar tools in the bank.

*January 23-Four men raid the **American National Bank of Bristow** stealing $6,900. Among the suspects are J. C. Whitehad, John Birchfield, Roy Brandon, Moss Birchfield, and his wife. John Birchfield and Whitehead are convicted and sentenced to twenty years imprisonment. Whitehead later escapes custody.

*February 11-**First National Bank of Noble** is robbed of $800. Thirty-three year old Walter Ball and twenty-five year old Frank Miller drove up and parked their roadster in front of the bank entering the front door of the lobby at roughly the noon hour on a typical cold blustery February day. The bank is occupied by the cashier and a single customer who are standing in the lobby, while the bank's president and his wife were going over the books in the back room. The two men, armed with handguns, rushed into the lobby screaming at the cashier to open the safe while waving their pistols in a wild manner. On complying with the robber's demands, the cashier along with the customer are forced to sit on the floor while the thieves scoop up the loot placing it into a cement bag before hastily departing the building and fleeing in their getaway vehicle. Bank President A. E. Ellinger, who was observing the heist from his

office, leaped into his own car and began boldly following the fleeing bandits even though he was unarmed and coatless. The nervous bandits, noticing they are being followed, speed up in an effort to loose their tail but subsequently miss a curve in the road loosing control of the roadster, smashing head-on into a large oak tree. Bailing out, the pair ran across an open field before stopping and hurriedly burying the cement sack containing the heavy coins while stuffing the paper money in their pockets. In the meantime, Banker Ellinger motors back to town and is met by a hastily formed posse. The posse members, who would soon number nearly one hundred, traveled to the spot where the bandits were last seen, and began beating the bushes. After an hour or so of searching, Cleveland County Deputy Sheriff J. W. Ballard spotted movement in a patch of tall weeds. When he called out for the pair to surrender, Walter Ball took a pot shot at the lawmen with a pistol. Ballard returned fire putting a well-placed slug directly through the desperado's heart. The outlaw's companion, realizing the jig was up immediately jumped up and threw his hands skyward with a shout of, "I give up, boys, don't shoot." When lawmen inquired of the surviving bandit what motivated him to attempt to rob a bank, he replied, "I just got a crazy notion." The lad then led the officers to the spot where they had buried the sack of coins. It was later learned the dead bandit was also a suspect in the robbery of the Bank of Barnsdall, which had occurred the previous year.

*February 19-The **State Bank of Sharon** is looted of $2,477 by two individuals. Charles E. Patterson is convicted of the heist and sentenced to ten-year term. "Big" Jim McGraw was listed as the second suspect.

*June 16-Three individuals rob the **Avard State Bank** of $532. On conclusion of the heist, a town merchant named Mrs. R. B. Patton rushed to the town fire-bell and began ringing it in order to alert the local citizens of the hijacking. When one of the robbers approached her with a high-powered rifle in hand threatening to "Put a slug in your gizzard" if she did not stop the racket, she replied," Go ahead and shoot." The salty lady defiantly continued banging the gong. Two individuals, "Big" Jim Callen and Raymond Miller, were arrested a month after the robbery in the aftermath of a shootout with federal prohibition officers in Kansas City, Missouri, and charged with the crime. McGraw was already charged with the hijacking of the Canute and Sharon bank robberies, which both occurred in 1924.

*June 30-Three men loot the **State bank of Greenfield** of $2,200. Elmer Stout is convicted and sentenced to twenty-five years imprisonment for the robbery. Father and son team of George and Joe Stewart are also named as suspects.

*June 30-The **Farmers and Merchants Bank of Loyal** is robbed of $1,822. George and Joe Stewart are once again listed as suspects.

*July 1-**First National Bank of Boynton** is robbed by three armed men of $4,000. John Cover, an out-of-work car salesman, is arrested several days after the event in possession of $1,900 of the bank's money. Frank Perkins of Okmulgee and Earl Thomas of Denver are also charged. All three plead guilty and are sentenced to ten years imprisonment.

*August 8-A lone bandit arrived at the **State Guaranty Bank of Sperry** by taxicab and entered the institution threatening to blow up the building with a bottle of what he claimed was nitroglycerin. After gathering up $774.44, the man forced a pair of bank officials and two customers into the vault. He escaped on foot and eventually made his way to freedom by flagging down a passing automobile.

*August 28-Three men armed with handguns rob **the Bank of Navina** of $700. After harvesting the loot, the trio escaped in a stolen Ford Touring car with Banker Albert Kinney in tow. Kinney was released at a point two miles south of town. Answering the alarm, the county sheriff along with Undersheriff Clay Oaks and Kingfisher Policeman Len McIntosh give pursuit. Five miles south of the little berg, the officers pass the car containing the raiders. The lawmen then halt and position their rig in a fashion, which blocks the road. When the hijackers approach their position Sheriff Block orders them to halt. The robbers answer with a pistol shot, the round embedding itself into the lawmen's car. The sheriff and Undersheriff, armed with high-powered rifles, return fire killing the driver and a passenger while the third officer, equipped with a shotgun, cut loose wounding a fleeing suspect. On searching the getaway car officers discovered the loot intact. The two slain outlaws are identified as George and Joe Stewart, the father and son team suspected in the recent robberies of the banks of Loyal and Greenfield. The wounded bandit is identified as Ralph Jones.

*August 31-The **Farmers National Bank of Yale** is hijacked by Jack Wilson, Ray Walker, and Freddy Davis. The 'take' is listed as $10, 400.

*September 16-The **Bank of Kendrick** is looted of $157 by Freddy Davis and Roy Brandon.

*The **State Bank of Mannford** is robbed of $180.

*The **First State Bank of Jennings** is looted of $2,105

*The **State Bank of Maramec** is robbed of $9,500 by Ray Terrill, Roland Williams, Jeff Duree, and possibly Harry Campbell.

*The **State Bank of Madill** is held up for $647

*The **Bank of Commerce at Barnsdall** is robbed of $600.

-1926-

**Eleven bank robberies noted. Unknown number actually robbed. The Oklahoma Bankers Association announces a $250 reward for the capture of bank bandits: Dead or Alive.

*March 11- A dry cleaner operator named Carson Rogers and a young farmer named Robert Mitchell entered the **First State Bank of Indiahoma** leaving a third man at the wheel of a Ford Roadster. The duo got the drop on Cashier Robert Benton. After scooping up roughly $1,400, the pair departed. The robbers changed cars a few miles out of town but are captured by a group of officers after they stop to change an ill-timed flat tire. The pair not only confessed to the Indiahoma raid but also admitted they had planned to rob the Bank of Cooperton but "got cold feet." Over time, the Bank at Indiahoma becomes a favorite target for hijackers.

*June 1-Two unmasked men, armed with big-bore revolvers, entered the front door of the **Wright City State Bank** at the noon-hour demanding the loot. After scooping up nearly $500 in bills, the pair exited the building fleeing in the direction of their getaway car, which was manned by a companion. Instead of finding a means of escape the duo found themselves surrounded by a shotgun toting band of officers, which included Oklahoma Bureau of Investigation Agents Luther Bishop and Claud Tyler along with McCurtain County Sheriff Richard Jones and a host of deputies. The car's driver had already been subdued and handcuffed to a nearby hitching post. The bandits, sensing the officers had them on the spot, dropped their pistols and raised their hands in submission. Not a shot was fired. According to a statement made by a spokesman from the State Bureau, a confidential informant had tipped off the authorities as to the time and place of the robbery. The three hapless bandits were transported to Hugo for safekeeping.

*June 9- A pair of bandits rob the **First National Bank of Brinkman** of $1,862 in cash along with $4,550 in Liberty Bonds before fleeing in a getaway car driven by a third man. An ex- employee of the Granite Reformatory named Arthur Bliss is later charged with the job. He had $500 of the bank's money in his possession when arrested.

*June 28-The **Kildare State Bank** is robbed of an undetermined amount by Blackie Lanier, Frank Thompson, and

Abner Hope. Mob Attorney J. Earl Smith is arrested for conspiracy but later released.

*June 30-The **Depew State Bank** is looted for $5,308 by the Kimes Gang.

*August 5-The **Farmers National Bank of Beggs** is raided for $4,680 by the Kimes Gang.

*August 25-**The American State and Covington National Banks** are held-up for $10,000 and $800 respectively by the Kimes Gang. Not a single shot is fired during the robberies. The event marks one of the few successfully double bank robberies on record.

*October 22-A lone bandit armed with a small caliber automatic pistol strolls into the lobby of the **First National Bank of Forgan** demanding all the cash in the tills. Only the cashier and a youth, who worked at the bank after school as a janitor, were in the building at the time. After harvesting some $1,500, the robber locked the pair in the vault before walking out of the bank, fleeing in a small Roadster. Apparently, the fellow overlooked several thousand dollars lying in an open safe.

*November 1-The **Farmers and Merchants Bank of Choteau** is robbed by three unmasked men of $4,000 just moments before closing time. Two men entered the bank while the third individual remained at the wheel of a Sedan parked in front of the financial institution. A bookkeeper and Cashier, along with five customers were forced to lie on the floor while the brigands scooped up all available cash. The bandits locked the witnesses into the vault on departing the scene. While one of the outlaws was described by bystanders as well dressed, the other was clothed in shabby attire. The hijackers fleeing auto was last seen passing through nearby Inola traveling at the rate of sixty miles per hour.

*December 12-Dave Brown and Paul Martin rob the **Bank of Jett** for an unspecified amount. Brown is captured and initially sentenced to death for his part in the robbery. Governor Henry Johnston later commutes his sentence to term of life.

-1927-

**Twenty-four bank robberies noted.
*January 10-At 7 in the morning six bandits forced a janitor to open a side door leading into the **Sapulpa State Bank**. On gaining entrance the outlaws took up positions throughout the bank. As employees arrived for work each were taken hostage. The bandits held sway over the financial institu-

tion for nearly two hours, leisurely looting every safe, vault, and cash drawer in the building. At approximately 9 a.m., the robbers locked nearly twenty employees into the vault before departing the area taking two bankers as hostages. The bankers were released at a location eight blocks from the scene of the crime. Officials estimated the take from the robbery amounted to over $41,000. Eyewitnesses later identify Matt Kimes as one of the looters. The Sapulpa heist is noted as one of the most carefully planned bank robberies ever perpetrated in the state.

*January 20-Two nervous youths dressed in Khaki trousers and light shirts, rob the **Citizens National Bank of Wann** of $446.20 at the noon-hour. According to witnesses, one of the men held a pair of pistols, corralling a trio of bank employees, while the other, armed with a single handgun, rifled the tills. As was the custom, the robbers locked the witnesses in the vault, which was rigged with an apparatus enabling the victims to open it from the inside. A large sum of money was overlooked by the high-strung bandits in their hurry to complete their business and depart the bank. The pair reportedly used a green roadster as a getaway vehicle.

*January 30-Two men loot the **Farmers State Bank of Clarita** of $950.

*February 7-Two men rob the **First State Bank of Loco** of $3,000.

*March 1-A pair of individuals robs the **Bank of Tuttle** of $5,000. A month after the robbery, J. C. Wilson is captured near Kiowa at the conclusion of a high-speed chase driving a stolen car. When searched, detectives discover $1,700 in traveler's checks that are identified as stolen in the Tuttle bank job on his person

*April 26-Four unmasked bandits enter the **First State Bank of Cushing** at closing time, while a fifth stands outside acting as a lookout next to the getaway car. The crowded bank was filled with a dozen employees and nearly twenty customers at the time of the heist. While two of the robbers forced the crowd into a back room, the other pair rifled the tills for nearly $10,000. When ordered to open the safe, Cashier John Wilson boldly refused. Thwarted by the obstinate banker the outlaws somehow managed to crowd the nearly three-dozen witnesses into the vault before departing the scene. After fiddling with the combination from inside the vault for some minutes the hostages were able to gain their freedom and give the alarm. The bandits were last seen driving south at a high rate of speed. Several eyewitnesses identify the notorious Ray Terrill as one of the hijackers.

*April 29-At noon a Ford Roadster pulled up to the front of the **Bluejacket State Bank**, two armed men dressed in Khaki trousers and blue shirts entered the bank while a third remained on guard at the getaway car. The pair confronted Teller Ben Horton, the lone witness in the building, forcing him to open the vault. While the robbery was underway, Cashier C. R. Spradlin, returning from his lunch, is accosted by the hijacker stationed outside and ordered to sit on the car's running board while his pals finish their business inside. Directly, the pair exited the financial institution with approximately $1,200 in their poke. The bandits sped out of town spreading about fifty pounds of roofing nails on the road in their wake. Witnesses promptly came forward stating the bandit's car carried a license plate that read 365F211. It turns out the car was stolen the previous night from an employee of the Carter Oil Company in Seminole. Craig County Sheriff Harry Campbell immediately organized a posse which began setting up roadblocks and scouring the countryside in search of the looters. Several days after the robbery, the Sheriff received a tip indicating one of the bandits was staying at a residence in Tulsa. That night Campbell, accompanied by a squad of Tulsa lawmen and Chelsea Officer Tom Dean, raided the home in question apprehending twenty-two year-old R. D. "Major" Taylor. The suspect had $215 in cash in his britches and the car parked in the driveway was positively identified as the one used in the Bluejacket heist.

On the evening of May 8, a party of Muskogee Police Officers making a liquor raid arrested Eddie Clanton, the son of a popular Vinita café owner, as well as C. H. Hill, and a female suspect, at a fleabag hotel in Muskogee. When searching the room officers uncovered $200 in cash as well as several quarts of bonded bourbon and a pair of loaded revolvers. After questioning the prisoners, Muskogee investigators suspected the pair was possibly the Bluejacket hijackers. They immediately contacted Craig County authorities. The following day Sheriff Campbell, accompanied by the witnesses from the bank heist, traveled to Muskogee where the bankers made positive identification of the suspects who were promptly transported back to Vinita for trail. On June 7, the trio was given their preliminary hearings and officially charged with armed bank robbery.

The following night, a jailor named J. L. Disney pulled the wrong lever in the Craig County Jail accidentally releasing the three who quickly overpowered him stealing his keys and pistol, beating him over the head repeatedly with a handy steel alarm clock. Once they had had their way with the jailor, the trio locked him in a cell and ran down the stairs to the street where they hijacked a milk truck driven by Frank Russill, forcing him to transport them to the edge of town where they released him after stealing a bigger car. Back at the jail, the courthouse janitor kept hearing a howling noise but ignored the commotion until it irritated him so much he decided to investigate. He followed the noise to the top floor jail discovering the poor jailor sitting bleeding in a locked cell. On being informed of the break, Sheriff Campbell again formed a posse and took to the field with fire in his eyes. He also announced a $300 reward for the capture of the escapees; the Craig County Bankers Association promptly matched the offer.

Several days later, a man came forward telling how the fugitives had forced him to drive them to Spavinaw. A few hours after receiving this information, an area farmer informed the laws the men were hiding in a barn located south of town. That night a posse made up of twenty-five Craig and Delaware County officers surrounded the barn. At dawn, a man was seen poking his head out the barn door. Lawmen opened fire. After feeling the heat of a dozen lead projectiles flying past his head, the man raced out of the building shouting "For G-ds sake don't kill me. I give up!" Minutes later his two companions surrendered peaceably and all three were hauled back to their cells. On March 20,1928, Clanton was convicted of the Bluejacket heist and sentenced to twenty-five years in prison, he was also handed a twenty-five year term for escape. C. H. Hill was also convicted; receiving an eighteen–year sentence while Taylor was hammered with a fifteen-year term. Clanton was given leave of absence from McAlester in 1932 due to his contracting TB, a common calamity in the nation's prisons during the era. He quickly hooked up with a prison buddy named Ford Bradshaw of Vian, who had recently been paroled on an armed robbery charge. He and Bradshaw would go on a twenty-month tear being suspected of pulling off a dozen robberies, several murders, and a host of lesser crimes as members of the so-called Cookson Hills Gang.

May 18-The **First National and Farmers National Banks of Beggs** are simultaneously robbed for $6,986 in cash and $7,900 worth of jewels by the Kimes Gang. City Marshal William McAnally is slain during the robbery. The event marks the second time in less than a year the Kimes Gang pulls off a rare double bank robbery.

* See previous article *The Kimes Boys* for further information.

*June 8-The **Bank of Agra** is robbed of $500 by two poorly dressed men.

*June 25-The **Avery State Bank** is robbed of an undetermined amount by two men. Both are eventually arrested by a hastily assembled posse.

*July 11-The **First National Bank of Mill Creek** is robbed of an undetermined amount by Jim Wilson and A. E. Holloway. Both suspects are eventually arrested and convicted of committing the heist.

*August 13- The **Bluejacket State Bank** is robbed of $400 by four men. Three of the suspects are eventually captured. A local attorney named Q.P. McGhee is charged with planning the job as well as harboring the fugitives in the robberies aftermath. The incident marks the second time in less than a year the bank is robbed.

*August 20-The **Douglas State Bank** is robbed by a lone bandit of $1,762. Earl Carr is arrested a month later working at a carnival at nearby Tryon and charged with the hijacking. The suspect had previously served a five-year sentence for auto theft and was currently on appeal bond concerning a charge of hog-theft out of Payne County.

*August 23-**First National Bank of Kingston** is held-up by four young men for $1,562.30. Two of the bandits are arrested thirty minutes after the heist in nearby Madill by Sheriff Ed Long and Chief of Police Crockett Long. The two give their names as Joe Leonard and Charlie Ross. Within 24 hours, the pair confesses to the crime and are both sentenced to twenty-five years in the joint. Now that's swift justice. Several days later, the other two hijackers are arrested in Texas. Most of the loot is recovered.

*August 30-A lone bandit walked into the **First National Bank of McCloud** where he subdued Assistant Cashier G. H. Jones with a pistol. The robber ordered the banker to, "Fill my sack." On departing the scene, the hijacker shut his lone victim into the vault, which failed to lock when shut. Jones easily freed himself and gave the alarm. The bandit, who had been observed by townsfolk loitering about town for several days before the robbery, got away with roughly $4,000. A large posse is mobilized but failed to capture the fugitive.

*September 2-Shortly after 2:30 in the afternoon a car containing four individuals stopped and parked a half block from the **Canadian Valley Bank of Asher**, three persons depart the vehicle and enter the bank while a fourth remains with the car. One man holding a pistol forced Cashier M.W. Hampton along with bank employees Horace Goss and Albert Baker and a customer named T. W. Watson to lie face down on the lobby floor while his companions loot the place for some $1,800. When the witnesses were forced into the vault Hampton used a phone, which had recently been installed to call the phone exchange. The young female operator who answered the call reacted by hoofing it to the McCarter Drug Store where she informed Clerk Bailey Browder of the ongoing raid. Browder grabbed a weapon and strolled into the street where he unleashed a volley of lead toward the bandits as they exited the bank. Although three of the robbers ignored the apparently poorly aimed projectiles, one of the hijackers returned

fire, a bullet striking the clerk in the midsection the round entering his right lung. Hearing the gunfire, the streets emptied and the hijackers rapidly departed town. Within minutes of the raid, a large posse of officers and vigilantes was formed and gives chase. That night a pack of bloodhounds from the state pen were added to the search. Several days after the robbery, the druggist succumbed to his wounds. Some time after the spectacular robbery and shootout a man named Tom Guest was arrested and charged with the murder of Mr. Browder. He was convicted and sentenced to burn in "Old Sparky" at the state prison. Later on, a twenty-one year-old-named W. J White was also apprehended and convicted of the robbery. The stolen money was never recovered. On July 17, 1930, society extracted justice from Tom Guest by executing him with a lethal jolt of electricity.

*October 1- Shortly before noon three armed men entered the **Macomb State Bank** forcing the occupants, Cashier C. R. Wallace and bookkeeper Pauline Carter, to "Hit the floor," while they looted the institution of some $2,500. The bandits reportedly made their escape in a crème colored touring car. The authorities immediately suspect the robbery is the work of a group of recent escapees from the severely overcrowded Seminole County Jail in Wewoka. The following day Seminole County Deputy Sheriff C. E. Majors and Wolf Township Constable Jim Villines were scouting the roads just south of Seminole when they spotted a car occupied by two of the jail breakers. The officers followed the pair to the doorstep of a boarding house located in the small oilfield community of Wilsonville. While Majors entered the front of the establishment, his partner attempted to gain entry through the rear door but found it locked. While Villines was struggling with the locked door, he heard the sounds of a struggle coming from within the house. Peering through a window, the officer observed Constable Majors grappling with one of the fugitives, who was later identified as Jack Bailey. Villines began shooting through the windowpane and suddenly his fellow officer hit the ground dead. In the meantime, Bailey and another escapee ran out the front door. Vallines chased the pair for several blocks firing at will. He later stated he observed Bailey fall to the ground but quickly regain his footing and make a dash into a wooded area. Sadly, Officer Majors was not the first nor would he be the last officer slain by gunfire in the raucous Seminole Oil-boom district during the decade of the roaring twenties.

*October 5-On receiving a tip inferring the **First National Bank of Pawhuska** was going to be robbed, eight Osage county officers took up round the clock positions inside the bank armed with shotguns loaded with buckshot. After holding their positions for several days, the posse was called off. The following day, two armed men entered the nearby **Liberty**

National Bank relieving the business of approximately $1,500 while an assembled crowd, unaware of the doings in the bank, gathered in front of a nearby business listening to the World Series on a radio. After shutting two bankers into the vault, the bandits left the bank and calmly strolled through the crowd before driving off into the sunset. Two area hooligans were later arrested and pled guilty to the crime. The pair implicated one of the bank employees of conspiring with them in the heist. Turns out, the robbery was an inside job.

*October 25- Two men armed with revolvers enter the **Bank of Sasakwa** while a third stands guard at their getaway car. The duo threatened the cashier, who was the lone person in the building, with death if he didn't "pony up." The banker did as instructed and the bandits fled the institution with $500 in their pockets.

*November 2-Three men identified as Raymond Wilson and brothers L. L. "Red" and W. R. Calloway rob the **Bank of Wynnewood** of $40,000. After entering the bank, Wilson covered a bevy of customers and employees while the brothers gathered up $40,000. The trio then retreated from the financial institution and made a clean getaway. All three were captured within months and convicted of armed robbery. Although the state urged the jury to put the Calloway brothers to death, the jurors decided on life sentences instead. Wilson received a twenty-five year sentence. Also arrested was Vivian Calloway, the wife of W.R., who is identified as the brains of the gang. Only $26,000 of the loot was recovered. The Wynnewood robbery was noted as one of the largest bank jobs in state history. Red Calloway died of Tuberculosis at McAlester in 1930.

*November 12-The **Farmers State Bank of Clarita** is robbed of an undetermined amount.

*November 22-Two unmasked men rob the **Citizens State Bank of Headrick** of $1,500. Several bankers and witnesses were locked in the vault before the duo fled the building joining a partner sitting in a running Hudson car parked in front of the bank. The bandits are last seen speeding toward Lawton.

*December 9-**First State Bank of Inola** is robbed by a lone bandit of an undetermined amount. Several days later, Officers Jim Burkhart and Oscar Jeffers arrested a suspect possessing $561 of the stolen loot and a pistol.

*December 22-Three individuals knock off the much-robbed **Carney State Bank for** the umpteenth time. Cashier George Jones fires four pistol shots into the bandit's departing green sedan. Robert Chastain, Ollie Harris, and Tom Antone are charged with the hijacking.

-1928-

**Twenty-five robberies noted-Oklahoma rated second behind California for bank robberies in 1928. Bankers were encouraged to carry guns to work especially shotguns. In nearby Texas, the bankers association began paying a $5,000 reward for each dead bank bandit. When the president of the Oklahoma Bankers Association demanded a similar reward be offered by his organization, Captain Frank Hamer of the Texas Rangers advised against such a move. He strongly criticized the Texas reward system, saying, "Offering that big reward has created a murder machine in this state. Frame-up jobs are becoming the norm. Fellows are hiring drifters to rob a bank then informing the authorities of their actions. When the "pigeon" is slain by waiting officers these cannibals are coming forward for their cut. These rewards have aroused the greed and desire of a small group of men who love money more than life."

*January 24-A pair of tough looking mugs entered the **Bessie State Bank** waving pistols about demanding the loot. Present in the building at the time was Cashier Ben Kiehn, a decorated hero of the First World War, accompanied by a female stenographer and a customer. Upon gathering up roughly $750, the duo shut the three witnesses into the vault, which failed to fully lock. Just as the bandits were withdrawing from the bank Kiehn pushed open the vault door several inches and began plastering the outlaws with gunfire from a pistol he had hidden inside the vault for just such an emergency. One of the desperadoes immediately hit the floor gravely wounded with slugs to the back and arm. The other thug reacted by engaging in a fierce gun-duel with the gutsy cashier. After a heated exchange of lead, Kiehn took a round to the head, the bullet striking him just below the left eye. He reacted by slumping to his knees mumbling, "Help" three times before falling dead. Taking advantage of the lull in the action, the unwounded outlaw grabbed his wounded pal and dragged him to their awaiting car that was described as a Jewett Sedan. The bandits were last seen speeding away in a westerly direction. Alerted by the storm of gunfire emitting from the bank a crowd of citizens entered the business discovering the dead cashier slumped against a cabinet but still clinging to his gun. A massive posse was quickly fielded, volunteers coming from a four county area. Hundreds of vigilantes armed with shotguns and deer rifles, set up a dozen roadblocks and beat the bushes for miles around the town. An airplane manned with a pilot and a spotter armed with a high-powered rifle equipped with a scope was sent aloft from the airport at Clinton. Around nightfall a man approached a farmhouse located a few miles west of town, which was occupied by Buster Peck informing him, "There's a man shot down there at the creek bank" before fleeing into the darkness. Peck rushed across the field toward the nearby dry creek bed where he spotted the glow of a small campfire. Approaching the fire, he discovered an individual lying on his side covered by an overcoat groaning in pain. He quickly informed the authorities who arrived in mass within a matter of minutes. The wounded man was identified as Fletcher Rickard. A physician was summoned and after examining the blood-soaked robber shook his head stating, "He won't last till morning." He was correct in his assumption. The man expired just moments before dawn. The deceased was positively identified by the witnesses from the bank robbery as being one of the hijackers. Fifty dollars of the $750 in loot was recovered from his pockets. The posse spent the next twenty-four hours scouring the area on foot fruitlessly searching for the man's companion. An individual named Frank Simpson was later charged with being Rickard's accomplice. Ben Kiehn, survived by his widow and a daughter, was buried with military honors at the Cordell Cemetery.

*January 25-On this date, three unmasked and heavily armed thugs entered the **Love County National Bank at Marietta** at a few minutes past noon looting the business for roughly $9,500. While in the process of holding up the place a young boy happened to be walking past the bank when he noticed a crowd of folks inside with their hands held skyward. Realizing he was observing a heist, the youth ran to the nearest telephone and rang up Love County Sheriff Sam Long at his home. Long, who was eating his lunch at the time, dropped his fork and grabbed his pistol heading toward the nearby bank as fast as he could. On his arrival, the lawman rushed into the financial institution and demanded the robber's surrender to which the shocked and surprised bandits answered with a burst of gunfire. Long pulled up short and began methodically returning fire. For the next several minutes the bank's lobby was the scene of appalling devastation, the shocking sounds of multiple gun blasts, accompanied by a crescendo of bright muzzle flashes, followed by the sickly smell of cordite and freshly spilled blood quickly filled the room. One of the bandits, later identified as Oscar Harrison of nearby Goose Creek, Texas, was struck by a pair of rounds to the head and dropped like a sack of rocks while the Sheriff took slugs to both the shoulder and neck. The surviving bandits then rushed past the wounded lawmen, one of the them pausing just long enough to pump a single round into the helpless officers stomach before jumping into a waiting car manned by a fourth confederate, leaving their wounded partner bleeding on the floor of the bank. Shortly after the robbery, the getaway vehicle was spotted at a location just south of town. John and Vernon Liddell, along with Claude Andrews, were arrested and charged with the robbery and assault. A warrant was issued for a fourth man identified as Haynie Liddell, a brother to two of those

already in custody. Sheriff Long died of his wounds a few days after the robbery.

The day after the robbery Claude Andrews led the local judge and county attorney to where he and his pals had buried the loot. Only half of the stolen money was recovered. Andrews later claimed the two officers of the court pocketed the missing funds. Although both the judge and attorney would be tried for theft, their separate trials ended in hung juries. Andrews plead guilty to armed robbery and he was sentenced to five years in the can. Vernon Liddell was acquitted while charges against his brother John were eventually dismissed. Brother Haynie remained a fugitive from justice until the afternoon of November 15 when he and a person identified as fifty-five year old Colbert Keel drove up to the First National Bank of Marietta in a small car. Entering the bank the pair lined up a passel of witnesses against a wall before looting the tills of approximately $10,000. When departing the building the two bandits forced the crowd of hostages in front of them through a side exit. On reaching the street the hostages suddenly split to the four winds rushing to the police station and various other locations where they breathlessly reported the robbery. Momentarily stunned at the loss of their human shields, the robbers grabbed Bank President Frank Conrad shoving him into their getaway car. Suddenly, a hastily formed posse made up of fifty armed citizens led by newly elected Sheriff A.W. Stafford surrounded the car and began pumping rounds from a hodgepodge of shotguns, pistols, squirrel guns, and deer rifles into the hijackers automobile. Banker Conrad, wounded by several rounds of buckshot, wiggled from the car and onto the street, taking cover behind a wheel while Liddell was struck by buckshot in the head and shoulders. His partner in crime was reportedly killed outright being literally perforated like a minnow bucket. Liddell would survive his wounds due to his wearing a steel vest while the wounded banker was listed in fair condition, although doctors feared he would loose sight in both eyes. On searching the bandit's car shortly after the raid officers found several boxes of ammunition, a first aid kit, a bottle of whiskey, and a bucket of roofing nails. A crude but effective deterrent if a posse happened to follow in their wake.

*January 30-The **Farmers State Bank of Clarita** is robbed of $950 by two men.

*January 31-The notorious Dick Gregg and two companions looted the **First Bank of Centralia** for nearly $1,500.

*February 21-The **American National Bank of Fort Towson** is looted by two individuals for $10,000 in cash and securities. Ollie Parks and E. I. Durfee along with Miss Billie Page are arrested in Paris, Texas, and charged with perpetrating the bank raid. The stolen money is not recovered

*March 3-Five men and a woman rob the **Bank of Commerce of Jenks** of $2,260. Robert Wheeler and Walter York, both of Tulsa, along with two brothers from Okmulgee are arrested and charged with the heist.

*April 18-The **First National Bank of Stonewall** is robbed of $1,750 by two men.

*May 29-A pair of unmasked men entered the **Hitchita State Bank** while a third stood guard at an automobile parked in front. One fellow approached the female cashier demanding to speak to the bank president then suddenly changing his mind he began fumbling with his shirt producing a revolver and informing the teller to, "Stand where you are and hand over all the money." His confederate quickly took up a covering position in the lobby. After gathering up approximately $1,000, the pair withdrew from the building and upon entering their car, a rubbernecker inquired of them what was going on. One of the bandits threatened to shoot him in the guts if he didn't back off and mind his own business. The trio then sped off in an easterly direction driving a Chevrolet Sedan, which had been stolen off the streets of Tulsa the previous night. An all points bulletin was immediately sent out to surrounding towns. Two local posses were promptly fielded and a dragnet began in hopes of capturing the robbers.

The trio abandoned the Chevy just east of town exchanging it for a Dodge vehicle. Soon after the auto-switch, one of the posses surrounded the trio but the outlaws ditched their car and somehow managed to slip through the net on foot. They soon ran across a farmer who they paid to drive them to the Pittsburg county community of Crowder where the bandits hailed a bus, which transported them to nearby McAlester. Shortly after their arrival, the gang split up.

The following day a fisherman reported a suspicious person had paid him $5 in nickels to row him across the Canadian River earlier that morning in his small boat. That evening, Officers John Floyd and S. A. Hamil arrested the same man at a boarding house in nearby Henryetta. The suspect possessed roughly $200 in coins and currency in his britches pockets. Upon questioning by McIntosh County Sheriff Erv Kelley the young man, who identified himself as twenty-one-year-old Roy Nicholson, folded up like a cheap suit snitching on his partners in crime. He stated, "I met those two fellows at a rooming house here in Henryetta. I had been in town three weeks. I got to talking to these guys and one thing led to another." He added, "I got cold feet during the robbery but by then there was nothing I could do about it. We had no plan for escape." He claimed he only knew his companions as "Skeet" and "Shorty." He further informed the Sheriff, "They went into the bank while I stayed outside. They had revolvers while I was unarmed." He told of spending the night in the bush, scurrying about the timber dodging the posse. According to witnesses, the young man appeared glad to have been captured and the whole affair at an end. The following day, Sheriff Kelley and a posse of fellow officers arrested Nicholson's confederates at a boarding house in Spiro. The men admitted their names were Otho Key and Jess Kimbrough. The pair had $550 of the stolen money on their persons at the time of their apprehension. When questioned, they admitted the robbery was their first bank job but they had had hopes of knocking off a few more in the future. All three suspects eventually pled guilty to the robbery and were each sentenced to twenty-five-years imprisonment. Sheriff Kelley received a $500 reward from the Oklahoma Bankers Association.

*June 6-The **Bank of Macomb** is robbed of an unspecified amount. John Brasher of Seminole is arrested and charged with the crime. The loot is recovered.

*June 12-Holding a revolver in one hand and a cement sack in the other, a lone bandit enters the **State Bank of Fay** demanding Cashier D.P. Karns, "Fill 'er up!" After gathering up about $1,000, the nervous young bandit locked Karnes as well as several other bank employees and a customer in the vault before departing.

*June 20-Three armed men loot the **Bank of Foraker** of $600 and successfully make their escape in a large touring car.

*July 20-Four individuals rob the **Bank of Hastings** of $1,000. Chief suspects are Ennis Fay Smiddy, R. L Park, Roy Anderson, and S. L. Scott.

*July 24-The **First State Bank of Lamont** is robbed of $1,300 by the Whitey Walker Gang.

*August 8-June 6 and 20 (Robbed on all three dates)-On June 6, a lone robber entered the **Bank of Breckenridge** threatening to shoot Bank President Fred Pralle if he didn't open the safe. The bandit got away with $1,000. On June 20, the same lone robber looted the financial institution for $1,150 but on this occasion, he separated the silver from paper money refusing to haul the heavy coins instead leaving it on the bank's floor. On August 8, a pair of bandits hijacked the bank for an undetermined amount. In December, Wesley Oaks was arrested and charged with participating in the August raid. Apparently, he dropped a dime on his crime-partner, naming Loren Norris, who was currently stationed at the Army Air Corps at Kelly Field in San Antonio, Texas, as his confederate. Norris was identified by the bank president as being the lone robber who struck the bank twice in June.

*August 9-On the morning of August 9, three men kidnapped a Muskogee ice crème salesman stealing his truck and tying him to a tree just outside town. The individuals then drove the stolen rig into the downtown district where one of the men entered the **Citizens National Bank of Muskogee** approaching Teller H. H. Bain demanding he, "Don't say a word, pass me those big bills and be quick about it!" Bain obeyed passing the fellow $3,334. On gaining the currency, the man began to exit the bank when Bain began vainly yelling, "Stop that man." The robber quickly joined his pals making a clean getaway.

*August 10–The much-robbed **Shidler National Bank** is looted for $4,148 by three heavily armed men.

*August 11-On this date, the notorious William Jennings Bryan "Whitey" Walker along with Owen Edwards and Curtis Black rob the **First National Bank of Allen** of approximately $2,000. The getaway vehicle is discovered abandoned in a wooded area just outside of town. Curtis Black is arrested a few days after the robbery. He eventually pled guilty to robbery with firearms and given a life sentence for the crime.

*August 29-Three men riding in a blue sedan parked directly in front of the **Shidler National Bank**. Two men exited the rig entering the bank while a third remained in the car smoking a cigarette. One of the bandits approached Cashier Harold Bobbitt ordering him to fill up a feed sack with paper money while the second bandit covered the lobby with a scattergun. When they departed the scene with $4,000 in their poke, the outlaws forced the cashier to accompany them requesting Bank Stenographer Mrs. R. J. Rust to, "Please be quiet and don't give the alarm for fifteen minutes or we will have to kill this young man." The bandits released the banker just over the Kansas border. When interviewed by the press the cashier stoically commented, "Just a nice ride in the country with a few minor inconveniences. The men made me keep my head down so I could not get a good look at them. They drove fast but safely." The following year R.E. Williams and Earl Stinnett are convicted of committing the heist while the third unnamed subject remained at large.

*September 13-At noon, a lone unmasked robber entered the **First National Bank of Billings** through the back door flashing a handgun toward two female bank employees who were the only persons in the place at the time. After gathering up around $300 in cash and coin, the gunman exited the way he had entered. The same bank had been robbed previously in July of 1927.

*September 17, Whitey Walker and Owen Edwards loot the **Nardin State Bank in Kay County** of approximately $1,000. The bandits kidnapped the bank's cashier and took him for a joy ride while a carload of trigger-happy vigilantes followed them out of town slinging lead their direction. The hijackers eventually lost the tail and abandoned their car and hostage a short distance from town. When the getaway car was discovered officers noticed the rear window was shattered and the car's steel body was riddled with bullet holes. When interviewed, the kidnapped banker stated that while on his wild ride he had overheard one of the bandits exclaim, "I'm hit!"

*September 22- Burglars strike the **Macomb State Bank** in the wee hours of the morning. The yeggs are unable to gain access to the vault so they plundered the safety deposit boxes for an estimated $100.The bank had suffered a daylight raid the previous October loosing $2,500.

*October 3-On this date three well dressed men knock off the **Canadian Valley Bank of Asher** for $3,386, taking twenty-year-old Alvin Baker and a female cashier hostage. The lady promptly freed herself by jumping off the car's running board while Mr. Baker was released near Konawa. A couple of days after the heist, L. L. Tomlin were arrested in the aftermath of a fight involving knives at a rooming house in Oklahoma City. He was promptly charged with the bank hijacking, as were two other subjects.

*October 16-Two men rob the **State Bank of Commerce at Gate** for $3,000. Both bandits are soon captured, as is an ex-employee of the bank named Albert Joyce who is charged with complicity. The loot is not recovered.

October 17-At the noon hour on October 17, three heavily armed desperadoes enter the **First State Bank of Prague** sticking up the lone cashier on duty for roughly $3,000 before taking the poor fellow hostage and exiting the building through the rear door and entering a waiting automobile. At a point four miles north and a mile west of the community of Meeker, the outlaws dismounted the car and entered a spanking new Ford. One of the bandits, later identified as Whitey Walker, turned to the cashier, and calmly said, "Now go on home." The baffled cashier drove the original getaway car back to Meeker and phoned the authorities, which set up several roadblocks and began beating the bushes in a futile effort to capture the outlaws.

*October 26-Two men drove up to the **First National Bank of Addington** in a small coupe, parking the rig in front of the financial institution. One man got out and entered the bank while the other remained at the wheel. Approaching Cashier Ray McTennis, the lone bandit demanded he fill up a grain sack with cash. When the cashier hesitated, the outlaw fired a single round into the ceiling for effect. Hearing the gunshot, Jefferson County Deputy Sheriff W. A. Fowler grabbed a rifle out of the trunk of his cruiser and cautiously approached the bank on foot. Observing a man armed with a pistol running from the bank toward a waiting vehicle, the deputy opened up with his rifle wounding the fleeing suspect. Although the man was noticeably staggered by the bullet's impact, he was somehow able to crawl into the car, which headed out of town at a fast clip. The officer then leaped into his own vehicle and gave chase blasting away with a pistol held in one hand while steering with the other. Suddenly, the getaway car came to an abrupt stop and the bandits baled out attempting to flee on foot into a nearby wooded ravine. Fowler eased over to the side of the road and taking a firm grip on his high-powered rifle shot one of the men in the head and the other in the torso. Both bandits crashed to the ground and lay still. One of the brigands, later identified as Claude Coffee of Fort Worth, was dead at the scene while the second subject, identified as Floyd Pruett, was severely wounded.

*December 6-Two youths hijack the **Bank of Kellyville** of $1,000. They are promptly run down by a posse of vigilantes and surrender after a short exchange of fire. The notorious Bill Pritchett is later charged with planning the robbery.

*December 21-The **Bank of Manitou** is robbed of $1,561 by the four Cunningham brothers, aided by their cousin.

-1929-

**Twenty robberies noted

*January 3-A pair of individuals loot the **Canadian Valley Bank of Asher** of $2,000 then kidnap the cashier and a female bookkeeper, holding both into the wee hours of the morning. Two men from Maud were later arrested and charged with the robbery. The event marks the second time the bank has been robbed in three months time.

*January 15-Bank bandit Whitey Walker is captured in Buffalo, New York.

*February 7-A lone bandit, described as 45 years-old, medium height, and wearing a sheepskin coat looted the **Bank of Macomb** for roughly $800. Besides the hijacker, Bookkeeper Pauline Carder was the only person present in the building at the time of the heist. Miss Carder was also present three of the past five times the bank has been hit in a little over a two-year period. She described the three robberies in an interview with a reporter from the *Daily Oklahoman* by saying: "The first robber was friendly. He smiled while he conducted his busi-

ness. He assured me I would not be harmed." The attractive young cashier continued, saying, "The second robber was wild-looking and most unpleasant. He forced a co-worker and me to lie flat on the floor while he robbed the safe. Sometimes I wake up in the middle of the night and I see his cruel eyes. Very distracting." Adding, "The most recent robber was like the first. All business and evidently intent upon getting away with the least excitement possible."

*March 20-**National Bank of Wynona** is robbed of $1,500 by Dick Gregg and others. Cashier D. C. Shewmaker and Clerk Jennie Briggs are locked in the vault when the bandits depart the scene. Shewmaker promptly escaped the confines of the vault grabbing an old army rifle he had stashed in a corner and ran to the street where he fired several ineffective rounds at the retreating outlaws.

*March 27-Three men rob the **Bank of May** of $1,265.

*April 9-Dick Gregg robs the **Keystone Bank** of an undetermined amount.

*April 12-Two men rob the **Quapaw Bank** of $8,000. William Bell and a nineteen year-old youth from Tulsa are convicted and sentenced to 25 years imprisonment. The loot is not recovered.

*June 16-Two lads aged fourteen and fifteen, one armed with a handgun, rob the **Bank of Union City** of a whopping $21. The pair is promptly captured and sentenced to a term at the Boys Reformatory at Pauls Valley. The heist may have set a record for the youngest documented perpetrators to be involved in an Oklahoma bank robbery.

*June 20-Two men on horseback loot the **Bank of Caney** of $750. Posseman catch up with the pair several miles outside of town. In the ensuing firefight, one of the desperadoes is wounded causing him to drop a burlap bag containing $250. Both bandits are eventually captured. This incident marks the last horseback bank robbery in Oklahoma history.

*June 21-Two young army deserters, Robert Yon of Altoona, Pennsylvania, and A. C. Heatly of St. Albans, New York, stole a automobile from a local park caretaker and began scooping the loop in downtown Moore. After a fashion, the pair dismounted the car and stood across the street from the **First State Bank of Moore** reconnoitering the situation. Meanwhile, a bank official contacted a city garageman named Roy Goss, who had been assigned by the local vigilante organization to provide security for the bank on that particular day, informing the mechanic that a pair of suspicious looking men was loitering in front of the bank. Goss armed himself and strolled into the financial institution taking up a position just off the lobby. Sure enough, just moments after Goss got in place the pair of "Jellybeans' came stumbling into the bank's lobby. Young Heatly stepped up to the teller's cage, whipping out a revolver and demanded the goods. Goss reacted by blasting the young fellow with a slug to the left side. Suddenly, young Mr. Yon desperately rushed to the counter snatching $150 in bills and ran for the rear door. He wasn't quick enough. Goss let him have it. The young robber hit the floor with a thud, dead to the world. Both the bank teller and Mr. Goss were paid $250 each in rewards from the Oklahoma Bankers Association. The bandit's body was shipped back to Pennsylvania for burial while twenty-year-old Heatly was remanded to the county jail where he was given medical treatment. Although he pled innocent to the robbery, he told newsmen, "If I'm convicted I'll take my medicine like a man."

*July 1-Two young men robbed the **Inola Bank** of $800 and escape in a small motorcar after locking the bank president and a customer in the vault. A passerby heard their cries and released them. The bank president stated the two bandits strolled into the building, one taking up a station in the lobby center while another approached the cage saying, "Stick 'em up Charley!" Pat Kendrick and Eugene Bowman, both of Wynona, were later arrested and charged with the heist. Kendrick was sentenced to twelve years in the slammer while Bowman died of TB prior to trial. The bank is robbed again on November 9 by three hijackers who relieved the financial institution of $600. On that occasion the bank president and his wife, along with a customer were taken hostage but released soon afterward.

July 10- Shortly before noon a young man entered the **Exchange Bank of Collinsville** inquiring of Bank President C. T. McCarty if he knew the whereabouts of a man named White. Before the banker had time to answer the lad produced an old-fashioned six-shooter ordering him and a customer named Arbuckle into the vault. The youth, now accompanied by a second robber, gathered up $4,400 from the safe and tills. Meanwhile, Town Marshal Harve Sims, noticing some unusual activity at the bank, approached the area on foot. Observing a car parked in front of the bank causing a traffic snarl, he ordered the driver to "Move on." Suddenly, the two bandits exited the bank, stopping just long enough to disarm the dejected lawman and order him to sit on the curb and, "Mind his own business." The getaway car was later discovered abandoned just outside of town. The following year, two subjects are arrested and charged with the heist. The stolen loot is never recovered.

*July 12-**Bank of Kendrick** is robbed of $600 by Owen Edwards and Freddie Davis, one-time members of the "Whitey" Walker Gang. The bank was previously robbed on September 16, 1925 by Freddy Davis and a companion.

*July 26- Late of a morning, four bandits hijack the **First National Bank of Hooker** for $9,822 fleeing in a Ford automobile driven by an accomplice. A large posse is promptly fielded, which soon discovers the abandoned getaway car covered with brush along side the nearby Beaver River. Although officers erect roadblocks and conduct a massive search throughout most of the Oklahoma panhandle region as well as bordering sections of Kansas and Texas, they discover no sign of the hijackers. It is later ascertained the robbery was the work of the notorious Cunningham brothers.*See previous article- *Brothers in Crime* for further details.

August 10-The **National Bank of Prague** is robbed by Golda McCollum and Blackie Hull of $3,400.
*See previous article-*The Sheik of Boynton* for further details.

*September 12-Goldie McCullom and Blackie Hill loot the **Peoples National Bank of Checotah** of $4,357.
*See previous article *The Sheik of Boynton* for further details.

*September 17–Three unidentified men enter the **First National Bank of Minco** forcing five witnesses into the vault before harvesting $5,000 from the cashier's cages. The robbers then exited the building hopping into a waiting automobile, which was later identified as stolen. Reports indicate the getaway car was driven by a lad of tender age. On releasing themselves from the vault, the hostages gave the alarm. A large posse hurriedly gathered and gave chase. At a point twelve miles east of Tuttle, the posse caught up with the robbers. The encounter produced a sharp exchange of fire. Following the short gunfight, the bandit's fleeing car was able to gain some distance from the pursuers. An hour later, lawmen discovered the getaway car abandoned in a weed-chocked ditch near the bridge over the South Canadian River. On closer inspection, officers noted the car had obviously been disabled due to the rear tire being shredded by gunfire. Bloodstains were found on the back seat. A few weeks after the robbery a young man named Freddie Davis was arrested and charged with both the July 12 robbery of the Bank of Kendricks as well as the Minco heist. The youth promptly turned informant, naming a one-time member of the now defunct Whitey Walker Gang, Owen Edwards, as the leader of the hijackers in both raids. Shortly afterwards, the young man, filled with remorse over his actions, hung himself in the Lincoln County Jail. A $1,000 reward was promptly

posted for the capture (Dead or Alive) of Owen Edwards.
*See previous article *Jim Keirsey* for further details.

*October 3-Two roughly dressed men armed with revolvers rob the **Bank of Avant** of $2,000 before escaping in a small car heading towards the Osage district. Several days later, officers arrest John Gordon in a cornfield just outside nearby Skiatook. He was positively identified as being one of the hijackers by several bank officials.

*October 9-Two bandits rob the **Farmers State Bank of Locust Grove** for $2,000.

* November 9- The **Inola Bank** is robbed by three hijackers who relieve the financial institution of $600. The bank president and his wife along with a customer are taken hostage but released soon afterward.

*December 20-Two characters enter the **First National Bank of Gracemont**, one armed with a shotgun and the other a .38 revolver. One of the men announced a holdup, ordering a bevy of customers and employees to stand still while his partner raked in roughly $1,600 from the tills. When ordered to open the locked vault, Bank President William Granger informed the robbers the vault could not be accessed due to it being on a time lock. While the pair was mulling over the bad news, a customer strolled into the bank and observing the situation quickly backed out into the street giving the alarm. Suddenly, the bank president lunged at a desk drawer withdrawing a pistol and sending a round at the bandit pair. Although the bullet missed its mark by a mile, the suddenly confused robbers took to their heels making for their getaway car. In a classic example of Murphy's Law, the looter's car sputtered and jumped before starting, giving the angry bank president time enough to empty his pistol into the carload of fleeing desperadoes, wounding one in both the shoulder and leg and the other took a slug to the arm. Finally getting their car to cooperate, the two raced out of town. Just a half-mile out of the village limits the bandits lost control of their rig smashing into a tree and were forced to flee on foot. Moments later, a large posse of armed vigilantes arrived on the scene giving chase. Cornered in a field, the unlucky bandits surrendered. The loot was recovered and the outlaws jailed. The robbers were identified as twenty-two year-old Joe Cherry of Ft. Smith, Arkansas, and thirty-one-year-old Oscar Logston of Tulsa. Cherry was listed as suffering only a slight wound to the arm while his partner was rushed to the hospital suffering a more serious wound. Apparently, the round that had hit him in the shoulder had traveled to a lung causing it to collapse. When Cherry was asked why the pair never returned fire on the posse or Banker Granger, he said, "I could have shot the banker but didn't have any de-

sire to kill anyone. What do ya know a pair of pacifist bank robbers!

*December 22-A lone bandit riding a motorbike robs the **Citizens National Bank of Fort Gibson** of an undetermined amount of money. Later that same day, R. C. Grower was discovered dazed and injured lying next to the road just outside of the community of Grayson. A damaged motorcycle was found in a nearby ditch. It seems he had lost control of the bike while rounding a sharp curve. He was identified by several witnesses as being the robber of the financial institution. The loot is discovered stuffed in his boots and the wrecked motorcycle was apparently stolen.

-1930-

**Twenty-nine bank robberies noted.
*January 6-At 1:30 in the morning, a heavy utility truck with a machine gun mounted on a tripod in the bed halted in front of the Minco rail depot. Three individuals dressed in overalls baled out entering the depot where they seized Constable Tom Chandler and a ticket man escorting them to the post office where they were gagged and bound. When the lawman attempted to resist he received a knot on his head for his troubles. The bandits then rounded up a half dozens citizens who were also held hostage while the trio broke down the front door of the **First National Bank of Minco** and cut their way into the steel vault with a torch. The hostages were forced to help the hijackers load the heavy safe on to the getaway truck, which departed town around dawn. The safe contained $3,500 in cash and negotiable bonds.

*January 6-The **Bank of Adair** is robbed of $2,467.

*February 24-The **First National Bank of Alex** is looted by three men for approximately $1,200. The entire affair was a comedy of errors. Two men entered the bank accosting Cashier Grady Harris and Bookkeeper Ethel Lawson and several customers forcing them to lie on the floor while they gathered up the loot. They then shut all but Harris in the vault taking him hostage in their getaway car that was driven by a third man. On departing town, the local marshal peppered the vehicle with shot. The officer pursued the bandits to a point two miles west of town where he again fired a fusillade of rounds into the rig. Feeling the hot rounds zinging past his head, the banker jumped off the fast moving car's running board into a ditch. A short distance down the road the car caught fire from a perforated gas tank. The bandits bailed out and two were quickly captured minus the loot. The third hijacker escaped on foot into the heavy timber of the nearby Washita River. That evening twenty-seven-year-old Ned Howell of Oklahoma City arrived at his residence driving a new car and boasting to his spouse of his exorbitant winnings at a poker game earlier that evening at a local pool hall. The wife's joy was somewhat dampened when she read the descriptions of the robbers of the Alex bank the following morning in the *Daily Oklahoman*. The description of the missing bandit perfectly matched that of her husband. Later that afternoon she informed her fellow workers at a local dry cleaning establishment how her spouse was indeed one of the hijackers. Naturally, they turned the unlucky fellow in to the police who promptly discovered $750 in cash hidden under a phonograph at his home. Mr. Howell and his companions, identified as C. H. Colson and Joe Jarbrouth of Amarillo, Texas, were all convicted of the heist and each sentenced to a ten-year hitch at "Big Mac."

*February 25- Three men dressed in dirty bib-overalls rush into the lobby of the **Farmers Bank of Bethany** waving pistols ordering five occupants to "Get them hands up and we won't hurt ya!" While one man stood in the center of the lobby, the other two looted the tills and cash drawers of $200 of silver, $1,000 in gold, and $3,700 of currency. According to witnesses, the bandit stationed in the lobby, who appeared very nervous, began issuing a string of profanities toward the small crowd of hostages. One of the bystanders admonished him, saying, "Quit cussing in front of these ladies." Once the hijackers got the dough, they quickly withdrew from the bank while ordering the victims to, "Give us five minutes before ya squawk." Piling into their stolen getaway car, which was parked in front of the building, the trio motored in the direction of Yukon at a high rate of speed. Within seconds of the bandit's exit, the folks from the bank rushed into the street spreading the alarm. The town constable gave chase but lost the thieves just outside of town. Five carloads of Oklahoma County Sheriff's deputies, armed with machineguns and shotguns, promptly took up the chase. Soon afterwards, a man named Leonard Wood was arrested and charged with the heist. When lawmen began checking his fingerprints they observed he had recently obliterated his fingertips with sandpaper making it difficult to match his prints with the ones left at the bank. Eventually, Scotty Ray and a man named J. W. Bainard were also charged with the crime. Ray was returned to the Texas pen to serve out a sentence while Bainard was sentenced to ten years for the Bethany job. Agents of the state crime bureau recovered the entire $4,900 taken from the bank. The robbery marked the third time the financial institution had been struck by hijackers.

*March 3-The peace and tranquility of the county seat town of Tahlequah was interrupted in the early morning hours by a terrific blast, which tore a gaping hole measuring five feet square in the roof of the **Liberty State Bank**. The explosion also shattered windows of businesses three blocks away. Officers rushed to the scene of the detonation but found not a soul in sight. It was later determined the yeggmen had miscalculated the amount of nitro to use in the blast. The effort marked the first bank robbery attempt in Tahlequah in the past fifteen years.

*March 3-A pair of unmasked men enters the **Lovell State Bank**, which was occupied by a single employee, Cashier H. C. Wehrenberg. After hitting the tills for $915 the bandits loudly complained of such a puny take, suggesting they had gotten over $4,000 on their last job. Midway through the event, a customer named Fred Fry strolls into the bank and was forced along with the banker to mount the running boards of a small getaway car. The captives were released a few miles south of town near the community of Crescent. No one was aware of the robbery until the hostages made their way on foot back to town and spread the alarm. A large posse was organized but to no avail. Wehrenberg described the bandits as "One wore grease stained overalls while the other a business suit." He further declared they were armed with revolvers but he noticed a sawed-off pump shotgun stashed in the getaway car.

*March 5-**The First State Bank of Alluwe** is robbed of an undetermined amount. Just days after this heist a bevy of suspects were rounded up and charged with this robbery as well as the January 6 hijacking of the Bank of Adair. The suspects included Chester Dykes and Ernest Royal of Picher along with Earl Osborn, and "Big George" Herrelson of Cherokee County Kansas. The quartet was also suspected of knocking off financial institutions in Arkansas, Missouri, and Kansas.

*March 20-Two penniless out of work drifters walked into the **Bank of Wheatland** demanding the "Johnny." With only a female cashier named Flossie Stewart and an elderly customer in the bank at the time, the pair had an easy time pulling off the heist taking some $3,000 in cash and coin before shutting the two victims in the vault and fleeing out the back door. Moments after entering the vault Miss Flossie hit an alarm button, which had been installed in the area for just such an occurrence. Within minutes of the heist, lawmen from all sides of Oklahoma County began rushing toward the bank.

In the meantime, the two desperados made a beeline toward the rail yards stopping just long enough to hide the heavy silver. At a point one half mile outside the city limits they were spotted by a posse led by Deputy Sheriff George Kerr. Firing several rounds into the sky was enough to halt one of the lads who thrust his hands into the air and surrendered. His companion turned on the speed running as fast as

172 / Taming the Sooner State: The War Between Lawmen & Outlaws in Oklahoma & Indian Territory 1875-1941

he could in an attempt to outdistance the lawmen. Kerr and several vigilantes soon caught up with the now exhausted young man. When ordered to give it up the lad reacted by firing a round, which whizzed past the deputy's head. Officer C. P. Lackey responded by hefting his Winchester to his arm and firing a well aimed round into the boys left shoulder. The wounded man was identified as twenty-year-old Earl Bolen. His pal gave his name as Clifford Garner. When questioned, young Bolen responded, "We are just a couple of country boys down on our luck. We robbed the bank in order get something to eat." Adding, "We had been drinking and hopping freights as of late. I have carried a two-dollar bill in my pocket since I was a kid for good luck. I refused to spend it." His partner added, "My pistol wasn't even loaded!" A real pair of amateurs. Both men were convicted of robbery with firearms and sentenced to ten years in the joint.

*April 10-The **First State Bank of Stonewall** is robbed of $2,343 by two men. Both subjects are eventually arrested and charged with committing the robbery.

*April 25- On this date, two men rob the **First National Bank of Tonkawa** of $84,000 of which $36,000 was jewelry and bonds and the rest in cash. The robbery was staged just moments after the bank's opening for the day. The bandits forced four employees and a quartet of customers to lie on the floor while they rifled the vault and cash drawers. On leaving the bank, the pair locked the crowd of witnesses in the vault. The hostages immediately called the cops reporting the heist from a phone that had recently been installed in the vault. A $1,000 reward was promptly posted for the men's capture. Several months after the heist, three prominent businessmen were arrested and charged with fencing the stolen bonds and precious gems. When detectives attempted to arrest a Tulsa lawyer named J. R. Owen, who was suspected of being a middleman in the transaction, he pulled a gun and shot it out with the coppers. Owens came out second-best in the gun-duel. Shortly after the raid, rumors began to surface implying the robbery was an inside job. The Tonkawa heist was one of the largest, if not the largest, bank robberies in Oklahoma to date.

* May 22-The much-robbed **Alluwe State Bank** was hit again by a trio of armed bandits whose faces were blackened with burnt cork. The outlaws made off with an estimated $2,500. Incidentally, the same bank was once knocked over by the infamous Poe-Hart Gang a decade earlier. Ironically, the owners of the bank were in the process of closing the institution for good and were scheduled to transfer the bank funds to Nowata the following day. The bandits abandoned getaway car was discovered six miles southwest of town. Officers discovered a jar of burnt cork and a pair of dirty overalls in the vehicle's back seat.

*May 27-Three men rob the **Bank of May** of $1,265 before fleeing towards the Texas border. Cashier A. J. Chase and Bookkeeper L. S. Smith are locked in the vault but soon escape.

*June 8- A young female, accompanied by two males, are confronted by Night Watchman Verdy Hicks and Deputy Sheriff James Payne as they attempt to break into the **First State Bank of Tuskahoma** during the early morning hours. One of the men is shot and killed while the others escaped into the darkness.

*June 20-Three young bandits dressed in overalls hijack the **First National Bank of Paden** located in rural Okfuskee County of $2,700. The bandits flee in a small red coup. All three were tracked down by investigators and charged with the robbery.

* June 25-**First State Bank of Lovell** is robbed by a pair of hijackers of $184. Both robbers are later convicted of the robbery and sentenced to ten years.

*July 3-Two men enter the **First State Bank of Maramec** at noon the day before Independence Day robbing it of $1,000. The bank's cashier, Mildred Grubb, and a customer named Ray Duff were the only ones in the building at the time. The bandits made their getaway in a large automobile that was found abandoned a dozen miles from the scene. The Maramec bank had been robbed twice before.

*July 9-The **Hunter Bank** is robbed of an unspecified amount by Alvin Payton and George Magness. Both men are later involved in the robbery of the Edna, Kansas, bank as well as a cop killing. Payton is one of eleven individuals involved in the 1933 Memorial Day Kansas prison escape.

*July 26-**Bank of Foyil** is looted by two men of $1,100.

*July 30-**First National Bank of Westville** is robbed by two men of $5,000.

*August 7-A trio of gun-wielding brigands rob the **Security National Bank of Coweta** of approximately $2,000. The robbers reportedly fled the scene driving a small red roadster, one man sitting in the rumble seat. A large posse led by Wagoner County Sheriff Clay Flowers was promptly fielded and an all points bulletin to be on the lookout for the hijackers was issued to area law enforcement agencies. A half-hour after the heist, an unmarked patrol car carrying veteran Tulsa Detectives C. O. Davis, J. W. Wilkerson, and Mark Lairmore sighted the villains motoring near the present day Tulsa airport. The officers took up the chase with vigor. Just moments into the high-speed chase, the bandit sitting in the rumble seat began taking pot shots at the cops with a pistol. An injudicious act on the part of the outlaw to say the least. The officer sitting in the passenger's seat of the opposing vehicle happened to be one of the most death-dealing lawmen to ever wear the star in Oklahoma. Mark Lairmore had put more than his share of sassy outlaws in boot hills across the state. Predictably, he reacted by licking his lips, unlimbering his .351 Winchester automatic rifle, and delivering a vicious barrage of slugs at an awe-inspiring rate. The fellow in the rumble seat made a perfect target. Lairmore shot him twice in the backside before turning his attention on the driver who he perforated as well. The driver slumped over while the speeding car spun out of control striking the guardrail of a bridge spanning Bird Creek causing it to land upside down half in and half out of the sluggish water. When Lairmore approached the wreck, the youth sitting in the rear, who was later identified as twenty-seven year old Eddie Cowden, weakly raised a shotgun aiming it at the officer who reacted by sending a slug into the boys jaw. Lairmore then tossed his rifle to a comrade, pulled his pistol and ran up to the wounded man stating, "Where's that money you stole kid?" Cowden meekly pointed to a sugar sack brimming with currency lying on the edge of the creek. In the meantime, his companions crawled off into a dark patch of woods illuminated only by a rising moon, leaving a broad blood trail. Lairmore commented, "They aint going anywhere." Within the next hour, Sheriff Flowers arrived on the scene leading a posse of over two hundred officers and vigilantes.

After repeated demands for the pair to surrender, Flowers said the hell with it and stormed into the thicket loudly declaring the duo had best give up or be shot on sight. He must have made a convincing augment. The two fugitives immediately came out of hiding begging the officers to spare their lives, saying, "We give up. We aren't fighting anymore." The pair, both suffering wounds inflicted from Lairmore's trusty rifle, was identified as thirty-three year old Reo Stertz and thirty-four-year-old Ralph Rhodes, both of Tulsa. A brief investigation turned up the fact their companion, Eddie Cowden, had a lengthy criminal record, and was a known user of narcotics. He had served three hitches in the Oklahoma penal system for charges ranging from possession of dope, burglary, and larceny. The youth was currently wanted for suspicion of robbing a Tulsa drugstore as well knocking off a pair of area filling stations. Cowden and Ralph Rhodes would eventually be sentenced to fifty-year terms at McAlester while their crime-partner would receive a thirty-year hitch. When interviewed by newsmen shortly after the gunbattle, Mark Lairmore was asked how he knew the fleeing car was that of the bank robbers. He sarcastically replied, "At first I didn't but when they started shooting at us I was pretty certain I had the right party."

* August 14- Two unmasked desperadoes loot the **Spencer State Bank** of $1,000 Cashier A. P. Pole suffers a bullet to the arm when he reacts a bit too slow to the robber's demands. A man and a woman are arrested the following day in connection to the heist but are soon released. Investigators apparently have few leads explaining the well-planned raid. In early December twenty-three-year-old Bryan Keene is charged in the case.

*August 22-Three bandits loot the **Farmers and Merchants Bank of Sparks** of $1,800 before making a clean getaway. During the robbery, Cashier Clarence Collier is forced to lie face down on the floor while the unmasked men ordered Assistant Cashier Ralph Cowan to gather up the cash. Upon completion of the heist, the two employees are locked into the vault, as was norm in these cases. The bank had not been robbed in six years. The chief suspect in the heist is Herman Cheveraux.

*August 28-Two youths hold-up the **First National Bank of Coyle** of $4,000. According to Cashier Fred Cook, who was the lone witness to the heist, a man walked up to his window and asked for change for a dollar bill As Cook turned to make change the bandit ordered him to lie on the floor. Moments later a second crook entered the establishment. After forcing the cashier to open the safe, the pair grabbed the cash and fled the building jumping into a small coupe. The duo abandoned the coupe several miles outside of town, speeding away in a large touring car.

* September 14-On several occasions, beginning in early September, Bank Cashier H. P. Lear observed several individuals enter the **First State Bank of Osage** and appear to measure up the place. Once he noticed a man enter the building and walk to the drinking fountain where after gulping several mouthfuls of liquid turned and took several measured steps from the fountain to the safe. His suspicions aroused, Lear approached Osage County Sheriff Ben McDonald voicing his fears of a pending hold-up or burglary of the bank. McDonald assigned a number of officers to keep a lookout on the financial institution. On the afternoon of September 13, Lear overheard a pair of individuals standing in the bank's lobby talking about burglarizing the bank the following evening. Once informed of the pending action, the lawman stationed a large posse around the bank building on the night in question. Half of the posse, operating under the leadership of Eugene Gum, the president of the Bankers Association, was posted on the roof of an adjacent a hotel, located across the street from the bank's front door, while the other half, led by Sheriff McDonald, took up positions to the rear of the banking establishment. Around 1:30 a.m. three yeggmen, as burglars were called in those days, were observed entering the building by jimmying

the bank's rear window. The Sheriff reacted by loudly calling for the men to surrender. The yeggs answered with an ineffective volley of shots. The lawmen opened up, firing a withering crescendo of rounds into the establishment that produced little effect on the well-entrenched badmen. Next, several tear-gas bombs were hurled into he bank. This strategy had the desired effect. Within minutes, the trio of bandit fled the building firing wildly as they ran. The posse let 'em have it. According to one source, it was like shooting fish in a barrel. Twenty-five-year–old Posey Mitchell was wounded sixteen times in the melee but miraculously survived. His companions, identified as S. J. Goin and Jim "Dusty" Miller, dived behind a car and shouted their surrender. The robbers were recognized as ex-crime partners of the late Dick Gregg. All three men were promptly convicted of attempted robbery and given stiff prison sentences.

*October 1-At 9:45 a.m., three armed and unmasked youths driving a Pontiac Roadster held up the **Bank of Salina** of $1,500. Three bank employees were the only persons in the building at the time of the hijacking. According to witnesses, while two male employees were lined up against a wall and told to, "Shut up and stand still," Teller Louise Griffith was ordered to, "Show us where the money is. We are desperate and have not eaten in three days." A posse made up of dozen-armed vigilantes was on the bandit's trail only moments after the conclusion of the robbery. That evening a Siloam Springs tire shop owner presented his self to the authorities, claiming four men had entered his business the previous evening, bound and gagged him before stealing his car, which matched the description of the one used in the heist. A few hours later, Mayes County Sheriff Charles Kelley and a Constable named Tom Bradshaw arrested two hitchhikers standing on the side of a road near Locust Grove. The pair, who had roughly $600 in bills on their person, was positively identified as two of the bank hijackers. Sheriff Kelley called the duo "Rank amateurs."

* October 14- At 2:30 p.m. two robbers enter the **Peoples National Bank of Westville** ordering the employees to lie on the floor while they scooped up $3,284 from the tills. During the robbery, a farmer named John Baker entered the bank from a rear door. He was also ordered to the floor at gunpoint. Unlike the other victims, he refused and began wrestling with one of the bandits. Taking advantage of the distraction, two of the bankers, Ed Adair and W. O. Bost, yanked out pistols and began peppering the hijackers, who reacted by bolting from the building piling into a yellow Pontiac Roadster. Meanwhile, the pair of gun slinging bankers took after the fleeing badmen and once again exchanged fire with the pair. Bank President F. S. Howard, who took a slug through his hand, quickly joined his fellow employees. After a spirited gun-duel, the outlaws were somehow able to get their now riddled getaway car in gear and

depart the area. Within minutes, every available man in the town limits showed up armed to the teeth and in hot pursuit. Shortly after the robbery, the bandit's vehicle was discovered abandoned three miles from town occupied by a dying bandit lying in the blood-soaked rear seat. The hijacker was identified as Tom Hayworth. It was later discovered the car had been stolen from George Cline of Yale, Oklahoma. No money was found either on the outlaw's body or in the discarded getaway car.

*October 31-Four individuals enter the **Oklahoma State Bank of Hastings** forcing an employee into the vault before gathering up the nearly $1,000 in cash and coin. The hijackers make a clean getaway.

*October 31-Three bandits rob the **First National Bank of Ft. Gibson** for $4,665 in cash. Before fleeing the premises, the robbers lock three employees into the vault. Moments later, the captives released themselves (By 1930 most walk-in vaults were equipped with an inside release mechanism) and ran into the street where Banker Charles Cobb fired five shots into the rear of the bandit's fleeing getaway car. When interviewed, Cobb firmly asserted he had hit at least one of the outlaws with his fire. The getaway rig, which had been stolen from the Miller Motor Company car lot in nearby Muskogee the previous day, was discovered abandoned later that day deep in the notorious Cookson Hills. Although the vehicle's rear window was shattered there was no blood found on the seats or floorboard. Muskogee County Sheriff Fred Hamilton asserted the outlaws had switched to a green Ford sedan. A few weeks after the robbery an Osage County ruffian named Dewey Parker who was scurrying about Muskogee with large amount of cash buying cars and luxury goods, was taken into custody for questioning. Parker was put in a line-up and identified by the Fort Gibson bankers as one of the perpetrators. It appears Mr. Parker turned informant giving investigators the names of his partners in the bank heist.

A warrant was immediately issued for a Muskogee businessman named Jack Preddy, who was also under investigation at the time for burning down a pair of dry cleaning establishments he owned in town for the insurance money. Since then, he had skipped town. Preddy was eventually apprehended in Texas and charged with robbing the Bank of Timpson, Texas, for $7,200. Although he was promptly indicted in Oklahoma on bank robbery and arson charges, Texas refused to extradite. In December 1931 newly elected Muskogee County Sheriff V. S. Cannon and Deputy Marsh Corgan captured a youthful Haskell County thug named Aussie Elliott and charged him with the Ft.Gibson heist as well. Several days later Leon Garhart was captured in Sheridan, Missouri, where he was living with a celebrated gun moll named Golda Johnson, the daughter of the notorious Charlie Johnson, a one-time associate of Henry Starr's. Garhart was extradited back to Muskogee and charged with the bank heist. His paramour followed him to town and the happy couple was allowed to marry at the county jail. Incidentally, Golda would later take up with Jim Clark, another noted Muskogee County bank robber. Aussie Elliott was eventually convicted of the Ft. Gibson bank job and sentenced to twenty years at the Granite Reformatory while Parker received twenty-five years.

*See the previous story *Bad Day at Sapulpa* for further information concerning Aussie Elliott.

November 12- The **Marland State Bank** is robbed by James Jackson and Carter Camp of $3,000. *See previous story *The Frame Up* for further details.

*November 22-Several industrious yeggmen tunnel under the **Bradley State Bank** gaining access to the vault but are unable to open the safe.

*November 26-At exactly high noon, Henry Lovett entered the **First National Bank of El Reno** armed with a pistol. On reaching the lobby, he ordered a passel of customers and employees into the vault. Suddenly, Cashier J. M. Burge pulled a gun from under the counter and blasted the bandit, a slug grazing his forehead. The bad man hit the floor with some authority but miraculously bounced back to his feet and began returning fire at the nervy cashier who ran from teller cage to cage exchanging potshots with the bandit. In the midst of this melee, twenty-eight-year-old high school coach named Dee Folliart entered the bank by a side door intent on conducting some financial business. Lovett, catching sight of the young man and thinking he was an officer, whirled about and fired a single shot which struck the man square to the chest killing him. Meanwhile, outside the bank's front entrance, bystanders began scrambling down the sidewalk and street in order to stay out of the way of stray bullets. The laws were notified and on their arrival at the bank, they quickly subdued the robber while he was attempting to flee. When informed that he had taken the life of the youthful coach, Lovett responded, "I'm sorry."

*December 8-In the dead of the night, burglars armed with crowbars, hammers, and chisels break into the **Luther State Bank** gaining entrance into the safe making away with $4,100 in cash and securities. A nearby resident later claimed he had heard a racket around midnight but assumed his next-door neighbor was doing some remodeling. The stolen money and bonds were never recovered and the looters remained at large.

*December 23-Just two days before Christmas a pair of

individuals loots the **American National Bank of Apache** of $2,500. After locking Bank Cashier John Eckert and Bookkeeper Nora Caraway, along with several customers into the vault, the pair took Cashier J. W. Pieratt hostage; eventually releasing him unharmed west of town near Saddle Mountain. When interviewed, the cashier stated, "A big fellow got behind the wheel while a little guy jumped in the back seat. I was forced to sit in the front with the loot in a sugar sack placed between my feet. The pair laughed and joked like old friends often times commenting on the condition of the farmland we passed. Saying 'Darn poor land I'd call it.'" Although one of the pair is eventually captured, the loot is never recovered.

-1931-

Overview of 1931- 47 robberies and six burglaries are reported.

*January 7–Four individuals loot the **Bank of Cyril** of $2,580 in cash along with $2,000 in traveler's checks. Three subjects, Charles Allen, Curtis Ivey, and Glenn Marshal are later arrested passing the stolen travelers checks in Texas. All three are convicted of the bank heist and given prison terms.

*January 8-On this date, three unemployed oilfield workers armed with handguns loot the **American State Bank of Porum** of approximately $3,800 at a few minutes after ten in the morning. According to reports, three customers and a janitor were forced to lie on the bank's floor while Cashier Dyton Dunaway was compelled to empty the tills into a flour-sack. The three bandits were described as dark, but not Indians, by Bank President R. B. Patton, who being unarmed, was forced to helplessly observe the robbery from the confines of his office. While making their getaway in a dark-blue Chevy coach, E. A. Plunkett, the Porum postmaster, emptied a pistol at the fleeing car but to no effect. A "Be on the lookout" warning was promptly issued via phone to the law enforcement agencies in surrounding communities. McIntosh County Sheriff John McQuillan overtook the bandit's car just east of Checotah on Route 266 and engaged them in a sharp but bloodless gunduel. The lawman pulled out of the chase after a bullet penetrated his radiator causing the motor to overheat. The hijackers were last seen speeding undeterred toward Henryetta. A check of getaway car's plates indicated it was registered to Allen Russell of Earlsboro. The vehicle turned out to be stolen.

H. J. Zufall, an eyewitness to the gunbattle, described it in this fashion, "I was driving along just on the outskirts of Checotah when a Chevy passed me going a pretty good clip then a Ford flew by traveling at a high rate of speed. At the time, I knew nothing about the robbery and was very surprised when the two cars halted right in front of me and began unloading lead at each other. I'd judge eight or ten shots passed between them. They paused only long enough to empty their guns then the first car moved off at a rapid rate followed by the second. By the time they had completed their shooting match a half dozen cars belonging to the posse had arrived and joined in on the chase. I just sat their dumbfounded for minute or two until I got my breath before resuming my trip."

Muskogee County Sheriff V. S. Cannon arrived in Porum less than a half-hour after the robbery. He immediately made contact with Investigator Erv Kelley and the pair began motoring toward the Seminole oilfield district. Ten days after the heist, Kelley and the sheriff arrested nineteen-year-old Albert Lee at Fort Smith, Arkansas. Some $695 of the loot was found hidden under his parent's garage at their rural residence near Bowlegs, Oklahoma. Lee immediately confessed to the crime and implicated twenty-one year old Ray Langford and A. L. Witham of Seminole as his crime-partners. He also allowed how the trio had previously robbed a store in Seminole, stole a car, then kidnapped a lawman near Tuskahoma only to release him a few hours later before turning to bank robbery. Within days of Lee's arrest, Arkansas lawmen captured Langford in Little Rock while Cannon and Kelley arrested Witham in Bowlegs. Langford had $665 on his person while Witham had only $54 in his possession. At his court hearing, Lee flung himself on the mercy of the court and with great tears whaling up in his eyes begged for mercy. District Judge W. J. Crump declared "Well son, you look like a good boy and since you made an honest confession I will go light on you." His honor then sentenced the youthful miscreant to twenty years at the Granite Reformatory. Langford was also sentenced to twenty years while Witham received a twenty-five jolt.

*January 14-Two fashionably dressed men entered the **First State Bank of Castle** through the front door and shut two bank employees into the vault while they loot the place of $2,300. Just as the robbers were about to leave town Marshal J.M. Van Zant entered the building but was quickly disarmed and joined the other hostages in the walk-in vault. After completing their business, the pair sped off in a small coupe.

*January 16-Two well-dressed thieves armed with revolvers sauté into the **Dover State Bank** announcing they wanted all the cash in the building before locking Cashier Alfred Sash, who was the lone witness to the event, into the steel vault. The bandits gathered up some $1,400 in cash and currency before departing. Meanwhile, Dr. I. E. Vincent and C. D. Mauk were strolling past the bank when they noticed the unusual activity. Believing a robbery was in progress, the pair rushed into Mauk's hardware store and began passing out Winchesters to several customers. Unfortunately, by the time the vigilantes had gotten into position on the street, the bandits had made their getaway.

*January 16-A pair of bandits enters the lobby of the **First National Bank of Maysville** where they were greeted by Cashier R. B. Grimmett, who was immediately ordered to lie on the floor facedown. When the outlaws notice Grimmett reaching for the burglar alarm one of then shot him in the side. The pair then fled the building after rifling the cash drawers for a couple of hundred dollars. Bank Vice President Walter Caudill was shining his shoes in the back room and failed to notice anything amiss until he heard the shot. Since he was unarmed, he could do nothing but watch as the bandits made their getaway. Once the robbers departed the scene, the wounded cashier reportedly walked unaided to the nearby doctor's office for treatment. Charles Allen was later captured and convicted. He received a sentence of thirty-five-years.

*February 26-The **First State Bank of Tuskahoma** is robbed of $1,914. Olen Bournes is convicted of the robbery and sentenced to a twenty-five-year term.

*February 27-The **First State Bank of Quapaw** is looted for $1,598.

*February 28-The **First State Bank of Carrier** is robbed of $472. George W. Gritton is convicted and sentenced to five years.

March 9-The **Bank of Earlsboro** is robbed of $3,000 by "Pretty Boy" Floyd, George Birdwell, and Bill Miller. The bandits departed the area in a small green roadster. This event marks Floyd's first Oklahoma bank robbery. *See previous article *Pretty Boy Floyd: The Phantom of the Cookson Hills* for further details.

*March 11-Two armed youths briskly stroll into the lobby of the **First National Bank of Harrah** shouting, "Get on the floor you bastards. This is a robbery." Moments later a retired doctor named W.E. Walker walked into the bank asking one of the bandits if he was the new cashier. "No," chimed the robber, " But I will take that money in your hand." After gathering up some $3,000 in currency and $250 in silver, the pair bolted from the bank heading toward their getaway car pushing several hostages in front of them. Unfortunately for the bandits, someone had hit the silent alarm. Several citizens took up arms and stationed themselves in strategic places in front of the bank. Among them was Walter Fallwell, who placed himself at the corner filling station, armed with a shotgun loaded with buckshot. Moments after exiting the bank, one of the men spotted the vigilantes and made a break for it running down the street while his partner stayed safely behind the hostages until he made it to the car. Spotting the fleeing robber, Fallwell shouted for a town barber George Miller, who was in the line of fire, to "Duck" just before delivering a full load of buckshot into the desperado's backside. The wounded bandit stumbled before fleeing into a barbershop. Moments later he crawled on to the street where he collapsed without uttering a word. Fallwell cautiously approached the fallen bandit then kneeled down and asked his name. The robber mumbled something unintelligible before taking his last breath. Meanwhile, the other hijacker sped off in his car using a crowd of shocked pedestrians and hostages as cover. The dead robber was identified by his mother as twenty-year-old Denver Graham of nearby Oklahoma City. She claimed the boy had been missing from home for a week. A quick check of area police departments proved the lad had never been in legal trouble before the day he was killed. Within hours of the gunbattle, Eugene Gum, the president of the Oklahoma Bankers Association, arrived on the scene handing Mr. Fallwell a check for $250. The standing reward offered for dead bandits. When interviewed, Gum, who seems to have been in a bloodthirsty mood that day, stated, "When I heard of the robbery and its results, I grabbed my checkbook and started to Harrah," adding "It's a shame the streets were so busy or I could have paid out two rewards." When the authorities searched the deceased robber's pockets, they discovered the $3,000 in cash, leaving them to believe the other bandit had the $250 in silver in his pocket. Soon after the bank heist, a subject named Ben Snyder was arrested and charged with the robbery. Although he denied any involvement in the hijacking, six witnesses positively identified him, as did a set of fingerprints off a soda pop bottle he had been seen drinking from which he had left at the scene. Snyder was convicted of robbery and sentenced to thirty-five years at McAlester.

*March 22-The **First National Bank of Tyrone** is looted of $47.

*March 30-The **First State Bank of Mounds** is robbed by two men of $622. One bandit sat in the getaway car while the other entered the bank armed with a pistol. Cashier Frank Crum and several customers were in the bank at the time of the heist.

*March 31-**Bank of Commerce** in Jenks is robbed by two men of an unspecified amount.

*April 8-Only moments before closing time, a lone bandit armed with a pistol entered the **First State Bank of Talala** while a companion sat at the wheel of a running car parked outside. The man locked Cashier Noah Whisunhunt and his assistant Miss Neil Dawson into the vault before gathering up some $600 in cash and coin. He then fled the premises joining his partner in the getaway car that sped off in the direction of

Tulsa. Whisunhunt soon freed himself and ran into the street where he joined three other armed citizens and gave chase. Just outside of town, the getaway car broke down and the robbers stole another vehicle, which was parked in front of a nearby farmhouse, all while under continuous but ineffective fire from the posse. After a twenty-mile high-speed chase, the outlaws finally outdistanced their pursuers and made a safe getaway. Bill Parker and Forrest Smith were later convicted of the robbery. Smith received a twenty-five-year sentence while Parker was given fifteen years.

*April 21-Charles Gibson single-handedly robs the **Community State Bank of Bristow** of $3,700. He was captured later the same day and eventually convicted and sentenced to a ten-year term in the state big house.

*May 12-Two men rob the **State Bank of Keota** of $2,000. The bandits escape in a stolen gray vehicle heading south. Twenty-one-year-old Jack Elliott is later arrested by Sheriff Stacy Moore while still in possession of the loot. Cashier E.E. Sewell, his wife, and a boy named Grady Merriman are the only ones in the bank at the time of the heist.

*May 20-Three men rob the **First State Bank of Pleasant Valley** of $614.The robbers take Banker C. M. Howland along with two customers hostage carrying them as far as the outskirts of town before releasing them. Several days after the heist the burned getaway car was discovered near the community of Meridian. At the conclusion of a short investigation conducted by operatives of the Oklahoma and Logan County Sheriff's Department, two men, identified as a father and son team were arrested and charged with the heist. Another individual was apprehended the following day. Witnesses positively identified the trio as the robbers of the bank. A search of the suspect's homes uncovered a sack containing $250 of the stolen loot.

*May 22-A pair of men later identified as "Big Bob" Brady and Clarence "Buck" Adams rob the **First State Bank of Roff** of $2,142. Brady, an Ada native, who would one day reach the heights of gangland notoriety, had already served a hitch in the Kansas prison system as well as two terms in the Oklahoma pen. He will later be associated with such criminal notables as Wilbur Underhill, Jim Clark, and Harvey Bailey.

*May 23-Three men hijack the **First National Bank of Luther** of $1,465. Shortly after they exited the premises, the trio was jumped by a group of armed vigilantes. Two of the bandits, later identified as Melvin Banes and Claud Fugate, quickly surrendered while the third man fled into a patch of woods located just off Route 66 on the outskirts of town.

When a Southwestern Bell telephone operator named Mrs. Ashley received a call from a local farmer reporting the whereabouts of the third bandit, she called up several businesses organizing a second posse who quickly surrounded the fugitive. When the bandit, identified as C. C. Gregory, refused to surrender, the vigilantes cut loose with a barrage of shotgun and rifle fire wounding the robber, who promptly surrendered. When interviewed by reporters from the *Daily Oklahoman* the following day, the spunky phone operator claimed rounding up posses was just part of her job, adding, "Excited, I should say not. It seems like I am always on duty when these things happen. This is the second robbery here and I handled calls for another one several years ago in Wellston." All three hijackers were convicted of armed robbery and while Fugate and Banes were sentenced to twenty-five years, Gregory got thirty calendars at the Oklahoma pen.

*May 27-The **First State Bank of Reydon** is robbed of $2,600.

*June 2-The **First National Bank of Britton** is robbed of $344.

*June 4-Two brothers, identified as Tom and Frank Carver, pulled up to the **Bank of Mounds** in a stolen car. When the pair entered the building flashing revolvers, a store-clerk named Lloyd Kelly spotted them and notified Town Marshal R. F. Crowder, who organized a posse, stationing a half-dozen armed men around the front door of the bank. After looting the financial institution of $600, the Carvers exited the building with two bank clerks (Frank Crum and H. C. Crews) in tow. Unfortunately, for them, they walked straight into the jaws of the group of armed citizens who made short work of the pair. Frank Carver was killed instantly while his brother took slugs to the back and shoulder. Neither of the hostages was wounded. Tom Carver later admitted the pair was planning to rob the Bank in Jenks the following week. He was sentenced to a fifteen-year term at "Big Mac." The stolen money was recovered.

*June 4-A lone bandit robs the **Security State Bank of Comanche** of $2,760. The robber entered the bank making a beeline to the teller's cage where twenty-year-old Lera Quitt was the lone employee on duty. After asking her to cash a check, he whipped out a pistol and ordered her to lie on the floor and be silent. He then ransacked the cash tills. Before departing, he picked up a bag of pennies the clerk claimed was gold coins. The robber ordered the terrified clerk to walk with him to his getaway car saying, "Act like you are my sweetie and you won't be hurt." On reaching the automobile, the robbers told her to "Lean against the car and smile" while he got in the rig and

drove off. The clerk later told reporters," I thought he was going to take me along, so I asked him if he was going to kidnap or shoot me."

*June 5- The **Citizens Bank of Okemah** is robbed by a lone gunman of $100. The man was quickly captured and sent to the insane asylum.

*June 17-A single bandit robs the **Farmers Bank of Orlando** of $993. Officers followed tire tracks leading from the bank directly to a farmhouse where they arrested a man named Ollie Blair while still in possession of the loot. Blair was convicted and sentenced to a five-year term. Another man who was accused of loaning Blair the car he used in the hold-up.

*June 18-A lone bandit described as dressed in overalls and stout in size hijack the **Bank of Inola** for $189 after locking Bank President Dennis Koenig in the vault. The robber flees in the direction of Tulsa driving a green Chevy.

*June 24 –The **State Bank of Roff** is robbed for the second time in a month by the same pair of unmasked men for $633. The perpetrators were "Big Bob" Brady and Clarence Adams. On this occasion, the pair walked into the lobby surveying the situation before Brady approached Assistant Cashier Fannie Tipton inquiring of the whereabouts of Cashier A.M. Stewart. When she replied he had the day off, the big thug yanked a pistol out of a newspaper he was holding in his hand and informed her " This is a stickup, sister!" Adams remained in the lobby while Brady went behind the cages and rifled the tills. The pair made a clean getaway. Miss Tipton was locked in the vault and it took the authorities nearly two hours to set her free.

*July 1-A trio of armed young men loot the **Community State Bank of Bristow** of $3,000 at the noon hour. The looters force two employees, Clyde Foster and Joe Britton, as well as a customer named Lem Conger to lie on the floor behind the cages while they scooped up the available cash. By the time the alarm is given, the bandits are long gone. A gray sedan used by the bandits is discovered abandoned just outside town the day following the hold-up. A month after the heist the body of one of the hijackers is discovered lying in a brush-pile deep in the notorious Cookson Hills. His partner, Bill Pritchett, was arrested in Bristow soon afterwards. The dead man, who had been deceased for roughly three weeks, is identified as Claude Peepers. According to the authorities, Prichett is wanted for several other robberies in the area. The outlaw is convicted of armed robbery and sentenced to five years incarceration. The money is not recovered nor is the third man involved in the holdup identified. This event marks the second time the Bristow bank has been robbed within the year and Oklahoma's twenty-fifth since the first of the year.

*July 10-The **Barnsdall State Bank** is robbed of $2,056 by "Big Bob" Brady, Buck Adams, Walter Philpot, and his son Frank.

*July 14-An attempt to rob the **First National Bank of Broken Arrow** is thwarted by lawmen. An officer is wounded in the melee, as is the would-be bandit, who is captured.

*July 21-Two youths attempt to rob the **Bank of Tuttle** but loose their nerve midway through the robbery. Bank President Floyd Kimble told a reporter, "One bandit was older and the other younger. They appeared nervous and when a crowd began to assemble in the street their courage failed them."

*July 25-**First National Bank of Brinkman** is looted of $1,229 by Arthur Bliss, Hubert Shannon, and Robert Poole. All three subjects are arrested and given lengthy prison terms.

*August 4- Pretty Boy" Floyd and George Birdwell rob the **Citizens State Bank of Shamrock** of $400. According to witnesses, Floyd entered the bank while Birdwell remained at the wheel of the getaway car parked directly in front of the bank. Only two persons, Etta Lewis and J.W. Martin, were in the building at the time of the heist. Bank officials claimed the bandits failed to take a large amount of money, which was stashed in a shoebox in the rear of the open safe. This robbery seems to have been a 'rather hurried and sloppy affair for a pair of such experienced hands.

*August 14-The **Farmers State Bank of Quinton** is robbed of $571. Harry Draper is later convicted and sentenced to a fifteen-year term for perpetrating the heist.

September 8-The **Morris State Bank** is robbed of $1,800 by "Pretty Boy" Floyd and George Birdwell.
*See previous story *The Unluckiest Bank in Oklahoma: The Morris Robberies* for further details.

*September 10-The **State Bank of Hitchita** is robbed of $900 by two pistol-packing bandits. A cashier identified as Mrs. Pence, was the only person in the bank at the time of the robbery. On October 8, 1932, a suspect in the robbery named John Wilson is arrested after a lengthy gunbattle with police taking place in Hartshorne. Wilson's partner, Harvey Jacques, is killed during the shootout.

September 15-The **Guymon Bank of Texhoma** is robbed by Bob Brady and Buck Adams for $5,300. Two weeks later, the pair is captured at Carlsbad Caverns, New Mexico, and extradited to Oklahoma where they are wanted for suspicion of robbing banks in Tuttle, Barnsdall, Roff, and Texhoma. Over $1,000 of the loot from the Texhoma, robbery is recovered. The same day that Brady is captured a pair of highway patrolmen pull over a car containing Walter Philpot and his son Frank along with Roy Adams. Adams and the younger Philpot react to the cop's presence by jumping out of the car with guns blazing. Officer Jack Cummings shoots both suspects. All three are charged with the recent Tuttle bank job but charges are later dropped when two other men confessed to the crime. Walter Philpot is also charged with participating in the Texhoma job. While awaiting trial "Big Bob" and Buck Adams saw through their cell-bars, attacking seventy-year-old Jailor C. K. Stinnett, who reacted to the assault by shooting Brady in the head. Brady recovers from his wound and is promptly convicted of the Texhoma robbery and sentenced to thirty-five-years at "Big Mac." The oversized badman escaped from the Oklahoma state prison on July 23, 1932, by hiding in a truckload of outgoing overalls. He is again captured in Kansas and returned to the state pen where he joins Harvey Bailey, Jim Clark, and Wilbur Underhill in the spectacular 1933 Memorial Day escape.
*See the previous article *The Underhill, Bailey, Bradshaw Gangs* for further details concerning Bob Brady.

*September 22–The **Tuttle State Bank** is looted of $500 by Luther Goodall, Ray Gibson, and Arthur Fraley. Members of the "Big Bob" Brady Gang are initially listed as suspects.

*September 22-Two unmasked men dressed in overalls rob the **Farmers State Bank of Waukomis** of $300. Cashiers Lewis Green and Leda Jung were in the bank at the time of the robbery.

*September 23-Two men rob the **Lindsay State Bank** of $3,500 and escape in a motorcar carrying Assistant Bank Cashier F. D. Stephens as a hostage. Stephens is released at a location fourteen miles southwest of town.

*September 29-"Pretty Boy" Floyd and George Birdwell rob the **First National Bank of Maud** of $3,849.The two bandits entered the bank shortly after noon and ordered Cashier Earl Martin and Bookkeeper Elizabeth Mahoney to lie on the floor while they looted the tills and vault. Several customers, identified as Sam Scroggins, Hal Bartow, and W. H. Hart, entered the bank during the robbery and forced to share some floor space with the bankers. All five witnesses were locked in the vault when the bandits exited the bank. Evidently, the pair overlooked a bundle containing $7,000 in bills, which was stashed in a desk drawer. According to witnesses, the bandits had stopped to change a flat tire on the side of the highway at a location just outside the city limits prior to making the raid. By the time a posse was organized by Sheriff W. A. Roberts, the hijackers were long gone

*October 14-The **Bank of Earlsboro** is robbed of $2,599 by "Pretty Boy" Floyd and George Birdwell. On exiting the financial institution, the bandits locked bank employees, L.F. Castell, C. A. Littleton, and Forest Anderson along with customers W.A. Seward and Wade Brown in the vault. The hostages were released shortly after the hijackers had departed by Duke Strain, a mechanic working at a filling station across the street. Floyd and Birdwell have previously raided the bank on March 9, 1931.

*November 2- The **Citizens State Bank of Headrick** is robbed by a lone gunman who was captured just outside the bank only moments after the robbery's conclusion. The perpetrator was identified as a local farmer named Sam Tinney, who claims his motivation for the robbery, was due to his family being in dire economic straits. Shortly after his capture, Tinney attempted to take his own life. The local judge felt pity for the man and handed him a light five-year sentence with a recommendation he be given an early release as soon as possible if he behaves himself. The great depression rages on claiming victims from one end of the state to the other and in this case a good man feeling responsible for his families suffering makes a poor choice and pays dearly for his unwise actions.

*November 5-The **First National Bank of Konawa** is robbed by "Pretty Boy" Floyd, George Birdwell, and a third man (Possibly Shine Rush) of $2,000. At noon a vehicle containing the trio pulled up in front of the bank disgorging Floyd and the unnamed confederate entered the financial institution while Birdwell remains in the car with a "Tommygun" openly displayed on his lap. The two bandits quickly took up positions in the bank covering four employees (H. W. Courtney, Lucille Nelson, William Tucker, Gene Douthitt) and two customers (Jessie Long and Leroy Head) with automatic pistols. Floyd forced Courtney to open the vault and after cleaning the place out of all available funds, the pair leisurely exits the scene strolling to their getaway car. In the meantime, Birdwell kept a fast gathering crowd at bay by waving about his "Chopper" and firmly telling the folks to, "People, stay calm and don't make no sudden moves and all will be well. Our business will be done momentarily." The carload of bandits then motored out of town without a cop in sight.

*December 24-The **State Bank of Sterling** is held-up

for $1,600 by a pair of unmasked bandits. A posse is quickly formed, but failed to track down the thieves.

*December 23-The **Morris State Bank** is robbed a second time in a year by "Pretty Boy" Floyd and George Birdwell. Over $1,100 is stolen.

*See previous story, *The Unluckiest Bank in Oklahoma: The Morris Robberies,* for further details.

*December 26-The **Central National Bank of Poteau** is looted of $7,000 by three men with the assistance of two females. Teller Mae Vasser was alone in the bank when the robbery occurred. The thieves compelled her to lie facedown on the floor while they scooped up the money and made their successful departure. Fred Sutton and a man named Kilgore were later arrested for the crime at a residence in Roswell, New Mexico. Sutton was convicted and sentenced to life in prison while Kilgore escaped custody.

-1932-
Oklahoma leads the nation in bank robberies in 1932 with sixty-three banks looted. Half the nation's bank robberies occurring that year take place in Oklahoma. Six bank robbers are killed and thirty-four are captured and imprisoned during the year. Over $100,000 in bank funds is stolen.

*January 2-A lone bandit armed with a cheap rusted pistol loots the **First National Bank of McCloud** of $750 before departing the area. Later that same day, the authorities receive information indicating the robber had driven to Fort Smith, Arkansas, where he attempted to charter a plane to fly back to his home in Tennessee. Rushing to the airfield, the authorities arrested a youth named Orville Burch who was promptly extradited back to Shawnee. When interrogated, the lad claimed he robbed the bank in an effort to garner funds for the care of his very ill and pregnant wife back in Tennessee. It appears the family was in a crisis due to Burch being unemployed and awash in medical bills owing to his wife's grave illness. After looking into the boy's statement and contacting the authorities in Tennessee, the victim (Banker N. Douglas), as well as District Attorney Clarence Tankersley asked Judge Eroy Cooper for leniency in the case. A delegation of Shawnee citizens also approached the jurist to demand clemency in the case. The Judge, stating: "Although I do not condone his acts, I cannot add to this boy's burden in life," sentences the boy to ten years but suspends the sentence ordering the youth to go back to Tennessee and sin no more. The great depression had many victims and Mr. Burch appears to have been one of them.

*January 3-The **First State Bank of Anadarko** is robbed of $238. Slim pickings indeed. Profits sink even for bank robbers as the depression deepens.

*January 6-At approximately 4 a.m., three men burst into the home of Town Marshal J. A. Jenkins forcing him at gunpoint to accompany them to the **Washita Valley Bank of Fort Cobb**. The trio entered the building by smashing the front window with sledgehammers. Although the burglars worked on the safe with crowbars and hammers for several hours, they were unable to crack the steel box. Around dawn, the burglars give up and flee town with the marshal in tow releasing the poor lawman about thirty miles distant. The three bungling yeggmen are arrested later that day in Chickasha.

*January 8-**Oklahoma State Bank of Konawa** is robbed of $2,998. This incident marks the fourth bank robbery in the state in less than a week. Clay Tollett and Coyt Morse are eventually charged and convicted of the robbery. Tollett is sentenced to thirty years while Morse got twenty-five. The state pen in McAlester is reportedly bursting at the seams with bank bandits by this time. Two days after this heist the premiums paid by Oklahoma banks for hold-up insurance in towns with less than a population of 5000 souls was doubled. While a great many writers over the past half-century have directly attributed this large increase in premiums directly to the crimes of "Pretty Boy" Floyd, it takes only a glance at the list of bank robberies and the vast number of folks involved to realize that while Floyd certainly contributed to the rise in rates his activities were by no means the major impetus for the action.

*January 14-At 1:45 p.m., two well-dressed men enter the **First National Bank of Castle**, one sporting a handgun, while the other was armed with a machinegun. Cashier C. Elliot and his assistant, H. H. Gray, were attending to business when they looked up and noticed the pair make their appearance shouting, "This is a holdup." According to Elliott, the men made short work of the cash on hand swiftly gathering up some $2,400 in currency and a small bag of silver. By chance, just as the bandits were about to depart, Town Marshal J. M. Van Zant strolled into the bank and was disarmed and locked into the vault with several other bystanders. The bandits forced the two bankers along with a pair of customers named Glenn Dill and George Morzatt to mount the running boards of the robber's black Ford Sedan for use as human shields. The four captives were released on the outskirts of town.

Meanwhile, just moments after the Castle heist was completed three unmasked men entered the First National Bank of Paden looting it of $2,543. Paden is located just twelve miles east of Castle. The bandits locked the witnesses in the vault before making their getaway. As usual, the bandits took a hos-

tage for cover. On this occasion, the captive wound up being Assistant Cashier C. L. Sutherland. The frightened banker was released near Boley. It was reported that during the Paden robbery a citizen on the street boldly walked up to the getaway car and tore off the license plate for use as future evidence.

Naturally, area newspaper reporters and editors had a field day loudly proclaiming both robberies were the work of Floyd and his faithful minions while ignoring evidence that indicated otherwise. Such as, the two sets of bandits had used dissimilar makes of automobiles, were dressed differently, had opposite physical descriptions, and could not of been in two places at once. While the media would eventually concede Floyd could not have pulled off both capers, they still insisted he was likely the brain behind the duel heists. Pure dribble, but a legend was in the making. For the next two years, nearly every bank robbery in Oklahoma would produce a newspaper headline stating, "Floyd robs bank!" Although it appears Floyd and Birdwell were indeed the looters of the Castle bank, the facts indicate, a habitual criminal named Harold Glenn Roy and two other individuals robbed the Paden bank. It would not be the last time Mr. Roy will be mis-identified with Floyd in the coming weeks.

*January 21-Three men rifle the **Dover State Bank** of $700. According to witnesses one man remained with the getaway car armed with a machinegun while the other two entered the bank, gathering up the loot before locking four persons in the vault (one was a state senator named W.P. Kimmerer). Pushing Cashier A. L. Fash in front of them, the pair jumped into the getaway car and fled town. The banker was released a mile and a half from town. Naturally, the newspapers quickly blamed Charley Floyd and friends for the heist. Three days later Billy Joe Harris and Harold Glenn Roy are arrested near Seminole on an informant's tip. Dover Bank Cashier Fash positively identified both as two of the three men who robbed the bank. In the meantime, a car matching the one used in the Dover robbery, which proved to have been stolen from a Earlsboro resident, was discovered burned to a crisp near the rural home of Harold Roy's mother-in-law, located three miles northwest of Seminole. Inside the incinerated car is the charred body of a man with a .38 caliber bullet wound to the back of the head. Officers quickly theorize the victim is "Pretty Boy" Floyd's chief henchman, George Birdwell. Rumors of a recent violent disagreement between the two bandits over Floyd's reputed "heavy drinking" quickly surface. Several persons who know Birdwell by sight are shown the burned corpse and all agree it well could be that of the lanky badman. Meanwhile, Seminole Chief of Police Jake Simms squashed the rumor by accusing Harold "Rabbit" Roy of the car torching. Sure enough, a few days later Roy admits he is responsible for the dastardly deed. According to Roy, he shot and killed a thirty-five-year-old war hero turned outlaw named Maurice Harkey in a drunken row fueled by a jug of homemade white lighting. Evidently, the main point of contention between the combatants concerned the pair's recent botched attempt to rob a Seminole filling station. After killing Harkey, Roy threw his body into the stolen car and soaked it in gasoline before igniting it. Roy was charged with murder and kidnapping along with robbing the banks of Paden and Dover. His partners in the two bank heists are determined to have been Harkey and Billy Joe Harris.

*January 27-Two individuals rob the **Bank of Sasakwa** of $3,066. No arrests are made and the loot is never recovered.

*January 30-A pair of heavily armed men pilfers the **Bank of Elgin** of $2,391. On February 1, two bandits are arrested at a Lawton tourist camp and charged with the heist.

*February 10-While one bandit stood in the street holding back a crowd of rubberneckers with a machinegun his two companions loot the **Bank of Haileyville** for $2,500. The robbers successfully make their getaway into the Jack Fork Mountain area. Pittsburg County Sheriff Bob Lackey quickly formed a posse and headed into the hills. Although the bandit's abandoned coupe is soon discovered, the bloodhounds are unable to pick up a scent leading the authorities to deduce the robbers switched to a second car. Refreshingly, the witnesses state none of the robber's matches the description of Charley Floyd.

February 16-This date marks a truly bizarre and desperate bank heist. At approximately 11:45 a.m. a lone gunman walked into the **First State Bank of Inola**, which had been robbed five times in the past two years, waving a pistol about ordering Bank President O. Koenig to "Pony up the cash." Little did the bandit know that the bank had recently established a new policy, which only allowed $30 to be on hand due to obvious reasons. Koenig, realizing the desperado would accuse him of lying if he handed him a measly few bucks, invited the bandit to come behind the counter and take what he could find, stating, "There is not enough cash in the bank to make it worth robbing." After the bandit had rifled the tills for a whopping $31.50, he fled the building cursing under his breath. Later that day Rogers County Deputies J. Hurt Flippen and Dick Patterson confronted a man who matched the robber's description at a nearby filling station. When ordered to halt, the fellow turned and fired on the officers with a pistol. Flippen in turn shot and killed the man. It was later determined the individual was fifty-year-old George C. Whitmire, who happened to be the Deputy Assessor of Adair County. No explanation was

ever discovered why this respected citizen committed such a foolish act. Incidentally, Deputy Flippen was slain in a ferocious gunfight with members of the Cookson Hills Gang later that year in Cherokee County.

*February 26-Two armed desperado's loot the **First National Bank of Alex**. When one of the bank employees made a break for the vault the lead bandit chastised him saying "You shouldn't make a run like that. Some rattle-brained bandit might shoot you!" Four bank officials were forced to lie on the cold concrete floor while the duo scooped up $1,596 before fleeing. The perpetrators, later identified as H. A. Kelly and Earl Parks, are soon captured hiding in the attic of an area farmhouse. Both men are convicted and sentenced to 25-year terms at McAlester.

*March 9-Four bandits loot the **Exchange Bank of Skiatook** of a whopping $7,950. No arrests are made or money recovered. As was the norm, the bandits are last seen motoring toward the Osage country at a high rate of speed.

*March 9-At the noon hour, a late model Chevy coupe, loaded with three men, parked their car across the street from the **Mill Creek State Bank**. Two individuals exit the rig and enter the building, which is occupied by Cashiers C. E. Penner and Virginia Dye, along with bookkeeper Paul Sparks. Just seconds after the suspicious-looking pair appeared, Mr. Penner hit the newly installed alarm. The duo, armed with pistols, forced the witnesses to lie on the floor while they rifled the tills for roughly $800. Unfortunately, for the robbers, while they were occupied with grabbing the cash the employees dived into the vault and locked the door. The outlaws reacted by firing several rounds into the steel vault door in frustration. Meanwhile, the Mill Creek Home Guard began forming outside the bank. Over a dozen armed vigilantes quickly took up positions. When the pair exited the bank, all hell broke loose. One of the looters, later identified as a forty-odd year-old farmer and former Deputy Sheriff named Fred Hamner took a load of buckshot to the head while his partner, a Wewoka police character by the name L. C. "Blackie" Smalley, was struck in the head by pistol fire.

Hearing the shots, the driver of the getaway car put the pedal to the medal in an effort to get out of town. Although he was wounded several times and the getaway car riddled, the driver was somehow able to slip out of harm's way. Officers followed the vehicle to a point a few miles south of town where they discovered it abandoned. Following a blood trail, which led to a barn, lawmen shouted at the fugitive, who was identified as Adam Richetti, to surrender or die. He wisely chose the former. A fourth man, W. A. Smalley, who turned out to be Blackie's brother was arrested later that day in Sulphur and charged with conspiracy. Back in Mill Creek, the hijackers were transported to the Sulphur Hospital where Hamner was pronounced dead on arrival. "Blackie" Smalley would survive to be sentenced to a forty-year hitch at the Oklahoma Penitentiary. A fellow inmate named Mose Johnson stabbed him to death on December 13, 1943. Adam Richetti recovered from his wounds and gained his freedom through the bail process. He would soon join up with the Charley Floyd Gang and hell would be in session.

*March 10-At noon, the favorite hour for bank jobs, two individuals armed with pistols enter the **Fairfax National Bank** looting the institution of $953. While one of the robbers held Bank President H. N. Cook along with Cashier Lester Postle and a customer named E. E. Shepard at bay, his companion looted the safe and cash drawers. On departing, the duo forced Cook to walk between them to their awaiting car before fleeing town. Cook was released at a point several miles outside the town limits. A few days later Muskogee County Sheriff V. S. Cannon received a tip from a local stool pigeon concerning a pair of individuals staying at a downtown Muskogee flophouse located near the Midland Valley Rail depot. The informant further claimed the men were responsible for the recent Fairfax bank job. Cannon, accompanied by Deputy Marsh Corgan and several Muskogee city officers, immediately launched a raid on the apartment capturing two heavily armed males and a pair of "ladies of the night" none of which offered any resistance. When interrogated they identified themselves as Roy Adams and Fremont McCullom.

When asked what were they doing in Muskogee, Adams foolishly allowed how they were in town to spring fellow criminals Leon Garhart and Dewey Parker out of the county jail. The pair was currently being held on charges of knocking off the Ft. Gibson bank in December 1930 with Aussie Elliott and Jack Preddy. The following day Cannon and his minions transported the two recently acquired prisoners to Fairfax where the two bankers promptly identified them as the bank robbers. Cannon later stated McCullom was also wanted along with the notorious Jim Clark for stealing some livestock from a trailer parked in an alley off South Main Street in Muskogee the previous year. The pair's female companions were questioned and released after being held for several days.

*March 11-The **Bank of Earlsboro** is robbed by four unmasked men of $163.

*March 16-A single individual unsuccessfully attempts to rob the **Luther State Bank**.

*March 23-At shortly after the noon hour, a car occupied by Charley Floyd and his sidekick George Birdwell parks in front of the **Bank of Meeker**. Floyd enters the building armed with an automatic handgun announcing, "This is a holdup," while his pal covers the front door.

Bank Cashiers M.G. McKee and E.E. Kinsey, along with two customers named V.F. Hall and W.E. Wiley, were ordered to stand next to a wall hands up while the wily Floyd rifled the tills for approximately $700. On entering the vault, the bandit inadvertently set off an alarm. Floyd and company immediately flee the building forcing the four witnesses to mount the getaway car's running boards. The moment he slid into the vehicle, Birdwell pulled a machine gun from out under a canvas tarp located in the car's backseat and began surveying the street for vigilantes. When none appeared the two bandits slowly drove out of town releasing the captives about three blocks from the bank.

*March 29- Two men, one apparently older than the other, rob the **Citizens Bank of Shamrock** of $600 at gunpoint. Upon completion of the raid, the pair seizes two bank employees (D.C. Sellers and R.A. Sellers) for use as hostages. They are released just south of town. Brothers Red and Tom Ernest, who are both later involved in the bloody May 1932, Morris bank robbery, are suspected of being the perpetrators in this heist. The loot is never recovered.

*April 4-The **Security Bank of Comanche** is burglarized during the night for $587, none of the funds is recovered.

*April 5- At exactly noon, three men, later identified as Chief Hatfield, Victor Hopkins, and J. T. Foster, park in front of the **First National Bank of Boynton** driving a mud-splattered blue-black Chevy Coach automobile sporting a broken right front spring. According to witnesses, Hatfield stayed with the running car while Foster took a position just inside the main entrance and Hopkins strolled into the lobby armed with a handgun-ordering bookkeeper Maxine Clark and a customer, who were the only folks in the bank at the time, to "Reach for the sky." Foster then entered the lobby leveling a pistol at Miss Clark while Hopkins looted the tills for $1,200. The victims were instructed to "Sit down and be good and no one will be hurt." After gathering up the cash, Hopkins ordered the pair of witnesses to enter the vault. When the frazzled bookkeeper expressed a fear she would suffocate, the bandits looked at one another, shook their heads in unison then told her to, "Just sit on the floor and be quite." Before departing the bank, the thugs cut the phone lines.

Once the robbers exited the institution, Miss Clark bolted from the bank screaming at the tip of her lungs. Contacted by phone, Sheriff V. S. Cannon and a posse of officers, which included Deputies Bob Martin, Robert Ledbetter, and Van Crooch took up positions on the highway just outside the

Muskogee city limits in attempt to cut off the robbers. A few minutes after setting up the roadblock the desperadoes came barreling down the highway at a high rate of speed and were met by a volley of rifle and shotgun rounds fired by the posse. The car veered into a ditch nearly turning over before bouncing back onto the road speeding into town. An hour later, the bullet-riddled getaway car was discovered parked in a lot next to the Muskogee Veterans Hospital. The rightful owner of the vehicle, who was a patient at the facility, was contacted and he informed the officers a couple of his pals had borrowed the car that morning to run a few errands. Within the hour the trio of badmen were arrested and sitting in a cell at the county jail.

*April 13-The **First National Bank of Medford** is robbed of an estimated $4,635.

*April 21- "Pretty Boy" Floyd and his sidekick George Birdwell rob the **First State Bank of Stonewall** of $944.

*April 27-**Indiahoma State Bank** is looted by three desperadoes for $4,194. The bandits are captured and funds recovered in short order.

May 2-Two characters parked in front of the **Bank of Union City** at a few minutes past noon, driving a car stolen the previous night from a farmer named J.E. Shutten. The men enter the institution armed with handguns and immediately issued the familiar "Hands up. This is a robbery." Three employees, President D. P. Richardson, Cashier Kenton Petree, Bookkeeper Miss Monty Kilgore, and a customer named Charles Brown occupied the bank at the time. After placing $1,260 of the bank's money in a sack the pair forced the four hostages in front of them while they strolled to the post office next door where they robbed the place of a whopping $6.00. Marching the quartet back to the bank, the robbers attempted to lock them into the vault but were unsuccessful due to Miss Kilgore's releasing a hidden spring, which prevented the heavy steel door from shutting. The gutsy teller then hit the alarm. The bandits reacted by fleeing the building and racing out of town in their getaway car. Responding to the alarm a hardware salesman named Elmer Ross ran into the street and riddled the rear of the robber's speeding car. He and Banker Petree then jumped into a vehicle and taking a shortcut, cut the bandits off at the pass so to speak at a point ten miles out of town. In the ensuing gunfight, the two antagonists fired an amazing amount of lead but surprisingly no one was injured. The bandits were finally able to shake free when their pursuers pulled out of the chase due to their running out of ammo.

A few miles up the road the hijackers were met by a carload of Oklahoma County Deputies who took up the chase. The bandits ultimately pulled over and abandoned their car fleeing on foot into a thicket just outside the town of Yukon. A search of the rig uncovered all but $500 of the loot. The officers warily approached the thicket. In the meantime, a pair of curious youths named Elmer and Alvin White, accompanied by their uncle arrived at the scene of the manhunt hoping to be part of the exciting activities. They should have stayed home. Next thing they knew a pair of fellows ran out of a creek bed commandeering their car and persons by force. After spending the next twelve hours driving in circles, the trio of hostages was finally released unharmed. On their arrival in El Reno, the three began telling a crowd of assembled reporters of their adventures in a matter-of-fact fashion, saying…"Wasn't nothing to it…no reason to be scared…they didn't look tough to me." A good example of phony bravado if ever was one.

The leader of the pair of bandits was later identified as being Frank Sawyer, described as an extremely violent, hot-tempered degenerate gambler who had slain two men in the past and had recently escaped from a prison work camp. Sawyer would one day become intimately involved with such underworld luminaries as Wilbur Underhill, Harvey Bailey, and Jim Clark.

*May 10-Several bandits loot the **Farmers and Merchants Bank of Sterling** of $362. One arrest is eventually made in the case.

*May 25- A lone bandit, covering his face with a handkerchief, confronted Bookkeeper Ray Monroe just moments after he opened the front door of the **First National Bank of Apache** at approximately 8 a.m., which happened to be the exact time the time lock is released allowing the bank's vault to open. The bandit successfully accessed the vault gathering up some $2,953 before splitting the scene never to be captured.

*May 25-A pair of bandits abruptly enter the **Bank of Commerce** of Claremore, which was occupied by Cashier H. O. McSpadden, forcing the banker to the floor before gathering up all the cash in sight and locking the lone witness in the vault. It was also reported the badmen took the time to brutally kick the poor banker a half-dozen times with heavy work boots prior to leaving the scene with about $1,100.

*May 27-Three armed men hijack the **Morris State Bank** of $1,130. One suspect is slain and another captured while a female cashier is severely wounded during the heist. * See previous story *The Unluckiest Bank in Oklahoma: The Morris Robberies* for further details.

*July 18-Three individuals rob the **First National Bank of Idabel** of $12,000 using machine guns. Assistant Cashier

C. R. O'Neal and a customer named Kate Allen are the only people in the bank at the time of the heist. It is the first ever bank robbery in Idabel. Several days after the raid, a carload of officers that include Constable Virgil Derby, W.H Wagner, and John Stephens spot the bandits motoring along the highway near Broken Bow. When the lawmen attempt to pull the rig over, twenty-six-year-old John Leonard open fires wounding Derby. The officers answer with a sustained volley of lead killing Leonard as well as John West and wounding twenty-one-year-old Ishmael Burns. Burns, who is described as a "cripple," flees the area outrunning the obviously slow-footed officers. He is later captured.

*July 18-A lone bandit robs the **Bank of Agra**. According to Bank President C. J. Allen, the robber of this institution entered the bank pulling a pistol from a brief case and began yelling, "Lay down on the floor,' before kicking me in the ribs." The banker added, " He looked like a lawyer and had a phony mustache." The man looted the tills for $300 before departing unnoticed. On August 2, Oklahoma State Investigator R. E. Maxey arrested a former Seminole police officer named J. C. Simmons who was promptly identified by the witnesses from the hold-up as the robber.

*July 19-Three robbers enter the **Dill State Bank** with guns drawn ordering Cashier's Claude Williams and Roy Brown to, "Get your hands in the sky!" Williams responded by triggering a recently installed gas bomb located in the lobby before flinging himself to the floor. The bandits, engulfed in tear gas, bolted out of the building without firing a shot jumping into a Chevy Coup coughing and hacking as they sped out of town. A posse was quickly fielded and soon discovered the coup abandoned near a thicket just north of town. The bandits, still suffering from effects of the tear gas, were easily spotted and rounded up. The outlaws were identified as Everett White, C.R. Quick, and twenty-seven year-old Clyde Mapes. When interviewed by reporters in the Custer County Jail shortly after his capture, young Mapes, his face and eyes still smarting from the gas, proclaimed he had, "Made a mistake." Adding, "I could find no work. I get nothing but bad breaks. I regret this will leave a blot on my child's name."

*July 28-Two thieves rob the **First State Bank of Grandfield** of $2,288. An ex-con named John O'Connor is arrested in September and charged with the bank heist. At his arraignment, O'Connor informs his honor, "I want to get back to McAlester where I can work in the fresh air. It's too stuffy in that county jail!" He got his wish by being sentenced to five years. The loot from the robbery is never recovered.

*August 2- A man and woman enter the **Guaranty Bank**

of **Texola** robbing it of $770. Apparently, the man scooped up the money while the lady in question held a revolver, which turned out to be unloaded, on several bank employees. The pair, later identified as a married couple, named Harris and Charlene Wilson, is captured only five hours after the hold-up in nearby Wheeler, Texas. It seems the couple only managed to spend thirty dollars of their ill-gotten gains, the other $740 was recovered. The pair admitted to the robbery and waived extradition to Oklahoma.

*August 10-**American Exchange Bank of Shidler** is robbed of an estimated $380 in a bloodless raid.

*August 14-A pair of hijackers steals some $935 from the **Wynona National Bank**. The suspects are soon captured and convicted.

*August 19-Five men rob the **Citizens Security Bank of Bixby** of approximately $1,000. Cashier Howard Dearston, who was alone in the bank at the time of the raid, reported three men entered the institution while two others sat in the getaway car. One of the individuals asked to change a sack of pennies for a half-dollar piece. While the banker was busy counting the copper coins, the man ordered him to fill up an old cement sack with cash, which he did. The bandits then forced him to accompany them to a sedan parked in a nearby alley. He was released five miles south of town. The bank had not been robbed for twenty-four years. On that occasion, the bandit's made their getaway on horseback. Although Dearston would initially identify one of the robbers as the notorious Fred Barker of the famous "Ma" Barker Gang of Tulsa, it appears he was incorrect in his assertion. The banker would later positively identify the bullets-ridden corpses of Cookson Hill badmen Kye Carlile and Troy Love as participants in the bank heist.

*August 22- A pair of fellows armed with handguns stroll into the **Wirt State Bank** relieving the institution of $1,000.On departing the scene, the desperados lock several bank workers and a couple of customers in the vault before taking Bank President George Smith hostage. Smith is released unharmed a couple of miles out of town. Several days after the holdup, the two bandits are captured at a boarding house in Clemscott. Although they were armed, the pair reportedly offered no resistance. They were transported to the county jail where Banker Smith positively identified them, as did a customer named June Wood

*August 22- -Just moments after the completion of the Wirt robbery two men enter the **First State Bank of Castle** taking some $776. The pair attempted to flee in a small coupe, which apparently refused to start. One of the bandits fled from the car running to the edge of town where he was promptly captured hiding in a cotton patch. His crime-partner eventually got the rig started then in an act of improvisation pulled up next to a citizen and asked him to, "Jump in so we can catch them bank bandits." The outlaw booted the unwitting citizen out of the car just outside town and leisurely motored to a location just south of Lindsey where he abandoned the car and somehow made his way to freedom. The loot was recovered in full when officers searched the captured bandit, who was identified as Kermit Snow. The robbery marked the second time the Castle bank had been looted in 1932.

*August 26- The **Tuskahoma State Bank** is burglarized for $183 in cash and coin.

*September 7-The **Webbers Falls State Bank** is robbed of $750.

*September 8-A pair of roughly dressed youths hijacks the **Fairfax National Bank** of $3,000. The pair locked ten witnesses in the vault before leaving the building. Bank President H. N. Cook as well as a delivery boy named Kenneth Bardfield are forced to accompany the duo in their getaway car to the edge of town where they are released unharmed. A hastily formed posse chases the bandits into the Osage Hills where they soon loose sight of them. The authorities suspect career badmen Aussie Elliott and Eldon Wilson of being the guilty party. This occasion marks the second time in a year the institution has been raided.

*September 9-A pair of bandits loots the **Bank of Wirt** for $532. Both suspects are captured and the money recovered.

September 27- Two robbers, possibly aided by a third, hold-up the **Bank of Vian** for $6,000. Although the authorities suspect Cookson Hills Gang members Ford Bradshaw and Charlie Cotner as being the guilty party, it appears more likely Sam Lockhart and an unknown companion are the actual hijackers.

*September 27-Three men and a female accomplice attempt to rob the **Farmers State Bank of Valliant** but the raiders are turned back by a party of heavily armed vigilantes. While the three male subjects are captured, their lady companion manages to escape the area on foot.

*October 1-A lone gunman robs the **Clayton State Bank** of $18 in cash and $140 in postage stamps.

*October 6-Two middle-aged men armed with pistols

enter the small, suburban **First State Bank of Dawson** accosting the lone employee, George Mays, ordering him to produce some dough. After collecting $150 in cash and coin, the pair flees in an older sedan.

*October 13-Four outlaws rob the **Exchange Bank of Skiatook** of $2,000 in mostly greenbacks. The event marks the second time in less than a year the bank has been robbed.

*October 28-Two male subjects dressed in blue denim overalls and driving a black sedan robs the much-looted **Maud State Bank** of $1,391. Bank President Bert Harris and several others were locked in the vault prior to the pairs exiting the bank.

*November 1-This date marks Charley Floyd and George Birdwell's final successful bank robbery in Oklahoma. The pair, joined by Aussie Elliott, robs the **Sallisaw State Bank** of an estimated $2,531. On departing the bank, Floyd takes time to parade up and down the streets of his hometown calmly pausing to chew the fat with a host of familiar faces.

*November 5-A pair of armed individual's loot the **Maud Bank** of $900.

*November 7-Five bandits rip-off the **Marlow Bank** for $4,287. On November 19, Louisiana authorities arrest Walter J. "Heinie" Henderson on a charge of burglary. The following day Oklahoma officers arrive in the area and place charges of robbing financial institutions at Maud on November 5 and Marlow on November 7 against him. When Oklahoma's governor requested Henderson's extradition, the authorities in the "Pelican State" declined, stating they preferred to prosecute him for a host of crimes committed in their state.

*November 7-The **American Exchange Bank of Henryetta** is robbed of $12,000. Suspects are Ford Bradshaw, Jim Benge, and Newt Clanton. Although half-dozen eyewitnesses positively identify Bradshaw as one of the hijackers, he is tried and acquitted of the crime by a sympathetic Okmulgee County jury made up of poor farmers.

*November 9-The **American Exchange Bank of Collinsville** is looted of $1,000 by several unmasked bandits.

*November 9-A single bandit robs the **Wirt State Bank** of $500 leaving the scene driving a small coupe. Within hours of the heist, the getaway car is discovered overturned on the highway near Hennepin, the loot and a pistol as well as several license plates are discovered in the wreck. Within minutes of the car's discovery, Officers W. A. Carter, Bill Ratliff, and Herschel Gilliam capture a suspect cowering in a nearby thicket, who is identified as thirty-year-old Charles Vandye. The bank was previously robbed on both August 22 and September 9, 1932.

*November 10-Three men enter the much-raided **Fairfax National Bank** announcing a hold-up, ordering everyone to "Hit the floor!" While the desperadoes are sacking up the loot ($1,000) a bank official named Matt Cook slips unseen out the rear door and gathers up a posse arming them with shotguns loaded with buckshot. As the robbers exit the bank, the vigilantes open fire. Witnesses reported seeing a bandit riding on the getaway car's running board being wounded and falling to the street. The outlaws stop and pick him up while at the same time returning fire. Bank Cashier W.C. Hunt is wounded twice in the melee. A week later, Anadarko Chief of Police Hoyt Shelby answers a disturbance call at a local domino parlor involving an intoxicated subject. When Shelby attempts to arrest the subject the man pulls a gun firing once before bolting out the back door into an alley. Shelby chases the fellow down the alley into the rail yards while still exchanging fire with the subject. Finally, the suspect hit the ground mortally wounded ending the foot race. The man was later identified as an ex-con named Raymond Guy of Oklahoma City. Upon inspecting the corpse, the authorities notice two fresh buckshot wounds. The following day several witnesses from the Fairfax bank job arrive on the scene and identify Guy as one of the bandits.

*November 23-On this date, Charley Floyd's pal, George Birdwell, along with C. C. Patterson, and Charles Glass are literally stomped asunder when they attempt to rob the **Farmers and Merchants Bank of Boley**. When a hitch in the heist occurs, Birdwell cold-bloodedly murders Bank President D. J. Turner. Another bank employee reacts to the shooting by pulling a hidden gun from the vault and slays the big cowboy. When Birdwell's companions attempt to flee, vigilantes armed with shotguns perforate them, killing Glass and severely wounding Patterson.

*December 5- A team of three bandits hijack the **Bank of Cyril** taking the financial institution for $4,000 before abducting Cashier L.W. Geist, along with bookkeeper Homer McCarty, and a farmer named P. A. Walker forcing them to accompany them on a wild ride in their getaway car. The hostages are released a few miles outside of town. The three robbers are later identified as George Noland as well as Lonnie Poe, and Millard Pack.

*December 13-Four unmasked men rob the **Yukon National Bank** of $2,500. According to Cashier Aaron Pitney, the leader of the bunch is cross-eyed. Within the week, Oklahoma County officers arrest all four subjects along with several accomplices. Apparently, a break in the case came when one of the bandits attempted to buy a new car with the hot cash.

*December 20-At approximately 6:30 a.m. two masked men hiding behind the **Webbers Falls State Bank** in an alley take janitor Link Gallahar hostage as he is opening the bank's rear door. The pair held the poor man at gunpoint until the arrival of Cashier S. L. Weatherly at 8 o'clock. Weatherly informed the pair the vault could not be opened due to it being on a time lock set to release at 8:30. The bandits calmly state they will wait. At the appointed hour, the safe sprang open and the thieves gathered up nearly $1,700 in mostly folding money before turning to the witnesses declaring, "We will lock you both in the vault." When the banker expressed a fear he would suffocate from lack of oxygen, the bandits declared, "We wouldn't do anything like that." The pair then left the bank the way they had come and sped away in a large Buick touring car. Witnesses observe the bandits crossing the bridge at Gore before speeding north up the well-known "Moonshine Trail" toward the Cookson Hills. A clamor was soon heard from the local media inferring Pretty Boy himself had carried out the robbery. Muskogee County Sheriff V.S. Cannon soon arrived on the scene and after conducting a short investigation firmly stated, "This is one holdup the pretty boy did not commit."

The following day the getaway car was discovered abandoned and the vehicle's owner identified as a local police character named Charley White who was promptly arrested. White, who had done a jolt at "Big Mac" for a 1922 Park Hill bank robbery, denied any complicity in the heist. Later that day, a young hooligan dubbed "Willi Boy" Choate was arrested for questioning but was soon released for lack of evidence. The following April Choate was pulled over for a traffic violation in Tulsa. He had on his person nearly $500 in cash wrapped in a band marked "Webbers Falls Bank" as well as a pistol. He was quickly turned over to Sheriff Cannon who began forcefully questioning the youth. Choate eventually admitted he and a twenty-one-year-old lad named "Rabbit" Collins had looted the bank. He also stated Charley White had allowed them use of his Buick for a $100 fee.

A few days after Choate's arrest, Collins was apprehended in Vian by Muskogee County Undersherrif Robert Ledbetter and transported to the county seat in Muskogee for questioning. Collin's story boiled down to, "Yea, we robbed the joint but we stole Charley White's car. He didn't know nothing." "Rabbit" was a stand up guy. The youth added, "After we robbed the bank we ditched the car and waded up the Illinois River a couple of miles where we hid most of the cash in a cave. We then split up. Later on when I re-visited the cave, the loot was gone. Choate had snuck back and stole it." So much for honor among thieves. Choate and Collins were eventually sentenced to ten years in prison while charges were eventually dropped against White.

*December 20-The **Citizens Bank of Wakita** is burglarized of an undisclosed amount by a pair of yeggs.

*December 21-On this occasion six men driving a pair of getaway cars knock off the **First National Bank of Lindsey** for $4,000 in cash along with $14,000 in bonds without firing a shot. In departing the bank, four persons, James Charles, O.M. McKoskey, John Costello, and an unidentified adding machine repairman were forced to accompany the bandits in their getaway. The four were released several miles out of town. It was reported the bank had not suffered a robbery since 1918.

In February, two brothers named Warden, along with Buster Murphy, and Ewell Brookshire were arrested and charged with the robbery. In order to save their hides, Brookshire and E.L. Warden turned state's evidence accusing a twenty-six-year-old lawyer named Henry Hinkle of plotting the robbery, saying, "He said it would be an inside job and they will be expecting us and the cash will be sacked up."

Attorney James Mathers, who defended Hinkle in court, called the pair snitches and accused them of perjury. Mr. Mathers, who had a long history of defending bank robbers, added, "This case is an outrage!" Maybe so, but his client was found guilty and sentenced to twenty years at McAlester while his co-defendants both received lesser sentences.

*December 21-Two men rob the **First State Bank of Indiahoma** of $1,000. Vigilantes promptly run the pair to ground. The cornered outlaws surrender after a brief firefight in which one of the bandits is shot in the leg. The stolen loot is recovered at the scene. The pair is later identified as brothers George and Earl Alford. A Duncan garage owner is charged with conspiracy when it is discovered he had loaned the boys a car for use in the raid for a fee of $25. Incidentally, the same bank was successfully robbed earlier in the year of $1,941.

*December 22- The **Bank of Hydro** is robbed by three bandits of $559.

-1933-

In an overview of bank robberies for the Year of our Lord 1933, the key terms are Underhill-Bailey-Bradshaw. There were twenty-three daylight robberies and fifteen burglaries that

year. A nearly fifty per cent decrease from the previous year's sixty-three bank raids. Nearly half of the daylight heists were perpetrated by a group of robbers that sprang from the Bailey-Underhill Gang, which was originally made up of five of the eleven 1933 Memorial Day prison escapees from the Kansas State Penitentiary in Lansing. These five, Harvey Bailey, Wilbur Underhill, Jim Clark, "Big Bob" Brady, Ed Davis, and their future associates, Ford Bradshaw, Newt Clanton, Charley Cotner, Charles Dotson, and the Eno brothers perpetrated nine of the twenty-three bank hijackings in Oklahoma as well as numerous others in Kansas, Kentucky, and Arkansas during 1933. Comprised of an ever-changing cast of characters, the remnants of the group continued operations throughout early 1934 as well. Several other jobs were committed by "Pretty Boy" Floyd and Wilbur Underhill imitators and associates. The Okmulgee robbery committed by Wilbur Underhill, Ford Bradshaw, Clarence Eno, Charlie Cotner, and Newt Clanton was the largest bank cash heist of the year with nearly $13,000 stolen followed by the $11,000 hijacking of the Clinton bank by the Bailey-Underhill group. The year marked the election of Franklin Roosevelt and the repeal of prohibition along with the advent of massive social and economic programs like the National Recovery Act, Agricultural Adjustment Act, and the controversial declaration of a bank holiday. The federal government finally decided to declare war on the depression and its accompanying crime problem. The so-called Midwest Crime Wave was at its height and the Bureau of Investigation (Soon to be renamed the FBI) began assuming new powers in the fight against America's Public Enemies. In rural Middle America, farm foreclosures hit an all time high. Tens of thousands of lost souls hit the highways and rails heading west in hopes of finding work. Vast sections of Oklahoma and Kansas nearly de-populated due to the ongoing drought and the appearance of a series of devastating dust storms. Unemployment skyrockets to record highs across the state. The rural poor, blaming the bankers and the rich in general for their economic plight, began cheering on the bank robbers of the period with gusto. Class warfare rears its hideous head throughout the state.

*January 16-Three men loot the **Depew State Bank** of $2,500. On departing in a new Ford V8 the gang took three bank officials and a pair of customer's hostage releasing them just south of town. Creek County Sheriff Willis Strange quickly surmises a cop-killer named Coleman Rickerson is the leader the gang of hijackers which includes badmen Lonnie Poe and Joe Milam. On January 30, the Depew robbers were nearly captured in a raid near Bristow at the home of one Charles McGinty. The fugitives escaped after a brief gunbattle with officers. Several days later, the same outlaws struck the National Guard armory at Konawa making off with a host of weapons including a case of Browning Automatic Rifles. A week later, a posse of Kansas officers raided the farm of George Ford near Eldorado, Kansas, capturing Lonnie Poe along with Joe Milam and a pair of Kansas thugs. According to Wichita newspaper reports, the raiders, who were armed to the teeth and ready for battle, were quite surprised, and a bit let down that the hoodlums had chosen to offer no resistance. Poe and Milam are extradited back to Oklahoma where they are charged with the Depew bank robbery. Poe is also charged with the recent Cyril bank job.

*February 2-In the early morning hours, a townsman named Jim Doyle who operated a blacksmith shop, which adjoined the **Spencer State Bank,** heard suspicious noises emitting from inside the financial institution. Grabbing his gun, Doyle carefully approached the bank visually searching the area. Suddenly, three persons exited the building through a smashed door. Taking careful aim the smithy fired several rounds at the fleeing figures, one man dropped to the ground dying instantly while his companions fled into the dark night. Apparently, the blacksmith's gun jammed allowing the other two to escape. The authorities later identified the dead man as George "Babe" Downer, who had recently been released from the federal penitentiary at Leavenworth, Kansas, where he had been imprisoned for the past decade for his participation in the 1921 robbery of a train at Edmond. Also convicted in the same case were the notorious Jeff Duree (The Ghost Bandit), his brother Dan Duree, and E. E. Dodge. On searching the slain robber's clothes officers discovered a note naming his crime partners. Several days after the failed burglary a posse led by Oklahoma County Deputy Sheriff Bill Agee and State Investigation Bureau Agent R. E. Maxey rounded up the rest of the gang in an Oklahoma City raid. It was later discovered Downer had been picked up on a liquor charge on January 25. He had given the officers a false name and made bond. According to his friends, the outlaw intended to skip bond before the authorities discovered his true-identity and sent him back to Leavenworth on a parole violation. He had evidentially joined in the Spencer heist in order to gain funds to finance his flight as well as pay off his bond, telling a friend," I want to shoot square with my bondsman. I won't leave him in a lurch."

*March 5-Newly-elected President Franklin Roosevelt declares a National Bank Holiday, closing the doors of every financial institution in the country for a ten-day period including those in Oklahoma. Naturally, the crime of bank robbery becomes extinct, if just for a few days.

*April 26- The **Security Bank of Comanche** is held-up by three bandits for an estimated $1,500. The robbers, using a machinegun to back up their demands, take five custom-

ers hostage when departing the scene. The identity of the three hijackers is quickly established as Coleman Rickerson, Clarence Garatley, and W. A. "Shine" Rush. Since Rush was a known associate of Charley Floyd's, a rumor soon surfaced implying the "Pretty Boy" was the mastermind behind the heist. Several days after the robbery Constable Bill Goss was engaged in searching the farm residence of Blackie Smalley (Brother-in-law of Adam Richetti, Floyd's current crime partner), located five miles west of Wewoka when suddenly he bumped into Coleman Rickerson and a companion. Rickerson, who was unaware of Goss's visit, refused to surrender and he and the lawmen promptly began exchanging lead. The outlaw came out second best, falling to the ground with a fatal case of lead poisoning. His pal, who was later identified as Clarence Garatley, reacted by taking to his heels. He was later captured hiding in a barn behind the house.

*June 1-Six men loot the **Bank of Chelsea** of $2,500. The raid began when a large blue Graham-Paige sedan pulled up to the main entrance disgorging six men. While two individuals, armed with sawed-off shotguns, placed themselves outside the main door, the other four entered the bank. Two subjects, armed with pistols, rushed the teller's cage ordering everyone to the floor while the other pair of thugs began aggressively looting the vault and tills. The moment the hijackers exited the bank, they were met by a blistering wall of lead. Having received a tip earlier that week suggesting the bank would be robbed, Sheriff John York had assigned a heavily armed posse made up of Officers Ed Chiles, Tom Dean, and Deputy Bob Walters to establish an position directly across the street from the financial institution. Although the two sides engaged in a hot exchange fire, miraculously, the outlaws were somehow able to get to their car and successfully make their escape unscathed. At first investigators speculated the robbery was the work of a group of recent escapees from the Kansas prison, but later concluded the hijackers were Clarence and Otis Eno, along with Glenn Roy Wright and others.

*June 8-Two men, one armed with a "Tommy gun" enter the **First State Bank of Bokchito** forcing several bank employees to lie on the floor while they loot the business of $2,000. The bandits flee the area in a small coupe, last seen heading into the Boggy River bottoms.

*July 3-Five well-dressed individuals, later identified as Harvey Bailey, Wilbur Underhill, Jim Clark, "Big Bob" Brady, and Ed Davis rob the First **National Bank of Clinton** of $11,000 in cash and $4,000 in bonds. The gang pulled up to the bank in a new Ford V8 double-parking at a side entrance. While Davis remained at the wheel, the others entered the bank; two taking up positions at both entrances while the other two entered the lobby announcing, "This is a holdup. Be quite and do as you are told," before herding the dozen employees and customers toward the rear of the building. After collecting the loot, one of the bandits informed two female customers, Georgia Loving and Thelma Selle, "Were going to take you two with us." Loving was placed in the backseat of the getaway car while Selle was forced to ride the running board. The pair of terrified ladies was released just outside of the town limits on the side of Route 66. The Clinton bank job marked the first of many bank heists to be committed by members of the notorious Bailey-Underhill Gang.

*August 9-The **Peoples National Bank of Kingfisher** is robbed of $6,000 by members of the Bailey-Underhill Gang. At just past one in the afternoon, a late-model black Ford V8 sporting red-wheel tires and spoke wheels, parked just outside the bank unloading three men. On entering the bank, Harvey Bailey took a position just inside the door armed with a machinegun while Bob Brady announced a holdup and Jim Clark leaped over the counter and began rifling the tills and vault. It was over in a matter of minutes. Withdrawing from the bank, the hijackers took three bank employees hostage (Marion Mitchell, Virgil Francis, and Burt Brigham), placing them on the running boards of the getaway car. After unloading the bankers just outside town, the outlaws met up with Wilbur Underhill, who had been driving about the area watching for coppers, and departed the area.

*August 13-Five desperate men kidnap a doctor named Jess Herman and a nurse, Jo Frey from the grounds of St. Anthony's Hospital in Oklahoma City, holding the pair hostage several hours before releasing them and stealing their car for use in an upcoming bank robbery. When the men attempted to hijack the **First National Bank of Fletcher**, they were driven off by gunfire and pursed by an angry posse to a farm located near Ft. Cobb where they were captured. Four of the bandits eventually pled guilty to robbery charges and sentenced to twenty-years each while the fifth hijacker, Lloyd Grable, chose to fight the charges. The decision turned out to be a mistake on the defendant's part. He was promptly convicted and sentenced to death. The case was later overturned on appeal. Grable, who had become a self-proclaimed lay preacher by this time, was sentenced to life.

*August 26-Two robbers loot the **McCloud Bank of Commerce** for $700. Two employees, J. E. Van Landingham and Ike Barrett as well as a customer named F. B. Williams are in the bank at the time of the raid.

*August 28- The **Logan County Bank** of Lovell is robbed by two well-dressed men of $300. Several days later,

Oklahoma City Detectives Newton Burns and Clint Miers arrest a pair of suspicious looking individuals at a traffic stop. When the car was searched, a packet containing $150 was discovered. Both men denied ownership of the cash. Since the pair's appearance matched the description of the two Lovell bandits, the cops hauled them in for a line-up. The witnesses from the bank robbery identified the pair as the guilty party. The suspects were identified as Coda McHone and Francis Hyde, both of Oklahoma City. Turns out, Mr. Hyde was a rouge attorney who had previously been convicted of forgery and attempted murder (He had once attempted to poison a client). Both men eventually pled guilty. While Hyde received a thirty-five-year sentence, McHone was handed a twenty-five-year jolt.

*September 15-Wilbur Underhill, "Big Bob" Brady, and Jim Clark rob the **First National Bank of Geary** of $1,497. According to reports, three fashionably dressed men brandishing automatic pistols enter the bank demanding Bank President John Dillon and several customers to move to the rear of the bank and "Keep your yaps shut!" After harvesting the dough from the tills and safe, the outlaws took three persons hostage forcing them to ride the running boards for approximately two miles before granting them their freedom. The car used by the hijackers is found abandoned near Watonga the next day. The vehicle was stolen off the streets of Tulsa the previous week.

*October 6-The **First National Bank of Frederick** is robbed by Bob Brady, Jim Clark, Wilbur Underhill, and Walter Philpot of $3,500. Brady and Clark are captured the following day in Tucumcari, New Mexico, after a brisk gun duel with officers.

*October 9-The **Farmers and Merchants Bank of Tryon** is robbed by Eugene Clark, James Camp, and Lillie Womack of $537. The two men, armed with pistols, entered the bank loudly informing Cashier Clarence Hall "This is a stick-up!" After rounding up the loot, the robbers took Hall, as well as two customers, Attorney William Vasser and Arthur McConnell, hostage forcing then to ride the running boards for several miles where they were released unharmed. According to the eyewitnesses, the driver of the getaway car was a woman dressed in bib-overalls. Since Clark, who was a was a minor acquaintance of the notorious Wilbur Underhill, was known to impersonate the noted bandit on occasion, investigators were initially convinced the infamous badman had led the bank raid. The theory was discredited when it was discovered Underhill had been positively identified as leading a gang of robbers in a raid on a Kansas bank the same day as the Tryon heist. Eventually, the three hijackers were captured and unfortunately for them, when they went to trial the prosecutor in the case was none other than bank robbery victim and recently elected District Attorney William Vasser. On the first day of Clark's trial Vasser announced, "We swapped horses. Now I'm in the saddle."

*October 11-The **International Bank of Haskell** is robbed of $1,500 by Wilbur Underhill, Ford Bradshaw, Charley Dotson, and either Jim Benge or Eddie Clanton. One man stayed with the getaway car parked in front of the bank while the others entered the building, Underhill placed himself in the center of the lobby flashing a "Tommygun" ordering Bankers W.A. Combs and Dennis Rainwater along with a single customer to "Get'em up or I'll give 'ya the works!" Dotson and Bradshaw went about harvesting the money in a business-like fashion. On departing the scene, the hijackers took the bankers hostages. Just before exiting the bank, Cashier Combs leaned over to a window and began rapping it with his knuckle and mouthing the words "Hold-up" to several citizens lounging on the street. Noticing the banker's gyrations, Ford Bradshaw slapped the man on the ear before putting the palm of his hand firmly over his mouth ordering him to "Shut up and calm down." The outlaws raced out of town at speeds of nearly 80 miles per hour, the terrified bankers placed on to the running boards hanging on for their lives, their suit tails flapping in the wind.

*November 2-**Citizens National Bank of Okmulgee** is robbed of $12,776 in cash and a $1,000 bond by Underhill-Bradshaw gangsters Wilbur Underhill, Ford Bradshaw, Clarence Eno, Eddie Clanton, and Charlie Cotner. According to reports, four nattily dressed men entered the bank while another individual (Eno) remained at the wheel of the getaway car. The bank was occupied at the time by Bank Vice Presidents J. H. McElroy and Crittenden Smith, along with employees Oscar Kirk, H.S Garst, Lillian Frye, Eunice Hunt, and a janitor named P. H. Benson. In what seemed to witnesses to be one sudden movement, the four hijackers rushed into the lobby taking up positions. Cotner, armed with a scattergun, stood at the front door, Clanton and Underhill stepped into the center of the lobby covering the bystanders while Bradshaw marched to the front of the lobby loudly announcing "This is a holdup, everyone move to the back of the building." Everyone froze in place except for Mr. Smith who approached the outlaw stating, "This is carrying a joke a bit far fellow." Just then, Underhill quickly crowded the banker angrily thrusting a large caliber automatic pistol into his face exclaiming, "This is no joking matter, pal!" adding "If you think this is a comedy, try not following orders and see what happens." Smith meekly responded, "That's all I wanted to know" before ordering his fellow employees to move to the rear of the room. After gathering the money from the tills and several small safes, Underhill ordered Cashier Kirk to open the vault. When Kirk informed the bandit the big safe was on a time lock, the fuming outlaw, the veins in his neck bulging, ordered the banker to, "Open it up, or I'll blow your

God damn brains across this building." A stony silence blanketed the room as the oversized outlaw considered whether to leave or kill the banker. Just then, Eddie Clanton broke the silence saying, "I think he's telling the truth Wilbur." Just then, a phone began to ring, the shrill noise shattering everyone's nerves. Unknown to the bandits, Bookkeeper Eunice Hunt was hidden, curled in a tight ball under her desk where the unanswered phone was located. She later told reporters, "I just held my breath and shook like a tree fearing I would be discovered and they would hurt me for hiding." After glaring at the cashier for several seconds Underhill finally acceded the point, announcing, "Alright, we'll take what we got and go." The bandits made a clean getaway.

*December 12-Wilbur Underhill, Elmer Inman, Ralph Roe, Houston Nash, and others attempt to burglarize the **First National Bank of Harrah**. The bandits, riding in a large Ford sedan accompanied by a winch truck, invaded the little town on a snow-swept evening taking Constable Jackson Smith hostage before breaking down the front door of the bank then attempting to winch the multi-ton iron safe from its moorings across the lobby and on to the bed of the truck. Halfway through the operation, the winch-cable broke and the heavy safe fell through the bank's wooden floor crashing into the basement leaving a large crater and the bandits scratching their heads. The outlaws departed the area with only their hat in their hands cursing their luck. Underhill was heard to mumble under his breath, "The hell with this business. I'll show you mugs how to rob a bank."

*December 13-**The First National bank of Coalgate** is robbed of $3,100 by the Wilbur Underhill Gang. The day after the Harrah fiasco, the gang's big Ford pulled up next to the Coalgate bank, disgorging Wilbur Underhill, Houston Nash, Ralph Roe, and Jack Lloyd. While one outlaw remained in the car, three well-dressed subjects entered the bank. Underhill took a position in the rear of the lobby, armed with an evil-looking Lugar machine pistol. Jack Lloyd approached Assistant Cashier Lillian Connell ordering her to "Open the safe, sister!" Cashier Oliver Browning answered the bandit stating, "The safe is on a timelock." Suddenly, Underhill elbowed his way up front and firmly thrust the cold steel barrel of the machinegun into Browning's face instructing him to "Open that safe, now!" The banker immediately popped open the steel box saying, "Go ahead." Just then, a customer named Milt House entered the bank. He was ordered to, "Get with the others face to the wall." After gathering up the loot, the hijackers fled back to their getaway car taking a customer named Frank Collettea as well as Milt House and Oliver Browning hostage, instructing them to "Jump up and hang on." The hostages were freed a few miles outside of town.

-1934-

**Twenty-seven bank robberies noted

The year 1934 was noted for a string of seven bank raids in Oklahoma involving the notorious Jim Clark Gang made up of Clark, Frank Delmar, Ennis Smiddy, and Aubrey "Red" Unsell. Clark, a recent escapee from the Kansas State Penitentiary, was a one-time partner of "Big" Bob Brady's as well as a member of the Bailey-Underhill Gang of bank robbers. In December, the infamous O'Malley Gang successfully pulled-off a rare double bank robbery in Okemah. The O'Malleys would go on to rob ten midwestern banks before their eventual destruction. On May 18, the Federal Bank Robbery Act is enacted making bank robbery a federal crime.

*January 4-The notorious Red Carson, who had escaped from the Osage County Jail in Pawhuska with Aussie Elliott and Eldon Wilson on October 23,1933, did the honors of conducting the seasons opener by leading a raid on the **First State Bank of Willow**. The robbery began with a brand new shiny Ford Sedan carrying four individuals parking in front of the bank unloading three of the occupants, who entered the building with guns drawn. While one of the bandits took up a position at the main door a second stood in the lobby with a shotgun covering two cashiers, named Ford and Osborn and a female bookkeeper named Jewell Patton. The third man leaped over the counter ransacking the institution of roughly $440. On completion of the raid, Carson informed Miss Patton, "Were going to take you for a ride, honey." The robbers then exited the bank and entered their getaway car, forcing their hostage to dust her rump in the backseat for a mile or so. Miss Patton described the brigands as, "One man was older and mean-looking (Carson) while the others were younger and more pleasant." Adding, "There were so many guns in the car there was hardly room to sit down." A week later, J. L. Harris, the Sheriff of Sumner County Kansas, received a tip indicating Carson, accompanied by a woman, had checked into a hotel located in Wellington. The Sheriff reacted to this startling news by contacting the Osage County Sheriff's office, where the badman was wanted for slaying a filling station attendant, requesting Carson's physical characteristics. He also learned the outlaw presently had a $50 reward offered for his capture (Dead or Alive). Satisfied they had the right man, the Sheriff went for the gold, so to speak. The following day he and a pair of officers confronted the outlaw as he exited the front door of the Antlers Hotel. Carson reacted in true badman fashion by pulling a revolver and firing a round, which struck the sheriff in the arm. The lawmen promptly returned fire riddling the bandit.

*January 25- A mud-splattered blue Plymouth Sedan carrying five passengers parked at the side of the **Central National Bank of Poteau** unloading three men who entered the bank while the other two stayed with the car. One fellow took up a position just inside the door while another covered Cashiers W. A. Campbell and May Vasser, who were the only persons in the institution at the time. The fifth bandit rifled the safe and tills of $1,200. During the robbery, three customers, J. N. Butler, B. T. Little, and Pat Folsom, entered the bank and were forced to lie face down on the floor. On completion of the heist, which took approximately five minutes, the hijackers ran out the front door and to the rear of the bank where they jumped into the waiting getaway car-fleeing town. Miss Vasser later described the three outlaws as well dressed and in there thirties. A citizen on the street took down the car's license plate, Oklahoma 495-385. The bank had not been robbed since 1931 when three men and several women looted the bank of $7,000. The getaway car was found abandoned the next day a mile south of the community of Page. It was located 300 yards off the road covered in brush. The license plate had been removed. At the time of the heist, officers could only speculate as to the identity of the bandits. One lawman openly speculated the infamous Cookson Hills Gang might have been responsible for the Poteau heist while another publicly stated it was definitely a Pretty Boy Floyd job. Decades later, true-crime writer/expert James Knight speculated how information he had garnered concluded him to believe the Barrow Gang (Bonnie and Clyde) was behind the robbery.

*April 10-A contrary sixty-five-year-old unemployed bricklayer named Jack Mann, armed with a small pistol, strolled into the **National Bank of Wagoner** robbing the place of $710. The budding Jesse James was captured in short order. When questioned by police as to his motive for committing the heist, the old man instructed the laws the bank owed him the $700 due to bank officers cheating him in a land deal a decade ago. When prodded as to where the loot was hidden, the elderly rascal informed the cops, "It's mine, and I'm going to keep it!"

*April 19-Three ex-cons hailing from Texas rob the **Farmers State Bank of Bethany** of $852. The following day officers in Lincoln, Nebraska, cornered the trio engaging them in a firefight. One of the badmen, identified as Aubrey Ray was slain as was a twelve year-old innocent bystander named Luceen Marshall. The other two thugs were captured. The following day Oklahoma County Deputy Sheriff John Adams journeyed to Nebraska demanding the pair's extradition back to Oklahoma. Nebraska authorities denied his request choosing to charge the pair with the murder of the child. The two subjects, identified as Sam Rivette and Walter Dean were subsequently convicted of first-degree murder and given life sentences.

*April 24-At roughly closing time, two men enter the back door of the **Bank of Sand Springs**, robbing the place of $2,000.The bandits took four persons, R.E. Bassett, Elsie Doule, Opal Willhour, and Lillian Rawson captive releasing them several miles out of town.

*April 26-A lone bandit, described as small in stature and dark complected, walks into the **Bank of Quapaw** threatening two bank employees named Vivian Bowman and Celia Sawyer to cooperate or face certain death. The man looted the cash till for a few hundred dollars before fleeing in a Ford sedan bearing Missouri plates. Officers express the opinion the bandit may have been the notorious Clyde Barrow of 'Bonnie and Clyde' fame who is slain by lawman in a Louisiana ambush just a few weeks in the future.

*May 9-The **Bank of Wetumka** is robbed by Jim Clark, Frank Delmar, Ennis Smiddy, and Red Unsell of $2,000.

*May 29-The **First National Bank of Stafford** is robbed by two individuals of $500. Although the authorities immediately suspect two of Charley Floyd's companions, Shine Rush and Adam Richetti, of committing the dastardly deed, Carl Melton and Ray Wilson are charged with the crime.

*May 31-The **Peoples National Bank of Kingfisher** is held up by Jim Clark, Frank Delmar, Red Unsell, and Ennis Smiddy of $3,000. While Clark remains at the wheel of the getaway car, Delmar and Unsell take positions in the bank's lobby, while Ennis Smiddy rushes to the front of the room scrambling over the tellers cages and begins to vigorously harvest the money from the cash drawers and safe. When departing the area the bandits take two bankers hostage releasing them a few miles out of town. This event marks the second occasion in a year's time Jim Clark has been involved in looting the financial institution.

*June 20-Seven highly intoxicated gunmen riding in several cars and a winch truck, armed with shotguns, automatic pistols, and machineguns, invade Crescent taking over the town, cutting phone lines and holding over a dozen residents hostage for several hours while they attempt to winch a heavy safe from the **Merchants Bank of Crescent** onto the bed of a truck. When telephone operator Clara Cunard refused to grant the bandits access to her office the hoodlums kicked her door down and dragged the poor woman into the street kicking and yelling. With daylight approaching, the hooligans give up and depart the area with little fanfare. Four of the seven invaders are identified as Jim Clark, Frank Delmar, Aubrey "Red" Unsell, and Ennis Fay Smiddy.

*June 13- A well-dressed man rushes into the **Bank of Welch** pointing a pistol at Cashier Floyd Booten, Miss Garnett Cellers, and a customer named Bee Holloway ordering them to the rear of the bank. The robber looted the institution of $300 before taking Miss Cellers hostage, releasing her three blocks away from the bank. The robber was later identified as a Missourian named George Ward who had kidnapped a young couple near Seneca, Missouri, the previous week and stole their car, which was used in the bank heist.

*July 12-At approximately ten in the morning two men, one described as old and grizzly, the other a youth, calmly enters the **First State Bank of Ketchum**. The older man pulled an ancient ivory-handled horse-pistol ordering Assistant Cashier Luther Gregory, the son of Bank President Elum Gregory, to "Reach for the sky!" His pal stood by the doorway armed with a small automatic pistol. Young Gregory, who was the sole occupant in the bank at the time, cooperated handing the hijackers some $300. On completion of the heist, the bandits mounted a four-door sedan and raced out of town with the banker in tow. About a mile past the city limits the looters released Gregory, who raced back to town on foot gathering up his father and a farmer named Oscar Blackwell. The three then sped into the bandits wake armed to the teeth hoping to catch up to the desperadoes. Meanwhile, back in Ketchum, the alarm was sounded and a large posse was fielded. After driving around in circles for several hours, the carload of bankers discovered the hijackers parked on the side of the road just south of Grove. One of the bandits was in the process of talking to an unsuspecting farmer while the other was changing the getaway car's license plate. Young Gregory, who was driving, pulled his 1932 Chevy Coup next to the bandit's vehicle for a closer look, still not totally certain the men were indeed the desperadoes who had held him up. The moment the Chevy stopped, the elderly bandit pulled his ancient six-shooter and lunged forward firing several rounds into Gregory's vehicle. His partner soon joined in the melee firing several rounds into the rig as well. While Gregory senior slumped to the floorboard suffering from several wounds to the chest, his son emptied his semi-automatic pistol into the old man and his sidekick while Blackwell, armed with a rifle, did the same. At the conclusion of the vicious gunbattle, the two bandits as well as Elum Gregory lay dead.

For the next week, officers rushed about attempting to identify the hijackers. They finally concluded the youth was Bill Quinton of Cherokee County while the older man was the infamous "Kaiser Bill" Goodman, the so called "Old Man of the Mountains," otherwise known as the "Fagin of the Hills." Due to the old man's habit of going under more names than Elizabeth Taylor, no one was certain of his legal name so they dubbed him John R. Goodman, which was the moniker he used most frequently. The "Kaiser Bill" nickname derived from the fact he sported a flowing mustache similar in style to that of Kaiser Wilhelm's of Germany.

Born somewhere in Pennsylvania around 1860, Goodman joined the U.S. Cavalry in the late 1870s under a phony name and was posted at both Forts Sill and Reno, Indian Territory, where he participated in the Indian Wars before deserting his post. He spent the next few years hijacking small trading posts, weary travelers, and such throughout Kansas, New Mexico, and the Indian Territory. It was long rumored he once participated in a train robbery with the notorious Dalton-Doolin Gang. According to several sources, he was incarcerated many times over the years in several state and federal penitentiaries. After the turn of the century, the old boy connected with the notorious Fred "Cottontop" Walker in the Cookson Hills of Eastern Oklahoma engaging in a bootlegging enterprise. In 1918, Goodman along with Walker and Levi 'Mount' Cookson knocked off the Farmers State Bank of Gore followed up by an unsuccessful attempt to loot the Bank at Gans with outlaw Bush Wood. He was arrested and convicted of the Gore heist shortly afterwards. While awaiting his removal from the Sequoyah County Jail to "Big Mac", he broke out of the institution going on the lam. Continuing his nefarious activities, he and Bush Wood paid a return engagement to the Gore bank in 1920. According to officers, the old man spent the next few years robbing stores in isolated settlements across the state with various crime partners until his 1924 arrest and conviction in Kiowa County for grand larceny under the name of Hale. When his real identity was discovered he was sent to McAlester to serve his term for the Gore job. In 1933 he was paroled and went right back to his old habits knocking off banks in both Midland and Mansfield, Arkansas, before looting several rural stores in Tulsa County. Lawmen, who knew of his activities, charged him with being the "Fagin of the Hills" acting as an instructor of crime to various Cookson Hills badmen like Ford Bradshaw, Kip Harbeck, and Kie Carlile over the years.

While Banker Elum Gregory was buried near Ketchum with honors, "Kaiser Bill" was dumped in a pauper's grave in Vinita with reportedly no mourners present.

*August 1- Shine Rush and Clifford "Jack" Boone entered the **First State Bank of Wayne** shortly after the doors opened, reportedly armed to the teeth, while Hugh Gilley sat at the wheel of a black sedan parked in front of the institution. Rush verbally warned the three bank officials present in the bank to, "Keep your hands down and keep quite. There's going to be a robbery." After gathering up roughly $600, the bandits take Bank President V. V. Haney hostage releasing him a few miles from town. According to news reports, the other witnesses to the robbery are Haney's wife, Vera, and a bank director named P.

J. Puckett. Three weeks later on August 29, Rush and Boone knocked off the Garber State Bank for $500. On October 2, a large party of officers raided a farmhouse located near Bristow in search of a fugitive named John Longacre, who had recently wounded a night watchman in a Stroud gunfight. While closing in on the suspect hiding in the residence, a second subject, later identified as Rush, suddenly appeared on the scene firing several wild shots at the lawmen with a pistol. Officers returned fire but lost the suspect in a foot chase through the heavy timber. Ten days later, a large posse of federal, state, and county officers raided a farmhouse near Norman capturing Rush. The outlaw was transported to the Garfield County Jail in Enid where he was promptly charged with the Comanche, Garber, and Wayne bank robberies as well as auto theft.

Shortly after Rush's capture, Jack Boone and Hugh Gilley were arrested. Boone was charged with both the Wayne and Garber heists while Gilley was charged with the Wayne job. Meanwhile, federal officers began questioning Rush in regards to the current whereabouts of his pals "Pretty Boy" Floyd and Adam Richetti. Evidently, they got a handful of nothing for their efforts. On November 10, six inmates broke out of the Garfield County Jail overpowering the guard by tossing a handful of crushed red pepper into his eyes. According to a jail spokesman, when the escapees inquired if Rush wanted to join them he declined the offer. On December 1, 1934, Rush pled guilty to robbing the bank at Garber and sentenced to a ten-year hitch at McAlester, while his companion, Jack Boone, received a five-year term. Judge J. W. Bird hammered Hugh Gilley with a ninety-nine year jolt before nailing a Garfield County farmer with a two-year sentence for harboring the trio in the wake of the Wayne job.

*August 1- Just hours after hijackers loot the First State Bank of Wayne, a trio of badmen led by Ennis Smiddy robbed the **First National Bank of Sentinel** of $1,500. Cashier W. O. Calloway, Assistant Cashier C. Yates, and Bookkeeper Mrs. Guy Marney occupied the bank at the time. All three were taken hostage by the badmen but released unharmed at the town limits. The trio was later identified as Smiddy, Aubrey "Red" Unsell, and George Flannigan. A month after the bank heist officers ambushed Unsell near the community of Hartshorne. Although lawmen did manage to wound the bandit, he somehow escaped apprehension. On September 10, a fast moving squad of federal, state, and local officers capture the outlaw near Duncan.

*September 6-At approximately 1:20 p.m., a lone bandit armed with a small caliber automatic pistol entered the **First National Bank of Custer** City approaching Bookkeeper Edna Berberness, inquiring who was in charge. She replied, Vice President M. O. Dawson and Cashier Fred T. Huster, who were both standing nearby. The bandit whipped out his pistol and nervously ordered the three to get down on the floor while shouting to a pair of customers, Julius Tatro and Chester Bender, who were standing in the lobby to, "Stand still. This is a real holdup and no joke about it." After gathering up roughly $800 in small bills, the hijacker fled from the building and departed town in a 1932 model Chevy Coach automobile driven by a cohort. A retired peace officer named W. O. Crow, who witnessed the event, jumped in his car pursuing the bandit for several miles south on Route 66 before loosing sight of the badman's car. Elmer Ford and Maurice Brian are later convicted of the robbery. Ford acted as the inside man on the job while Brian drove the getaway car.

September 10- Ex-members of the Wilbur Underhill Gang, "Jack" Lloyd and Ralph Roe, rob the **Farmers National Bank of Sulpher** of $3,000. According to eyewitnesses, the pair strolled into the bank's lobby armed with handguns forcing Teller Kathryn Patton and Cashier David Collins, along with a trio of customers to the floor. After gathering the loot and placing it in a sugar sack, the bandits took Collins hostage forcing him to ride the running board for several miles before kicking him off the running car. Both Roe and Lloyd are later captured and sentenced to ninety-nine years in prison for committing the Sulpher bank job. Roe drowned in a December 16, 1937, escape attempt from Alcatraz while Lloyd died of prostrate cancer on June 15, 1964, at the Federal Medical Center for Prisoners at Springfield, Missouri.

*October 4-Three bandits led by the notorious Ennis Smiddy enter the **First State Bank of Ryan** at 10 a.m. announcing to three bank officials and a customer, "This is a holdup!" The folks in the bank at the time were Rose Hughes, Oliver Anderson, Tom Hughes, and an unidentified customer. While the heist was ongoing, two persons, E. L. Worrell Jr. and Charles Rose, entered the institution and are both detained at gunpoint. The robbers were unsuccessful in their attempt to open the safe and fled the bank with a measly $300 in cash and coin. Four of the captives were taken hostage and forced to ride on the running boards of the getaway car for a mile or so before being released.

*October 6-A gray sedan containing a quartet of highwaymen force a vehicle transporting money from the **First National Bank of Miami** to the bank in Picher off the road one mile north of Commerce, Oklahoma. Occupants of the bank car were identified as Clarence Miller and Mrs. R. M. Chambers, both employees of the First National. Unfortunately for the robbers, the bankers were only carrying roughly $300 in silver at the time. The bandits stole the loot plus the ladies purse and the keys to the car before speeding away.

*October 19- Two men forcibly enter the home of Banker Will Lauderdale forcing him and his wife to accompany them to the **First National Bank of Yale** where he was forced to open the vault. The robbers scooped up some $1,200 before leaving the financial institution. While Mrs. Lauderdale was driven back home and released, her husband was forced to ride with the bandits to a point four miles out of town before he was released. By years end all three bandits had been captured and tried. Richard Marlow and twenty-one-year-old Henry Harrison were sentenced to ten-year terms while a Pawnee resident named Merlin Venable received a one-year term for driving the getaway car.

*November 1-Three men led by Ennis Smiddy enter the **First State Bank of Temple** announcing, "This is a holdup. Don't touch anything!" According to witnesses, one man stood in the lobby while another positioned himself at the door, while a third began rifling the tills. After taking roughly $1,800, the bandits flee the bank taking four bank officials, M.F. Ray, C.S. Worthan, V. A. Dowlen, and John Nelson as well as a customer named Jess Knight hostage, forcing them to mount the getaway car's running boards. The captives are released at a point one mile from town. An hour after the robbery the bandits speeding automobile is spotted racing through nearby Ardmore.

November 8- The **First National Bank of Okeene** is robbed by three bandits of $1,165. Jim Clark's old pal, Ennis Smiddy was suspected to have been the leader of the hijackers. Smiddy is captured on Christmas morning opening presents with his family at their farmhouse near Waurika. The badman would later admit participating in the hijacking of eight banks, Crescent, Wetumka, Temple, Ryan, Kingfisher, Sentinel, and Okeene, Oklahoma as well as Saint Jo, Texas. His next residence is the island bastille located in San Francisco Bay called Alcatraz. The badman died at the prison infirmary of liver disease in 1941.

*November 26- Two well dressed youths, enter the **First State Bank of Ryan**, which is currently occupied by Cashiers Oliver Anderson and Tom Hughes, robbing it of $250. The lads, described as looking like "collage boys", take Anderson hostage. A posse of vigilantes is promptly organized but has to standby helplessly as Anderson is used as a human shield by the bandits as they make their getaway. The bank had previously been robbed earlier that year for $300.

November 28-The **First National Bank of Fairland** is looted by three unmasked men for several hundred dollars. Vigilantes take a couple of ineffective pot shots at the trio as they depart town in a black sedan. Cashier K. S. Milbourn and bookkeeper Mrs. M. G. Campbell are present in the bank at the time of the robbery.

*December 12- At mid-day, three jovial bandits enter the **Bank of Canton** getting the drop on bank officials O. P. Willis and Mrs. Merle Wahl. When Willis informed the outlaws the safe was on a time clock set to open at 4:15, the bandits pulled the window shades and sat around shooting the breeze with the bankers. Around 4 o'clock, they were joined by State Senator Bert Willis, who was also a cashier at the bank, along with two customers named John Jacobs and Lee Seifried. The trio was instructed to, "Come on in and join the watch party." At the appointed hour, the thieves opened the safe and fled the bank with $1,000.

*December 22-Two banks, the **Okemah National and the First National of Okemah**, are robbed simultaneously of $19,000 by members of the notorious "Irish" O'Malley Gang.

* See previous article, *Irish O'Malley and the Ozark Mountain Boys* for further details

* December 24- Area badman Buster Cooper robs the **Quapaw Bank** of $300 at the beginning of a weeklong crime spree. In the next several days, Cooper and Bob Johnson (Both members of the Irish O'Malley Gang) hijack several motorist as well as rob a couple of rural stores before ending up in Picher where they are involved in a high-speed chase that concludes in a gunbattle in which two lawmen are wounded. After wrecking their car, the two outlaws split up and Cooper retreats to a friend's house where he is soon confronted by a heavily armed posse led by Ottawa County Sheriff Dee Watters. The officers lay siege to the residence, firing several rounds of tear gas and a couple of hundred bullets into the place in less than an hour's time. Deputy Gerald Hodge enters the home and is fatally shot by the wounded outlaw. Cooper is riddled by waiting lawmen when he attempts to flee the structure.

Outlaw and Lawmen Cemeteries

Oak Cemetery

Although located in Fort Smith, Arkansas, this well-kept burial ground is intimately associated with numerous individuals connected to the Indian Territory. The thirty-acre facility, which was established in 1842, is the final resting place for some twenty-eight persons who were hung on the Fort Smith gallows. Most had committed crimes occurring in the Indian Nations. Over one hundred federal deputy marshals who " Rode with Parker," are buried there as well.

Clifford "Kip" Harbeck who at one time participated in robbing banks with several bank depression-era robbers, including the legendary Oklahoma bandit "Kaiser Bill" Goodman. Harbeck was shot and killed while attempting to escape from the notorious Tucker Prison Farm. Photo by Naomi Morgan.

Jacob Yoes, US Marshal out of Fort Smith court 1886-89, then 1890-93. Photo by Naomi Morgan.

Captain James Mershon who once rode with Parker. Photo by Naomi Morgan.

Fort Smith National Cemetery

Like Oak Cemetery, this burial grounds holds the human remains of numerous characters connected to the Indian Territory such as….

Judge Isaac Parker. Photo by Naomi Morgan.

Deputy Federal Marshal Floyd Wilson, slain by outlaw Henry Starr. Photo by Naomi Morgan.

Grave of Attorney J. Warren Reed, remier antagonist of Judge Parker. Photo by Naomi Morgan.

Ball Cemetery-Nowata County

Walter Jarrett one-time crime partner of outlaw Elmer McCurdy. Jarrett was the eldest of the eleven brothers of whom at least seven were criminals. Walter was killed in the aftermath of an Osage County bank robbery. Photo by Naomi Morgan.

Albert "Ab" Connor, leader of the Cedar Creek Gang, was slain during a grocery store robbery near Coffeyville, Kansas. Connor was married to Hazel Jarrett, sister to the notorious Jarrett brothers. Hazel wed depression-era outlaw Wilbur Underhill in 1933. Upon her death, her ashes were buried next to Ab Connor's final resting. Photo by Naomi Morgan.

Ethan "Al" Spencer, charismatic 1920s bandit, slain by US Marshal Alva McDonald. Photo by Naomi Morgan.

Levi (Lee) Jarrett, member of the Poe-Hart and Cedar Creek Gangs, was killed in a car crash. Outlaw brothers Roger (Buster) and Glenn Jarrett lie nearby in unmarked graves. Photo by Naomi Morgan.

Right: DickGregg, 1920s desperado, killed in bloody Tulsa gunbattle with police. Photo by Naomi Morgan.

Okmulgee Park Cemetery-Okmulgee

Dick Farr, who rode with Parker as a deputy US marshal prior to becoming Okmulgee police chief. Farr was involved in numerous gunfights including the infamous "Okmulgee Burning" incident, throughout his long career as a lawman. Photo by Naomi Morgan.

George Fee, slain by depression-era bandit Wilbur Underhill in 1926 robbery. Photo by Naomi Morgan.

Entrance to Ball Cemetery-Final resting place of many an outlaw. Photo by Naomi Morgan.

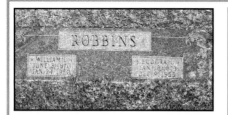

"Wild" Bill Robbins, who served as Deputy Federal Marshal under Judge Parker before serving as a Muskogee County Deputy Sheriff. In 1916, he was employed as a deputy for Okmulgee County. Robbins was one of the officers who slew three members of the notorious Poe-Hart Gang near Nuyaka in 1917. Photo by Naomi Morgan.

John Lung, a member of the posse who killed Oscar Poe, Will and Harry Hart in a shootout near Nuyaka. Lung was slain by an unknown assassin in a Sapulpa parking garage in 1922. Incidentally, Poe and the Hart twins are buried in unmarked graves located just a few feet from Lung's final resting place. Photo by Naomi Morgan.

Arthur Gooch, last man hung in Oklahoma, 1936. Photo by Naomi Morgan.

Henry Klaber, Okmulgee chief of police slain in shootout in 1908. Photo by Naomi Morgan.

"Big" John Russell, Okmulgee County Sheriff in the 1920s, prison warden, and pioneer rancher. Russell shot and killed four men in the line of duty. Photo by Naomi Morgan.

Mark Lairmore, celebrated lawmen from the 1920-30s, died of a heart attack at the age 60. Shot seven men in his career. Photo by Naomi Morgan.

Summit Cemetery-Guthrie

Outlaw Elmer McCurdy, the mummified outlaw. Courtesy Roger Bell.

Final resting place of Bill Doolin. Courtesy Roger Bell.

Charley Pierce-Doolin Gang member slain by the Dunn brothers along with "Bitter Creek" Newcomb for reward. Courtesy Roger Bell.

"Little" Dick West-Doolin Gang member slain by lawmen. Courtesy Roger Bell.

Greenhill Cemetery-Muskogee

Lawman Sam Tulk. Photo by Naomi Morgan.

Samual Morton Rutherford, pioneer attorney and US Marshal (1895-97) who served the Muskogee Court, Indian Territory. Rutherford was killed in a tragic car accident. Photo by Naomi Morgan.

Bushyhead Wood, member of the "Kaiser Bill" Goodman-"Cotton" Walker Gang of bank robbers circa 1918-23. Photo by Naomi Morgan.

Kelsie Morrison, one-time member of the bank robbing Blackie Thompson Gang. Morrison was also involved in the Osage mass-murder case. In 1925, he was convicted of murdering Anna Brown at the behest of W.K. "Big Bill" Hale. Although sentenced to life imprisonment, he was paroled in 1937. Upon gaining his freedom, he traveled to Fairfax, Osage County, where he was killed in a gun-duel with a pair of city cops soon after his arrival. He is buried next to his mother. Photo by Naomi Morgan.

John Barger, a long-serving Muskogee County Sheriff, city police officer, deputy sheriff and partner of Joe Morgan at the time of Morgan's murder. Photo by Naomi Morgan.

Muskogee County Deputy Sheriff Joe Morgan, slain in 1924 in Texas attempting to bring the Lawrence brothers to justice. Photo by Naomi Morgan.

Sam Neal, Muskogee officer who was slain in 1916. His killer was executed via the electric chair. Photo by Naomi Morgan.

Webster Reece, the Muskogee County Deputy slain by Carlile Gang in Standing Rock gunfight September 17, 1932. Photo by Naomi Morgan.

Will Laurence was hung in Arizona for the murder of Phoenix Officer Haze Burch. Also participated in the murderers of Muskogee County Officer Joe Morgan as well as a Montana lawman. Photo by Naomi Morgan.

John "Marsh" Corgan was a tough, no-nonsense Wagoner County Sheriff, as well as Chief of Detectives and later Chief of Police of Muskogee. Corgan committed suicide in 1936. Photo by Naomi Morgan.

Ben Bolton, Muskogee Chief of Detectives, slain by the O'Malley Gang during a 1935 bustout from the Muskogee City-Federal Jail. Photo by Naomi Morgan.

Susie Sharp was slain by members of the Cookson Hills Gang on Braggs Mountain in 1932. Her sensational murder sparked a furious manhunt that ended in the violent deaths of Officers Frank Edwards, Webster Reece, Andrew McGinnis, and J. Hurt Flippen, as well as three badmen in a series of running gunbattles taking place in Cherokee County. Photo by Naomi Morgan.

Homer Spaulding, an Okmulgee City detective killed by members of the Barker Gang.

*Author's Final Comment

As a shameless follower of the "Fifty year rule," a theory suggesting historians wait at least fifty years after a happening to fully chronicle the event, thus giving a researcher the opportunity to gain a fuller perspective of the subject matter, I will leave the rest of the story to future historians. It is my fondest hope folks enjoyed reading this book as much as I enjoyed writing it...until we meet again...R.D. and Naomi Morgan, Haskell, Oklahoma.

John "Ed" Hensley, a Muskogee PD detective slain by escaped convict Charles Martin.

Romie Hinson, a Muskogee PD detective killed by an irate taxi dirver. He was the second Muskogee officer slain in the line of duty in 1934.

Sources

Books

Bailey, John Harvey & Haley, J. Evetts, *Robbing Banks was my Business*, Palo Duro Press 1973.

Berry, Howard K. & Jones, Richard, *He Made It Safe To Murder: The Life of Moman Pruiett*, Oklahoma Heritage Association 2001.

Bearss, Edwin & Gibson, Arrell, *Ft. Smith: Gibraltar on the Arkansas,* Norman 1969.

Beggs: The First 100 Years, Bell Books 2003.

Biles, J. Hughes, *The Early History of Ada*, Oklahoma State Bank of Ada 1954.

Breuer, William B, *J. Edger Hoover and His G, Men*, Praeger Publishers 1995.

Burton, Arthur T., *Black Gun, Silver Star: The Life and Legend of Frontier Marshal Bass Reeves*, University of Nebraska Press 2006.

Butler, Ken, *Oklahoma Renegades: Their Deeds and Misdeeds*, Pelican Publishing, Gretna, Louisiana. 2000

Cordry, Dee, *Alive If Possible…Dead If Necessary*, Tate Publishing 2005.

Croy, Homer, *He Hanged Them High*, Duell, Sloan & Pearce, 1952.

Duvall, Deborah L., *Tahlequah and the Cherokee Nation*, Arcadia Publishing, 2000.

Edge, L. L., *Run the Cat Roads*, Dembner Books 1981.

Elliott, David Stewart, *Last Raid of the Daltons*, Coffeyville Historical Society 1892.

Esslinger, Michael, *Alcatraz: A Definitive History of the Penitentiary Years*, Ocean View Publishing 2003.

Franks, Kenny A., *The Rush Begins: A History of the Red Fork, Cleveland and Glenn Pool Oil Fields*, Oklahoma Heritage Association, Western Heritage Books 1984.

Franks, Kenny A., *Ragtown: A History of the Greater Healdton, Hewitt Oil Field*, Oklahoma Heritage Association, Western Heritage Books Inc.

Gibson, Arrell Morgan, *Oklahoma: A History of Five Centuries*, University of Oklahoma Press 1981.

Gibson, Arrell M., *Harlow's Oklahoma History*, Marlow Publishing 1972.

Gregory, George, *Alcatraz Screw: My Years as a Guard in America's Most Notorious Prison*, University of Missouri Press 2002.

Hanes, Col. Bailey C., *Bill Doolin: Outlaw O.T.,* University of Oklahoma Press 1968.

Helmer, William & Girardin, G. Russell, with Rick Mattix, *Dillinger: The Untold Story*, Indiana University Press 1994.

Helmer, William, with Rick Mattix, *The Complete Public Enemies Almanac*, Checkmark Books 1998.

Hinton, Ted, *Ambush: The Real Story of Bonnie and Clyde*, Shoal Creek Publishers 1979.

Hoig, Stanley, *Night of the Cruel Moon: Cherokee Removal and the Trail of Tears*, Facts on File 1996.

Hope, Wellborn, *Four Men Hanging: The End of the Old West*, Century Press 1974.

Jones, W. F., *The Experiences of a U.S. Marshal of the Indian Territory*, Starr, Hill Associates 1976.

Knight, James with Davis, Jonathan, *Bonnie and Clyde: A Twenty, First Century Update*, Eakin Press 2003.

Koch, Michael, *The Kimes Gang*, Authorhouse 2005.

Lamb, Arthur H., *Tragedies of the Osage Hills*, Raymond Red Corn 1935.

Louderback, Lew, *The Bad Ones: Gangsters of the '30s and Their Molls*, Fawcett 1968.

McConal, Patrick M., *Over the Wall*, Eakin Press 2000.

McKeown, Roy S., *Cabin in the Blackjacks: A History of Ada, Oklahoma,* no date.

McReynolds, Edwin, Marriott, Alice, Faulconer, Estelle, *Oklahoma: The Story of its Past and Present*, University of Oklahoma Press 1967.

Morgan, R.D., *The Bad Boys of the Cookson Hills*, New Forums Press 2002.

Morgan, R. D., *The Rise and Fall of the Poe, Hart Gang*, New Forums Press 2003.

Morgan, R. D., *The Bandit Kings of the Cookson Hills*, New Forums Press, 2003.

Morgan, R. D., *The Tri, State Terror: The Life and Crimes of Wilbur Underhill*, New Forums Press, 2005.

Morris, Jon W., *Ghost Towns of Oklahoma*, University of Oklahoma Press 1977.

Morris, John, *Drill Bits, Picks, and Shovels: A History of Mineral Resources in Oklahoma*, Oklahoma Historical Society 1982.

Norton, Virginia Patty, Sutton, & Layton R., *Indian Territory and Carter County, Oklahoma, Pioneers including Pickins County, Chickasaw Nation, Vol. I 1840, 1926*, Chickasaw Historical Society of Southern Oklahoma and the Southern Oklahoma Genealogical Society.

Owens, Ron, *Oklahoma Justice: The Oklahoma City Police*, Turner Publishing 1995.

Parnell, Percy R., *The Joint*, Naylor Co., 1976.

Patterson, Wayne with Alt, Betty, *Slaughter in Cellhouse 3: The Anatomy of a Riot*, vanderGeest Publishing 1997.

Purvis, Alston Tresniowski, *The Vendetta*, Public Affairs 2005.

Ramsey, Winston G, Editor, *On the Trail of Bonnie and Clyde: Then and Now*, 2003.

Sabljack, Mark & Greenberg, Martin, *Most Wanted: A History of the FBI's Ten Most Wanted List*, Bonanza Books 1990.

Samuelson, Nancy B. , *The Dalton Gang Story*, Shooting Star Press, 1992.

Shirley, Glenn, *Heck Thomas: Frontier Marshal*, University of Oklahoma Press, 1962.

Shirley, Glenn, *Law West of Fort Smith: A History of Frontier Justice in the Indian Territory, 1834, 1896*, Henry Holt and Co. 1957.

Shirley, Glenn, *West of Hells Fringes: Crime, Criminals and the Federal Peace Officer in Oklahoma Territory, 1889, 1907*, University of Oklahoma Press –Norman 1978

Shirley, Glenn, *Gunfight At Ingalls*, Barbed Wire Press 1990.

Shirley, Glenn, *The Fourth Guardsman*, Eakin Press 1997.

Shirley, Glenn, *Marauders Of the Indian Nations*, Barb Wire Press 1994.

Svenvold, Mark, *Elmer McCurdy: The Misadventures in Life and Afterlife of an American Outlaw*, Basic Books 2002.

Toland, John, *The Dillinger Days*, Random House 1963.

Trekell, Ronald, *History of the Tulsa Police Department*, Privately published 1990.

Unger, Robert, *The Union Station Massacre: The Original Sin of Hoover's FBI*, Andrews, McNeal 1997.

Vaughn-Roberson, Courtney & Glen, *City in the Osage Hills: Tulsa, Oklahoma*, Prevett Publishing 1984.

Wallis, Michael, *Pretty Boy: The Life and Times of Charles Arthur Floyd*, St. Martins Press 1992.

Watkins, T. H. , *The Great Depression: America In The 1930s*, Little Brown and Co. 1993.

Welsh, Louise, Townes, Willa Mae, & Morris, John W., *A History of the Greater Seminole Oil Field*, Western Heritage Association 1981.

West, C. W. "Dub", *Outlaws and Peace Officers of the Indian Territory*, Muscogee Publishing 1987.

West C. W. , *Persons and Places of the Indian Territory*, Muskogee Publishing 1974.

Worster, Donald, *Dust Bowl: The Southern Plains in the 1930s*, Oxford Press 1979.

Articles and Periodicals

Bell, Roger, "Mose Miller: Outlaw of the Greenleaf Hills," *Oklahombres*, Fall 1995.

Bell, Roger, "Bud Ledbetter's Muskogee Gun Battle," *Oklahombries*, Fall 1995.

Bowman, Ruth Fisk, "Death by Hanging: The Crimes and Execution of Arthur Gooch," *The Chronicles of Oklahoma*, Summer 1984, Oklahoma Historical Society.

Burkholder, Edwin and Anderson, Joe, "Blasting the Lawless Cookson Hills," *Official Detective* –Six part series, Summer/Fall 1945.

Burton, Art, "Indian Police of the Indian Territory," *Oklahombres*, Winter 2005.

Butler, Ken, "The Outlaw Tom Slaughter," *Oklahombres*, Fall 1995.

Butler, Ken, "Outlaw Joe Davis," *Oklahombres*, Spring 1999.

Butler, Ken, "The Cunningham Brothers: Bank Robbers and Petty Thieves," *Oklahombres*, Summer 1999.

Cordry, Dee, "The Last Days of Bill Doolin," *Oklahombres*, Spring 1996.

Cordry, Dee, "The Killing of Sheriff W. A. Williams," *Oklahombres*, Winter 1993.

Cordry, Dee, "In the Line of Duty: The Story of the Keirsey Lawmen," *Oklahombres*, Summer 2000.

Edmondson, Linda and Larason, Margaret, "Kate Barnard: The Story of a Woman Politician," *The Chronicles of Oklahoma*, Summer 2000, Oklahoma Historical Society.

Foreman, Carolyn and Thomas, "The Light Horse in the Indian Territory," *Oklahombres*, Fall 1998, Previously printed in the *Chronicles of Oklahoma*.

Fulbright, Jim, "Tale of the Gun: W. D. 'Bill' Fossett," *OKOLHA*, Volume I , Spring 2004.

Haines, J. D., *U.S.* "Deputy Marshal Bud Ledbetter," *OKOLHA,* Spring 2006.

Keen, Pat, "Temple Houston: Oklahoma Lawyer and Shootist," *Oklahombres,* Winter 2001.

Koch, Michael, "Life and Times of Henry Starr," *Oklahombres,* Fall 2002.

Koch, Michael, "The Tri, State Terror: The Saga of Wilbur Underhill in Oklahoma," Four part series, *Oklahombres,* 1994.

Lambert, Dan, "Smashing the Barker, Karpis Mad Dogs," *Startling Detective,* May 1934.

Mattix, Rick, "Bonnie and Clyde in Oklahoma," *Oklahombres,* Fall 1992.

Mattix, Rick, "Southwest Lawmen Slew Dillinger," *Oklahombres,* Fall 1994.

Mattix, Rick & Wm. Helmer, "Evolution of an Outlaw Band: The Making of the Barker, Karpis Gang," *Oklahombres,* Fall 1995.

Mattix, Rick, Machinegun Kelly, Oklahombres, Fall 1992.

Reading, Reba, The Choctaw Nations Lighthorsemen, Frontier Times, May 1977.

Reck, Gloria Schouw, "The Lynn, Long Shootout of 1932," *Oklahombres,* Winter, 2003.

Samuelson, Nancy B. , "The Three Guardsmen and US Marshal Nix," *OKOLHA,* Volume III Spring 2006.

Samuelson, Nancy B., "Bill Power and Dick Broadwell: Members of the Dalton Gang," *OKOLHA,* Fall 2006.

Turpin, Bob, Bruner's Graveyard, *True West,* April 1977.

Webb, Michael, "Pretty Boy Floyd's Visit to the Gateway City," *Oklahombres,* 1998.

Whitehead, Terry, "Sideshow Outlaw: Elmer McCurdy," *Oklahombres,* Spring 1999.

Williams, Nudie E. , "Black Men Who Wore the Star," *Chronicles of Oklahoma,* Spring 1981, Oklahoma Historical Society.

Woods, Walter E., "The Last Turn in Ben's Road," *True Detective,* September 1963.

Newspapers

The author made use of hundreds of archival newspaper articles. Although too numerous to credit them all, I would like to single out the *Tulsa World and Tribune, Muskogee Phoenix and Times Democrat, Joplin Globe, McAlester News Capitol, Seminole Producer, Kansas City Star, Okmulgee Democrat and Daily Times, Dallas Morning News, Shawnee Morning News,* and *The Daily Oklahoman* for their excellent work reporting events big and small concerning crime and punishment occurring in Oklahoma and surrounding states.

Other

National Archives, NARA, San Bruno, California, Alcatraz Records

National Archives, NARA, Kansas City and Fort Worth, Texas

Three Rivers Museum, Linda Moore and Roger Bell, Muskogee

Oklahoma Law Enforcement Memorial, Dennis Lippe

Oklahombres

OKLAHA

Missouri Department of Corrections

Oklahoma Department of Corrections

Kansas Department of Corrections

Fort Smith Historical Society

Fort Smith National Historic Site, National Park Service, Linda Gray

Oklahoma Historical Society

Kansas Historical Society

Missouri Historical Society

Muskogee Public Library: Grant Foreman Research Room, Thanks Wally

About the Author

R.D. Morgan has written six books concerning Oklahoma lawmen and outlaw history including *The Bad Boys of the Cookson Hills* and *The Tri State Terror: The Life and Crimes of Wilbur Underhill.* He has also penned dozens of articles for historical journals, magazines, and newspapers on the subject. Morgan was recently engaged as a historical consultant for the production of the documentary "Crime Wave" for the History Channel. He is currently working on his seventh book, *Irish O'Malley and the Ozark Mountain Boys.* The author, his wife, Naomi, and two faithful dogs reside in Haskell, Oklahoma.

Index

A

Ada, OK, 44
Adair, OK, 17, 170, 171
Addington, OK, 157, 168
Aggas, Clara, 105, 107
Agra, OK, 163, 186
Alcatraz, 68, 141
Alex, OK, 171, 183
Alexander, Bill, 140
Allen, OK, 168
Alluwe, OK, 29, 172
Anderson, Joe, 52, 53, 76
Ardmore, OK, 5, 7, 18, 29
Arkoma, OK, 133
Ary, Jack, 59, 60
Asher, OK, 163, 168, 169
Avant, OK, 171
Avard, OK, 159, 160
Avery, OK, 158, 163

B

Bailey, Harvey, 89, 90, 112, 113,
    118, 130, 132, 141
Baldwin, Skeeter, 125
Ballew, Bud, 26, 29
Barger, John, 62, 63, 201
Barker, Arizona (Ma), 54, 56,
    79, 80, 82, 83, 85, 86, 91,
    125
Barker, Arthur (Doc), 61, 79,
    80, 81, 82, 84, 88
Barker Fred, 79, 80, 82, 86, 91,
    94, 123
Barker Herman, 55, 61, 79, 80,
    83, 85
Barker Lloyd, 83, 79, 85, 86
Barnsdall, OK, 180
Barrow, Buck, 135
Barrow, Clyde, 119, 134, 137
Bates, Albert, 113
Beggs, OK, 35, 65, 69, 127, 163
Benge, Jim, 132
Bessie, OK, 165
Bethany, OK, 172, 193
Bertillon System, 39, 138
Billings, OK, 168
Birdwell, George, 98, 112, 116
Bishop, Luther, 48, 49

Bixby, OK, 186
Blake, "Tulsa Jack", 17, 18
Bluejacket, OK, 163, 164
Bokchito, OK, 190
Boley, OK, 102, 188
Bolton, Ben, 125, 202
Bookman, Henry, 146
Boulware, Laf, 38
Bowlegs, 48, 67
Bowline, Link, 59
Boyd, Percy, 136
Boynton, OK, 71, 72, 161, 184
Brackett, Charlie, 56
Bradshaw, Ford, 31, 36, 102,
    104, 118, 130, 132, 136, 143
Brady, (Big) Bob, 76, 118, 130,
    132
Braggs, OK, 29
Brandon, Clyde, 66
Breckenridge, OK, 167
Brandon, Roy, 60, 68
Brinkman, OK, 161, 180
Bristow, OK, 64, 157, 160, 178,
    179
Britton, OK, 179
Broadwell, Dick, 17
Broken Arrow, OK, 180
Brodie, Jack, 56
Brumley, Tom, 114, 117
Bruner, Heck, 4, 22
Bryant, Charley, 6, 16, 17
Bryce, Jelly, 118, 120, 124
Buck, Rufus, 11, 23, 26
Bullock, Charles, 37, 39

C

Camp, Carter, 78
Campbell, Cal, 134, 137
Campbell, Harry, 54, 80, 87, 92,
    142
Caney, OK, 169
Cannon, V.S., 116
Canton, OK, 197
Canton, Frank, 4, 19
Carlile, Tom (Kie), 57, 76
Carolin, Dupert, 115, 117
Carnes, Clarence, 142, 143
Carney, OK, 159, 165

Carrier, OK, 177
Carson, Red, 116
Casey, Bert, 26
Castle, OK, 101, 177, 182, 186
Catoosa, OK, 157
Cedar Creek Gang, 35, 37, 57
Centralia, OK, 166
Chandler, OK, 13
Chase, Vivian, 51, 125
Checotah, OK, 18, 71, 170
Chelsea, OK, 190
Cherokee Bill (Crawford
    Goldsby), 6, 11, 23, 25, 32
Chickasha, OK, 182
Choteau, OK, 162
Christie, Ned, 21, 23
Chuculate, Perry, 57, 67
Clanton, Ed Newt, 118, 129,
    133
Clark, Jim, 112, 118, 130, 132,
    133, 134, 142
Claremore, OK, 21
Clarita, OK, 162, 166
Clayton, OK, 187
Clifton, "Dynamite Dick", 17,
    18
Clinton, OK, 190
Coalgate, OK, 133, 192
Coffeyville, KS, 17, 57
Coker, Sam, 49, 91
Cole, Theodore (Teddy), 142
Collinsville, OK, 170, 187
Colvin, Ralph, 118, 131
Comanche, OK, 179, 184, 190
Commerce, OK, 136, 177, 185
Conner, Albert (Ab), 26, 37, 49,
    55, 57, 199
Cook, Bill, 6, 23, 24, 27
Cookson, Mount Levi, 30, 195
Cooper, Russell, 127
Corgan, John Marsh, 202
Cotner, Charley, 53, 118, 132
Covington, OK, 66, 162
Coweta, OK, 173
Coyle, OK, 174
Creekmore, Bill (King), 26, 37
Creighton, Jimmy, 92
Crescent, OK, 194
Cromwell, OK, 48

Crump, George, 4, 11
Cunningham, Emanuel, 73, 74
Cunningham, Forrest, 73, 74
Cunningham, Jess, 73, 74
Cunningham, John, 73, 74
Cushing, OK, 65
Custer City, OK, 194
Cyril, OK, 176, 188

D

Dalton, Bill, 15, 17
Dalton, Bob, 6, 15, 17
Dalton, Emmett, 6, 15, 17
Dalton, Frank, 15
Dalton, Grat, 6, 15, 17
Daniels, Danny, 61
Darrow, Ross, 59
Daugherty, Roy "Arkansas
    Tom", 17, 18
Davis, Ed, 118, 130
Davis, Freddie, 53, 62
Davis, Joe, 26, 33, 34, 56
Davis, Lee, 114, 117
Davis, Lucky, 11, 23
Davis, Volney (Curley), 80, 84,
    142
Dean, Tom, 76
Deckard, Newt, 34, 35
Delmar, Frank, 133, 142
DeNoya, OK, 157
Depew, OK –66, 162, 189
DeVol, Larry (The Chopper),
    80, 92, 95
Dewey, OK, 158
Dill, OK, 186
Dillinger, John, 102, 121, 124
Doolin, Bill, 6, 13, 18, 28, 36,
    200
Dotson, Charlie, 132
Dover, OK –18, 177, 182
Doyle, Jess, 80, 84
Downer, George (Babe)
Drake, Raymond, 143
Drumright, OK, 48, 59, 60, 65
Duncan, OK, 73
Dunn, Bee, 17, 19
Dunn, Jess, 41, 42, 140, 141
Duree, Dan, 54

Duree, Jeff, 48, 49, 54, 55, 61, 88
Durrill, Grover, 56

E

Eads, Bill, 70, 76
Earlsboro, OK, 98, 100, 177, 181, 184
Edgmon, Orin, 31
Edwards, Owen, 49, 53, 62, 66
Elgin, OK, 183
El Reno, OK, 176
Elliott, Aulcie (Aussie), 115, 117
Elliott, M.E., 46
Enid, OK, 95
Eno, Clarence, 31, 130, 132
Eno, Otis, 130, 132
Eureka Springs, Ark., 13, 18, 56

F

Fairfax, OK, 184, 187, 188
Fairland, OK, 196
Farr, Dick, 26, 34, 199
Fleagle, Jake, 53
Fletcher, OK, 191
Flournoy, Lee, 51, 80, 125
Flowers, Clay, 76
Floyd, Charley (Pretty Boy), 31, 55, 76, 95, 119, 123
Floyd, Ruby, 101, 104, 106, 107
Ford, Tab, 140
Fort Cobb, OK, 182
Fort Gibson, OK, 175
Fort Scott, Kansas, 7
Fossett, Wm., 4, 12
Frederick, OK, 130, 191
French, James, 46
French, Jim, 6, 20, 24

G

Gage, Wesley, 76, 114
Garhart, Leon, 175-76, 184
Garrett, Buck, 26, 29
Garritson, John, 37
Gates, Douglas, 118, 122
Gates, John, 118, 122
Geary, OK, 191
George, Buck, 38
Gibson, Russell, 70, 71
Gilmore, Dewey, 125, 126, 127, 129
Glover, B. V., 46
Goodman, "Kaiser Bill", 26
Gooch, Arthur, 46, 53, 200
Gossett, I. B., 73

Gracemont, OK, 157, 171
Grady, Mont, 58
Grammer, Henry, 36, 37
Granite, OK, 42, 54, 64, 93
Greenfield, OK, 160
Green, Will, 56, 80, 83
Gregg, Dick, 49, 55, 58
Guest, Tom, 149

H

Haileyville, OK, 183
Hale, William K, 62
Hamilton, Ray, 59
Harbeck, Kip, 198
Harrah, OK, 37, 133, 177, 192
Hart, Harry, 37, 38
Hart, William, 37, 38
Haskell, OK, 28, 132, 192
Hastings, OK, 167, 175
Headrick, OK, 165, 181
Heady, Dan, 126, 127, 128, 130
Henryetta, OK, 187
Hitchita, OK, 167, 180
Hooker, OK, 170
Houston, Temple, 14, 15
Hueston, Tom, 17, 18
Hunter, OK, 173
Hydro, OK, 189

I

Idabel, OK, 185
Indiahoma, OK, 185, 189
Ingalls, OK, 17, 18, 19, 28
Inman, Elmer, 61
Inola, OK, 160, 165, 170, 171, 179, 183

J

Janaway, Carl, 142, 145
Jarrett, Buster, 57, 199
Jarrett, Earl, 49, 57
Jarrett, Floyd, 57
Jarrett, Glen, 199
Jarrett, Lee, 26, 35, 37, 57, 199
Jarrett, Walter, 35, 199
Jenks, OK, 167
Jennings, OK, 159
Jett, OK, 162
Johnson, Charley, 33, 56
Johnson, John E., 26, 27, 30
Johnson, "Pussyfoot", 26

K

Karpis, Alvin, 82, 86, 89, 91, 94, 95, 123, 124
Keating, Larry, 34, 25
Kelley, Erv, 76, 101, 107, 108, 109
Kelly, George (Machinegun), 76, 11, 114
Kelly, Kathryn, 112, 113
Kellyville, OK, 169
Kendrick, OK, 170
Keota, OK, 178
Ketchum, OK, 194
Keystone, OK, 169
Kiersey, Jim, 53
Kimes, George, 49, 65, 68
Kimes, Leroy, 68, 69
Kimes, Matt, 49, 65, 68, 70
Kimes, Roy, 68, 69
Kingfisher, OK, 12, 130, 133, 191, 194
Kittrell, Troy, 105, 107
Klaber, Henry, 34, 35, 200
Konawa, OK, 100, 181, 182
Kuykendall, Mallory, 143

L

Lairmore, Mark, 66, 67, 76, 200
Lamont, OK –157, 167
Langford, Ray, 177
Ledbetter, Bud, 4, 26, 28, 32, 62
Lenox, U. S., 59
Lawrence (also spelled Laurence), Babe, 62, 63
Lawrence, Bill, 62, 63, 202
Lawson, Jimmy, 88, 92
Lighthorse, Native American, 5, 15
Lindsey, OK, 180, 189
Littrell, Jess, 26, 37, 40
Lloyd, Jack, 142
Lockhart, David (Ed), 49, 55, 57
Lockhart, Sam, 58
Long, Crockett, 13, 108, 111
Lovell, OK, 172, 173
Lung, John, 26, 38, 39, 200
Luther, OK, 176, 178, 184
Lynn, Wiley, 13

M

Macomb, OK, 164, 167
Madsen, Chris, 4, 13, 14, 18
Maledon, George, 9
Manitou, OK, 169

Maples, Dan, 22
Marlow, OK, 74, 187
Marietta, OK, 166
Marland, OK, 176
Marshal, Joe, 64
Maud, OK, 100, 180, 187
Maxfield, Bud, 33, 56
May, OK, 173
Maysville, OK, 177
McCain, Rufus, 142, 143
McCloud, OK, 164, 181, 191
McCollum, "Goldie" Ben, 49, 71, 72
McCurdy, Elmer, 35, 36, 200
McDonald, Alva, 49, 54, 55
McGhee, Q. P., 83
Medford, OK, 185
Meeker, OK, 101, 184
Melton, "Red" Virgil, 127, 129
Miami, OK, 196
Milam, Joe, 189
Mill Creek, OK, 163, 183
Miller, Bill (Killer), 98, 99
Miller, Jack, 127, 128
Minco, OK, 53, 170, 171
Moody, Stella (Boots)
Moore, Eugene, 134
Moore, OK, 169
Morgan, Joe, 62, 63, 201
Mounds, OK, 178, 179
Morris, OK, 105, 107, 180, 181, 185
Morrison, Kelsie, 201
Muldrow, OK, 31

N

Nash, Frank, 55, 56, 76
Nave, Fred, 62
Navina, OK, 161
Neal, Sam, 201
Newcomb, "Bitter Creek", 6, 16, 19
Newton, Joe, 48
Newton, Willis, 48
Nix, E. D., 4, 18
Noble, OK, 160
Noland, George, 67

O

Okeene, OK, 196
Okemah, OK, 127, 179, 197
Oklahoma Bureau of Identification and Investigation, 49, 75
Okmulgee, OK, 132, 192